Mar 2010

We are hap
book help you see the importance of
following
God's plan to
train your
children—
We wish you the best —

love you —

Training Up a Child

Following God's Plan

11 Essential Components to Building a Child

by Gwendolyn M. Webb

Published by The Old Landmarks
P.O. Box 19414
Oklahoma City, Oklahoma 73144

Grateful acknowledgment is given to Dr. Leila Daughtry-Denmark for granting permission to Gwendolyn M. Webb to use quotations from her book *Every Child Should Have a Chance* in the Addendum of this book. The publication of Dr. Denmark's material does not permit quotation therefrom in any other work.

Grateful acknowledgment is also given to Madia L. Bowman for granting written permission to use quotations from her book *Dr. Denmark Said It!* in the Addendum of this book. This publication of Madia Bowman's quoted material does not permit quotation therefrom in any other work.

All Scripture quotations are taken from the King James Version of the Bible.

ISBN 0-9727308-O-X

The ideas, procedures, and suggestions in this book are intended to supplement, not replace the medical advice of trained professionals. Readers are advised to consult their own doctors or other qualified health professionals regarding treatment for their child or themselves. The author and the publisher expressly disclaim responsibility for any adverse effects arising from any person reading or following the information in this book.

To order books:

Call -   1-800-272-3100

Write -   The Old Landmarks
            TUAC Division
            P.O. Box 19414
            Oklahoma City, OK 73144

I dedicate this book

In loving memory of my Christian parents, Euty Farice Bruce Sr. and Iris Geraldine Bowers Bruce, who followed God's plan to construct their home, gave me life, and, with their loving care, trained me how to live it.

To my Granddaughter _____

To my Great Granddaughter _____

To my Great-great-Granddaughter _____

I entreat you, sweet one, to remember that God's plan for the human family will never change. The design was made in heaven, recorded in Holy Writ, and will remain on its pages until the end of time. God left us His Word to be "a lamp unto our feet and a light unto our path," from which we shall all be judged.

It is my eternal prayer that you will be among the saved, and that on the pages of God's "Book of Life" your name will be written.

I love you forever!

CONTENTS

Acknowledgements

To God, my Heavenly Father, who answered my every prayer that preceded the writing of each chapter of this book.

To my husband, Kermit, who has encouraged me to be a conqueror over what seemed to me to be unconquerable--writing this book. He is my King and he has made me his Queen. He never insisted I work a career job all day and perform my "God-assigned" duties at night. He has honored me as the "weaker vessel." Thank you, my darling, for fighting life's battles while the rest of us remained sheltered in the quiet and peaceful confines of our home. You have been our spiritual guide while leading us, protecting us, and providing for us. We will love you eternally and ask God to reward you generously.

To "the winners," who shared many secrets of how they won with their children, and whose advice and suggestions inspired the major topic outline for this book.

To all my family members and former students whose real-life stories I have been permitted to use in my teaching and in this book.

To the women students who originally heard these lessons taught and urged me to put them into book form.

To the readers, who continually encourage me to keep *Training Up a Child* in print.

To Leonard Jackson, my editor and friend, who has helped to refine this manuscript.

Preface

It has been twenty-five years since I first wrote *Training Up a Child*. A generation has passed and many women have either read the book or attended a TUAC class. Often I receive phone calls from new mothers who were recipients of the TUAC teachings. They will say, "My mother raised me by the principles she learned from your book. I just gave birth to my first child and I want to train her the same way. Do you have a copy of the book I can order?"

When I began this revision, I was asked, "You aren't going to change your principles are you?" " I like your book just like it is." "Don't change anything." To which I replied, "Of course I'm not changing the teachings! How could I? God's plan for the human family can't be changed."

What I have chosen to do, however, is to enrich the contents of *Training Up a Child*.

Dr. Leila Daughtry-Denmark has agreed to let me improve this new edition of *Training Up a Child* with her Addendum. This addition will teach you how to care for the physical needs of your children.

According to the American Medical Association, Dr. Denmark is the oldest practicing physician in the United States. She has practiced medicine for seventy-plus years, thus being America's most experienced pediatrician. She has dedicated her life to serving little children.

Dr. Denmark was born in Bulloch County, Georgia, February 1,1898 and graduated from Tift College in 1922. She was the third female to graduate from the Medical College of Georgia in 1928. Dr. Denmark became the first intern at the Henrietta Elgeston Hospital for Children in Atlanta. Since that time she has been in continuous practice of medicine, specializing in pediatrics.

She married John Eustace Denmark in 1928, only seventy-two hours after she received her medical degree. She says they got married on Monday; she got up and cooked breakfast on Tuesday, and immediately started work at Grady Hospital in Atlanta. Mr. Denmark served as vice president of the Federal Reserve Bank of Atlanta for more than sixty-two years.

Mary, their only child, was born in 1931 and Dr. Denmark practiced what she preached and is still preaching. She set up a clinic and worked out of her home, treating patients, tending to her husband, and rearing her daughter.

Among Dr. Denmark's contributions to professional journals, her research papers on diagnosis, treatment, and immunization of whooping cough have been particularly notable. Her study began in 1933 and continued for more than eleven years. This research led to her receiving the Fisher Award for Research in 1935.

Dr. Denmark is a true humanitarian. She volunteered a day's work every week for fifty-six years at the Central Presbyterian Clinic in Atlanta to give needed care to poor people. She has never charged more than $10 for a first visit or $8 for each visit thereafter. Generations of families have brought their children to Dr. Denmark for her wisdom and experience. Some travel hundreds of miles for their children to be treated by her. She stays busy but in her own estimation has never worked a day in her life. She says that by its very definition, work is not fun and what she does is fun.

Dr. Denmark has lived through two world wars and has seen the age of the horse and buggy transform into a high-tech world of high anxiety, but she says the most significant change in her lifetime has been parents giving up responsibility for their children. She says, "Parents are pursuing materialistic goals--new cars, bigger houses--to the neglect of their children. Parenting has gone out of style and it's wrecking this nation!"

She reminds us, " More than half of our nation's babies went to day care today; many have eaten between meals and many are sick. They'll come home tonight to a tired mother and a tired father. And the parents will say to me, ' I'm firing my doctor because he just doesn't keep my baby well.' But no doctor under the sun can keep that baby well. It needs the love and nurturing of its mother. It needs to be fed right. If you bring a baby into this world, that's your responsibility. But all that's changed today. Parents let other people take care of their babies."

She recalls one family she helped. "The family was so poor they picked up coal along the railroad tracks to heat their home. But that mother raised the most wonderful kids. It's not poverty that's harming our children. It's parental neglect. Mothers have deserted their children. They're out making money instead of making people. Without parental guidance our children can't make it." she declares.

She advises against putting children in day care, where she thinks they are deprived of attention and catch illnesses. "Day care is supporting the pediatricians in the country today." she reveals.

"I believe in women having freedom. But with our freedom we have abandoned our children and wrecked our nation. We won that freedom when we won the right to vote in 1922, but what have we done with it? We can now kill our babies and 40 percent of women who work outside the home lose their husbands. Is that progress?" she asks.

In the addendum portion of this book, *Dr. Denmark Speaks,* you will read how to take care of the physical needs of your child. Following her advice, your little one can be healthy and can more likely be kept out of the doctor's offices. She will teach you preventive medicine, thus potentially saving you thousands of dollars in medical bills over the years.

From Dr. Denmark's instructions, you will learn how to produce a child who can be healthy in body and mind.

One of her patients has said, "Dr. Denmark has convinced me and multitudes of others that motherhood is a sacred calling, a divine vocation, not a job or burden. We do what she tells us and our babies rarely get sick. She is a Christian missionary in the highest sense."

After working with Dr. Denmark and "living" within the pages of her book, *Every Child Should Have a Chance,* for so many months, I have come to the definite conclusion, when **Dr. Denmark Speaks** we all should listen.

The Birth of Training Up a Child

The birth of *Training Up a Child* was not planned ahead of time. Its actual beginning was the day my husband and I decided to leave our jobs in the South and move north to engage in mission work.

We were newlyweds at that time. I had worked as an elementary school teacher and my husband was a minister. We were both young and wanted to travel, go different places, and see new things. My husband applied for a new preaching position and was accepted. We left family and friends and soon arrived at our new home in the Northwest. The towering evergreens, pristine mountains, clear rushing streams and the ocean were overwhelmingly beautiful! We had never experienced such splendor before and loved our new home!

We had not worked with our new congregation two months, when one cold winter day the phone rang in my husband's study. He answered and heard the voice of a distraught, troubled woman. She told him: "I desperately need help! My husband has deserted us. I do not know where he is. He is an alcoholic and may be in jail. We are strangers in this area. I am alone with seven children and we do not have anything to eat. The utility company has notified me that if we do not pay our bill, they are going to shut our gas off. I have no money and no way to keep my children warm. Will your church help us? "

My husband got her address and took immediate action. He informed the men of the church who served on the benevolence committee about this family's crises. The next day they visited the family and witnessed the deplorable conditions in which they were living. The children were undernourished and reportedly were scavenging for food in garbage cans. They were half-naked, had no shoes, and were sleeping where they could on the floor. There were only two half-beds to accommodate seven children. The beds had mattresses but no bedding. There was nothing at the windows except a few blinds that were broken and hanging in disarray. There were one chair and a broken-down couch in the living room. The baby was suffering from second-to-third-degree burns on her buttocks. She was not wearing a diaper when her older, retarded sister had set her on a hot oven door.

All the children demonstrated noticeable symptoms of physical, emotional, and social maladjustment. There were obvious marks and scars of physical injury on their bodies. Development of social skills did not exist. They constantly clamored for attention and attempted to climb into the car with anyone who visited them and was preparing to leave. All seven of the children interacted with one another much like a starving litter of puppies. Their ages ranged from eighteen months to twelve years. The three boys were the oldest and the four girls were the youngest.

The brothers severely mistreated their little sisters. They would knock them down and push them across the room. It was disturbing to behold their aggressive, brutal, behavior. They would threaten, "I am going to kill somebody when I grow up!"

The church paid the utility bills for the family, delivered food to their house, and initiated a clothing drive. Within a week, all children were clothed and warm, and there was plenty of food in their house. Eventually, the alcoholic father returned home.

On Sundays, church members picked up the mother and her children and brought them to worship. The children were so out of control, however, they had to be separated and seated with different families in an attempt to prevent them from disrupting the worship service. The boys crawled on the seats, under the pews, and periodically interrupted the assembly with loud talking.

One Saturday afternoon this dysfunctional family's trouble reached a climax. The father had left his family again. My husband and I happened to stop by to see how they were getting along and the mother was walking around in the yard in what appeared to be a dazed condition. She had threatened to kill herself and all of the children. When we asked, "What can we do to help?" She said, "If you will take the children for a few days, when my husband comes home, maybe we can decide what to do."

The next morning an appeal was made to the congregation, for anyone who could to provide temporary shelter for these children. By evening six of the children had been placed in Christian homes. However, no one volunteered to care for the oldest boy, who was both mentally and emotionally retarded.

In a few days the father and mother appeared at the church office. When they visited their children and the families who were caring for them, they asked if we could keep them just a little while longer. They remarked that they had never seen their children so happy and well cared for.

A few weeks passed before the parents made contact again. We learned that they had taken their oldest son and left the state. Those of us who were caring for the children were in a precarious situation. It was a serious risk to be caring for abandoned children with no legal authorization.

When we realized this circumstance was turning into something more than a temporary act of Christian benevolence, we notified the State Department of Public Assistance and asked for help. We were informed each family must undergo home studies and become licensed by the state as foster parents. My husband and I were caring for two of the "little girls," who were three and four years old. The state offered us remuneration for the services we were rendering, but we refused to accept it. We had not engaged in this benevolent service for money. Our only intention was to help two hungry, abused, children.

The mother finally returned alone to visit her children. She was immediately urged to accept state assistance, and the church offered to help her find a place to live so she could personally care for her children. She refused and left again.

Days turned into weeks and weeks into months. What we originally believed would be a temporary act of benevolence was turning into a permanent arrangement. We grew more sympathetic to the "little girls" and we began to see some signs of improvement in them. We obtained medical assistance to treat their staph infections, boils, and worm infestation. All six children were helped in the same way and they all saw each other three times a week at worship services.

The "little girls" finally stopped hiding behind furniture, telling fantasies, and chewing on their hands. They learned some table manners, how to distinguish colors, tie their shoes, and to count. They liked for me to read to them, dress them in pretty clothes, and take them places.

Since the State Department of Human Services was involved, they had final control of the children. The mother and father eventually divorced and were living with new partners hundreds of miles away. The mother moved in with a man who had four children. That relationship, however, did not last for very long.

More than three years had passed when the natural mother decided she was ready to retrieve her children. The state had other ideas. They were not going to release the children to her until she proved that she had the ability to care for them. A court trial ensued. After the testimony was heard, the Juvenile Judge ruled her an incompetent mother. He ordered that all the children stay in their present foster homes. Once more, she left the state.

I did not start teaching school again, as my hands were full trying to advance these children to normalcy. I kept them out of school an extra year and continued to work with them at home, giving them more time to develop and experience a quiet, stable life. Four years passed and the "little girls" were seven and eight years old.

My husband and I were planning another major move. A new baby was coming and we were making plans to leave the Northwest. We wanted to move closer to our mothers, who were widowed and getting older. The "little girls" were getting more adjusted to us. We cared about them and had much time and effort invested in their well being. To us it was unconscionable to desert them. If they did not remain with us, we knew they would be moved from foster home to foster home, which would further disrupt their lives and tear down what we had attempted to build.

We requested that the state help us make legal arrangements to take them with us when we left the state. The authorities advised us that would only be possible if we adopted them. It had been many months since the natural mother of the "little girls" had contacted us. Since her whereabouts was unknown for the length of time required by law, the state declared the children abandoned and we were permitted to adopt them. Our new baby had arrived and all five of us moved together to a new home.

In time the natural mother re-established contact with all of the foster parents. The older siblings, one by one, and by their own choice, left their foster homes and were re-united with their mother. That left the three youngest girls who had not been returned to her. The mother learned where we had moved and began writing letters, and contacting us by phone. The baby girl, who was deserted at eighteen months, stayed with her original foster family until she was grown. She and her husband established a Christian family and have children of their own.

The "little girls" lived with us for approximately eleven years. When they were teenagers, they experienced a great deal of disturbance and confusion. They went to visit their siblings and spent some time with their natural mother, who was married to yet another man. They also lived with a grandmother. Periodically they returned to visit us. In spite of their turbulent years, they each achieved a high school education and completed some college work.

The youngest of the "little girls" is deceased. She died during a surgery while in her early thirties. She left a son and two daughters with their Christian father. The oldest of the "little girls" is married, has a son, and works with her husband in their family business.

It was during those early years in the mission field that my husband and I had our first experience with parenting. It was a shocking encounter to walk, you might say, into the back door of the school of parenting. It was those trying years of struggling to help abandoned children that inspired me to study carefully the subject of child-rearing. I combined my experience of growing up in a Christian home, studying the Bible, interviewing successful parents, reading books about parenting, as well as direct experience, and produced the manuscript for this book.

When I mention the "little girls," the reader will know to whom I am referring. During the eleven years I mothered them, I learned more than I could have ever learned sitting in a university classroom studying child and adolescent psychology. If it had not been for that hands-on experience, I am sure I would never have written this book.

Introduction

OUR YOUTH ARE DISTURBED

Every era has recorded sad commentaries on its youth. More than two thousand years ago, Socrates described the youth of his day in this way:

"Children now live in luxury, they have bad manners, contempt for authority; they show disrespect for elders and love to chatter in place of exercise. Children are now tyrants of the household. They no longer rise when an elder enters the room, and they contradict their parents. They chatter before company and gobble up the food at the table; they cross their legs and tyrannize their teachers."

Our time is no different. We are reminded daily of the deterioration of our youth. In California, over an eight-year period of time, there was a two thousand percent increase in the use of narcotics and drugs. Juvenile arrests are increasing seventy percent faster than the population. Shoplifting, grand larceny, gang warfare, emotional maladjustment, sexual freedoms, and teenage suicides are all indications of disturbed youth. [1]

PREVENTION IS THE ANSWER

The old saying, "An ounce of prevention is worth a pound of cure," still holds true. If a state is experiencing an increase in forest fires, the solution is not to increase the number of smokejumpers or to purchase larger fleets of aircraft that spread fire retardant chemicals. Men of good judgment advocate decreasing the fire hazards by clearing the underbrush; eliminating open campfires in the dry season, and advising tourists not to throw burning cigarettes from their cars. In other words, their approach is to eliminate the conditions that increase the danger of forest fires.

By the same token, if a community or nation is troubled by an increase in juvenile delinquency, it is not an effective solution to build bigger and better jails, increase the police forces, and spend millions of dollars on institutional care.   Wise citizens should discover the source of the problem. In most cases, negligent parenting is the cause of troubled children. To solve this problem parents must be taught more effective and better methods of parenting.

WHY TEACH PARENTS?

Emotional disturbance, mental illness, increasing social and behavioral problems all point to a failure of popular methods of child training.

Society demands at least sixteen years of education to teach in public schools. A doctor must study approximately twenty years in order to practice medicine.   Carpenters, plumbers, clerks, and soldiers all undergo months and even years of apprenticeship to learn their work.

For parenting, society requires no teaching. It is the most difficult and important job on earth; yet it is almost entirely preformed by amateurs. Society's prerequisite for producing and rearing children used to be marriage, but tragically, single parenting and out-of-wedlock births are widely accepted as a part of our present culture. 2

It is for these reasons that we need to educate parents.   The sole purpose of *Training Up a Child* is to help you be a better parent, have a peaceful home, and rear healthy, happy, responsible, and productive children.

THREE PHILOSOPHIES OF CHILD REARING

There are three basic philosophies of child rearing:

(1) *Autocratic* -In this method, the parents are the authority.   The children may have ideas and suggestions, but, when decision time arrives, the parents' word is final. Hassling and arguing are simply not permitted. The word of the parents is law.

(2) *Democratic* - In this setting everyone is on an equal plane. The parents aren't the authority, and neither are the children. If conflicts arise, the family attempts to work out its disagreements so that everyone in the family will be happy. The proponents of this theory suggest this can be accomplished by learning proper communication skills.

On one occasion I paid a significant sum of money to attend a class that advocated this theory of child rearing. In my opinion, my money was wasted.   Neither time nor energy would last long enough to guide children effectively down this uncertain path.

(3) *Laissez-Faire* - With this philosophy the child is left to himself. He is free to do as he pleases. He will be what he will be; so why be bothered? The only thing parents feel they can do is hope that through chance he will turn out all right.

The autocratic philosophy, in which the parents are the authority, is the approach I advocate in *Training Up a Child*. The Bible permits me to promote no other method.   God says, *"Children, obey your parents in the Lord: for this is right."* Ephesians 6:1. Again it reads, *"Children, obey your parents in all things: for this is well pleasing unto the Lord."* Colossians 3:20.

SIX THINGS TO UNDERSTAND

There are six things I would like you to keep in mind as you read.

(1) *I make no personal claims to being an authority on child rearing.* When I wrote this book, I did not believe I was endowed with special wisdom on the subject. I had the good fortune of being reared in a Christian family, but I also had an intense interest in the subject of parenting. I set out to learn all I could about the topic.

Christians should always search for truth on every important subject and ask God to help us find it. It was God's providential guidance that helped me locate Dr. Denmark. I learned about her from a television documentary and later became personally acquainted with her. This book has been enriched a great deal with her medical knowledge and practical philosophy of living.

(2) *This study does not answer all questions for every child.* Parents who have a mentally or physically challenged child will need to learn special skills that are not addressed in this book.

If you are fostering or parenting an adopted child whom you took after he was twenty-four months old, you should seek professional *Christian* counseling. Your child missed the "falling in love with you" years and the TUAC car of Love will not function properly. You will need help beyond what is written in this book.

It is because you missed your child's bonding and attachment years that I am implying that you may experience conflict as you attempt to parent this child. Your child experienced separation from persons to whom he had grown attached. His former environment was all he had ever known, and being taken away from it caused him to experience *rejection*. He can't spell or pronounce the word, but he knows its meaning and how it feels. He will yearn for what he has lost; (no matter how bad his former conditions may have been) he may reject you, and in his heart blame you for his pain and sorrow. He will wonder, "Where is my real family and why can't I stay with them?" Unless this emotional wound can be healed, you may perform all the duties of a mother, but will remain in his mind only a temporary parent.

It is for these reasons that you should seek the assistance of trained *Christian* counselors who know proper approaches to healing these deep emotional wounds. This third person can provide a support system you both need. When we experience a broken bone or are bleeding from a wound, we seek help from one who is trained to help us heal. The scars may always be there, but we can go on with life without a noticeable limp or a running sore. Don't be too proud to seek help nor develop a fairy tale mentality by believing that all the problems will eventually vanish and everyone will "live happily ever after." Parenting a troubled child presents a different set of challenges than parenting a child that you have nurtured from birth.

(3) *Rearing children is a human relationship.* No two children are exactly alike and no two parents are the same. In this book, I present a set of guidelines that parents may implement in various ways.

(4) *The focal point of the instruction is designed for a child from birth to twelve.* The earlier you implement these principles, the better it will be for you and your child. I have specialized in teaching the *Training Up a Child* principles to new mothers. The many older women, who have commented, "I wish someone had taught me these principles fifteen years ago," have convinced me of the need to teach new mothers as early as possible.

A key point to remember in "Training Up a Child" is to start training your child at birth.

(5) *Decide what you want your child to be as a teenager, and begin training him early.* The relationship you establish with your child from birth to twelve will determine the kind of relationship you will have with your child for the rest of your lives. If you want your son to be a gentleman at fifteen, then you must start training him when he is five to open doors for others, let ladies go first, and not to strike little girls. If you desire your daughter to be your co-worker in homemaking at fourteen, then you had better teach her to help dust, make the beds, and stir the pudding at age four.

(6) "Training Up a Child" is written for new mothers. This does not imply that Daddy is not welcome to read it. He is. In fact, Chapter Four is lovingly dedicated to fathers. To apply the *Training Up a Child* principles properly, the cooperation of Daddy is absolutely essential.

The reason I concentrate on teaching mothers is that I believe the mother has, by far, the overwhelming opportunity to mold and influence the life and character of her children in their formative years. I agree with Professor Burton L. White of Harvard University. He conducted a project to determine what produces bright, happy, and socially attractive children. These were the conclusions of his research: The brightest, happiest, most charming children spend their earliest years listening to adult conversations, roaming freely around their homes, and spending a lot of time sharing. *The single most important factor in this is the mother.* She has a greater influence over a child's early experiences than anyone else. A rich social experience is the best thing you can provide to insure a good mind. For the child, this means seeking attention from the mother, following her around, and learning cooperation. [3]

Never forget " the hand that rocks the cradle, rules the world."

WHERE I FOUND AUTHORITY FOR "TRAINING UP A CHILD"

Since I make no claims of being an absolute authority on parenting, I will explain how I assembled the material for this study.

First, I used the Bible. It is my personal belief that the answers for the questions of life are found within the pages of "The Book," the Bible. When we buy an appliance or purchase a new piece of equipment, we get an instruction book that tells us how it is to be used. The Bible is our instruction book. God does not bless us with children and then neglect to instruct us in how to train them effectively.

Second, I appealed to select older couples who, from my observation, had joyful results with their parenting. "What rules did you follow in rearing your children? What pitfalls did you seek to avoid? What are some mistakes you see young couples making today?" were just a few of the questions I asked. I refer to these couples throughout the book as "the winners." It is they who have helped me formulate this book's major topics as arranged in the fourteen-chapter outline.

Third, supplementary material from various sources has been added. Some of the illustrations will be personal, and I have tried to mix in good common sense along the way.

My gratitude for this book is first to God, who designed the principles, and second to "the winners" for confirming that these standards are practical and workable.

PARENTS MAKE CHILDREN

Chapter One
Parents Make Children

As a prerequisite to the ideas and instructions that follow, I direct your thoughts to the manner in which parents make children. I chose this chapter title because it provides many thoughts we should consider before entering into the main study.

There are three ways the statement, "Parents Make Children," can be interpreted. By putting the emphasis on each word separately, three areas of discussion are addressed that hold vital information for parents.

DISCUSSION #1- <u>PARENTS</u> MAKE CHILDREN

By accentuating the word *parents* in the above statement, I refer to the physical making of children. It is the answer our mother gave us many years ago when we asked for the first time, "Mother, where do babies come from?" We can all remember, in our formative years, when the subject of sex aroused our keenest curiosity. Now that we are adults and our knowledge on the subject is advanced, there is no need for a lengthy discussion on the topic.

The miracle of childbirth forever leaves us humble and in awe. We know that children are created of their parents' flesh, blood, genes, and chromosomes. This union determines hair, skin, and eye coloring. A child's physical and mental abilities, skills, talents, and personality attributes are also an endowment from his biological parents.

Even though we have little control over the physical aspects of the *how* our children are made, we do have control over *when* they are made. We should use good judgment to control our family size so that it fits our parenting abilities, and we should *never forget our children did not ask to be born.* They are here because of us.

During moments of anger, we can be unfair with our children and they may defend themselves by asking, "Why did you have me if that is the way you feel about me?" Actually, it is a legitimate question and, serves as a reminder that their birth and very existence is truly our responsibility. We, therefore, should exert a deep interest in doing our best to train them properly.

DISCUSSION #2 - PARENTS <u>MAKE</u> CHILDREN

By emphasizing the word *make* in the chapter heading, I point out that children are what we make them. Parents physically make children, but more importantly, they are the making of their children. As crops are products of the soil, so children are products of their home environment.

The following are three ways we *make* our children. I have chosen for each thought a symbol that will serve as its reminder throughout the book.

WE MAKE OUR CHILDREN

I. By what we are ourselves.

II. By the way we train them.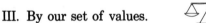

III. By our set of values.

Thought I - We Make Our Children
By What We Are Ourselves

"Nothing is more important in establishing parents' authority with their children than the example which the parent sets with his own life." [1] How many times have you heard the old sayings, "like father, like son," and "like mother, like daughter"? The Bible supports this thought when it says, "*As is the mother, so is her daughter.*" Ezekiel 16:44. And, "*He walked in the way of Asa his father and departed not from it.*" II Chronicles 20:32.

I have heard preachers say to young people, "Young man, before you marry a girl, go into her home and observe her mother. That is the way she will be some day." And, "Young lady, before you marry a boy, observe his father. That is the way he will be some day."

Our children are images of us. Our speech, manners, and actions are reflected back to us by our children's imitation. A little boy will often carry himself and develop a walk almost identical to his father's. A little girl will take care of and play with her dolls in the same manner her mother takes care of and plays with her.

Parents Can and Do Change

What we are as parents can and does change from time to time. We never remain exactly the same. It is interesting to note that our constantly changing will, in a sense, actually cause our children (the oldest, middle, and the youngest) to have different parents. Let's consider three ways this change in parents takes place.

(1) *We can change by acquiring new knowledge.* We obtain new knowledge through our experiences, and by trial and error. Many parents express regret over the way they dealt with their first child. "If I had it to do over, I would certainly do differently," they explain. Due to parents' acquiring experience and new knowledge they may deal differently with children who are born later than they did with their first child.

We acquire additional knowledge through instruction. I have had the opportunity to teach many women one simple principle that can revolutionize their marriage relationships. That principle is: *"Don't try to change your husband.* As his wife, you must accept him as he is. If he changes, it will have to be his idea." A woman can go through her married life with the false idea that if she nags, coerces, and pouts long enough, she will get her man to turn from what she considers his erring ways.

The only workable, practical way for a woman to improve her marriage is to devote her time to putting her life in order. When she does this, a surprising thing will happen. When she becomes beautiful, sweet, and has an agreeable disposition, she will draw her husband to want to be with her and please her. This works on the same principle that bears are attracted to honey. Obtaining one bit of new knowledge like this can transform a home that has been in turmoil for years, into a haven of peace.

Many people gain knowledge through reading and research. The purpose of this book, and hopefully the reason you are reading it, is to help you obtain new knowledge that will improve your parenting.

(2) *We can change by allowing God to work in our lives.* When one becomes a Christian, his life is transformed. The Bible refers to this change when

it speaks of "putting off the old man and putting on the new." I have known families in which the father and mother became Christians later in life. Their older children were grown, but the younger ones were still in the home under parental influence. Consequently, the younger ones also became Christians. The older ones who had already left home and missed their parents' altered influence did not become Christians.

When one allows God to work in his life, a simple early Morning Prayer can change his day entirely. To explain God's wonders in this area of conversion is as impossible as counting the stars of evening or numbering the sands on the seashore.

(3) *We can change through determination.* An individual who possesses determination not only acquires new knowledge, but will work to develop the self-mastery needed to implement it in his life. It is one thing to "know," and another to "do." My doctor can tell me to lose twenty pounds in order to maintain good health. I know what I should do, but will I have the determination to control my eating habits and bring about the suggested weight loss?

The principles you will be learning may be decidedly different from what you have ever heard before. The question is, "Do you possess enough determination to put them to work for you?"

Tell Me About Yourself

I am establishing the fact that we will make our children what we are. I want you to do a little exercise with me. You will need three things: (1) A mirror, (2) a pencil, and (3) a Bible. Take these items and proceed as follows: Look in the mirror. Take a good long look. Now take your pencil and write ten sentences that describe the real *you.*

1. I am _____.
2. I am _____.
3. I am _____.
4. I am _____.
5. I am _____.
6. I am _____.
7. I am _____.
8. I am _____.
9. I am _____.
10. I am _____.

When you are finished, open your Bible and read Proverbs 23:7a.

How Did You Score?

Psychologists say our self-image (what we think of ourselves) is the key to our personal adjustment. If you visited in a psychologist's office and he read on your list that you had said positive things about yourself that would indicate that you have a good self-image. He would classify you as "well adjusted." If you said negative things about yourself, you would be diagnosed as having a poor self-image.

How did you score? Did you list positive things such as: "I am a good wife. I am a loving mother. I am happy. I am intelligent. I am pretty. I am a good cook"? Or did you write uncomplimentary things like: "I am lazy. I am ugly. I am unhappy. I am six inches too tall. I am a failure as a wife and mother. I am not talented"?

Look What Can Happen

If you have a bad self-image, it's likely your child will develop a bad self-image as well. Perhaps your daughter has heard you run yourself down for years. "I hate this red curly hair. I've never been able to do a thing with it." "I 'm so flat chested that I might as well have been a man." "My shoes are so long and wide they look like boxcars." Now, see what happens! Your daughter has reached her teens. She has red curly hair, wears a size 32 AA bra, and a 10 B shoe. She concludes: "I am unattractive. Something is wrong with me."

You want your daughter to be well adjusted. But training her to have a good self-image when you do not, is as difficult as standing two steps above her on a stairway and reaching down to try to lift her higher than yourself. Try the lifting experiment. It is almost impossible.

Where's Your Pull?

If the things we do not admire about ourselves are in an area, we can do something about, then quietly set to work and change it. If not, then we must accept ourselves and count our blessings.

It is unfortunate that many things people dislike about themselves is self-inflicted.   Being overweight, for example, brings deep despair to many. Feeling self-conscious about one's size can cast a negative reflection on one's entire life. Being lazy is another self-inflicted problem that brings depression to thousands.

We are building our children's self-image by what we are and how we feel about ourselves. Are we pulling them down with a negative and pessimistic attitude that finds fault not only in ourselves but in others as well?   Are we like the artist who paints the entire world in grays, browns, and blacks?

Or are we pulling our children up with a positive and optimistic attitude that looks for and finds the good and wonderful things about our own lives and the lives of each of our children?

We must never forget that our *attitudes* will determine the *altitude* we will gain for our little ones and ourselves.

Thought II - We Make Our Children By the Way We Train Them

In order for you to continue with this study effectively, it is vitally important that you have an accurate understanding of the word "train." God says, *"Train up a child in the way he should go: and when he is old, he will not depart from it."* Proverbs 22:6.

Training Defined

Just what does it mean to train?   Training consists of two steps that involve three major activities.   The first step is *teaching*; the second is *discipline.*

Let's talk about teaching. Teaching covers two of the three activities. The first thing one does in teaching is to show how a procedure is done. Then the teacher explains the details of the lesson.

After a child has been taught, he is ready for the last step in training - - discipline. The word discipline comes from the word disciple, which means "a follower of." The child is now ready to practice what the teacher has taught. *For a child to be well trained, he must follow what the teacher demonstrates.*

For example: Suppose you want to start training your two-year-old to put his toys away. First, you will show the child how to pick the toys up and how they are stored in the toy box. You will talk to the child as you go through the process of showing him the steps in putting his toys away. "Now, Jimmy, you put this toy away," you direct him to the toy box. The child puts the toy away, following what he watched you do and heard you say. You have taken Jimmy through his first lesson in putting toys away. Jimmy will be trained over a period of months and years of following your procedure. Each time you tell Jimmy to please put his toys away, he will know exactly what to do. (Whether he *follows* your instructions will depend on how well you study and apply the principles that will be taught in Chapter Eight.)

Perhaps this diagram will help you fix the training process in your mind:

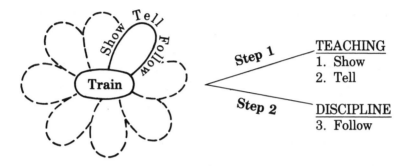

Follow the dotted lines on the flower and as you draw, repeat over and over the three activities in training. Show, tell, and follow. Show, tell, follow me, Jimmy. Show, tell, and follow. Show, tell, and follow me, Susie. On and on we go, training a child in the thousands of lessons and skills he will learn over an eighteen-year span of time.

Two Types of Discipline
It is important to point out two types of discipline.
(1) *Self-Discipline* - This is when a child follows you willingly, and does what you show and tell him to do. He does it because it is something he wants to do. His will and yours are in agreement. When a child exercises self-discipline, training is most enjoyable.
(2) *Imposed Discipline* - This is when a child decides he doesn't want to do as he has been instructed, and you must compel him to follow your lessons. You gain your child's obedience by imposing discipline upon him. (You will be taught how to impose parental discipline in Chapter Eight.)
If you are a new parent, do not expect that your child will always exercise self-discipline with regard to your teaching. Obedience does not just happen! During the first six years of a child's life, especially during his "negative and discipline years", (Read Chapter 7 in the Addendum) there will be many times you will need to impose discipline on your little one in order to train him. However, the sooner you impose discipline to make him follow your instructions, the more quickly your child will develop and exercise his own self-discipline and good judgment.

Let's Practice Training

Using the show, tell, and follow steps, let's begin practicing training.

(1) *A Computer Typist* - Suppose you are an efficient typist and a young lady comes to you who is interested in learning to type. If you agree to undertake the task of training her, what procedure would you follow? (Step 1 - *Show)* You would take her to a computer keyboard, show the home keys, proper finger placement, and all the features of the machine. You would demonstrate your typing skills. (Step 2 - *Tell)* All of the preceding action is accompanied by verbal instructions. While you typed, you would explain all the dos and don'ts of typing on a computer. (Step 3 - *Follow)* It is now time for your student to follow your teaching. (She will never learn to be an accomplished typist until this is done.) She must sit down at the computer keyboard and start the long, tedious task of learning to type. After considerable time and practice, she will eventually become a competent computer typist.

(2) *A Swimmer* - In a more abbreviated form, let's apply our steps of training to a swimmer. (Step 1 - *Show)* We dive into the water, show the proper breathing technique and the head, arm and leg movements involved in swimming. We swim and let our student watch. (Step 2 - *Tell)* We explain the dangers and all the safety precautions to take while swimming. (Step 3 - *Follow)* The student must get into the water and try to do everything she observed and heard. She will never be a swimmer until she becomes successful at following all of the steps she has been taught.

Heredity vs. Environment

In closing this section, let's consider the controversial idea of heredity versus environment in child development. Many couples declare it was through a misfortune of heredity that their wayward child happened to turn out like ol' Uncle Zeke or Aunt Matilda on Grandpa's side of the family. The laissez-faire family environment they provided in their child's formative years had little or nothing to do with their child's going astray.

Dr. William E. Homan says, "This idea of heredity provides too much sand for head burying. If a child studies spelling sixteen years under a teacher and ends up a non-speller, you have to think the teacher was to blame." He further says, "Heredity plays a part in a child in that the child can have varying degrees of talents, skills, and personality attributes. *These only make more or less easy or difficult our job in training."* 2

Homan is saying that Jimmy may need to have discipline imposed upon him only once or twice to get the message that he must follow your command to put his toys away. Due to Jimmy's congenial nature, little discipline will be needed to gain his obedience.

On the other hand, strong-willed Susie may be altogether different. It may require repeated sessions of imposed discipline to impress her that she must follow your instructions to place her toys in the toy box. It may be that she just doesn't learn quickly; but more than likely she has a determined, headstrong make-up, and will engage in a battle for control with Mother. Whatever the case may be, a mother interested in training Susie will patiently, but firmly, impose discipline upon her until she obeys Mother's instructions.

I believe environment plays the dominant role in the making of children. Few people would take the risk of adopting a newborn baby if they knew the child was destined by heredity to turn out wrong. When a couple desires to adopt a baby, the adoption agency will give them information on the natural parents' talents, skills, and personality traits (just as Dr. William E. Homan suggested). The adopting couple will be told if the biological parents were musical, athletic, mechanical, artistic, et cetera. That is essentially all they will ever need to know.

However, as I wrote in the introduction, don't expect that a good Christian environment is going to cure all the ills of children you took after they were older and had passed out of their "falling in love" years. Parenting these emotionally deprived children will require outside help for you and them.

Thought III - We Make Our Children by Our Set of Values

Our set of values is the invisible balancing scales we use in determining the things we accept or reject, the things we believe or disbelieve. Every word, action, thought, or feeling that passes through our lives, we weigh on the scale of our values.

Decisions Decisions Decisions

I have mentioned how God endowed Daddies and Mothers with the responsibility of being boss. Being the one in charge is not an exalted position in which we sit on a throne with servants constantly ministering to our whims. The opposite is true. We are the servants who must know the answers, be on the job, and alert to serve.

We must make hundreds of thousands of decisions while rearing our children. The decisions I make and circumstances I arrange for my children's lives will not be exactly the same as you will make for your children. Each child is a unique individual and every family will confront different sets of circumstances. The basic rules of discipline and training, however, must be applied to each child.

It is as impossible to expect that all parents will handle their children exactly alike, as it would be to suppose the world could be blown apart and fall back into its original condition. Even brothers and sisters from the same family do not have exactly the same experiences, go everyplace at the same time, nor face identical events.

For this reason you will learn a set of principles, but all parents will implement them in their own manner.

From Big Things to Little Things

From little questions to big problems you make decisions and explain to your children the difference between right and wrong. Suppose, while your son is playing, he becomes frustrated with his truck, kicks and throws it, and uses a curse word he learned from the boy next door. This incident is sifted through your set of values. Is this behavior acceptable or not? Unfortunately, some mothers would weigh it acceptable. Others would weigh it absolutely non-acceptable. It may be okay with some parents for their children to kick, throw things, and curse when they are angry, but this sort of behavior is not acceptable with those who follow God's plan.

Let's take another example. The question is asked, "Is it important for children to go to college?" Some people weigh this question and, according to the knowledge and experience they have had, they decide, "Yes, I will insist that my children get a college education." Others might answer "No, it isn't important for our children to attend college."

These variations in parental values will make a difference in the course of life their children take. The little boy who was not taught to control himself and went into a rage will more than likely become the man who will have no inhibitions about striking his wife and cursing his children when things do not go his way. The young man who was constrained and disciplined when he allowed his emotions to get out of control will grow up to be an adult who is better equipped to control his anger when facing life's frustrations.

Tip Your Scales

Read the following situations and weigh them on your scale of values. Do you judge the following actions to be right or wrong:

1. Johnny is jumping on the couch.   Is this acceptable or non-acceptable?

2. Jane is throwing a temper tantrum.   Do you approve or disapprove?

3. Billy will not stay in bed.   Is this okay or not?

4. The children are fighting.   Is this permissible or not permissible?

5. Can Bobby bring a garden snake into the house?   Yes or no?

6. Sally wants to wear Make-up, bra and hose when she is nine.   Do you agree or disagree?

7. Jerry refuses to go to worship with the family.   Shall his wish be granted or not?

We continually make decisions that influence our children's lives.

Understanding how values vary from family to family will help you answer your child's question the next time he comes to you and complains, "Mother, our neighbor Sammy doesn't have to go to bed at seven o'clock. Why do I have to?"

Take time to explain to him why. You may say, "The answer to that question, darling, is that my set of values is different from Sammy's mother's. I send you to bed at seven o'clock because all seven-year-old boys and girls need twelve hours of sleep to keep healthy. Also, when you go to bed at seven o'clock, I can get you up at seven o'clock so you can eat breakfast with Daddy before he goes to work."

DISCUSSION #3 - PARENTS, MAKE <u>CHILDREN</u>

By placing stress on the word *children* in this discussion, I am strongly suggesting that you let your children be children.

As a mother of little ones, you are not marking time, you are racing time. How rapid the development is from diapers to dolls, bottles to bears, cribs to cars; and the brief hours of primary school followed by high school and college. 3

This poem titled "Making a Man" 4 describes all too accurately the days in which we live.

> Hurry the baby as fast as you can,
> Hurry him, worry him, and make him a man.
> Off with his baby clothes, get him in pants,
> Feed him on brain foods and make him advance.
>
> Hustle him, soon as he's able to walk,
> Into a grammar school; cram him with talk.
> Fill his poor head full of figures and facts,
> Keep on a-jamming them in 'til it cracks.
>
> Once boys grew up at a rational rate,
> .Now we develop a man while you wait,
> Rush him through college, compel him to grab
> Of every known subject a dip and a dab.
>
> Get him in business and after the cash,
> All by the time he can grow a mustache.
> Let him forget he was ever a boy,
> Make gold his god and its jingle his joy.
>
> Keep him a-hustling and clear out of breath,
> Until he wins - - nervous prostration and death.
> > - - Nixon Waterman

Shame On Us

Why is it that parents feel they must rush their children into growing up? Many attempt to push their babies to walk too soon, believing, "There must be something wrong with my child. The neighbor's baby was walking when he was nine months old, and mine is almost thirteen months old and isn't walking yet."

For two years I taught remedial reading classes in elementary school. While working in that program designed to help children overcome reading problems, I learned how important the crawling period is in a baby's life. Parents should insist their baby spend a lot of time on the floor crawling. The action of moving arms and legs in forward and backward synchronized motion plays an important part in the development of both the right and left sides of the brain, which in turn will help the child learn to read later on. When a baby is crawling on all fours and he picks up one hand, there are receptors in the semicircular canals of his ear that sense where his head is in space. That information is sent to his brain, and the brain creates networks of connections as a result of that movement. His brain is actually being stimulated to grow as a result of the crawling motion.

I suggest that you allow your baby to crawl for as long as possible. It is not too late for a child to begin walking at twelve or thirteen months old.

Some parents are concerned that their three- and four-year-olds will be educationally deprived if they do not enroll them in a pre-school. I suggest you listen to the conservative educators who say that daily pre-school in the life of a child serves little more purpose than being a baby-sitting service for the mother. Your child will be better served if he stays home with you.

Dr. Denmark teaches that you should not send children out of the home until they are six and sometimes older. I agree with that counsel and followed it myself. Let your child (boy or girl) be *six* before sending him/her to Kindergarten. Your child may be the oldest in the class, but they will also have a chance to be the best in the class.

Other parents allow an eight-year-old to paint herself with lipstick and make-up, and a nine-year-old to wear a bra long before it's needed. We rush our children into dating at twelve and thirteen. (This practice is more common than one might imagine. Some mothers have actually been known to encourage their children's dating activities by furnishing and driving the cars for their twelve- and thirteen-year-olds' dates.)

Shame on us if we have been guilty of pushing our children to grow up too soon. Too many parents are robbing their children of the most glorious, beautiful, and peaceful time of their lives - - their childhood.

It's a Small World After All

I don't know how many of you have experienced the thrill of taking your children to Disneyland in Los Angeles, California, or Disney World in Orlando, Florida. If you have, you can relive with me a part of that fantastic adventure.

The boat ride into the small world actually brought goose bumps to me. It was a thrill I shall never forget. As our family sat in the little boat, being drawn along through the water, we began hearing the song, "It's a small world." Soon we saw in every direction hundreds of animated dolls, representing all the countries of the world, dancing and singing. The music grew louder and louder. Soon we were completely surrounded in a child's world. It was simply terrific! I wished this voyage into never-never land could have lasted all day! The joy of being a little boy or girl should be a happy, lasting experience. Do not rush your children through it too quickly.

Between Two Worlds

Yes, there is a wide chasm between a child's world and that of an adult. That is the way it should be. God did not intend for a child to be burdened with problems, heartaches, and weighty responsibilities that await him in his adult life.

I often thank the Lord for my happy childhood. When my mother was living, I wrote her expressions of gratitude for the years she stayed home with me. She provided for me that protective and loving shield every child so desperately needs. I am positive that it was that foundation that has played a major role in my ability to face confidently the challenges of adult life.

Permit your child to enjoy his childhood as long as he can and you make sure you are there to enjoy it with him.

Summing It Up

When John the Baptist was born, the question was asked, "*What manner of child shall this be?*" Luke 1:66. I ask you, "What manner of child will yours be?"

First, he'll be your flesh and blood, made of your genes and chromosomes.

Second, he'll be (1) what you are yourself, (2) what you train him to be, and (3) what your set of values weigh out for him.

Third, he will be a child for as long as he can, if you will only allow him.

Keep On The Track
As You Train

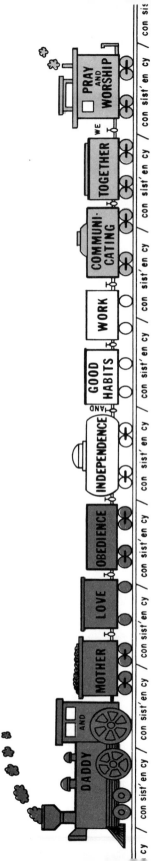

TRAINING UP A CHILD

"Train up a child in the way he should go, even when he is old he will not depart from it."

Proverbs 22:6

Chapter Two
Keep On The Track As You Train

This little train has been such an important part of my *Training Up a Child* classes that I feel I must include it in the book. At the time I decided to use *Training Up a Child* as the theme for this book, I could think of nothing more fitting than to use an old-fashioned steam locomotive as a visual aid. Reinforcing teaching with pictures is a part of my teacher training that has always stayed with me.

The little train (I call it my Home Express) teaches three lessons I want you to learn. Once you have committed them to memory, you will be ready to plunge into the heart of our study.

LESSON 1

As you look at the little Home Express, you will notice a label on each car. Start at the engine, then proceed to the back of the train, and carefully read each label. Observe how you can build three sentences as you go.

Sentence 1 - Daddy and Mother love obedience.

Sentence 2 - Independence and good habits work.

Sentence 3 - Communicating together, we pray and worship.

You have just learned the eleven essential components that are needed in the life of every child. Please fix them firmly in your mind.

Each time I teach a *Training Up a Child* series, I begin the first lesson by requesting that my students save up all their questions. I say, "Please don't ask me any questions about what you should or should not do with your child. As we cover each lesson, I feel sure you will be able to answer your own questions from these eleven categories of study." That has always held true. I have never had a graduate of TUAC who could not locate the area that would help her solve any problem she has experienced.

I remember one lady who enrolled in my classes as a desperate last resort. She and her husband had paid many visits to a professional counselor who charged them a large fee for each hour of counseling. Their five-year-old was tearing their home apart. After completing the TUAC class, she told me she had been helped tremendously and that she now understood what they were doing wrong.

Another TUAC graduate said, "The time I spent in TUAC has probably made more difference in my life than any other single experience."

LESSON 2

The second lesson I would like for you to learn from our little Home Express is that every single car on the train is essential. You cannot give up any of these eleven principles. One builds upon the other. Each segment depends on the development of the one prior to it.

For example, if you and your child do not have mutual love for each other, the child will reject your training. You must love the child and he must return your love in order for your Home Express to travel successfully down the track. One may say, "I've tried to get obedience, but I have failed. I will work on everything else but obedience." Forget that idea. If you cannot gain obedience from your child, you will be unable to get him to work, communicate, or follow any of the other TUAC principles for you either. So please keep in mind that for you to train your child successfully *all eleven ingredients are essential.*

LESSON 3

The third key point you must remember in *Training Up a Child* is that all of the principles must be exercised with consistency. Be sure to *keep firmly on the track as you train your children.*

Listen! Can you imagine the wheels on the locomotive saying, con *sist'* en cy, con *sist'* en cy, con *sist'* en cy, as it rumbles along? Accentuate the second syllable and it can be a fun exercise to keep you reminded of con *sist'* en cy.

While watching television I heard a panel of educators discussing the word consistent. They concluded that in actuality it is impossible for one to be completely consistent.

The dictionary definition of consistent is: "keeping or inclining to keep to the same principles." If these educators believe that it is impossible to be perfectly consistent at all times, I agree.   But, the definition of consistency is being inclined (that means being willing) to keep the same principles. Incline does not suggest perfection, but willingness.

Remember that *consistency is not perfection in applying our eleven principles, but a constant willingness to apply them.*

ASSIGNMENT

1. Take some time to be alone with each of your children. Tell them how much they mean to you. Children love stories, and will enjoy hearing you describe your experiences when you were a little girl and your dreams about the children that you would have. Let them hear you say, "I always wanted a little boy (or girl) just like you. I am so glad God gave you to me."

2. Make a card to remind you that you are making your children what they are. Place it on your kitchen windowsill. Write the caption I WILL MAKE MY CHILD. Draw the following three pictures:

    Mirror - By what I am myself

    Flower- By my training

    Scales - By my set of values

3. Write a report describing what you want your child to be when a teenager.

Section I

Daddy and Mother

Love

Obedience

DADDY and MOTHER

Behave in Your Beehive

Chapter Three
Daddy and Mother

As our Home Express goes cruising along, its destiny is somewhere ahead. Daddy and Mother are in the engine at the controls. The safety of the remaining eight cars depends on the skill of those in the engine. I repeat! *The success of ALL the remaining principles in TUAC depends on the success of the Daddy and Mother relationship.* Is each willing to bear his or her responsibility? Are they willing to work together?

WHICH WAY
High in the Canadian Rocky Mountains is a rushing stream called Divide Creek. As it flows down the mountain, it is a splendid sight. Unfortunately, because a huge boulder obstructs its path, its glory is short-lived. The smoothness of its flow is shattered when it rushes into that mighty rock. When the water strikes the rock, it must divide. Some flows left to Kicking Horse River and eventually to the Pacific Ocean. The rest rushes to the right to Bow River and on to the Atlantic Ocean. The boulder determines "which way" the water will go. 1

I compare fathers and mothers to that boulder. They are in the middle of the stream of their children's lives, acting as the object to determine "which way" their children will be directed to go.

Because this relationship is so vital, it is absolutely essential that we learn what Daddy and Mother must be. In order to have some fun with this lesson and to impress its points, I've titled it, "Daddy and Mother, Behave in Your Beehive."

GOD SAYS ORGANIZE
The autocratic home must first of all be properly organized. God gives the pattern for that organization in I Corinthians 11:3 - *"The head of every man*

is Christ; and the head of the woman is the man; and the head of Christ is God." Do not forget that order.

> God
>
> Christ
>
> Man
>
> Woman

This particular Scripture does not address children, but previous passages we have noticed, such as Ephesians 6:1 and Colossians 3:20, have already confirmed that they are under Daddy's and Mother's authority.

Any time Daddy's, Mother's, and the children's positions are not in proper sequence, there is serious trouble. The family will not function well, nor be happy. Parents are uncomfortable and the children are discontent. Society suffers, and the nation deteriorates.

God has designated that men bear certain responsibilities and that women must assume others. Even though men and women are not the same in purpose or responsibility, their roles are of equal importance. To argue one is more important than the other is foolish. God does not approve of anything less than a "100% - 100%" marriage. Our purpose is to learn how to become a "100%" Daddy or a "100%" Mother.

God did not plan for our homes to be marred by confusion and disorder. *"God is not the author of confusion, but of peace."* I Corinthians 14:33

When we observe the sun, moon, and stars moving with precise order and direction, and the dependability of the changing seasons, we witness proof of God's orderliness.

SEVENTY-FIVE PERCENT? YOU'RE KIDDING!

One morning as I was going about my household chores, our doorbell rang. When I opened the door, I met two pleasant ladies who were standing on our front steps.

"Good morning! Are you the lady of the house?" one asked. "Yes, Ma'am, I am," I replied.

"We are in the neighborhood this morning calling on young mothers. Do you have any children?"

"Yes, I do," I answered.

They inquired, "Do you have a few minutes that we may visit with you?"

I noticed they both carried briefcases. I was not sure if they were taking a survey or selling something. But if they wanted to talk about my family, they were welcome. So, I cordially invited them in.

I learned my guests represented a leading encyclopedia company. After approximately fifteen minutes of listening to their sales presentation, I was sold.

"A set of encyclopedias would be terrific aids for helping me answer the multitude of questions I am asked!" I reasoned.

I expressed my excitement about their books, so they made an appeal for me to purchase a set.

I was enthusiastic about the thought of owning that beautiful set of encyclopedias, but not so much that I had forgotten who makes the final decisions about large purchases at our house. I explained to them that I would love to have a set of their encyclopedias, but they would need to talk to my husband.

I knew he was occupied upstairs, so I dashed up the stairs, turned on my wifely charms, told him about the encyclopedias, and asked if he would please listen to the ladies' appeal. My husband was adorable! "Sure, honey, I will listen to their story," he agreed. He followed me downstairs, into the living room, and I introduced him to the women.

The whole encyclopedia sales story was repeated. This time I was ready not to walk, but to run, and get the checkbook and write a check for the down payment.

Decision time was at hand. My husband, as any good autocratic leader should be, had been polite and a perfect gentleman. Furthermore, he had played the game fairly. He did not make a snap judgment. Fifteen minutes of his time had been spent gathering information, and he was aware of my enthusiasm for purchasing the encyclopedias.

It was now his responsibility to weigh the matter and make a decision. His decision was, "No! We can do quite well without the books. There is a library nearby that has several sets of encyclopedias for any research we might need to do."

I was disappointed, but I knew perfectly well, that the husband's having the final say is the only way to obey God's law and keep order to the family. (I must add that my husband is very generous with me and seldom denies any request that I make to him.)

The ladies gathered their materials and prepared to leave. While they were in our home, I had been puzzled about their door-to-door approach. Why did this encyclopedia company, which was one of the largest in the country at that time, send representatives to neighborhoods to make sales appeals to young mothers? So, before they left, I asked them about it. They replied, *"We do this because our experience has proved that seventy-five percent of our sales are made to the woman of the household."*

I was amazed! I asked myself, "Do seventy-five percent of young mothers act as chief decision-maker in the American family? Do they actually finalize a purchase involving that much money without first consulting their husbands?"

Perhaps this startling statistic points to a chief cause of the problems many families experience today. When women usurp the family's financial authority, men should object. Why should the head of the house be held responsible for a large debt of which he does not approve?

What do you think about it? After reading God's order for the home, do you suppose the fact that women are occupying the leadership position in so many homes has any connection with the domestic problems our country is now experiencing?

Chapter Four
Daddy Bee

There are four major responsibilities Daddy should bear in order to maintain proper organization in a home. His responsibilities are:

1. Be the head of the home.
2. Be the protector
3. Be the physical provider.
4. Be the spiritual leader.

RESPONSIBILITY NO.1 - BE THE HEAD OF THE HOME

Yes, Daddy, according to God's decree, you have the responsibility of being the head of your family. This includes being the one by whom and through whom all major decisions and orders of the family's business are approved.

You are the king of your domain! You are to make or sanction the rules of the household! You give the ultimate yes or no! Your word is final! If conduct and activities of which you disapprove are going on inside your home, you need to set your house in order. If a family member ignores your leadership, he or she should be put back in proper position.

Sociologists and psychologists tell us that, if all homes had a strong male figure, the juvenile crime rate would plummet. One of the questions I have been asked most often by the women I have taught is "What do you do if your husband is complacent and will not assume the responsibility of leading his family? What can I do if he shifts the important decisions to me and refuses to discipline the children?"

I always answer these questions by directing the woman to the Bible. *"For the husband is the head of the wife, even as Christ is the head of the church...as the church is subject unto Christ, so let the wives be to their own husbands in every thing."* Ephesians 5:23 and 24. Other Scriptures as

Genesis 3:16, I Corinthians 11:3, and I Timothy 2:12 leave no escape for a husband. He is commanded by God to assume the leadership position in his household. If he refuses, or is slothful in fulfilling this responsibility, God will hold him accountable.

Be A 3F Man

If it were possible, I would shout over the most powerful public address system on earth and give every man in America three tips about how to become the head of his home and persuade his family to follow his leadership. He must be a 3F man. It is as simple as 1-2-3. Here's the secret.

(1F) - BE FAIR. A man launching out to lead his wife and children must first of all be fair. The following are six important ingredients of fairness all successful leaders must practice:

(a) *Listen* - Before you make final decisions, be fair and listen to your family's wishes about a given subject. You are not compelled to grant all they ask for, but have the courtesy to listen to their wishes. Every member of the family should enjoy the privilege of being heard.

(b) *Especially Listen to the Wishes of Your Wife* - Remember that she is your co-worker. She is not your equal in power or responsibility, but she is your equal in importance. Grant her desires whenever feasible or possible. Consider her suggestions and thank her for them. Appreciate her for the invaluable contributions she makes to your home, and with regularity TELL HER HOW GRATEFUL YOU ARE.

(c) *Don't Expect of Your Wife and Children What You Are Not Willing to Do or Be Yourself* - A good leader will always strive to be that which he would have others be.

(d) *Take Care of Your Family's Needs Before Your Own* - Your family's willingness to follow and respect your leadership will be built upon the example they see of your willingness to meet their needs.

Follow General Andrew Jackson's example of leadership. The story has been told that in the battle of New Orleans, as he was making his way through his army, he noticed a soldier who had no boots.

He stopped his horse and asked the man, "Private, where are your boots?"

The soldier replied, "General, sir! I have no boots."

At that point, General Jackson dismounted from his horse, took off his boots, and gave them to the man.

"If anyone in this army does without boots, it will be me," Jackson replied.

An honorable leader is like that. His family's needs are met first. If there are sacrifices to be made, he will be the one who makes them. He will not spend most of his income on something he wants and then bring the scraps of his wages home to his family. Neither will he give them only his leftover time. He will come home to be with his wife and children rather than go other places and spend his time with other people and projects.

(e) *Be the Financial Manager* - If you are the leader of your family, you must bear the burden of managing the family income. Any man who will bring his hard-earned money home and turn it over completely to his wife and expect her to manage it is openly surrendering his leadership. Your wife can act as secretary and tend to the tedious and time-consuming task of check writing; but the who, where, when, and what to pay should be determined by the husband.

This is not to say a woman should have no financial responsibility. As you designate how the family income is to be spent, be fair and provide your wife with money to spend as she chooses. You will have a happier wife if you express your confidence in her by allowing her to have her own personal account. Each month deposit a fair portion of your monthly income into the bank for her to manage on her own.

A separate budget for each of you is a successful solution many couples have found to handle family finances. Your wife can be responsible for the food, clothing, household and personal items. You pay the monthly utility bills, house payment, insurance, income taxes, and lawn and car expenses. A separate budget plan helps each of you to have added incentives to be thrifty and work to have money left to save or invest.

Disagreement about money is one of the four major causes of divorce. This one fair gesture of providing personal accounts for wives would solve a great deal of discontentment among homemakers. Few things are more humiliating for a hard-working and intelligent woman than to be lowered to the level of the children and be forced to get approval for every penny she spends.

(f) *Don't Forget That Your Business Is Your Wife's Business, Too* - Be thoughtful enough to consult her, or at least inform her, if you decide to sink your life's savings into the stock market or other investments. Out of respect for your wife, keep her informed about the family business. In the event of your death, you do not want your wife to be confronted by red tape, complicated legal questions, or a lawyer who may be cunning enough to take much from her that you worked all your life to obtain.

(2F) - BE FIRM - The second tip I give to a man aspiring to be a leader is to be firm. One distinct mark of a leader is that *he will not allow himself to be pushed around*. He just will not tolerate it!

We women can be quite pushy and domineering. Often, we are only testing. Once we learn our husband will not stand firm, we begin to feel stronger and more capable of leading the family than he is.

What would you think of the president of your local bank if he allowed a teller or the vice-president, to come in every morning and take control of his office? Would you consider a private school for your child if every time you visited the school and asked for the principal, a first-grade teacher appeared and informed you, "I'm the boss around here." I am sure you would not approve of either of the above situations. Men must not allow their wives to push them out of their position as the head of the family.

Women respect firmness and hate wishy-washyness. Oh, she may be that way herself, but she cannot stand it in her man. So, YOU, Daddy, leader, captain, and king, be fair and be firm. *Be Firm and Make What You Believe Are Wisest Choices, Stick to Them, and See That Your Orders Are Carried Out.* The only circumstance under which you should change a decision is when valuable information arrives late and convinces you that your initial decision was unwise. You will then correct your mistake. However, make these occasions few, or you will appear to have poor judgement.

Do not misunderstand what I am saying. When I commend firmness, I *do not* mean that you should ever use physical force with your wife. No man should physically mistreat his wife under any circumstances. At the point when a husband resorts to cuffing his wife around physically, he is no longer an effective leader. Neither is he a man. A woman cannot respect a brutal man, much less feel obligated to submit to his leadership and authority.

(3F) - BE FAITHFUL - A woman can endure almost any hardship, but there is one pain that is devastating when inflicted on her. It will crush her spirits, torture her mind, and shatter her nerves. If you wish to crush your wife and break her heart, you do not need to raise your hand against her. Just do not love her. Avoid her. Never compliment her. Make her feel that she is inferior to other women and constantly criticize her. Treat her with contempt. Give her the silent treatment. Be more attentive to other women than you are to her. Make her feel she is unworthy to be married to such a great man as you. And, of course, the ultimate humiliating blow is to choose another woman to take her place.

On the other hand, if you want your wife to adore you and follow you to the ends of the earth, *Be Faithful to Her and Love Her.* Her life depends on it and, in more than one way, yours does, too. God commands, *Husbands, love your wives, and be not bitter against them...give honour unto the wife, as unto the weaker vessel, and as being heirs together of the grace of life; that your prayers be not hindered."* Colossians 3:19, and I Peter 3:7

Compliment your wife to others. Show her affection in the presence of family and friends. Tell her how much better she does some things than your mother did. Tell your children, in her presence, how fortunate they are to have such a wonderful mother. *The greatest gift you could ever give your sons and daughters is to love their mother deeply.* Often tell your wife, "I love you." This does not cost you anything, but you will reap a thousand percent dividend in return. And remind her that of all the men in the world you are the most fortunate to have her for your wife.

A man who is FAIR, FIRM and FAITHFUL to his wife and children has learned the indispensable formula for manhood and leadership.

My Husband a 3F Man

My husband taught me soon after we were married that he intended to be the head of our family and that he would not permit me to dominate him. I've often thought, since that occasion, what a shame it is that more husbands will not impress their family that they are not "Mr. Milktoasts," softies, or push-overs.

After our Acapulco honeymoon was over, and we descended from the clouds, I began to establish some negative patterns of wifely behavior. Becoming a nag appeared to be one of my natural talents. I had plunged headlong into exercising it freely when one day, to my astonishment, my new husband, who is a mild, quiet man, interrupted one of my irritating recitals. He informed me in a clear and understandable manner that he was not going to put up with it. His speech went something like this:

"I am a reasonably intelligent man, maybe not a genius, but smart enough. My vision is excellent - - 20/20 to be exact. Furthermore, I am still young and haven't suffered a hearing loss. As long as you are not in the closet with the door shut and I in the shower with the water running, I should be able to hear you. Once you express your views and wishes to me, that is sufficient.

I will be happy to consider them, but I refuse to be nagged constantly. Do you understand?"

I admitted that I did and, since that day, I have understood where my husband has drawn the boundary lines. I would not be honest, however, if I did not confess that it is still my nature to want my way. There are times I have to bite my tongue, and even show my frustrations a little, when my husband makes a decision with which I do not agree. But on that day, many years ago, my husband pledged his fairness, proved his firmness, and daily provides his faithfulness.

RESPONSIBILITY NO. 2 - BE THE PROTECTOR

The second responsibility of an autocratic daddy is to provide ample protection for his family. He protects them by providing not only physical shelter, but emotional protection as well. Fear and feelings of insecurity are devastating emotions that trouble many families. If one who is afflicted with them, is not relieved, it may adversely affect him physically, emotionally, or psychologically.

A woman afflicted with fear and uncertainty may develop digestive disorders, resort to tranquilizers, or break out in a chronic rash. An insecure child may develop behavior problems or a speech impediment. If he has asthma, it may be aggravated, or he may be affected with any number of other physical and emotional ailments.

God instilled within men the ability to minimize their family's fears and feelings of insecurity. Human nature, mixed with common judgment, tells the family to seek refuge in the protective arms of Daddy. With his deep, strong voice he can drive away any intruders. His shoulders are so broad, and his hands and arms are so strong, that he can fight off the biggest bear in the forest and sweep us away to safety. If a family moves to a new locality, they have confidence that Daddy is wise enough that he will provide a comfortable house in which they will live when they arrive at that big intimidating city. The family may fall asleep and not be afraid because Daddy is near. These are the silent sentiments of a child.

My Childhood

My daddy was an A-1 protector. I remember very few times that my father was absent at nightfall. In addition to keeping up our farm, his extracurricular activity that I remember the most was the meetings he was required to attend as a member of the local board of education. I dreaded those nights when he had to be away. Perhaps I was a child who needed an extra amount of security, but I never felt that all was well until daddy returned home. It was only when my daddy was home that I could relax and rest peacefully.

Homes Without a Daddy

In order for Daddy to be the protector, it is logical that he must be in the presence of those he is protecting.

Dr. Bennett Olshaker, in his book, *What Shall We Tell the Kids?*, writes, "It is crystal clear to anyone who works with upset children or who cares about the problems of young people that the lack of a father is a prime cause of difficulties in many boys and girls." [1]

Divorce and separation are reaping a devastating toll on the American family. It is for these reasons that many homes are deprived of a father. Tragically, many families are being robbed of a feeling of security because they are left unprotected.

When Daddy Is Home But Not At Home

It is possible for Daddy to be in the home physically and at the same time not really be home. That may sound like a contradiction, but it is not. A daddy can absent himself from his home in at least the following three ways:

(1) He may have a job that takes him out of town for most of the week.

(2) He may be engaged in so many activities, in addition to his regular job, that they consume a major portion of his extra time.

(3) He may be bodily at home, but his thoughts and spirit are not there. His attentions are not focused upon the members of his family but are elsewhere.

In a survey of eight thousand high school seniors, it was learned that their number one problem was trouble at home. Their major complaint was that they seldom saw their dads. "Dad's too busy." "He's too busy playing golf or reading the newspaper." [2]

In his book, *You Can Be a Great Parent!* Charlie Shedd promised his infant son, "When I'm with you, Peter, I'll really be with you." [3]

Daddy, Come to Supper

To illustrate how a daddy can be at home but not be home, I will share this story:

A family was gathered around the table for the evening meal. The members had been separated all day; so they had accumulated several exciting events they wished to share. Soon after the meal was in progress, everyone became actively engaged in chatter and conversation, everyone, that is, but Daddy. As he ate, he was entertaining himself by peering over his shoulder watching the Monday night football game on television.

The smallest male member of the family was just beginning to talk. In his little boy way, he attempted to join the conversation. The family members suddenly began to notice the excitement that was coming over the baby. They stopped their talk briefly to pay attention to what he was trying to say.

He started his narrative and was going full steam ahead when he stopped to address a major point to his father. He was completely unsuccessful in gaining his father's attention. Daddy was involved in a touchdown play and did not even hear Junior. The more the baby tried unsuccessfully to gain this father's attention, the more fretful he became. As a last resort, and with all the volume he could muster, he yelled, "Daddy! Come to supper!"

With that burst of frustration from his child, Daddy got the idea. He came to supper, not only in body, but in spirit, too. Daddy gave his full attention to his precious, persistent toddler.

Remember Twelve

Have you ever heard a father express disappointment over the lack of interest his teenage son showed in his companionship? During the boy's formative years, daddy looked forward to the time when his son would become a man. "We will have more in common then," he reasoned. But now that the boy is approaching manhood, he rejects his dad. What went wrong?

Unfortunately, that father failed to hear the tip, "Remember Twelve." If you don't become a bosom buddy with your boy before age twelve, you will seriously damage your chances of ever enjoying a close relationship with him. In the teenage years, your son will wish to spend most of his time with friends his own age.

If, on the other hand, a father is wise enough to make his son his number one companion from birth through age twelve, his son will never reject him. Dad will always be one of his favorite companions, and his son will remain loyal to his father throughout his life.

A father should plan "special times" when he and his son can go places together. Leave Mom and the rest of the family home and go to the mountains and camp for a few days. Purchase airline tickets and spend a week touring Washington D.C., or go explore old abandoned gold mines in the mountains. Taking time to engage in these kinds of enjoyable activities together will build everlasting memories.

Fathers make an error in judgment when they consider the babbling of their babies to be trivia, which he may ignore. The rock throwing, kite flying, bike riding, rabbit hunting, playing catch, and horseback riding in the pre-adolescent years are activities that build the bridge over which your son will let you pass into his future world.

Resign Today

An autocratic home must be blessed with the watchful protection of a daddy. If you are a traveling salesman, a cross-country truck driver, or are over-burdened with social activities, consider changing to another job, or cutting back on unessential social entanglements. Arrange your life so that you can be home with your family in both body and spirit. Your child's spiritual, physical, social, and mental well being critically depend on you.

Fathers must not make the same mistake that the prophet Samuel made. Samuel was a good man, but the Bible tells us, "*And his sons walked not in his ways, but turned aside after lucre, and took bribes, and perverted judgment.*" I Samuel 8:3. The Bible indicates that Samuel's mistake was being absent from home too often to properly influence his sons. "*And he went from year to year in circuit to Bethel, and Gilgal, and Mizpeh, and judged Israel in all those places.*" I Samuel 7:16. Samuel was an unfortunate example of Song of Solomon 1:6, "*They made me the keeper of the vineyards; but mine own vineyard have I not kept.*"

What's the Matter with Steven?

Some years ago, I heard a widely known speaker relate a personal story that I have never forgotten. His purpose was to convince the men in the audience that there is no substitute for Daddy's presence in the home.

When this man's children were small, he was working vigorously to earn a doctor's degree. His study was so time-consuming that he was leaving his family early in the morning and arriving home late at night. During the brief time this ambitious father was at home, his children were usually asleep.

One night his wife shared with him a growing concern she had about their oldest son, Steven. "There is something wrong with his throat," she told her husband. Of course, her worry aroused Dad's concern and he insisted she take Steven to their pediatrician as soon as possible. Steven was taken to the doctor's office for an examination.

The doctor checked him thoroughly and gave him all the usual medical tests. After completing the examination, he pronounced Steven in good physical health.

The doctor then requested a private conference with Steven's mother in his office. During the visit, he inquired about their home life. After asking several more questions, the doctor was able to determine his young patient's problem. "How much time is his daddy spending with him?" he asked. She frankly replied, "None! He is working on a doctorate and is gone from early in the morning until late at night." The doctor dismissed her with this practical prescription: "Take this message home to your husband. Tell him he will have to choose between the books and the boy. Steven is suffering from an emotional upset. His father's companionship is the medicine that will cure him."

When she delivered the doctor's message to her husband, he went to a secluded place and knelt in prayer to God. He pledged to the Lord that if He would help his little boy regain his health, it would be the boy and not the books. He started coming home early to spend time with Steven. He installed a light in the drive so they could play ball together after dark. His son's throat was soon back to normal.

That lesson was so impressive to that father that it became a habit for him to return home from his demanding schedule and play with his children. His fortunate children never suffered again for lack of Daddy's attention.

Oh yes, today Stephen, who is a law school graduate, is a judge and another of this man's sons is a practicing pediatrician. The father who once needed to spend more time with his children became an outstanding winning parent.

RESPONSIBILITY NO. 3 - BE THE PHYSICAL PROVIDER
From near the beginning of time, it has been God's decree that the man is to make the living for his family. (Genesis 3:17- 19, 23, Exodus 21:10, and I Timothy 5:8.)

The man is equipped with the physical and emotional stamina to fulfill this obligation. *Being the physical provider for the family is Daddy's responsibility.*

God made this rule when He told Adam "*to till the ground from whence he was taken; in sorrow shalt thou eat of it all the days of thy life; thorns and thistles shall it bring forth to thee.*" This decree was made because Eve believed Satan's lie and disobeyed God's command. Adam erred by following Eve's example and ate the fruit, which God had forbidden. Because of their disobedience they were both expelled from the paradise they had enjoyed in the beautiful Garden of Eden. Adam was ordered to work by the "*sweat of his face,*" and Eve was told, "*in pain thou shalt bring forth children; and thy desire shall be to thy husband, and he shall rule over thee.*" Since Eve was so easily deceived, Adam was appointed to be her leader. At this time, God appointed Adam (man) as the provider and manager and Eve (woman) as the obedient wife and mother.

Do Not Weaken Your Headship

A man weakens his headship when he does not make adequate provisions for his family. Being a good provider strengthens a man as the head of his house. (We just learned how God joined the two together.) It is the husband's ability to make the livelihood that wins his mate's confidence in him as her leader. If a man is weak, inept, and *demands* that his wife help provide the living, she loses confidence in his leadership. When the husband is the one who *insists* that his wife work outside the home, she in most cases, will lose some admiration for him, may even resent him, and will never be content with this unfair arrangement.

In his book, *Man of Steel and Velvet,* Aubrey Andelin says, "When a woman works because it is her husband's idea, a great harm comes. His suggestion that she work casts doubts in her mind as to his adequacy as a man. If he must lean on her, she will question his ability to solve his problems and face responsibility that is his. This brings insecurity." 4

For many years I have observed the festering anger that develops in the hearts of mothers who are *forced* to take jobs out of the home. The tasks, for which God gave her special talents, she must now neglect. She feels abused to return home after a tiring day's work and then be required to cook, clean, serve, entertain, and cater to her family's needs. It especially infuriates her to watch her husband relax in front of the TV or read the paper while she is forced to do all of the work she should have enjoyed doing if she had the privilege of staying home throughout the day. There is little peace or contentment for a mother in a home unfairly ordered in this fashion.

The idea that Daddy is to be "the bread winner" has never been challenged in the history of the world until our present age. We now have a generation of young men who believe it is as much their wives' responsibility to help make the living as theirs. If we are to stand as a secure nation, we must reject this misguided notion. Until women are allowed to return to the home where they belong and work to build physically, spiritually, and emotionally fit children, we are plunging toward disaster for our country.

The American Home Is Being Destroyed

Some time ago, there was a gathering of former presidents, state governors, city mayors and hundreds of prominent people from all 50 states to address one of the most pressing dilemmas facing America.

Their task was to solve the problem of 15 million young Americans. "These young people are at risk of growing up unskilled, unlearned, or, even worse, unloved," said the chairman of the President's Summit for America's Future. "This problem has the potential to explode our society," he warned.

He was not exaggerating. Fifteen million in a total population of about 60 million youth is a huge number. Mostly these young people come from dysfunctional families and fall victims to the poisons of the street. Every year 3.4 million of them try drugs and half a million attempt suicide. Many of them will drop out of high school and will become functionally illiterate in a country with free universal education. Violent crimes committed by these youngsters have become such a problem that Congress passed a juvenile crime bill that allows people as young as 13 to be treated as adults in the criminal justice system.

What was the committee's solution to this daunting problem? It is seeking to find mentors--adult volunteers who will take care of these children. But what happened to these children's parents? They were not killed in a war or by a plague, or some other natural disaster. Their problem is self-inflicted. In the United States mothers are leaving the home to take jobs on the factory floor, in the show room, or in the office. Our society is belittling the task of homemaking and is losing its homemakers. With the free mixing of men and women in the work place, one thing leads to another.   The American home is gradually being destroyed.

What Is a Wife to Do?

I have taught enough women to learn that many of the American mothers who have joined the working force are not leaving their houses and children in someone else's care simply because they prefer it.

After hearing me teach lessons on the importance of mothers remaining in the home, young women have come to me with tears in their eyes. They sorrowfully asked, "What are you supposed to do when you want to stay home with your children, but your husband *insists* that you go out and get a job?"

What *IS* a wife to do when her husband will not take the responsibility of earning the living for the family? As we see the divorce figures rising in our country, many women are answering that question this way: " If I must earn my own living, what do I need with a husband? I will leave the relationship. If I am freed from meeting all of his demands, my burdens will be much lighter."

Your Wife Already Has a HUGE Job

If you are a father with a child who is still at home, you must understand that your wife has a job--a HUGE job! The moment the two of you decided to bring a new life into the world, your wife's vocation changed.

Homemaking and mothering are vitally important jobs and only women are uniquely qualified to perform them. It is not by chance that bearing children and nursing them are purely feminine tasks. God has given women the special talents and the psychological makeup that is needed to nurture children. There is no substitute for mother's milk or mother's love.

It is impossible to extract and bottle motherly compassion.   Her patience, kindness, willingness to sacrifice her own comforts, her natural affinity for children, and the children's natural affinity for the mother are the combination for successful child rearing.   A mother understands her children's problems, even when they cannot express them. She uniquely senses their physical and emotional needs. No day-care center or nursery can replace the mother.

Mothers are the silent workers who are indispensable for building the character of the next generation. A Christian mother, who understands the crucial nature of her responsibility, will tutor her children with faith and moral values, as only she can. She will raise children with courage, honesty, truthfulness, patience and perseverance, love and kindness, faith and self-confidence. On the other hand, a society without mothers and homemakers will produce at-risk youth.

Please, Daddy, Let Mama Stay Home

Fathers will *insist*, or allow, their wives to work for at least one of the following seven reasons:

(1) He and his wife have set their standard of living too high. His earning power is not sufficient to reach their material goals.

(2) Perhaps they are both "thing" collectors and always want added luxuries that they cannot afford.

(3) It gives a husband added security for his wife to work.

(4) His own mother worked outside the home; therefore, he feels it's the natural thing for his wife to do.

(5) He may feel his wife has too much time on her hands. He reasons that, since she is always "running around", she might as well use her time for something constructive.

(6) He sees very little that she has accomplished when he gets home after a hard day's work. He reasons, "If her homemaking duties don't require any more effort than this, I will help her find something that will more profitably occupy her time."

(7) His wife may have a college degree or be skilled in a particular field. He doesn't want her to neglect her profession.

Maybe none of the above is your reason for encouraging your wife to forsake her home in favor of adding another paycheck to your family income. God's principles remain the same. *It is still your God-ordained responsibility to make the living for your family.*

Again, may I say, if you are a daddy who *compels* your wife to work outside the home, please permit me to act as your children's guardian ad litem, pleading in the court of domestic tranquillity, "Please, Daddy, let your children's mother stay home. They desperately need her, and no one else can take her place."

Think Essentials

It is my conviction that there isn't a living man who is physically and mentally sound who cannot carry out God's order to make a living for his family. He may not be able to provide all the luxuries that allure many modern Americans, but he can provide the essentials of life. Anything beyond this, he must weigh on his scale of values. He must answer the question concerning luxuries: "Can we get along better without them?"

Children would overwhelmingly vote to live without large houses, fancy cars and fat bank accounts in favor of having a happy life at home. *"Better is a dinner of herbs where love is, than a stalled ox and hatred therewith."* Proverbs 15:17 It is never "things" that build happy memories and firm foundations for children. I was not impressed with the model of car my daddy drove when I was a child, but I will always remember some of the stories he used to tell me while I sat on his knee. A child will always remember the times a daddy played hide-and-seek, told stories, popped popcorn, and played games with him.

Two Extremities

When I consider money and providing adequate provisions for the family, I am reminded of the words of Van Dyke, who said, "Our poverty comes not from the smallness of our provisions, but from the largeness of our desires."

In the past, I have known men who represented both extremes of the income scale. Yet their decisions to bear the responsibility of providing for their families and letting their wives tend to the homemaking produced happy results.

One such family with whom I was acquainted lived in very humble circumstances. The husband's efforts were mainly devoted to the ministry, for which he never received more than modest wages. He supplemented his earnings by working as a carpenter and doing odd jobs. His wife never worked outside the home. They reared five children, and those who were interested obtained a college education. Their food was sufficient, their clothes were plain, their house humble, but the children they raised were admirable and would be the envy of thousands of affluent families.

Another man and his wife with whom I was acquainted were materially wealthy. This father devoted his life to tilling the soil and owned vast acreage's of land worth hundreds of thousands of dollars. His wife never worked away from home. They reared five children and some of them also obtained higher degrees of education. Their food was abundant, their clothes elegant, their house was elaborate. Their children brought them delight and would also be the envy of multitudes of parents.

How could each of these men, representing two extremes of the income scale, produce the same results of a successful family? The secret is obvious! They each set priorities! Each man organized his family according to God's plan. Each considered his opportunities and the talents he possessed. Each worked hard at his chosen profession and *taught his family to live within his income.*

I'll Never Forget Sarah

Sarah was a little girl who once lived across the street from us and often came by our house on her way to school.

She never appeared to be a happy child, but one particular morning I remember sadness clouded her pretty little round face and dark brown eyes.

Compassionately, I put my arms around her and asked, "What is the matter, sweetheart? Is something wrong today?" Holding back the tears, she replied, "Mrs. Webb, I like to go to school, but I hate coming home!"

Little Sarah explained her despair. Both her parents were attending a doctors' convention in a distant city. (Her mother was a pediatrician and her father a neurologist.) Sarah was one of the multitudes of unfortunate children who must come home to a baby-sitter or an empty house every day.

She and her little brother and sister were the most neglected children on our block. They had material "things" galore, but one of the most vital ingredients of their lives was missing, the watchful, nurturing, care of a loving, stay-at-home mother.

Our Men Deserve a Standing Ovation

Multitudes of men in America deserve an ovation for the way they daily leave their homes, go fight the battles of life, and earn a living for their families. All young fathers are not abandoning their manly responsibility. One young homemaker was recently discussing with me how grateful she is that her husband provides for her and their child. She added, "You know, it makes him proud, and he feels better about himself because he takes care of us." That is so true! That is the way God intended families to be.

I suggest we wives honor our faithful husbands by saying, "Thank you! We love you, and will appreciate you eternally, for your undying loyalty in working so hard for us."

This poem, titled "Only A Dad," 5 is an outstanding tribute to our working daddies.

> "Only a dad, neither rich nor proud,
> Merely one of the surging crowd,
> Toiling, striving, from day to day,
> Facing whatever may come his way,
> Silent whenever the harsh condemn,
> And bearing it all for the love of them!
>
> "Only a dad, but he gives his all,
> To smooth the way for his children small,
> Doing with courage stern and grim,
> The deeds that his father did for him.
> This is the line that for him I pen:
> Only a dad, BUT THE BEST OF MEN!"
>
> --Edgar E. Guest

RESPONSIBILITY NO. 4 - BE THE SPIRITUAL LEADER

Once more I direct your attention to God's plan for the family. "*But I would have you know, that the head of every man is Christ; and the head of the woman is the man; and the head of Christ is God.*" I Corinthians 11:3 The order is:

God

Christ

Man

Woman

Notice that God reigns supreme. Christ was under God's authority and voluntarily submitted to Him when He chose to come to earth and surrender His life for the sins of the world. (Philippians 2:5 - 8)

Woman is under man's authority. A woman is to submit *willingly* to her husband's leadership, as Christ *voluntarily* submitted to God's headship. Hopefully, by the time a woman finishes this study, if she has not done so already, will willingly submit to her husband's authority.

What does this mean to a man? To whom is he accountable? Christ is the head of man. Man is answerable to his Savior. *An autocratic daddy must be a follower of Christ in order to maintain God's proper order for the family.*

Since Christ is the head of man, it compels a husband to live in a close relationship with his Lord. He must study to know Christ's will so that he, being the head of his wife, can take her by the hand and lead them both in paths of righteousness toward salvation. It is his responsibility to yield to Christ's authority and lead an exemplary life of obedience to God.

Ephesians 6:4 says, "*Fathers, provoke not your children to wrath: but bring them up in the nurture and admonition of the Lord.*" It is Daddy's responsibility to announce, "Get up, boys! Get dressed. We are all going to worship this morning." Or, "Come on, children, gather around. We are going to read the Bible before you leave for school today."

Daddy, Heaven's Reflector

God created the home in order to teach us a little bit about Himself. The association children experience with their fathers will subconsciously teach them what they may expect from their heavenly Father.

Our Heavenly Father is an invisible spirit. His throne is in heaven, even though His presence is with us constantly. A child subconsciously reasons that God, whom he has not seen, must be like his father whom he sees. Now he understands what God is like. 6

I remember something our son said at age two. It impressed me so much that I have not forgotten it. He was sitting in his high chair. When there was a pause in the family conversation, he looked over at his daddy and said, "Some day I be Jesus, like Daddy."

A father and mother may possess dominant features, which can teach a child two of God's attributes. God is firm. When He says something once, He means it. If a father leads the home with that sort of firmness, a child associates that same consistency with God's commands.

God expressed compassion and love for us. He gave His only Son in order to bring forgiveness and salvation to the world. A mother possesses a beautiful ability to teach this quality. When a child's heart is broken or his spirits downcast, a mother can be compassionate, tender, and loving. When a child consistently receives these graces, he will make the association that God also is sympathetic and forgiving.

He Is So Distant to Me

In his book, *Help! I'm a Parent!*, Dr. Bruce Narramore relates a counseling experience he once had with a female patient. In one of his sessions with the lady, he asked her to describe her father. "He is loving, kind, just, and a fine gentleman . . .but I feel he is so distant," was her response.

Weeks later, and without her realizing it, he asked her identically the same question, only this time with reference to God. "He is loving, kind, just, and omnipotent, but He seems so distant," she replied. 7

Unconsciously this woman used almost the exact words in describing God that she used to describe her father. It is interesting to note that her father had failed to build a close, warm, relationship with her; consequently, she considered him a stranger. Undoubtedly that void of fatherly warmth and security in her early life had a great deal to do with her need for psychiatric counseling when an adult.

There's No Confusion in This Order

Notice that, according to God's order, everyone in the family is in a position of submission. When each remains in his proper place, submitting to the one who is his leader, law, order, and peace will prevail.

> God (is Head)
> Christ (obeyed God)
> Man (obeys God and Christ)
> Woman (obeys Christ and Man)
> Children (obey Daddy and Mother)

There is no confusion in a family that is ordered after this infallible plan.

An Example of a Strong Spiritual Leader

Throughout my husband's years in the ministry, there have been two times when our family's tranquility was suddenly interrupted. Those stressful moments arose because a few men became discontented about some Biblical truths he had preached, or because a personality clash had developed. These men decided they would take care of the matter by exerting their power. They accomplished this by issuing him orders that he would have to vacate the church office and move his family out of the church-owned house. It did not seem to matter to them that they had not bothered to consult "the church," or that it was the dead of winter and the holidays were only two weeks away. We were still compelled to leave and find another work.

It takes a strong and determined *leader* to endure this kind of unjust treatment, but my spiritual guide never let it get him down. As long as he was convinced the Lord was on his side, he did not mind standing alone. Each time these situations developed, the Lord WAS on his side, never forsook him, and my faith in my husband never wavered. If I had wrung my hands in despair, wept over rejection, and developed a troubled spirit, perhaps he would not be preaching the gospel to the thousands that he reaches by his widely listened-to daily radio program.

During our storms of life, I never had a doubt that he would be able to protect and provide for us. Since the beginning of our marriage, he has known that I fully trust in his ability to take care of us. All I needed to do was remain calm, support his decisions, be his "sounding board," be in control of all my domestic chores, nestle close to his side at night, and sleep comfortably. With his determination to respect the Bible, and God as our ultimate protector, we have never gone hungry, been deprived of adequate clothing, or experienced homelessness.

Lord, Open Our Eyes

I shall always believe that any Christian man who is sound in body and mind can earn his family a living. God will help him! It requires commitment, determination, a deep abiding faith in God to providentially guide his life and open doors of opportunity to him, and an obedient wife who is supportive of his decisions. His leadership, like Abraham's, may call for him to move his family *"unto a strange new land that I will shew thee"* and his wife must be ready to go with him. She must be *"even as Sara when she obeyed Abraham, calling him lord."* I Peter 3:6

For years, I have observed that many men in the Lord's Army have weakened their headship. This hinders them from entering into difficult fields of battle and creates a spiritual dearth in the Lord's Kingdom. When our officers should be traveling into new fields to labor, "which are white already to harvest," they do not go. Why, you ask. It is because, somewhere along the way, the man decided to put his wife to work outside the home to help with the burden of providing for the family. Her job is too secure and carries with it too many benefits for them to leave it. His wife's job hinders him from launching out into more challenging works in which he could achieve much greater success.

Remember that necessity is and always has been the mother of invention. *Most men will do what they HAVE to do.*

A minister of the gospel understands that his wife is the "weaker vessel" and God assigned her work to do inside the home and church. He should refuse to accept a full- time-work with any congregation that is unwilling to pay him a salary adequate enough to support his family. Congregations need to understand that their minister must set a proper example of God's order for the family. How can an evangelist effectively preach Christ's plan of salvation, the acts of worship, proper order for church government and then fail to be a proper Christian example in ordering his family?

The trouble is that many of God's people have fallen into step with the world and many husbands no longer follow God's order for the home. Why doesn't he permit his wife her God-ordained place as *"keeper at home and guide of the house"*? How can he rightly expect his wife to assume part of the responsibility that God assigned to him?

Have we missed the tenor of the Bible teaching concerning the family? Was it not Christ's life, death, and resurrection that brought us the "good news of the gospel"? Was it not from His teaching that elevated woman to a place of honor and protection? The scripture commands husbands, "give honour unto the wife, as unto the weaker vessel." Our forefathers had no difficulty understanding this concept!

May the Lord open our eyes of understanding that we may once again properly order our Christian homes.

Questions

Because it is difficult for us to be objective about ourselves, I suggest in closing this chapter that Mother Bee answer the following questions "yes" or "no." Daddy Bee, I will ask you to do the same for her by answering the questions at the end of Chapter Five.

I use this quiz to review the need for Daddy Bee to accept his honorable responsibilities as the head, protector, physical provider, and spiritual leader of his home.

Yes   No   1. When your husband is home, do you send the
                children (if they don't go voluntarily) to him for
                permissions or decisions unrelated to you?

Yes   No   2. Does Daddy have the final word and make
                decisions?

Do all family members respect and obey him?

Yes   No   3. If your child was asked, "Who is the boss at your house?" would the answer be "Daddy" and no doubt about it?

Yes   No   4. Would you say you are married to a 3F, rather than a 2F, or 1F man?

Yes   No   5. Does your husband spend his after-work hours at home with the family, rather than becoming involved in too many outside interests?

Yes   No   6. Can you truthfully say that your husband is home enough in the evenings to be considered an A-1 protector?

Yes   No   7. Does your husband earn the family living?

Yes   No   8. Would your husband object to your taking a job outside the home?

Yes   No   9. Is your husband a Christian?

Yes   No   10. Does your husband take your family to worship regularly?

If you answered all the questions **Yes**, you and your children are residing in the courts of a *King*. Walk the halls of your house proudly and remember, "It is not everybody who gets to live with a King."

Chapter Five
Mother Bee

There are four major responsibilities Mother must meet to maintain proper organization in the home. Those responsibilities are:

1. Be a helpmeet.
2. Be in submission.
3. Be a keeper at home.
4. Be the guide of the house.

RESPONSIBILITY NO.1 - BE A HELPMEET

"And the Lord God said, It is not good that the man should be alone; I will make him an help meet for him." Genesis 2:18. Helpmeet also means helpmate. Meet means suitable. Mate is wife. One, therefore, must become a suitable wife.

One of the first things we must recognize about being a suitable wife is that suitability varies from man to man. There are some virtues that all men appreciate. Then again, there are specific characteristics that appeal to different men individually. To allure a husband, a woman must acquaint herself with the attractions that appeal to all *men*, and then be wise enough to adapt them to the specific pleasures of her *man*.

If you are concerned about whether or not you are a suitable wife, don't worry! If you practice the secrets of what a male desires in a woman, it is possible for you to be a delight to the heart and soul of almost any man. It makes little difference if he is from Annapolis, Amsterdám or the Andaman Islands.

All you have to do is to become a 3A woman. This is a simple concept to explain.

Be a 3A Woman

Before explaining the three A's, I emphasize again that you will discover that there are common qualities that almost ALL men adore. How you go about fulfilling these basic manly desires, will be determined by the unique disposition of your husband. Soon, you will learn how to fulfill his specific needs. This insight will come about with observation and intimate association.

The important thing for every wife to remember is that her sole responsibility is to HELP MEET these 3A desires in the manner most pleasing to her husband. What her father, brothers, uncles and grandpas like is strictly immaterial. Those men's likes and dislikes should be the concern of their helpmates.

1A - Attract

ALICE ALLURE

Once upon a time in a land obscure,
Lived a lovely young maiden named Alice Allure.

Alice was most fair, of that we are sure;
Her countenance did shine like one who was pure.

She arose in the morning not lazy and late,
But lighted her lamp to avoid possible fate.

At the light and birth of each new day,
Alice went to her closet to choose her array.

Her clothes were chosen from colors most bright;
She worked for everything to be just right.

As she leisurely sat in her dressing room chair,
She carefully maneuvered the comb through her hair.

Her make-up was applied with just the perfect touch,
Being ultra-cautious not to get too much.

Her teeth and shoes were always ashine,
As she waltzed down the steps of the winding incline.

Soon she was whisked away in her crimson Capri,
Disappearing to search for her nobleman free.

This poem describes a young, unmarried woman. In addition to our innate feminine nature, we also observed examples of Alice Allure from the fairy tale characters of Cinderella and Snow White. They tell us, "Be beautiful, find your prince, marry, and you will live happily ever after."

It is appropriate to encourage girls to be as physically attractive as possible. Before marriage a man is mainly attracted to a woman by her physical appeal. Seldom does he carefully investigate a young lady's character or disposition before he is attracted to her. He is first allured by a woman's outward charms and later will be especially grateful if his wife possesses inward beauty as well.

Your size, height, hair, face, fragrance, complexion, personality, and posture were part of that which initially drew your husband to you.

Step 1 to being a suitable wife is to never cease working to be attractive for your husband. You must continue to work to charm and fascinate him with your femininity. Supply daily the fuel of romantic allure that first ignited his interest in you. During the days of your courtship you selected your clothes, styled your hair, and wore your cosmetics in a way that was appealing to him. After you are married, it is still important to apply a perfume and warmly greet him at the door when he arrives home from work. And don't forget to *keep your figure trim for him.* These are feminine charms that keep your husband's desire alive for you.

What is Your BMI?

Half of all American adults are either overweight or obese, and many men are turned off by wives who let themselves go physically. If the shapely woman he married is now hidden under excess pounds, he may be less than enthusiastic to introduce her as his wife. Remember that every man desires a wife of whom he can be proud. Do you still resemble the woman your husband married, or have you allowed your weight to balloon out of control?

If your Body Mass Index (BMI) is within its proper range, then your answer to my question is "no." One's BMI is the most common guideline used to determine whether he or she is underweight or overweight.

Take this test to determine your BMI. It will tell you the proper weight for your height.

1. Write down your present weight _____.
2. Write your height in inches _____.
3. Use a calculator and multiply your weight X 700.
4. Divide that figure by your height in inches.
5. Divide that figure by your height in inches again.
6. You now have your BMI number. Write it here _____.

If your BMI number is 18.5 to 25, your weight is normal. Anything under 18.5 is underweight. If your number is above 25, you need to lose weight. A BMI of 30 to 35 is obese, and anything over 35 is considered severely obese.

Here is another formula that will help you know if you need to shed a few pounds. Remember that your weight X 15 = Your Daily Calorie Intake, which maintains your present weight. If you want to lose one pound a week, eat 600 fewer calories per day than your present daily intake. If you want to lose two pounds a week, eat 1200 fewer calories per day than your present daily food intake.

The good news is that if you will begin following Dr. Denmark's Food for a Day Plan you can restore your health and drop any extra pounds you need to lose. (Read Chapter 10, Gem #2 in the Addendum)

Attract God's Way

Since God gives instructions to women about how to become attractive, I would be negligent not to include them. He reminds us, in our desire to be beautiful, to be cautious. There are right and wrong ways to attract a man's attention to oneself.

God commands women "*to be chaste.*" (Titus 2:5) This means we are to be pure and decent in character, conduct, and the way we dress.

For the preservation of morals, and the well being of society, God commands us to keep our physical, feminine charms discreetly concealed. In the marriage relationship, before our husbands, is the place where we may disrobe. "*Marriage is honorable in all, and the bed undefiled.*" *Hebrews 13:4*

A Christian woman must be devoted to preserving her chastity. She understands that her manner of dress and conduct are an outward reflection of her character. She also knows that if she, because of exposing her body, causes any man other than her husband to lust for her, she is guilty of sin.

Work to be attractive for your husband, but your dress and behavior before others must be modest and chaste.

God's Dress Code

Few subjects have generated more debates among present-day Christians than the subject of modesty. It seems that few people can agree about what is or is not modest apparel. How short is short, and how long is long? In the end, most people use their own judgment.

Why not follow God's dress code and be safe about it? His approved dress code is explained in Genesis 3. We read a description of Adam and Eve's judgment for acceptable dress (and it is still the opinion of most today.) After they had eaten the forbidden fruit, their eyes were opened and they realized they were naked. *"They sewed fig leaves together, and made themselves aprons."* Genesis 3:7

The word "aprons," is translated from the Hebrew word *chagora*, which means loincloths that covered the part of the body which modern swimsuits cover. The first two human beings covered their bare essentials and imagined that was sufficient.

However, Gods standard is much higher and He corrected them: *"Unto Adam also and to his wife did the Lord God make coats of skins, and clothed them."* Genesis 3:21. This garment, according to the Hebrew word, *Ketonet*, was a long covering that reached, at the least, from the **shoulders to the knees.** This is God's definition of being properly clothed.

The Zondervan Pictorial Bible Dictionary, describe this *Ketonet* as the *tunic coat* worn by the Hebrews. It was a shirt-like garment, which was worn in the home and on the street. When worn to do hard manual labor, it was sleeveless and cut off at the knees..

A careful study of appropriate dress during Bible times reveals that no clothing worn by male or female ever revealed more of the human anatomy than from above the shoulders and below the knees. It was in the Garden of Eden that God gave His rule for suitable dress. He made no difference between how much of man's body should be covered and how much of woman's body can be exposed. Both sexes should be clothed modestly.

If Mother Eve could see the modern dress of her sons and daughters in the Western world, she would be appalled that they did not learn from her mistake.

2A - Adapt

After a woman makes herself attractive for her husband, the second thing she must do is adapt for him. Adapt means to make fit or suitable, adjust, modify or alter for a different use.

A wife must fit her life to her husband's. *"For the man is not of the woman; but the woman of the man. Neither was the man created for the woman; but the woman for the man."* I Corinthians 11:8 and 9 Properly adapting to geographical locations, houses, her husband's occupation, salary, his habits (good or bad), her new in-laws, and friends are all a part of being a responsible HELPMEET.

Most couples have many similarities. Their lives blend together, but there will be times when they have opposing views. It is when these differences arise that a wife must devote much effort to adapting.

Adapting to your husband does not mean you become like him. It means you allow him freedom to be himself. You will not attempt to dominate him or constantly demand that he change.

The following are four examples of opposites that exist in marriages. After acquainting yourself with these accounts, you will be ready to learn how to cope with each case by three steps.

Example 1 - Jim comes from a home in which his mother picked up his clothes that were left on the floor, as if she were his servant. When Jim married, he continued to leave his shoes in the middle of the floor, toss his clothes across a chair, and leave a mess in the bathroom. Sue grew up in a meticulous home. Her father and brothers picked up after themselves. How is Sue going to adjust to Jim's sloppy habits?

Example 2 - Janet was trained to go to bed early and rise early. Her family went to bed early and each morning rose in time to have breakfast together. Everyone was off to work or school on time. Promptness was an essential part of her life. Jack, her new husband, stays up late, falls asleep on the couch, and comes to bed late. In the morning he gets up late, never wants breakfast, and must rush to get to work on time. How can Janet adapt to Jack's irritating habits?

Example 3 - Helen's husband, Wayne, is a television fan. When he gets home from work, he watches TV from his recliner most of the evening. He seldom stays at the table to eat with the family. He prefers eating in the living room as he watches the evening news. Helen thinks TV is a waste of time and seldom enjoys watching it. She feels that the evening meal should be valued as one time in the day the whole family can be together. How can she adapt to Wayne's television habit?

Example 4 - Tom has a night job. He must get his rest from 8 A.M. to 4 P.M. Esther does not like being home alone at night. Things are further complicated when she has to work at keeping their children, ages two and five, quiet during the day when Tom is sleeping. How can Esther adapt to Tom's work schedule?

Step 1 - Verbally Ask

The first step a wife must take to solve a difference she has with her husband is to communicate to him what it is that troubles her. Often one whose behavior offends his mate is unaware that his behavior is disturbing to her. This happens with the ones we love. *Any time your husband is doing something that is offensive or disturbing to you, tactfully tell him how you feel.*

Your approach to solving problems should be well thought out. What you perceive to be your husband's shortcomings is a serious matter to you. However, if you attack him in an aggressive manner (like a woman wielding a rolling pin) you will likely make the situation much worse.

Be honest about your feelings. Tell your mate in a gentle, quiet, and loving way exactly what is disturbing you. Ask him kindly, and tactfully, " Would you consider doing something about it?" Promise him that you do not plan to press the point, but you feel better knowing that he understands your feelings.

The Wind and the Sun

A man is much more likely to respond to his wife's kind and gentle approach concerning a problem than a harsh, blunt, forceful one. I am reminded of the fable of the sun and the wind. They were engaged in a contest to see who could be the first to make the old man walking along the dusty road take his coat off. The wind argued it wouldn't be hard at all. He blew and blew with all of the force he had. The old man only wrapped his coat around him more tightly and walked directly into the wind.

The sun took a different approach. He radiated all the warmth he could muster and shone down with all his brilliance. The day grew so warm and pleasant that the old man soon removed the coat from around his shoulders and proceeded with his journey.

This old fable furnishes women a special bit of wisdom about how to deal effectively with their men. If you want to draw your husband close to you, use a warm approach. If you are blunt with him or pressure him, he is more likely to ignore your requests.

Ask, Don't Agitate

Remember that there is a difference between asking and agitating. Older women can confirm this truth to young wives: *Your husband will never change if you become an agitator and a nag!* Don't forget that truth. In order to avoid the temptation to agitate, start applying this TUAC principle today: *"Say what you have to say once, never more than twice, unless you're asked."* (We will learn in Chapter Eight how this same principle should be applied to the children.)

God set the principle of "saying something once" with Adam and Eve. He didn't threaten or warn them over and over by saying, "Now, if you eat the forbidden fruit one more time, I really will cast you out of the beautiful garden!" He told Adam *one time* that he was not to eat or touch the fruit of the tree of knowledge of good and evil. (Genesis 2:17) After that, He granted Adam freedom to obey or disobey.

Watch for His Reaction

Once you have used a kind and gentle approach, expressed your feelings, and asked your husband for his consideration, then observe his reaction. If he accepts your suggestion and expresses a willingness to alter his behavior, be grateful, and thank him. When he tries, but on occasion slips and forgets, honor his position as head of the home and apply Steps 2 and 3, shown below.

If your requests irritate your spouse or he grows hostile to your suggestion that he change, drop the subject and go to Steps 2 and 3.

Step 2 - Mentally Accept

If the husbands of Sue, Janet, Helen, and Ester express no interest in altering their behavior, these women must adapt pleasant mental attitudes and accept conditions as they are.

Most women ignore the idea of accepting minor differences of habit and views that exist between them and their husbands. They disregard the principle of speaking about a grievance once or twice and dropping it. They will often worsen the situation by constant nagging. They may even go to Step 3 and physically adjust to the situation, but still refuse mentally to accept their husbands as they are. *"It is better to dwell in a corner of the house top, than with a brawling woman in a wide house."*

Proverbs 21:9 I remind you of the old saying, "keep a man in hot water long enough and he will become hard boiled."

A wife's refusal to accept her husband's manner of living keeps her irritated and unhappy. She may continually pick, scold, and find fault with her man. She can carry on to the point that he will avoid coming home and seek other companionship. Reportedly, some women's unpleasant behavior have even driven their husbands to drink.

A woman who is an agitator is usually blind to her destructive behavior. She believes the reason her husband doesn't come home or drinks too much is that he doesn't love her anymore or has lost interest in things around home. It may be true that he no longer desires her company, but she refuses to accept the reality that it is the constant clamor she has created that has driven him away. "*Every wise woman buildeth her house: but the foolish plucketh it down with her hands.*" Proverbs 14:1

My, Oh, My!

A few years ago, I read of an unusual occurrence. This is a true story about a man who lived in a small southern community. He had a day off and made plans to enjoy it fishing. The morning he was to leave, he arose early. While his wife was preparing a lunch for him, he was digging worms and assembling his fishing gear. By sun-up, he was by the river ready to fish.

As he put his bait on the hook, he was puzzled because the little worms bit his fingers. "My, oh, my! I did not know little worms could bite like this!" he thought. Being inexperienced at fishing, he did not take it too seriously and continued to bear the discomfort of the little stings.

By lunchtime, he could stand it no longer. He was faint and did not feel like eating. He gathered his tackle together, got into his car and started home. When he arrived, his wife met him at the door. His whole body was swelling and he was desperately ill. She helped him back into the car and drove him to the hospital. He died that evening.

Upon investigation, it was discovered that those innocent looking little "worms" he was using as bait were not worms at all. They were actually baby rattlesnakes! Bit by bit they injected enough poison into the man's system that it ultimately killed him.

A wife who refuses to accept her husband and thinks she can force him to change may accomplish the same result as the rattlesnakes. Her nagging will, little by little kill his love.

Step 3 - Physically Adjust

If a woman accepts her husband, she will discover ways to adjust and love him even though he is not absolutely perfect. And, he will love her in return.

(1) Sue can joyfully pick up after Jim and be thankful that he is such a successful accountant and is earning his family a good living. As their children grow up, she can train them to be neat and pick up their clothes.

(2) Janet may choose to stay up late with Jack. Enjoying her loving companionship may inspire him to respond more readily to rising early in the morning. She may help him get off to work sooner by laying his clothes out for him. She can get up earlier than Jack and prepare a hot nutritious breakfast. His habit of not eating breakfast may be because no one ever bothered to prepare one for him. If she tires early, due to staying up late, she may choose to take a short nap in the afternoon.

(3) Helen can make sure the vacuuming is done before Wayne gets home. She may plan her work so she has time to sit with him in the evening. Her mending or letter writing may be saved for that time. A TV can be located near the dining table so that Wayne will not need to miss the news at mealtime.

(4) Esther could ask Tom if he would install a security system in their home. She could call their local police department and ask if they will patrol their neighborhood. She must provide the children a play area away from Tom's bedroom. She should choose quiet games and toys, turn the TV low, and train the children to stay away from the bedroom while Daddy is sleeping.

These types of suggestions often anger women. They feel unfairly imposed upon or mistreated. At first it may seem that way, but the rewards of "giving" pay rich dividends.

Jesus said, "*Give, and it shall be given unto you; good measure, pressed down, and shaken together, and running over..*" Luke 6:38

Try it and you will discover it works. If you nag and fuss at your mate, matters will not grow better, but worse. You will only achieve more misery for yourself, your husband, and your children.

From Sweet Cream to Sweet Dreams

Some women stubbornly refuse to make necessary physical adjustments that are needed as a marriage grows. Such was the case of a lady who attended a series of lessons I taught about improving marriage relationships.

Her marriage of thirteen years was unhappy and in serious jeopardy. Her husband had asked her for a divorce. She and her two young children were facing the bleak prospect of a fatherless home. She was bewildered about what had brought her marriage to the edge of destruction. She had been first-rate at attracting her husband. She was pretty, so that was not the problem. One would look at her and ask, "What more could a man want in a wife?"

This lovely lady favorably impressed me. Every week she brought me a quart of fresh sweet cream from their farm that nestled in the foothills of the Cascade Mountains. Having been reared on a farm myself, I really enjoyed her weekly treat. I churned the cream into butter, an activity that my mother had taught me when I was a child.

However, I was unaware that living in the country was the wedge that was driving her and her husband apart. Since their move to the country, his job had changed, and all of his business was now transacted in the city. Living in the country made it inconvenient for him to do his work. He insisted on moving, but she dearly loved their country lifestyle. To her it seemed he expected too much by asking her to give up the home she loved. She reasoned that he could commute to work and leave her and the children undisturbed to enjoy their paradise on the farm.

This lovely young housewife may well have been the most disturbing student I ever taught. She upset me so much with her weeping in class that it was difficult to continue with the lecture each week.

After she was convinced that their problem was a result of her unwillingness to adapt and agree that the family should move closer to her husband's work, she willingly made the change. Happily, her marriage and home were saved.

They sold the farm and moved into the city. The last time she called me, they were happy and their home was again peaceful. She had learned just in time that being a suitable wife meant being a mature adapter and that the farm and cows were not nearly as important as a contented husband and peaceful home.

You Can Start Over

If you have been married for several years and have not made adjustments for your husband, what should you do? You can start over! Every day is a new day. Make a commitment that you are going to accept your husband as he is and will not waste your time trying to make him over.   Instead, turn your attentions to yourself and make yourself over. See just how beautiful a person you can become.

Step 2 in being a suitable wife is to adapt by verbally asking, mentally accepting, and physically adjusting to your husband's life.

3A - Appease

After a woman chooses to work to stay attractive for her husband and adapts to his life, she must then learn to appease him. An appeaser is one who satisfies an appetite or desire. In Chapter Four men were told how they must fulfill your need to be loved. A wife's body and spirits thrive on love, and no one can give it to her better than her husband. I have pointed out that a man is to be the head of his home. He is the protector. He should be strong, manly, and courageous. He is to work hard to make a living for his family. " What an independent creature!" you say. But is he really?

You are going to discover if you haven't already, that God has placed men in a dependent state. On whom must he rely? The answer is his wife! He is the king, but he must depend on his queen for much of his contentment and well being.

Just as she in her frailty must look to him for love, protection, and material provision, he must depend on her for nourishment that will renew his strength.   A husband's body and spirits thrive on proper nourishment, and no one can give this to him better than his wife.

"Let every one of you in particular so love his wife even as himself; and the wife see that she reverence her husband." Ephesians 5:33

Two for the Body and Two for the Soul

Men hunger for four types of nourishment. Two for the body and two for the soul! Leave one out, and he'll fail to reach his goal.

NOURISHMENT NEEDED FOR MEN

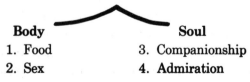

Body	Soul
1. Food	3. Companionship
2. Sex	4. Admiration

Food, sex, companionship, and admiration are hungers for which a husband depends on his wife to satisfy. He cannot completely and satisfactorily fulfill these desires without a warm, caring, loving wife.

Drives, for the physical and emotional needs of life, are so intense, that some men surrender to pressure from their wives. An assertive wife can hold her husband at bay, or coerce him to meet her demands by denying him fulfillment of these intense hungers. A wife who employs these tactics, especially withholding sexual fulfillment, rebels against God, and endangers her marriage and her own soul.

A woman seeking to establish an autocratic home, be obedient to God, and be a HELPMEET for her husband will provide proper nourishment for her husband. *Step 3 in being a suitable wife is to appease and satisfy your husband's desires for food, sex, companionship, and admiration.*

Weapons for War or Presents for Peace

A woman may use these favors as weapons of war or gifts for peace. She may deny them to her husband and use them as her most effective tools for a battle of wills in which she is determined to have her own way.

A woman's physical strength is less than a man's, so she fights in more subtle ways.

She may serve liver (which he detests) for dinner because he arrived late for dinner three evenings in a row. She may deny sex because she is angry because he spent his evening bowling with his friend Harry instead of accompanying her to a flower show.

She may refuse to go with him to his annual company banquet. That will show him! When he arrives alone, his boss and associates will know he has trouble at home. And to worsen their marriage relationship, she can turn her admiration into burning scorn when her husband decides it is unfeasible financially to travel across country to spend Christmas with her family.

Prime the Pump

Perhaps ignorance is one reason a woman neglects to give her husband the proper nourishment of love and attention he needs to make him happy. It is possible that she had no intention of denying him her affections. Even so, it does not alter the fact that damage is done. Many marriages are in shambles due to a lack of proper emotional nutrition because the wife has failed to nurture a warm, loving, relationship with her husband.

A wife often possesses the power to resurrect a dead marriage and must be willing to exercise it. After she has followed 1A of being attractive and 2A of adapting, her last secret to reviving a happy marriage is to supply the four needs essential to her husband. Over a period of time, as his confidence is restored, he will repay her with adoration. Cast the bread of your love on the water and your husband will return it to you in many ways.

This is another application of the principle of "*give, and it shall be given unto you*" applied in marriage. The old-fashioned water well worked on this same principle. You may grasp the well handle and pump and pump, but the well will not give water until water is first freely given (called priming the pump). When it is primed, the well gives much more water in return.

A wise wife chooses to start the blessed process of giving. When she primes the well of her home with the living water of love and concern, she discovers that abundant love and care are returned to her, pressed down and running over.

Appease, Don't Displease

The following is a list of the four gifts a husband needs.

(1) *FOOD* - An old cliche' our grandmothers and mothers have passed down is, "The way to a man's heart is through his stomach." I suggest, however, that unless you plan food to please your husband's taste, you will not reach his heart. So remember the following rules:

#1 -P*repare food your husband likes.* If you don't like some of the foods he enjoys, plan something else for yourself. Don't attempt to force him to change. #2 - Serve *his meals on time.* If one must wait, let it be you instead of him.

(2) *SEX* - Dr. David R. Reuben provides excellent counsel to a wife who is seeking to be her husband's HELPMEET. First, he suggests "she must understand that as far as men are concerned, the most powerful incentive on earth is sex. The passion of a male is nine times stronger than that of most females, and "the wife who refuses to give her husband reasonable sexual satisfaction is literally inviting him to go elsewhere. The woman who does her best to meet her mate's sexual needs goes a long way toward making him immune to the allure of other women." Dr. Reuben further says that "sex isn't too difficult for a woman to give if she will remember that satisfying a man sexually is ten percent ability and ninety percent accessibility." [1]

Wives have a God-given responsibility to fulfill their husbands' sexual needs. *To avoid fornication, let every man have his own wife, and let every woman have her own husband. Let the husband render unto the wife due benevolence; and likewise also the wife unto the husband. The wife hath not power of her own body, but the husband; and likewise also the husband hath not power of his own body, but the wife. Defraud* (that means deprive) *ye not one the other, except it be with consent for a time...and come together again, that Satan tempt you not for your incontinency."* (I Corinthians 7:2-5)

I believe the soundest advice I ever heard concerning the sexual relationship of marriage was given by a Christian mother. It was her daughter's wedding day and nearing time for the wedding ceremony to begin. During a quiet moment, this mother revealed to her daughter one of the secrets of a happy home. She told her that until this time, she had encouraged her to guard her purity with her life. Now she wanted her daughter to understand that from this day forward she was freely and without reservation to give herself to her husband. "Make him a warm and affectionate wife, and NEVER refuse to satisfy his sexual desires" was her final advice. That is one secret to producing a happy husband.

(3) COMPANIONSHIP - I once heard a man say, "I'd rather live in a world full of troubles with the woman I love, than in heaven with all men." That statement expresses the strong desire men have for the companionship of a woman.

A wife should prefer being with her husband above anyone else on earth. He should come first. The moment she would rather spend her time with her children, parents, brothers, sisters, neighbors, or friends, she stops being the best possible HELPMEET for her husband.

No husband wants to stand second, third, or tenth in line for his wife's attention. After a man has worked all day, he desires that his wife recognize his presence when he returns home. Many men enjoy the comforts of home so much that they stay up late at night to enjoy them as long as possible. If your husband loves home that much, stay up with him and keep him company. If you need extra rest, take a nap during the day; but don't make a practice of going to bed and leaving him alone.

Some men, because of job requirements, have to go to bed early and get up early. I knew a man who had to rise by 4:30 A.M. for years. His wife adapted to his schedule, and they had a beautiful marriage relationship. She was not only a good companion who went to bed and got up with him every morning, but she met his desire for good food by preparing his favorite breakfast each morning before he left for work. She never considered it an imposition, but was an outstanding companion and adapter.

Sadly, some couples begin to grow apart early in their marriage. This often happens when a wife allows the children to take precedence over her husband. A young child's needs are demanding and often immediate. A wife should tend to their urgent needs and then get back to being with her husband. Never permit your children to drive a wedge between you and your husband.

More and more we learn of couples getting a divorce after thirty or forty years of marriage. The wife often has made the mistake of allowing the children to take priority over her husband. As a result, over the years, the husband developed a world without his wife. They kept their home together for the sake of the children. When the children are grown and leave home, he and his wife discover they have little left in common.

A good rule of thumb for every wife to remember is to spend at least half of her recreation hours with her husband. Do what he wants to do and go where he wants to go. If your husband likes to ride motorcycles, ride with him. If he likes to fish, bowl, play golf, or target-shoot, keep him company. If you don't like to participate, you can learn to keep his score and be his "cheer leader." The point is for you to be with him. And, never forget there may be another woman somewhere who would love to take your place.

(4) *ADMIRATION* - If you want to put a bounce in your husband's steps and keep a song in his heart, compliment him *EVERY DAY*. Admiration is the most neglected item of the nourishments needed by men and, surprisingly, is the one that requires the least amount of time and effort. It takes minutes and hours to groom yourself, prepare and serve food, be an active sex partner, and be his companion. But furnishing your husband with one word of *PRAISE* a day only takes a few seconds!

Admiration is a man's ego food. If he doesn't receive it, he may react in multitudes of negative ways. Some men may act tough, are arrogant, appear to be conceited, or become obnoxious. Others may be quiet and subdued. All men need admiration, but a woman who marries a man who was injured emotionally in his childhood must give extra doses of admiration. If she consistently praises his good characteristics, she will win his constant devotion, and love.

Praise and admiration appear to be little things, but they are like salt for the food, air in the tires, or spark plugs to the engine. They are essential, if a man is to function happily.

Never conclude there are no positive things you can say about your husband. If he has breath in his body, you can praise and admire something about him. Compliment his:

Devotion	Mechanical Skills	Intelligence
Honesty	Fatherhood	Mustache
Faithfulness	Hair Style	Masculine Voice
Physique	Occupational Skills	Being a Strong Protector
Clothes	Manners	Speaking Ability
Muscles	Being a Good Provider	Money Management

These are only a few suggestions to help you get started. Select one positive thing a day that applies to your husband. *Take thirty seconds, look him in the eyes, give him a squeeze, and tell him what you appreciate and admire about him.* On the third day, give your admiration a different touch. Take thirty seconds and direct your complimentary remarks about him to the children. Make sure he hears the compliment. On other days, put a note of appreciation in his lunch or give him a love call at the office. Variations for expressions of admiration and appreciation are as broad as your imagination.

Remember in giving admiration that everyone is ignorant--only on different subjects. Discover the subjects about which your husband is intelligent and *praise him daily on his accomplishments in his fields of expertise.*

If your father, uncle, or Mayor Jones is a "handyman" around the house and your husband is not, this does not mean he is inferior. There are areas in which he is unskilled. So please! Don't show lack of judgement and tact as a wife by dwelling on your husband's deficiencies.

In A Nutshell

Briefly I will sum up the three steps to being a HELPMEET. Following these principles will help you be a delight to your husband, and it is to him only you must concentrate.

A 3A woman will:

1A - *Attract - Adorn herself in a way that pleases her husband.* She will work at being pretty, sweet, clean, and neat. She will practice self-control and not allow herself to get overweight and never become obese.

2A - *Adapt - Fit into his life.* She will give her man freedom to be himself and will never nag him. She will learn how to ask, accept, and adjust her activities to fit his mold. She will not stand in his way, but be his helper along the way.

3A - *Appease - Be his lover.* She will love to (1) Cook for him, (2) Make love to him, (3) Go places and be with him. (4) *TELL HIM DAILY* what makes him the greatest man in the world for her.

RESPONSIBILITY NO. 2 - BE IN SUBMISSION

In order that there be no misunderstanding, God clearly tells women the position they are to maintain in the marriage relationship. Again and again the Bible says, *"Wives, be in subjection; wives, submit yourselves; wives, be obedient to your own husbands; women are not to usurp authority over men; and, wives, be subject to your own husbands in everything."*

Read the following scriptures and familiarize yourself with God's commands to wives:

> Ephesians 5:22-24
> Colossians 3:18
> I Timothy 2:12
> Titus 2:5
> I Peter 3:1-5

Being a submissive wife means yielding to the power and authority of your husband. When differences of opinion or judgment arise, a wife is to step aside and abide by her husband's decision. She may express her views, but she should not pout or shout if she does not get her way. She applies Steps 1, 2, and 3 to adapting and helps meet his final decisions.

If he declares the children are not to jump on the couch, she sees to it that his orders are carried out. If he says the children are not to play with the children next door, an obedient wife will not allow it through the day and then call them home just prior to the time he arrives from work. If Daddy says Jeremy can't have new shoes until next month's paycheck, an obedient mother will not rebel and proceed to purchase them on credit.

An obedient and submissive wife is one who WILLINGLY carries out the wishes, and decisions of her husband.

Why Submit?

The reason a woman must be submissive is that God commands it. And God commanded it because it is the only practical way to preserve harmony in the home.

The world recognizes the pattern of submission. Order cannot be maintained in any other way. No store, bank, school, sports team, library, government, army, or any other institution can operate without organization. Each employee and department head must be willing to submit to his or her superiors. If employees refuse to follow instructions, the business will fail.

Homes are no exception. They are the most important human organization on earth. The only differences between individual families and huge corporations are that there are billions of them and they operate on a smaller scale. While a shoe or airplane factory manufactures products that are worn out quickly, homes produce children who will live for eternity. It is more important for families to be properly organized than any other business.

Once I was a guest on a local television program in the city where we lived. The hostess of the show interviewed me for a few minutes and then turned the telephone segment over to me. I remember I had just emphasized the point that the only way to maintain order in a home is for wives to submit to their husband's authority. The first call I received was from an irate young woman. She was upset with what I had said and demanded to know by what authority I would air such ridiculous propaganda. When I replied, "God is my authority," she replied, "Well! That's a pretty poor authority if you ask me.!" I felt sorry for that lady. One could tell from the tone of her voice that she was an unhappy person and desperately needed God and His principles in her life.

God, our supreme authority, knew a home would be confused and self-destructive if it were not properly ordered. For this reason, a woman should *willingly* follow her husband's leadership.

On the Day of Judgment

If a woman considers her position of vice-president as dishonorable, she will resent it. If she considers it a blessing, she will treasure it. It is all in her state of mind.

Take, for example, a man who is district supervisor for a reputable company. If you belittle him for being district representative instead of state supervisor, the man will be insulted. His rank may not be the highest in the company; nevertheless, he is proud of it.

You would not belittle your insurance agent because he is not the president of the company. Neither is it humiliating for a woman to willingly submit to the rule of her husband. Just because he is the manager, that does not mean his wife's job as assistant manager is unimportant. God equipped men with the disposition and physical strength to bear the heavier responsibilities as head of the home. What woman with sound judgment would want to assume the responsibility and pressure God appointed her husband to bear? It is my conviction that on the Day of Judgment, God will, in part, determine my eternal destiny on how well I submitted to my husband.

Even though it is sometimes difficult for you to abide by decisions with which you may disagree, *it is the only way that works. Someone must have the final say, and God has decreed that one is your husband.*

If the idea of submission is a new concept to you, perhaps it will encourage you to learn this truth: *The more submissive a wife becomes, the more likely her husband will be open to her suggestions.*

A submissive wife who pleases her husband will often observe him adopting her point of view. Many weeks may have passed since they discussed an important matter and then one day she will notice that he followed her wishes. Her influence was so gentle, that her husband happily chose to please her and place her desires above his own. This kind of woman does not mind if she does not receive a lot of recognition and glory, but rejoices that she is able to be such a significant influence on her husband.

A Mother-Dominated Home
When a woman consistently overrides her husband's decisions, her domineering behavior will lead to domestic disaster. When children witness their strong-willed mother overpower their father, they witness the weaker vessel overpower the stronger. This tears down their structure of reason. Even a toddler has enough sense of balance to know that the bigger and stronger blocks hold up the smaller and weaker ones.

There are men who build huge corporations, manage multi-million-dollar businesses, and guide scores of employees through a working day. Yet, when that same successful man comes home, his wife decides he is incapable of knowing when his son misbehaves, or when his daughter is late coming home from a school function.

The results of mother-dominated homes are devastating. When children grow up in a home in which Mom consistently bosses Dad, their sense of proper order is pushed off track. Studies have proven unwed mothers, drug-addicted teenagers, homosexual sons and daughters have often grown up in a mother-ridden family.

Mother, a Measuring Rod

The obedience (or submission) a mother gives to Dad is an example for their children. The respect she gives to her husband is an additional incentive for their children to respect and obey their father. If Mother Bee disobeys Daddy Bee, why shouldn't Baby Bee disobey both him and her? If a wife is defiant toward her husband, the children will practice the same rebellious behavior when their father gives them commands.

A mother's behavior should be a living model of God's plan. Children cannot see God, so their image of what He is like is developed by observing their parents.

This poem, titled "Measuring Rods," 2 expresses the idea:

> I know what Mother's face is like,
>   Though it I cannot see:
> It's like the music of a bell,
> It's like the way the roses smell,
> It's like the story fairies tell---
>   It's all of these to me.
>
> I know what Father's face is like,
>   I am sure I know it all:
> It's like his whistle in the air,
> It's like his step upon the stair,
> It's like his arms that take much care,
>   And never let me fall.
>
> And so I know what God is like,
>   The God whom no one sees:
> He's everything my mother means,
> He's like my very sweetest dreams,
> He's everything my father seems---
>   But greater than all these.

What If He?

Many women try to justify refusing to follow their husband's leadership. The following are examples of the questions they ask: *WHAT IF HE* --Isn't a Christian and I am? Drinks, or is an alcoholic? Engages in salacious behavior? Is not as smart as I am? He has little education and I have a college diploma? Refuses to be a leader and avoids making important decisions? Has poor judgment and I have lost respect for him? Wastes our money? Refuses to adequately support our family? Spends large amounts of money on himself, and neglects the children, and me? Won't pay our bills?

I am sympathetic to a wife in these unfortunate situations. However, there are two questions she must answer. Why did she marry this man? And is she partly at fault because she has not been a cooperative HELPMEET for him? In our culture our mates are not chosen for us, so a discontented wife is responsible for the choice she made.

If she hasn't been a 3A woman, her husband's unsatisfactory conduct may be a reaction to her own shortcomings. If she had responded to him in a more agreeable, loving manner, it is possible their problems would never have become serious.

Three Alternatives

God gives three alternatives to a wife who finds herself in a difficult situation in her marriage.

Alternative I - She may repent. If a woman has failed to be a cooperative HELPMEET for her husband, her soul is in danger. She must correct her shortcomings and become a suitable wife.

Alternative II - She may be patient and receive God's promised blessings. (Read I Peter 2:13 - I Peter 3:1) In Chapter 2 of I Peter, God teaches submission of citizens to civil rulers, and obedience of servants to masters, and reminds us how that Christ, being perfect, suffered, and submitted His will to the will of his Father.

Servants were instructed not only to be good slaves to the gentle masters, but also to endure, without resentment, any suffering wrongfully administered by a harsh, cruel, or perverse master. The Bible teaches us that, when one suffers for doing well and takes it patiently, this is acceptable with God. *"For what glory is it, if, when ye be buffeted for your faults, ye shall take it patiently? But if, when ye do well, and suffer for it, ye take it patiently, this is acceptable with God."* I Peter 2:20

I Peter 3:1 reads, *"Likewise ye wives, be in subjection to your own husbands."* We are to be submissive to our husbands in the same way as citizens are commanded to be subject to kings and governors, servants to masters (whether good or bad), and remember that Christ is the supreme example of one suffering wrongfully for doing good.

Even if a Christian woman is married to a non-Christian man, she is still to stay in her position of submission to him as long as he does not attempt to force her to live in disobedience to God.

She is daily to remain faithful to his leadership. Day after day and week after week she is to buy, prepare, and serve him his food to his specification. She is to neatly groom herself, the house, the children, and his clothes. She should be a warm and affectionate sexual partner. She should not purchase items of which he does not approve. Her example of love and submission is the means by which her husband may eventually be won for Christ. *"Ye wives, be in subjection to your own husbands; that, if any obey not the word, they also may without the word be won by the conversation of the wives."* I Peter 3:1 As a result of her obedience, they will both in time be blessed by God.

Alternative III - She may withdraw from her husband's leadership. If a woman is being forced to live in wicked and ungodly conditions, God does give her the choice of separating from her husband. *"And unto the married I command, yet not I, but the Lord, Let not the wife depart from her husband; But and if she depart, let her remain unmarried, or be reconciled to her husband; and let not the husband put away his wife."* (I Corinthians 7:10 and 11) Notice that if a wife does separate herself from her husband, she must remain unmarried or eventually be reunited with her husband.

If reconciliation cannot be accomplished, the separation will be permanent. *If a woman makes this choice, it is vitally important that she understand that marriage to another man is forbidden.* (Read Romans 7:2 and 3)

There is one cause Christ gives as justification for divorce and remarriage, and that is fornication. *"And I say unto you, Whosoever shall put away his wife, except it be for fornication, and shall marry another, committeth adultery: and whoso marrieth her which is put away doth commit adultery."* Matthew 19:9

If fornication was committed against her and she is contemplating divorce, she should analyze her situation carefully. She must examine her heart and honestly answer the question, "Have I failed to be the HELPMEET I should have been? Is it partially my fault that he sought the companionship of another woman?"

Don't Leave the Mission Out of Submission

I have stressed the prefix *sub* in the word submission, but what about *mission* in the word submission? What message does it hold for a wife?

Mission is defined as a special purpose. The purpose for which a woman marries is so she may follow a new special mission in life.

When we were single, we did almost everything for ourselves. Where am I going; what do I want to do; were our most important questions. However, when we took our marriage vows, I, me, and mine changed to we, us, and ours. The marriage relationship involves a woman's exchanging her Identification, occupation, and habitation from I, teacher, apartment keeper, to wife, mother and homemaker.

So far, you have learned how to fulfill your mission as a WIFE. Now you will advance to instruction about motherhood and homemaking missions.

RESPONSIBILITY NO. 3 - BE A KEEPER AT HOME

The Scripture leaves no doubt that God's designed mission for a wife and mother is to be a "keeper at home." *"That they (the older women) teach the young women to be sober, to love their husbands, to love their children, to be discreet, chaste, **keepers at home**, good, obedient to their own husbands, that the word of God be not blasphemed."* Titus 2: 4-5 The Greek definition of "keeper" is "one who watches or guards."

God is speaking to a young woman when He says, *"I will therefore that the younger women marry, bear children, **guide the house**, give none occasion to the adversary to speak reproachfully."* I Timothy 5:14 The Greek definition of "guide" is "to show the way, direct, and manage."

The words *house* and *home* are used interchangeably throughout the Scriptures. In some passages, house and home refer to the **people** who compose a family unit. (John 4:53 and I Timothy 5:4) In other passages, house and home means the building or **structure** in which people live. (Matthew 8:6 and Luke 15:8)

As I discuss being a "keeper at *home*," I am addressing the mission of guarding and keeping watch for the welfare of family members. "Guiding the *house*" is applied to directing the affairs of the dwelling and caring for the family's material possessions.

Mother, Stay With the Home

The nine remaining TUAC principles are dedicated to helping mothers to be watchful for their children's welfare. As a prerequisite, I must devote time to establishing one vital point.

In order to watch and guard her children, Mother must stay with them. Daddy's responsibility is to provide for the family. This will necessitate, in most cases, his being away from the family members several hours a day. In his absence, Mother must take complete responsibility for the children and see to it that their physical and emotional needs are all met.

It is the mother's *presence* in the home that means everything to the child's feeling of well being. Even though she is busy with homemaking tasks, her *presence* provides the security for her child and helps him develop normally.

"The Winners" Said It Was a Mistake

"The winners" predicted thirty years ago that it was a mistake for mothers to forsake their homemaking responsibilities and accept employment outside the home. Today, America is reaping the havoc caused by mothers who have left their children to be cared for by others while they joined the work force. Every other home in America is destroyed by divorce and as a result many young people are suffering from emotional and physical ill health. Their diets are composed of food from frozen dinners, boxed mixes, or junk foods prepared by fast food restaurants. They no longer have access to their mother's nutritious home cooked meals.

We now have a generation of young people, many of who are confused. They live in a culture that has blurred the roles of male and female to the point that they are unable to clearly distinguish the difference between masculine and feminine responsibilities.

There are those who argue that we must have women in the work force to survive economically as a nation. If that is true, there will always be enough single, childless or widowed women or those who have finished rearing their children to fill those jobs. No MOTHER should ever forfeit her opportunity to mold the lives of her children to "grow the nation's economy." Nurturing the life she was responsible for bringing into the world is her best opportunity to leave her positive influence on this earth.

It is imperative for the mothers of America to work at home and build healthy, strong children or we will cease to have a powerful, free homeland, and a viable workforce. If we continue the trend of destroying our families and health, our once great nation will one day be remembered only on the pages of history books. Calvin Coolidge, former U.S. president, said, "Look well to the hearthstone. Therein lies all hope for America."

When Daddy Must Be Away

Occasionally a Daddy's occupation requires him to be absent from his family more than he would like. Doctors, ministers, and military men, for example, must go to the aid of people or the nation when they are called. A family can survive this kind of intrusion into their private lives IF Mother will stay with her children and maintain a positive attitude. If she cheerfully explains, "Daddy can't be with us now because he is helping bring a little baby into the world (or, he is teaching a family about Jesus or he is away helping to protect our country). I am so proud we have a daddy we can share to help others, aren't you?"

Children will seldom resent their father's frequent absences if it is explained to them in that way. They can survive if Daddy has to be gone when duty calls; but when mother vacates the home, too, the children are in serious trouble.

A newspaper article put it this way, "The day both parents decide to get a job, the baby sitter, the police department, and the juvenile authorities adopt our children."

When A Mother Goes To Work

A mother who leaves her home and goes to work in the business world relinquishes her mothering mission into the hands of others for eight to ten hours a day, This is a mistake for at least the following four reasons:

(1) *She is disobeying God.* The most important reason a mother should not abandon her home for another job is that God has said she should not. When she disobeys a divine command, she weakens her spiritual influence.   As her children grow older and read God's word for themselves, they will see the inconsistency between their mother's example and God's written word.

If her circumstance is one in which she is working because of her husband's insistence, God will hold him, as the head of the home, responsible for the decision.

(2) *She reduces herself to less than a fifty-percent-on-duty mother.* In a week, a young child has approximately eighty-four waking hours. If his mother works out of the home, she spends forty or more of these hours on her job. She will use another five hours dressing and getting ready to leave for work.   If she lives a long distance from her place of employment, additional irretrievable hours are spent traveling to and from work. When all of this time is calculated, she only has enough hours left to be less than a half- time mother.

(3) *She divides her interests.* When a woman accepts a day job, and is paid thousands of dollars a year by an employer, she is expected to give her first energy and best services to her occupation. Birthday parties, Timmy's first steps, Jamie's first word, Alice's play at school, and Pete's afternoon football game often must be sacrificed on the altar of her profession. Even more heartbreaking than missing her children's special events is the fact that she is exhausted at the end of a working day. She has given her best to her employer and customers. Her husband and children will get her leftover time and energy.

Five years of working experience taught me that truth. I did not have children during those years. Had I been a mother, I am certain that my job would have come first. If I had children, they would not have received a warmed-up mother, but a worn-out mother.

(4) *Her child's best interests are not met.* The daily helter-skelter, pressure, and rushing madly about of a working mother would give anyone a migraine headache. Furthermore, pressure turns many naturally sweet dispositions into sour ones. The scolding and shouting, "Hurry up and finish your breakfast, I am going to be late to work!" "Come on, you are too slow!" " Where is your coat?" "Haven't you gotten your shoes on yet?" All of this scrambling and tension creates a miserable atmosphere for the whole family.

Once a mother delivers her precious child to a part-time caretaker, the turmoil doesn't end. Her helpless little one is often greeted by screaming, crying, emotionally disturbed, and sometimes physically sick children with whom he must interact all day.

There isn't a child who would not give everything he possesses to exchange that kind of hectic existence for a quiet and peaceful life in his own home. Nothing on earth can be compared to the quiet, tranquil, and peaceful spirit that is produced in a child when he is permitted to play quietly in the secure atmosphere of his home.

"Please Mama, Don't Leave Me"

I am acquainted with a man who, when a child, was cared for in an all-day nursery school. This was before such care was as common as it is today. He describes his memory of clinging to his mother and crying, "Please Mama, don't leave me." The people overseeing him did not have his welfare uppermost in their minds. They forced him to eat sauerkraut, which was nauseating to him. When he vomited this repulsive food into his plate, he did not receive sympathy from his unfeeling callused caregivers.

This man is a grandfather today. He still will not touch sauerkraut because of this early cruel experience. Under no circumstance would he have required his wife to vacate their home for a day job and leave his son.

Millions of precious little Annies and Andys are abandoned each day by their parents to impersonal care provided in day orphanages. Far too early these helpless little ones are abandoned to a "hard-knock life" which may leave permanent scars on their souls. Determine that you will dedicate your energy to building the peace and security in your children that will equip them to fight the battles of life with courage and confidence.

Are You Planning to Stay Home?

When my husband and I adopted the "little girls," we were living near a beautiful city in the Northwest. We had undergone quite a rigorous procedure before the adoptions were finalized. The adoption service caseworker had made several visits to our home and learned our entire family history; her home study required counseling sessions for both my husband and me.

Our social worker's office was located near the top floor of a skyscraper with an exquisite view overlooking the city. One morning while we were there for one of our meetings, she expressed her desire to have a clear understanding with me. She knew that I had worked as an elementary school teacher in the past, so she asked me this question, "Mrs. Webb, are you planning to stay home to care for these children?" She was pleased when I replied, "Yes, those are our plans." She gave me the impression that if I had answered otherwise, she might not have approved the adoptions. (During those years, private agencies did require adoptive mothers to remain home with their adopted newborns.)

This conscientious lady carefully elaborated to me about why she had such strong feelings about mothers remaining in the home to nurture their children. Many of her professional services were performed before a judge in juvenile court. Her office was only a few doors from the courtroom. She said, "In my judgment, the majority of the juvenile cases we deal with in the courts could be eliminated if mothers would return to the home."

She then proceeded to give me counseling based on her own personal experience. She was a mother who had reared four children. She was privileged to stay home with her older two children until they were grown. For reasons beyond her control, she was forced to seek employment outside her home and abandon her two younger offspring to someone else's care. She sadly reminisced, "Today they are all grown. My two older children have happy homes and are very well-adjusted. The two younger ones are not so fortunate. They have problems that will be with them throughout their lives. I recognized the problems were developing as they were maturing, but I simply did not have the time to help them as I should have."

After listening to our caseworker's sad testimony, I was more convinced than ever of the need to share this professional woman's unhappy experience with others. The importance of staying home with your children is one of the major points I am determined to share with new mothers and one of the main reasons I have devoted many years to writing this book.

Why Mothers Work Away From the Home

There are two basic reasons that mothers seek employment outside the home. They are *money* and *boredom*. One motive is understandable the other completely unjustified.

(1) *Money* - Desire to supplement the family income is understandable. In some cases, it is essential. If one's husband is in bad health or is unemployed for a prolonged period of time, it may be necessary for his wife to seek a temporary job outside the home. Many women who do not have a husband who provides for them must work for a salary. Prices never seem to decline. They only increase. For these reasons many women feel pressure to help with the family expenses by earning an additional salary.

It is encouraging for me to read God's description of a virtuous woman. (Proverbs 31:10-31) The Bible gives us the term "virtuous woman." More specifically, she was a homemaker. The Biblical description of her responsibilities is the same as those of a homemaker today. Her husband occupied a responsible, respected position in the city and he trusted his wife to manage the home.

She did handwork, shopped for food, rose before daybreak and prepared food to feed her household. She planted a garden, set aside time for personal study, increased her faith, and shopped so that her cabinets were always well stocked with provisions. She ministered to the poor and needy, spun her own material, made her family elegant clothes, took care of her health, dressed well, and even made her own candles to be sure there was a plentiful supply to provide light for her house at night.

After doing all of that, she still had time to bring in added income for the family. Proverbs 31:24 tells us, *"She maketh fine linen and selleth it; and delivereth girdles unto the merchants."* Perhaps her extra income was used to buy the land she purchased. Proverbs 31:16

There is nothing wrong with a mother earning extra income for the family. What does matter, however, is where and how it is done. God's virtuous woman is an example of how this can be satisfactorily accomplished. Notice that she did not join the merchants or the men at the gates of the city. Her work was done within the framework of her home.

I can imagine the worthy woman weaving the linen and sewing the girdles while caring for and nurturing her children. When she was ready to go to a village with her product, her children probably traveled with her. The "girdles" the worthy woman made were a square yard of woolen, linen, or silk cloth cut into a triangle, then folded into a sash-like belt about five to eight inches wide and approximately 36 inches long. They were worn with the *Ketonet* I mentioned earlier. They were drawn about the waist, and the tapering ends tied in back. It not only girded the loins but its fold formed a pocket in which small articles were carried. Both men and women wore them.

There are numerous ways a woman may begin a home-based business and earn added income without leaving her children. I have learned that, by being a homemaker, I am free to engage in interests that I never thought possible before. When I have pursued the opportunities God provided for me, they have led to adding income to our family budget. I have not planned any of them, but they keep coming. When God chooses to open doors for me, I can enter them or reject them. It is my choice.

Many enterprises afford women the opportunity to sell their products at their leisure. Tupperware, Amway, and Mary Kay are three such businesses. Other companies now make it possible for women to stay at home and perform their work with a computer. You may be an artist, music teacher, seamstress, cake decorator, photographer, writer, hairdresser, or candle maker, You may knit, crochet, make quilts, or be a private tutor. All of these talents can be performed without leaving your children in the care of others.

(2) *Boredom* - When a woman says she is bored with staying at home, she is admitting that she does not understand how to be an effective Homemaker. She obviously needs to seek training to learn how to be a good cook, to create things with her hands, sew, decorate, perform benevolent deeds for others, be an exciting wife to her husband and a loving mother who understands how to successfully train her children.

Please understand, when I discuss working to keep your home, I am talking about tending to the emotional, mental, physical, spiritual, and social needs of each of your children. A mother who gets bored listening to, feeding, teaching, reading to, singing to, and playing with her children is absolutely unacceptable.

For many years I did not understand why God instructed older Christian women to teach the younger women to love their husbands and their children (Titus 2:4). I believed that love for one's children should come naturally, but becoming a good wife and mother demands skills one must be taught. If a girl does not learn them from her mother (and millions do not), how will she ever learn them if someone does not teach her? The fact is that without a teacher she may never learn them at all.

Millions of marriages could be saved if only women were successfully trained how to be loving wives, mothers, and homemakers.

It Is Just Not Fair!

Some homemakers actually feel sorry for themselves. They are convinced that their husbands have a much more gratifying work than they do. They reason his world is exciting! Mine is monotonous! He engages in exhilarating conversation with other adults. I must listen to baby talk all day! He gets to dress up, drive to work, and attend interesting meetings. He is a part of making the world go around, while I am home with flour on my face and cleaning dirty faces and bottoms. I am capable of bringing home a paycheck as large or larger than my husband's! Why must I wash, cook, clean, discipline, and listen to children? The work I do is never finished. It is the same ol' routine day in and day out! I work an eighteen-hour day while my husband only works an eight-hour day. He comes home, kicks off his shoes, relaxes, or engages in things that he enjoys and waits for me to serve him dinner. I'm too tired to think! All I want to do is go to bed so I can get a little rest. Life is just not fair!

Mothers, I assure you, that your work is not mundane. It is heavenly! Every moment you spend with your children, every kindness you do for them, or for any helpless person, is a blessing. You are performing work for Christ. He has no hands but your hands, no feet but your feet to do His work today. And in eternity you will stand before Him and His holy Angels. One day your children, if properly trained will be your greatest honor and delight.

Where Is Mother?

A home without Mother is like a day without sunshine, a song without music, Christmas without presents, a fireplace with no fire, or a table without food. She is irreplaceable; no one can successfully be her substitute.

If God has blessed you with children, make a commitment today to stay at home and be a one-hundred-percent mother for them.

WHERE IS MOTHER?

Our little one lay mid snow-white sheets,
    And smiled in peaceful slumber sweet.
Soon he opened his blue eyes wide
    And he saw me standing by his side.
His baby lips quivered, loud he cried,
    "Where's Muvver?"

Small Anne was playing in the yard,
    She ran too fast and fell so hard.
Up the steps she ran past me,
    With bleeding hands and aching knee.
Tears in her eyes, she could not see;
    She cried, "Where's Mother?"

When Jack comes in each day from school,
    Throws his coat and cap upon a stool - -
Into the kitchen he quickly flies,
    Thinking of cookies and apple pies.
If she's not there, he always cries,
    "Where's Mother?"

My lovely daughter came up the steps
    And right by my chair she swept;
She asked not for sister, or brother,
    But asked the same old question over,
    "Where's Mother?"

I was their Dad and I could not see
    Why they asked for Mother instead of me.
But the next day when I came from town,
    Before I laid my burden down,
I asked the children standing ' round,
    "Where's Mother?" [3]

In The End, IT IS FAIR

If God gives you children, IT IS FAIR that YOU care for and supervise them. You may think that you will not have time for yourself, but you will. Your mothering, depending on how many children you have and the way you space them, will be complete in approximately twenty to thirty years.

Your husband's responsibility of providing a living will not end. As long as he lives he must bear the obligation of providing for you. Those years you thought he was resting while you were working ' round the clock will, in the long run, even out for both of you.

After thirty-one years of mothering and being a caretaker for my elderly mother, I now have more time for my personal interests. My husband, however, still works. He says God will determine when he retires.

In the end, IT IS FAIR!

RESPONSIBILITY NO. 4 - BE THE GUIDE OF THE HOUSE

God assigned the mission of guiding the house to women. (I Timothy 5:14) A house is the building in which a family lives. Since God understands the value of specific assignment of work, He assigned the responsibility of the inner workings of the house to women.   He endowed us with talents that enable us to be capable managers, directors, and organizers. We can and should do a superior job of caring for the family's domestic needs. It is the husband's duty to earn money in order to provide for his family's physical needs. The wife is to guide, organize and make certain that family goods are properly conserved and utilized.

Mother is the one who should know where the clean towels are kept, when dinner will be served, and where coats are hung.

Stop Buying So Much "Stuff"

Young families will be more content if they cut their budget and stop buying so much "stuff." Quit making unnecessary purchases that create financial burdens and cause worry and strife.

I have heard it said about some women, "She can throw more out the back door with a teaspoon than her husband can bring in the front door with a scoop shovel." I hope that cannot be said about you.

(1) Save on Food - Follow Dr. Denmark's nutritional plan and save money on your food budget. When you cook from scratch, stop purchasing snack foods, sugary drinks, boxed mixes, prepared "pop in the oven" dinners, and other unwholesome food items that undermine one's health, you will save a great deal of money. Cook and puree your baby's food. Stop buying expensive baby food contained in bottles that must be disposed of by the basketfuls. When you resolve not to frequently patronize restaurants and cook nutritious meals at home, your family will be healthier and become wealthier in the process.

(2) Save on Transportation - After you have sliced your kitchen budget, go to the garage and evaluate your transportation. Does your family purchase new cars that cost thousands of dollars extra, plus spending much more money on more costly insurance rates, tags, taxes, plus high interest rates? Why not purchase a previously owned car with low mileage and in good condition? Cut back to only one car. When you stay home as a homemaker, your family can get along comfortably with one car. This is especially easy when your children are small.

(3) Save on Clothes - Go into your bedrooms and take inventory of the clothes in your closets. Often clothing is an easy place to slash the family expenses. Many families purchase far too many clothes. Think about it! How many clothes can you wear at one time? Many families discover it is preferable to have a few well-made, attractive clothes to cramming their closets with many garments that they seldom or never wear.

When I am tempted to stuff my closet with too many clothes, I consider my roots. When I was a small child, our family of eight lived happily in an eight-hundred-square- foot house with one small closet. Once when my mother was taking me to purchase a new pair of shoes, I remember sincerely asking her, "Mother, my shoes don't look too bad. Do you think they will sell us a new pair?"

I am not suggesting you deny your children attractive apparel, however, there are areas in which you can avoid extravagance by refusing to buy unnecessary clothing.

It should be the goal of every family to live within a reasonable budget, pay for a home, and rid themselves of debt. This may not be possible if you purchase material things, which you cannot afford.

I Am Learning We Have a New Name

I have recently learned that a new name is being coined to identify "homemakers." Those of us who keep full-time watch over our children and houses are being referred to as "domestic engineers." A domestic engineer writes the following:

The Job of a Domestic Engineer 4

Domestic engineering is a home-based career that comes without a handbook of standard operating procedures; a job that can only be learned by doing. No experience is necessary yet the eagerness to learn and grow through hands-on training is a plus. The goal of this position is to put into the world young adults with good strong values, kind hearts, caring dispositions and the desire to make the world a better place than it is today by living their lives in a decent, honest, God-fearing manner.

This is a position of authority, discipline and influence. Needing to have the ability to set realistic goals and to establish a good support system for every youngster. Acknowledging that every child is an individual with his/her unique personality. Everything that is seen is absorbed into young minds, therefore, it is best that actions be thought out thoroughly before acted upon. Young minds and hearts should be filled with the love for God and the desire to do right. This position requires the ability to administer medications and dress wounds. The willingness to get dirty under the hood of a car or fix the chain on a bicycle. The skillful art of preparing meals and tending house must also be known and taught through a caring way to both the boys and the girls. A shoulder to cry on, a listening ear, a caring heart, being able to forgive, patience and plenty of words of praise are also skills one must possess. Being able to say, "NO!" at certain times, even if it hurts, is a task in itself. To instill in young minds that it is _not_ okay to hate, yet it is okay to have their own opinion. Possessing the ability to solve problems and to be a mediator in times of disagreement is a plus. Knowing the ABCs and 123s is helpful when tutoring. Yet the biggest skill that means the most not only to the youngest but also to teens, is the ability to give a big hug and say, "I Love You!," just because.

I have been a Domestic Engineer for 15 1/2 years. Every day is a new day with new problems and surprises, some good and some bad. The experience I have gained goes beyond what words can describe. With every new child, there is more to learn and more to pass on. There is no monetary pay, bonuses, or vacations just the satisfaction of knowing that there are four good kids growing and learning and preparing themselves, with our help, for life in our world. Hazards to this job are, but are not limited to, graying hair, sleepless nights, and at times, feeling of failure . . . This is a job I will never quit.

by Tracey Rogers

I like being called a "domestic engineer" and may start signing my name Gwendolyn M. Webb, D.E. The sound of it makes me feel important and the signature would make sure that people ask questions. The next time you must fill out forms asking for your occupation, you may want to use this new title.

Woman Power Converted to Electric Power

The work of a "domestic engineer" is relatively easy and enjoyable when compared to the requirements of keeping a house and home in past generations. Our great-grandmothers scrubbed clothes on a rub board. Today, it takes only a few minutes to do the family laundry with an automatic washing machine. Permanent-press clothes have done away with the drudgery of ironing shirts and skirts for hours. Today one rarely sees clothespins and a clothesline, because electric dryers have taken over the work of drying clothes. While an electric dishwasher is humming away cleaning the dishes, Mother has time to spend on-line with her computer. Many floors are covered with beautiful thick carpet or attractive tile. The creaky wood floors with the wide cracks are relics of the past. Brooms are used to sweep the garage and sidewalk. Vacuum cleaners now efficiently clean our floors in a matter of minutes.

The convenience of storing food in refrigerators and freezers has reduced shopping time to one trip a week to the supermarket. We are able to cook our food and warm and illuminate our houses by the simple flip of a switch.

We must admit that the modern "domestic engineer", to a great degree, exchanges electric power for womanpower. Because of modern conveniences, some women feel that they have been freed to work outside their homes.   They strongly affirm there is not enough housework left to occupy their full time.   Therefore, they seek other challenges and work outside their homes.

Thirty Times Yes and I Will Believe You

If you are a mother who claims that staying within the confines of your house is not challenging enough for you, answer these thirty questions. If you answer "yes" to each one, I believe there is a chance you have nothing left to do in the way of housework.

Yes	No	1. Are your windows shining inside and out?
Yes	No	2. Are all of your walls free of fingerprints and marks?
Yes	No	3. Have you shampooed your carpets and furniture within the last six months?
Yes	No	4. Do you make quick breads from scratch, rejecting the boxed ready mixes?
Yes	No	5. Do you prepare three well-balanced meals a day?
Yes	No	6. Are you caught up with all your correspondence?
Yes	No	7. Did you plant a garden last spring?
Yes	No	8. Do you can or freeze some of your food in the summer?
Yes	No	9. Did you make any of your children's school clothes?
Yes	No	10. Did you bake and decorate the birthday cakes for the family this past year?
Yes	No	11. Is your house decorated with beautiful flowerbeds?
Yes	No	12. Do you bake any of your yeast breads?
Yes	No	13. Did you make your Christmas gifts last year?
Yes	No	14. Are all of your drawers and closets cleaned and well organized?
Yes	No	15. Is your oven clean?
Yes	No	16. Have you re-arranged your furniture in the past three months?

Yes   No   17. Are your recipes copied and organized in a recipe box or book?

Yes   No   18. Are your kitchen cabinets cleared and clean before you go to bed each night?

Yes   No   19. If you have sterling, have you shined your sterling pieces within the last six months?

Yes   No   20. Does some of your own handwork decorate the walls of your home?

Yes   No   21. Could your husband say he has not had to ask, "Where is a clean shirt, underwear, or trousers?" in the last month.

Yes   No   22. Do you consider it a waste of money to buy disposable diapers and have chosen instead to wash cloth diapers?

Yes   No   23. Do you spend time visiting and encouraging the elderly?

Yes   No   24. Are your floors waxed and shining?

Yes   No   25. Have you washed the light fixtures throughout your house and replaced burned-out bulbs in the past year?

Yes   No   26. Are your family snapshots well organized in albums?

Yes   No   27. Is your mending basket empty--no holes in socks, missing buttons, or dresses that should be re-hemmed?

Yes   No   28. Are the children's schoolwork--report cards, pictures, papers, and artwork -- being preserved in scrapbooks?

Yes   No   29. Have you taken a dish of food to a neighbor who was sick or lonely in the past two months?

Yes   No   30. Do you spend time trying to help a needy child?

Questions For Daddy

At the end of Chapter Four, I promised Daddy Bee that he could answer the following questions about Mother Bee. This quiz will serve as a review of Mother Bee as a submissive HELPMEET, keeper at home, and guide of the house.

Yes   No   1. Does your wife choose her clothes, style her hair, and wear her make-up in a manner that is attractive and pleasing to you?

Yes   No   2. When your wife is unhappy about something you have or have not done, does she calmly talk to you about it rather than punish you with the silent treatment or seethe in anger?

Yes   No   3. Does your wife accept you as you are and never nag you to change?

Yes   No   4. Does your wife stay home with your children because that is what she would rather do?

Yes   No   5. Does your wife prepare and serve your food in a way that pleases you?

Yes   No   6. Is your wife a warm and affectionate partner who is always enthusiastically willing to fulfill your sexual needs?

Yes   No   7. Would your wife rather be with you sharing your hobbies and recreational activities than be with someone else or somewhere else?

Yes   No   8. When you disapprove of a particular way your wife is managing the house or children, is she willing to change?

Yes   No   9. Does your wife make you feel that you are the greatest and most important man in her life?

Yes   No   10. Do you look forward to coming home to a clean, sweet-scented, attractive wife and a well-organized house?

If you answered yes to each of the above questions, you and your children have a Queen for a wife and mother. Shower her with words of appreciation, crown her with honor, and praise her before all. Remember that it isn't every man and child who has the privilege of abiding in the presence of a Queen.

Gwen's

Special Health

&

Food Unit

GWEN'S SPECIAL HEALTH & FOOD UNIT

America's Distressing Health Condition
Dr. Don Colbert, M.D. in his book, *What Would Jesus Eat?*, writes, "Approximately half of all Americans alive today will die of heart disease, and approximately a third will develop cancer at some time in their lives.

"As a physician, I have a strong conviction that America's fast-food diet and its dependence on processed foods is the primary reason for the epidemic of the widespread and serious diseases we see in our society today. These adverse health conditions include this top fifteen list: obesity, heart disease, cancer, diabetes, hypertension, high cholesterol, attention deficit disorders, gastroesophageal reflux disease, gallbladder disease, diverticulosis, diverticulitis, arthritis, chronic fatigue syndrome, fibromyalgia, and addictions. *Almost all other degenerative diseases could be included in this list.* It is difficult to find a family that has not been affected by one or more of these diseases. It is also difficult to find a family that doesn't consume a significant quantity of fast-food meals or a significant percentage of processed foods. As a physician, I do not see this as a coincidence." [5]

In her book, *Healthy Kids*, Marilu Henner states, "During the past twenty-two years, since I've been studying food and health, I've seen the amount of chemistry in our food go from bad to worse. Visit any grocery store and, at random, pick up a box of prepared food from the shelf and read the label. It's horrifying. I am always joking that you should not eat anything that needs a paragraph to describe it or says, "Continued on the next can." But when we are talking about giving this chemical-laden, sodium-heavy, sugar-sweetened, nutritionless food to our children--it's not funny. I can honestly say without hesitation that the amount of chemistry in our food is killing us. We are eating our way to a future marred by heart disease, diabetes, cancer, and obesity." [6]

Our Body God's Temple
*"Know ye not that your body is the temple of the Holy Spirit...**glorify God in your body**."* I Corinthians 6:19 & 20
When the Holy Scriptures teach that our bodies are temples, that should impress us. A temple is a beautiful structure. We admire temples. A temple should be carefully maintained and guarded. As a

Christian, I must take excellent care of my body. My body is the earthly house in which the Holy Spirit dwells.

Our earthly temple, our husband's temple, and all of our children's little temples must receive the most excellent care we can give them. We all must be fed, bathed, groomed and clothed, and make sure our bodies are in excellent condition. When others observe us, they should see an attractive example that they are inclined to imitate.

Mother, You Are in Charge

Mother, when God assigned you to be the "keeper of your home" and "guide of your house", He put you in charge of safeguarding your family's physical temples. Preparing wholesome food is the best way to safeguard the physical health of your family. This is achieved when you prepare nutritious meals and serve them at the proper time. The aroma of wholesome food whets a healthy appetite and unites the family around the kitchen table. A child's preference of food is formed during his first four to five years of life. The food you serve him will determine his choice of food for the rest of his life.

The task of preparing and serving food, and cleaning up after three meals a day will consume four to five hours of your working day. That does not include the time it takes to purchase and store the food. While you are training your children to help in the kitchen, it will take even longer. As they grow older, however, you will reap a reward when they are able to perform many kitchen chores without your help.

When I tell you that it takes a mother twenty-eight to thirty-five hours each week to prepare food for a family, I am not describing an inexperienced cook, or one who has a poorly equipped kitchen. I am describing a woman whose kitchen is equipped with all of the modern conveniences such as: a garbage disposal, microwave oven, dish washer, stove, refrigerator, freezer, toaster, stainless steel cookware, pressure cookers, a food processor, electric skillet, and a large variety of other kitchen utensils. Even with this modern equipment, it will still take hours of her time IF she prepares the right kinds of nutritious foods for her family.

How Did My Mother Keep Me Healthy?

I was born at home, never taken to a doctor's office, nor examined by a physician until I was sixteen. I would not have been examined then, except the law demanded all student athletes have physical examinations.

When one observes how often children are taken to visit doctors today and the large amount of money spent on doctor bills, one may wonder, "How did your mother keep you so healthy?" It was not by chance or through good genes that I enjoyed robust health. The answer lies in the fact that my mother fed our family nutritious foods in their natural state. Food as God created it!

My Mother breast-fed me when I was a baby, and our family drank fresh water, pumped by our windmill. My Mother mixed and baked our bread. She prepared all of our food from "scratch." Our vegetables were grown in her garden or the "truck patch" my father planted. The black-eyed peas, corn, beans, onions, radishes, lettuce, fresh mint, beets, turnips, and rhubarb were not contaminated with chemical sprays. The beef and poultry we consumed were raised on our farm. In those days, farmers did not inject animals with bovine growth hormones, steroids, or antibiotics. Our free-ranging chickens raised on grain and grass produced our eggs. Our family's butter was churned from the cream our cows produced.

I maintained excellent health because I was fed a wholesome diet of nutritious food. By keeping me healthy, my parents saved a great deal of money on doctor and medical bills.

Selecting Proper Nutrition Is Difficult For Today's Domestic Engineers
You may say, "Meal preparation is more convenient now than it was for your mother. Our food is already mixed and measured. It is ready to eat from the cartons, cans, or heated from frozen packages. It isn't necessary for me to be a scratch cook. Preparing meals does not take me as long as it did your mother."

Contrary to what many believe, it is far more difficult for domestic engineers today to feed healthful food to their families than it was in previous generations. Women who lived in the past did not need to "beware" of as many hazardous materials lurking in their food as there are today.

In today's world, choosing healthful food is similar to driving your car through an obstacle course. The path you must travel has dangerous hazards strewn in the roadway. If you run into these dangerous objects, they have the potential to harm you. As you travel, you must constantly slow down, swerve, and stop to avoid perilous pitfalls. There are no signs warning you where these hazards are, so you must be careful to avoid them. If you are careless, before you are halfway through your journey, you will meet with disaster. If you miss a hairpin curve, you will plunge your car over a cliff and crash.

This dramatic illustration describes the conditions you face as you push your grocery cart down the aisle of your local super market. Refined "dead food" is all around you. It is perched on every shelf and in every aisle of food stores. You pick them up and place them in your grocery cart without realizing the good nutrition has been removed from them. You assume they are healthy for you. (After all, our government looks out for our welfare, doesn't it?) You pass down the cereal aisle and pick up your favorite cereal and fail to notice that you are buying three kinds of sugar--white sugar, high fructose, and corn syrup, plus coloring agents Yellow 5, Yellow 6, and Yellow 40. You buy cookies for your baby. How could you know that "partially hydrogenated" oil is hidden inside them? How dare the food processors put dangerous substances in food for babies to eat!

The point is this. If you don't become an educated shopper, you will be like the car that crashed. You and your family are at risk of poor health and in the worst case your lives could end prematurely.

The Fast Food Giants Are Out To Get You

Women in past generations didn't have a fast-food industry sitting like vultures on the fence waiting to undermine their children's health. You do!

Every day, the fast food giants are ready to snatch your children's appetites. You must combat an endless stream of advertisements glaring from billboards, in magazines, on Internet and television screens. These profiteers do not mind damaging your children's health by serving them "dead bread," fatty meats, French fries dripping with "partially hydrogenated" fat and soft drinks loaded with sugar. They entice you to buy their tasty products. What they give you in return for consuming their wares is a child whose health is damaged just a little bit more. They are bold! They "target" your children. Fast-food restaurants lure them with attractive playground equipment, toys and other gimmicks.

The soft drink industry is ready to addict you and your children to unhealthy products. They advertise that their drinks "refresh you." Instead, they addict you. Many beverages are loaded with caffeine and sugar, and, "sugar free" drinks are sweetened with a chemical called aspartame.

"NutraSweet, or aspartame, contains two amino acids: phenylalanine and aspartic acid, as well as methanol. In the body, these elements produce substances that are identical in composition to wood alcohol and formaldehyde (yes, formaldehyde is the embalming fluid). Aspartame is known to have addictive tendencies. Many anecdotal studies have been published reporting that the more diet drinks one consumes, the more one craves diet drinks. One irony associated with these sweeteners is that they tend to be related to increased sugar consumption. NutraSweet especially has been shown to increase the craving for sugar." 7

Dr. Tim O'Shea writes, "How many people do you know who drink at least one 12-ounce soft drink per day? If the sugar from each bottle could be crystallized, it would amount to 10 teaspoons." 8

To be a "Domestic Engineer" Is To Be a COOK

A young life relies on its mother for nourishment. The newborn infant, baby sparrows or infant kittens all use their cries to attract their mother's attention for food. If these new lives are to be sustained, a compassionate mother must meet their needs. Mothers in the animal world are guided by simple instinct to nourish their young. Human mothers face a much more challenging task. They must learn how to feed their families properly. Our world is continually changing. New philosophies and modern methods constantly emerge. After a wise mother considers her options, she will choose a good system and a nutritious menu of foods to nourish her family.

In her Food for a Day Plan, Dr. Denmark teaches what each body needs to stay healthy. (Read Chapter 10, Gem #2 in the Addendum) Her outline is simple and easy to remember. When you walk into your kitchen to prepare a meal, all you have to keep in mind is to serve a PROTEIN, STARCH, FRUIT, and WATER. For lunch and dinner, add the VEGETABLES.

Feed your family breakfast using the above combinations. In another five and one-half hours serve a nourishing lunch. Provide plenty of fresh water to drink throughout the day. After another five and one-half hours, serve dinner. After you have served three nutritious meals to your family, you can send them to bed with perfect confidence that you have done your best to keep them healthy.

Furthermore, Dr. Denmark advises us not to snack between meals or allow children to snack between meals. After eating a hearty meal, it is like closing the lid on the washing machine. *Do not open the lid* and throw anything else in until the cycle is finished. In our case the cycle of digestion will not be finished for five and one-half hours. If your child refuses to eat at mealtime, then he has five and one-half hours to build his appetite. If his hunger does not return, your child may be getting sick.

Being a successful "domestic engineer" involves being a conscientious cook. Feeding all family members properly will be especially time-consuming when you are nursing a baby or cooking special food to puree for a toddler. (Read Chapters 5 & 6 in the Addendum)

PROTEIN

You should serve a complete protein at each meal. A complete protein is a food that contains all eight of the essential amino acids your body requires. These essential ingredients must be delivered to your body via the food you eat. Your body does not manufacture them. (Notice Dr. Denmark says **a** protein. It isn't necessary to serve an assortment of proteins at each meal.)

There are several foods from which you may select when choosing a complete protein. Your protein sources are *eggs, the meat of animals, fish, fowls, or dairy products.* From vegetables you may choose soy (which is a complete protein in itself) or you may combine *beans* and *whole grains* together and that will create a complete protein. Combining *seeds* and *nuts* with *beans* can also form a complete protein.

In the Bible, there is an account of Daniel and his three friends, Shadrach, Meshach, and Abednego, who were taken into Babylonian captivity.

The king of Babylon selected Daniel and his companions for special training. Because they were talented and perfect physically, they were selected for special treatment. "*The king appointed them a daily provision of the king's meat, and of the wine which he drank; so nourishing them three years, that at the end thereof they might stand before the king.*" Daniel 1:5

However, "*Daniel purposed in his heart that he would not defile himself with the portion of the king's meat, nor with the wine which he drank.*" Rather, "*he requested of the prince of the eunuchs...Prove thy servants, I beseech thee, ten days; and let them give us pulse to eat, and water to drink...Then let our countenances be looked upon before thee, and the countenance of the children that eat the portion of the king's meat...so he consented to them in this matter, and proved them ten days. And at the end of the ten days their countenances appeared fairer and fatter in flesh than all the children which did eat the portion of the kings meat."* Daniel 1:12-15

It is significant, that, after the test, which involved eating simple wholesome food, Daniel and his friends appeared to be in much better condition than those who consumed the rich, fatty diet of the king's dainties. Also remember that throughout his life Daniel was physically healthy and mentally alert.

The definition of pulse is course grain, peas, beans, and the like.

I enjoy making up different pulse recipes by combining whole grain and bean combinations. Many people do not like to cook beans because it takes too long. They have also been taught that beans must be soaked overnight. Cooking with a pressure cooker will solve both of those problems. One can take beans (legumes) directly from their packages, rinse them, place them in a pressure cooker, add a sufficient amount of liquid and seasonings and in about an hour they will be cooked and ready to serve. Pressure cooking also preserves the nutrients.

Things to Remember about Preparing Protein Food

1. When available, buy beef, chicken, and eggs that come from free-range animals, that have been fed on grass and grain, and kept free of steroids, growth hormones, and antibiotics.

2. Cut away all fat from your beef before cooking. God commanded, *"Speak unto the children of Israel, saying, Ye shall eat no manner of fat, of ox, or of sheep, or of goat."* Leviticus 7:23 The only fat to be consumed is the fat which is marbled inside the meat.

3. Also cut away all fat and skin from chicken, turkey, or other fowls before cooking.

4. Eat generous amounts of fish. The omega-3 fatty acids in fish are good for the heart and brain. Consuming Cod Liver Oil is a common treatment for arthritis. Choose fish from the ocean, as they are less likely to be contaminated.

5. Broil, poach, or bake your meat protein. Seldom fry meat. If you do choose to fry beef, chicken or fish, use extra virgin olive or canola oil.

6. Treat butter and cheese as a condiment. Use cheese sparingly and on rare occasions. If you like, you can whip extra virgin olive oil in with softened butter (1/4 to 1/2 part oil to 1/2 part butter.) It makes the

spread last longer and the mono-unsaturated fat in the olive oil is good for you.

7. Eggs are healthful. They contain choline, which helps brain function and memory. Lecithin is embodied inside an egg and is the substance that emulsifies (breaks up) the cholesterol of the egg yolk. Eggs comprise folic acid, B vitamins, antioxidants, and unsaturated fats.

8. Soy can be purchased in the form of miso, tofu, tempeh, milk, yogurt, flour, and nuts. Switching from cow's milk to soymilk is an improvement any family can make to build its health. If you are one who must have half-and-half or dairy cream, switch to soymilk creamer. The White Wave Company produces an excellent soy creamer.

9. Be careful of the fat contents in the hamburger you buy. Buy hamburger with less than 10% fat and add a little extra virgin olive oil if it sticks to the skillet.

10. Add these seasonings to one pound extra lean hamburger, ground turkey or chicken to make a breakfast sausage. *Sausage Seasoning Mix* - Combine 3/4 t. thyme, 1/8 t. cayenne pepper, 1/2 t. sage, 1t. marjoram, 1/8-t. coriander, and 1/2-t. sea salt. *Italian Sausage Mix* - Combine 3/4 teaspoon each of fennel, black pepper, parsley, basil, marjoram, and 1/2-t. sea salt.

Take Special Care to guard your little girl from eating meat containing steroids, hormones, and antibiotics. It is believed that these second-hand contaminates cause girls to be thrown into early adolescence, and they begin to menstruate years earlier than normal.

So that you will know, God forbade the Israelites to eat any animal that did not chew the cud and part the hoof. Swine and rabbit are in that category. God also commanded His people to eat only "clean" fish. Clean fish had both scales and fins. Fish that do not fit that category are catfish, clams, mussels, oysters, scallops, crabs, lobsters, shrimp, prawns, and crayfish. Unclean fowls like vultures were to be avoided. God created "unclean" creatures to be scavengers. They were designed to clean up the land and sea. Read Leviticus 11:1-23

Christians are not bound by the dietary laws that were given to the Israelite people; however, there were good reasons for the laws God gave and they are recorded for our learning. Romans 15:4

Do Not Drink Cow's Milk

Dr. Denmark is adamant in teaching that one should not drink cow's milk after weaning. She has researched the subject extensively and has treated many thousands of children who have suffered a variety of health problems caused from drinking cow's milk. Anemia, ear infections, allergies, hemoglobin loss, juvenile-onset diabetes, acne, flatulence, constipation, mucus, runny noses, bronchitis, asthma and obesity are just a few of the health problems she believes are caused by drinking cow's milk.

She is not alone in this conclusion. Dr. Don Colbert writes "Are you aware that the human being is the only mammal that continues to drink milk as an adult? Other animals, it seems, are smarter than we are in that regard. Only their young drink milk." [9]

"My Family Thought We Had the Nectar of Life"

T. Colin Campbell grew up on a small dairy farm of 210 acres, nestled among glorious green pastures near the Shenandoah Valley in northern Virginia.. Almost from the moment he learned to walk, he followed the footsteps of his father, Tom Campbell, as he tended the farm's 20 to 30 milk cows. Eventually, young Colin was given the chore of "stripping" by hand any milk from the cows' udders that the milking machine left behind. He also learned how to operate the family butter churn and, on special weekends, helped man the hand-cranked bucket used to make ice cream.

The Campbells were a simple family, without much money, but considered themselves blessed to have milk straight from the cow. "We thought we had the nectar of life," Campbell says, "I was proud of the fact that somehow, every day, I could drink a gallon of milk, or more."

Campbell went on to devote his life to nutritional research. Two decades ago he contributed to the first federally funded report on the relationship of diet to cancer, an influential study that helped establish the nutritional importance of grains, fruits, and vegetables. At age 66 he is nearing retirement as a nutritional biochemist at Cornell University. He is also president and CEO of Paracelsian, a company that promotes holistic health and sells assays to measure dioxin like chemicals and evaluate herbal products. Campbell lives on a quiet residential street and, by all appearances is like most of his neighbors. But these days not one drop of milk touches the lips of anyone in his household, and his refrigerator is stocked with soy cheeses, sorbet, and rice milk. "People might think we're nuts," he says. "But non-dairy beverages and foods are pretty good once you adjust to the taste."

Like most Americans, Campbell once assumed that dairy products were not only wholesome but also an essential part of the daily diet for anyone desiring good teeth and strong bones. After years of scientific research, however, he's now convinced that cow's milk is responsible for a share of our nation's medical woes. The fact that fats in dairy products can contribute to hardening of the arteries and heart disease has long been common knowledge. But Campbell worries that stocking up on skim milk and low-fat yogurt--or going organic because of concerns about cows exposed to pesticides, antibiotics, and bovine growth hormone--may offer only limited protection against the potential health hazards of milk. Unlike most nutritionists, he questions the much-touted health benefits of milk. And he believes his research raises issues his colleagues have tended to ignore.

What Does The Bible Say About Milk?

Many Biblical passages speak of milk from kine (cows), goats, sheep, and camels.

One day while Abraham and Sarah were dwelling on the plains of Mamre they received unexpected guests for lunch. Three angels visited them in the form of men. Abraham and Sarah extended warm hospitality to them by quickly preparing a meal. The dinner they served consisted of Sarah's homemade bread, beef, butter and *milk*. Genesis 18:6-8.

What kind of milk Abraham and Sarah served is not specifically mentioned, but no two kinds of milk are alike. The milk of each species of animal is tailored to meet the needs of that species. Human milk contains the nutrients to build not only a healthy body, but also a healthy brain. To nourish rapid brain growth, human milk is rich in special long-chain poly-unsaturated fatty acids but low in saturated fats. A baby's brain grows more during infancy than at any other time, doubling its volume and reaching around 60 percent of its adult size by one year. Cows produce milk that is high in saturated fats that encourage rapid body and bone growth, but is low in the fats that support rapid brain growth.

Goat and sheep milk is the two types of milk mentioned in the Bible which were consumed by humans. *"And thou shalt have goats' milk enough for thy food, for the food of thy household."* Proverbs 27:27 *"Who feedeth a flock, and eateth not of the milk of the flock?"* I Corinthians 9:7 Notice that the milk stipulated in these passages was to come from small animals-- *goats* and *flocks*, which would include sheep.

Concerning cow's milk, the only thing I discovered that people used were the by-products of butter, cheese and curds.

Problems with Today's Milk

Today there are several large problems with consuming cow's milk. Few people drink any milk other than cow's milk. It is bad enough that humans drink milk that God designed to grow a forty-five pound calf into a three hundred pound animal in six to eight months, but our government demands that milk be pasteurized and homogenized before it is sold to the public. These two processes further damage the milk and the human beings that consume it.

Pasteurization requires milk to be heated to 145 degrees for thirty minutes in order to kill harmful bacteria, but in the process beneficial bacteria are also killed. Heating denatures the enzymes in milk and alters the structure of the protein. Pasteurization also decreases the ability of the calcium in milk to be absorbed. Many believe that the changes made in the milk by pasteurization are the reason that so many people are allergic to dairy products.

Homogenization is a process by which whole milk is put under great pressure that breaks the butterfat into tiny droplets. The purpose of this is to mix the cream so that it will not rise to the top of the milk. The butterfat becomes so miniscule that it easily passes into our bloodstream and causes triglycerides and cholesterol to rise. All of this damages blood vessels, while it paves the way for plaque buildup in our arteries. The butterfat droplets of milk in its natural state, (non-homogenized) are so large they are not absorbed nearly as well.

The average American family does not have access to cow's milk in its natural state. Dairy farmers have told me they are not allowed to sell their milk directly to the public. The middlemen who come to their farms and purchase their milk make them sign contracts that prohibit them from selling to anyone else.

I agree with Dr. Denmark, Dr. Colbert, T. Colin Campbell and many others who have concluded that cow's milk was not designed for humans. I am not as large as a cow and have no desire to obtain that size. I use a brand of soy or rice milk called Better Than Milk. I use it for drinking, to make gravies, puddings, soups, ice cream, and in any recipe that calls for milk. My guests eat my food containing soy or rice milk and never know the difference. Little do they know they receive zero saturated fat and cholesterol, yet get sufficient amounts of potassium, carbohydrates, protein, calcium, and Vitamin B12.

I still use sparingly some of the protein products that are made from cow's milk--butter, cheese, and fat-free yogurt. If I were to ever decide to use animal milk for protein, I would choose non-pasteurized goat's milk.

STARCH

Starch is another food Dr. Denmark teaches must be consumed at each meal. We get starch from *whole grains* and *potatoes*. The whole grains that are the most familiar to us are wheat, rice, corn, oats, rye, barley and millet. Less familiar whole grains are amaranth, buckwheat, and quinoa. To make these grains more palatable, we have learned to turn them into *breads*, *cereals*, and *pastas*. Potatoes are also prepared in a multitude of ways.

My goal is to persuade you to purchase and consume whole grains and products made from whole grains with no added artificial sweeteners, flavors, preservatives, coloring agents or "hydrogenated" or "partially hydrogenated" oil.

Modern men have learned to refine grains. That means they know how to strip the grains and separate the various parts. A grain of wheat for instance has three parts. The outer shell is the bran, which makes up 15 percent of the kernel. It is rich in fiber, minerals, and vitamin B. The next layer is the wheat germ, which makes up 3 percent of the kernel and it is rich in Vitamins E and B. The inner core of the kernel is called the endosperm. It makes up 80 to 85 percent of the grain.

Flour is made from the endosperm. The bran and germ are removed from white flour and are mainly used in animal feed. In order to please most of today's public, refineries go even further and put the flour made from the endosperm through a bleaching agent. That makes it whiter, but further destroys the few vitamins that remain. In all of this milling and bleaching twenty-two important nutrients have been removed from the kernel of wheat. When you pick up a package of bleached white flour in the grocery store, you are buying dead food. Oh, but they enrich it, you say! The thiamin, niacin, riboflavin, and iron they put back into the flour or bread products is usually derived from coal tar and has little actual vitamin enrichment at all.

Dr. James Duke has made the comment that the human equivalent of fake food today is bleached white flour. 98% of spaghetti, bread, pastries, and pancakes are made with bleached white flour. Frequently, such products are caramel-colored to make you think you are eating 100% whole-wheat products.

When you buy bread, pasta, and cereal products, read the label. If it does not say, "whole wheat" or "whole grain," you can assume it is made completely or partially with refined flour. Only 2 per cent of the flours consumed in this country are whole grain. The other 98 per cent are processed.

It Was A Must for Me

Many years ago I learned that it was a "must for me" to bake my own breads. No store-bought biscuit, pancake, waffle, cornbread, or muffin mix is as healthy for my family as the ingredients I combine in homemade breads. How can I use only nine ingredients and make delicious biscuits when a boxed mix or can of biscuits purchased from the store requires a paragraph two inches long, typed in fine print, to explain the ingredients contained in the product? Most of the information printed on those boxes and cans is so tedious and incomprehensible the average person never takes time to read it.

I can walk into my kitchen, turn my oven on to 450 degrees, combine 1 cup fresh-ground whole wheat flour, 1/3 cup wheat bran flakes, 2/3 cup unbleached white flour, 3 teaspoons of baking powder, 1 teaspoon sea salt, 2 tablespoons sucanat, (sweetener) 1 1/2 teaspoons Enter-G Egg Replacer, (optional) 1/3 cup canola or extra virgin olive oil, and 2/3 cups soy or rice milk, mix and roll them out between waxed paper, and cut them with a can. I place them on my oiled baking stone and the biscuits will be baked in 12 to 14 minutes. I know exactly what my family is eating and the bread is ready by the time breakfast is prepared.

I also encourage you to bake your own yeast breads. Grind your choice of whole grains to make flour and add different kinds of seeds like flax, sesame, and sunflower. Use extra virgin olive or canola oil, sea salt, filtered or distilled water, and honey along with yeast. It only takes a few good ingredients to make leavened bread, not twenty or twenty-five unknown substances that are listed on packages of store-bought bread.

Prepare hot cereals from whole oats, cracked wheat, brown rice, grits, millet, or barley. Cream of Wheat, Farina, Cream of Rye, or Malt-o-meal all are good.

When you shop the cold cereal aisle at the market, look for whole grains with no added sweeteners, coloring agents, preservatives or "partially hydrogenated" oil. When you purchase them for future consumption, store them in your refrigerator or freezer. Bugs like food that is full of "life", so don't give them a chance to move in and share your groceries.   My family loves my homemade granola cereal.   I encourage you to look for a recipe your family likes. Homemade cold cereals are much less expensive than cereals you buy in the grocery store.

Things to Remember About Starch

1. Buy whole grains from a health food store. They stock whole grains that have not been sprayed with pesticides. When you buy food from a natural food store you can feel confident you are getting the most wholesome grains available.

2. Remember this saying, "The Whiter the Bread the Sooner You're Dead."

3. Compared to bread made with whole grain wheat, white bread is missing: 96% of Vitamin E, 78% of dietary fiber, 72% of magnesium, 62% of zinc, 50% of folic acid, 72% of chromium, 78% of vitamin B-6, plus phytochemicals.

4. The nutrients removed from white bread are critical to immune function, cell communication, appetite control, preventing "free radicals," fetal brain development, plus 500 other functions.

5. *Use unbleached flour* as fill-in flour. It is made from the endosperm of wheat and is allowed to age naturally without the use of chemicals or maturing agents. If you combine it with whole grain flour when making breads, the bread will be more light and fluffy. Unbleached flour is good to thicken gravies and use for items that need to be rolled in flour.

As I speak about using unbleached flour, it reminds me of another example of the absurdity of today's packaged foods.   It takes 6 tablespoons of unbleached flour, 3/4 teaspoon sea salt, 1/2 teaspoon course ground pepper, and 3 cups of soymilk or chicken or beef broth heated to a thickening boil to make delicious gravy. On a package of Biscuit Gravy Mix, 23 ingredients are listed to make 3 cups of gravy.

6. Always serve brown or wild rice. Never purchase polished or white rice.

7. I keep a 50-pound bag of wheat in my chest freezer and grind fresh flour, as I need it.

I grind the wheat and use it immediately, because as soon as grains of wheat are burst they begin to oxidize. The same thing happens when you remove the peel of an apple or banana. When these foods are exposed to air, they begin to deteriorate. To take full advantage of the nutritious benefits in wheat is why I grind the wheat and use it immediately. I also grind other grains like barley or rye to use in my homemade loaves of bread. I use a Vita Mix machine to grind small two-cup portions and a Bosch machine to knead my dough. You can view both of these machines on the Internet. Type in Vita Mix and Bosch Kitchen Mixers and punch search.

8. Do not remove the skin from potatoes. It has nourishment and adds fiber to your diet.

9. Barley, rice, and potatoes are three balanced starches rich in complex carbohydrates that fuel the body with a steady flow of energy. If a man is doing hard labor, these foods will help sustain his energy from one meal to the next. When I grew up on the farm, we had a lot of "meat and potato" men.

10. Beware of store-bought whole grain crackers. Most of them contain "hydrogenated" or "partially hydrogenated" oil.

11. There was a study done in which men ate three helpings of barley a day in the form of cereal, bread, cake, and muffins and lowered their LDL (bad) cholesterol 15% in six weeks. Another group of men who ate the same products made with wheat or bran flour did not experience a drop in their cholesterol counts.

VEGETABLES

Dr. Denmark says you must eat vegetables for lunch and dinner. She suggests serving plenty of dark green leafy vegetables that contain an abundance of iron. She also recommends vegetables from the colorful carotenoid vegetables-- those that are red, yellow, and orange in color. Alternate them from meal to meal with the green leafy and crucifer vegetables.

Green Leafy Vegetables include spinach, mustard greens, turnip greens, beet tops, parsley, and watercress.

Magnificent 7 Crucifers are noted for reducing cancer. They are cabbage, broccoli, cauliflower, kale, brussels sprouts, bok choy, and collard greens.

Colorful Carotenoids include carrots, tomatoes, squash, sweet potatoes, and beets. Diets rich in foods that contain carotenoids are associated with a decreased risk of both cancer and heart disease.

Vegetables Mentioned in the Bible are cucumbers, leeks, onions, and garlic. The Children of Israel had these vegetables in abundance while they lived in Egypt. They longed for them when they were on their journey to the Promised Land.

Dried Beans (Legumes) are known as "the poor man's meat." They are high in protein, but need to be mixed with grain to make a complete protein. Beans contain no fat, and can lower cholesterol. They are good to stabilize blood sugar and contain high fiber, which helps to prevent constipation. The following is a list of a variety of beans: brown beans, peas, lentils, garbanzo, lima beans, green peas, black-eyed peas, white beans, navy beans, black beans, and kidney beans. On the food pyramid the government places beans in the protein section. They must assume anyone eating beans will also include bread made of grains in their diet. Cornbread and beans are a familiar staple for those of us who live in the South.

Things to Remember About Vegetables

1. Buy organic-grown vegetables if you can find them. Purchase locally grown vegetables when they are in season.

2. The United States Department of Agriculture suggests that one eat three to five helpings of vegetables a day.

3. Include plenty of garlic in your cooking. Garlic is the most natural healing food known to man. It benefits the human body in so many ways that it is a good idea to take a daily garlic tablet supplement.

4. Cook with onions liberally. Like garlic, they comprise a host of beneficial properties. Onions are known as the healing herb.

5. Parsley will help block allergy attacks. If you have garlic breath, munch on parsley and it will help rid you of the odor.

6. There is no better way to preserve the flavor and nourishment in vegetables than to cook them in a four-quart pressure cooker. The green leafy, crucifers, and carotenoids will cook in one to three minutes once the pressure is built up in the cooker. The dried beans will cook in an hour or less after the cooker is pressurized. Some smaller beans will cook in ten to twenty minutes while beans like garbanzo (chick peas) require a full hour.

7. Splash a little Bragg Liquid Aminos on your vegetables after they finish cooking for a change of taste. Dab on a little butter, butter/olive oil spread, or Smart Balance when they are hot.

FRUITS

Dr. Denmark says if your food budget is tight, fruits are the place you can make a cut.   Purchase apples and bananas before any other fruit. Either of these fruits will complete a well- balanced meal.

Apple Facts - The old saying, "An apple a day keeps the doctor away," has medicinal support. *Apples are called the all-around health food.* Apples help suppress your appetite if you are trying to lose weight and they help stabilize your blood sugar. They are high in pectin. You will experience fewer upper respiratory infections if you eat apples. Apples have been proven to lower bad cholesterol and high blood pressure. They help prevent tooth decay, and hinder the growth of cancer cells. It is preferable to eat apples raw with the peeling on.

High Antioxidant Foods- Prunes and raisins are the top two foods that are the highest in antioxidants. Blueberries and blackberries are third and fourth on the list of potent antioxidant foods

Things to Remember about Fruit

1. Eat organically grown fruits when you can. Since we should eat the peel of apples, this is especially important to remember.

2.The United States Department of Agriculture informs us that we need to eat two to four helpings of fruit a day.

3. People who consume the most fruits and vegetables usually have the lowest rates of cancer, hypertension, heart disease, diabetes, and arthritis.

WATER

The last of Dr. Denmark's requirements for a complete meal is to drink water. She teaches that a child does not need anything to drink except water, served at room temperature and drunk when he is thirsty. Iced water retards the digestive process.

Water is vitally important for the human body. It carries nutrients to all cells of the body and is needed for circulation, digestion, absorption, and excretion.

Dr. Denmark suggests that adults drink hot water with a meal in place of coffee. Sipping on hot water is very soothing and satisfying and avoids caffeine. Hot water also aids the digestive system. If you are dieting, drink warm water when you feel hungry and it will help suppress your hunger.

Invest in a water clean-up system. We cannot trust that our water is as pure as it should be. I question drinking chlorine-treated water that is left unfiltered before it is piped into our homes. We have lived in places where the fumes from chlorine were so strong that they would sting my eyes when I drew bath water.

To relieve fears of drinking and cooking with unsafe water, my husband and I installed an under-the-counter water-filtering system. With this system, our water is cleaned three times. It is taken through a fine filter, then through charcoal, and the last step is reverse osmosis. I periodically have our water tested to make sure it is close to 100% pure. There is a convenient five-gallon holding tank under the kitchen counter and a spout that is mounted on my sink.

One last tip about clean water. If you bake bread, use distilled or filtered water in your dough. You will be amazed how much better your yeast works. Yeast does not like chlorinated water.

Those Sweet Treats

Dr. Denmark concedes that it does not hurt children to have an occasional sweet treat. However, she does not eat them herself. Desserts once or twice a week will not harm a child; in fact, it gives them something to look forward to at mealtime. I do have some suggestions about how to keep our sweet treats as healthful as possible.

1. *Throw out all white sugar.* There is no reason anyone should use refined white sugar. Stock your kitchen with an unrefined sugar that retains all of its vitamins, minerals, and trace elements. There are several sweeteners from which to choose. Sucanat, turbinado, and stevia are my favorites. Stevia is a sweetener that comes from a perennial shrub of the aster family. It is so concentrated that it only takes one-half teaspoon of liquid stevia to sweeten a quart of lemonade. Sucanat or turbinado can be used in any recipe that calls for sugar.

2. *Use honey, maple syrup, molasses, or maple granules* on pancakes, waffles, French toast, or cinnamon toast.

3. Use *butter or extra virgin olive or canola oil.* If a recipe calls for shortening, use butter or a non-hydrogenated vegetable margarine like Smart Balance. When a recipe calls for oil, there are many choices. I use extra virgin olive or canola oil for most things because they are mono-unsaturated. I make pie crusts with canola oil.

This healthy pie crust recipe will make enough dough for one double crust or two single crust pies: Mix together in a bowl 2 cups unbleached flour plus 3 tablespoon soy flour and 1 teaspoon sea salt. Whisk 2/3-cup canola oil and 1/3 cup boiling water together and pour into the flour and salt mixture. Work the mixture with your hands into a ball. Divide the dough in half. Roll each piece between wax paper and shape into the pie pan. Bake at 450 degrees for 10-12 minutes. Children love this dough rolled out flat and fit onto a large cookie sheet sprinkled with sucanat and cinnamon. Bake at 450 degrees for 10 minutes and break into pieces.

4. Use the above healthful ingredients, along with your choice of flour, sea salt, and free range-eggs to make cookies, muffins, pies, or cakes. You will deliver good nutrients to your family when you serve wholesome sweet treats.

5. For an occasional treat serve lemonade. Mix 1/3 cup of fresh-squeezed lemon juice with 4 cups filtered water and sweeten with 1/2 teaspoon of liquid stevia. It contains no calories, and health-building nutrients are in the lemon juice.

6. Drink small amounts of purple or red grape juice. Serve it to your children at mealtime as a fruit replacement. Grape juice is so high in calories and vitamin C that it only takes a few ounces per serving. Purchase pure red or purple grape juice that has no sugar added.

The Bible encourages drinking grape juice. The nutritional benefits enclosed in those small nuggets are abundant. Grapes are an excellent source of antioxidants, help lower LDL (bad) cholesterol levels, and contain properties that help fight cancer and heart disease. With all of these nutritional aids we can understand why the Apostle Paul instructed Timothy, to drink juice from the grape. Paul told him it would be good for his stomach and would help his frequent infirmities. I Timothy 5:23

Some may believe I am misrepresenting that Scripture by not using the word "wine." I use the term "juice of the grape" because many people associate wine with an alcoholic content. I do not believe that is the correct meaning of I Timothy 5:23. Paul would not have prescribed a beverage with alcoholic content for one suffering with a stomach problem. Alcohol is an irritant! The Greek word *oinos* translated wine in this passage simply means "juice of the grape."

I Believe In Vitamins

After I have fed my family the most nutritious diet possible, I have always given natural vitamin supplements to everyone. I have given many spoons of Shaklee's Liqui-Lea vitamins made for children. During the years my elderly mother lived with us, I made sure she received daily vitamin supplements. Her physical health visibly improved.

My husband and I have taken natural vitamin supplements most of our married life. Some might say we concentrate too much on nutrition, but our only purpose is to do our best to stay in good health. We want as many active years as God will allow us to accomplish His work.

In the first printing of *Training Up a Child* , I included the following practical advice from Dr. Linus Pauling, a Nobel Prize winner in Chemistry: Dr. Pauling taught that as much as twenty years can be added to the life span of an individual if he will follow five simple suggestions. (1) Daily supplement your diet with liberal amounts (500 to 1,000 mg) of Vitamin C. (2) Daily supplement your diet with liberal amounts (400 to 800 IU) of Vitamin E. (3) Be sure you have an adequate intake of all other vitamins and minerals. (4) Sharply reduce the amount of sugar you consume. (5) Avoid using tobacco. Adding up all these benefits, Dr. Pauling concluded that the increased intake of Vitamin C would add eight years to your life, the proper intake of Vitamin E and other vitamins and the decreased intake of sucrose would add an additional eight years, and the other four years would be gained from not smoking. [10]

What Is Hydrogenation?

In closing this food unit, I must explain hydrogenation. I have mentioned it six times previously and warned you to avoid products that contain "hydrogenated" or "partially hydrogenated" oils.

Fats are an important part of our foods and are needed to keep our bodies healthy. We get energy from fat and it builds new cell membranes. It insulates us from the cold, and builds a shock absorber to protect our bones. It helps us absorb vitamins and is necessary to build healthy hair and skin.

Saturated fat comes from animal sources. Animal fat is solid and will remain that way at room temperature. We have learned that God said to cut the fat from meat and that it should not be eaten. Cow's milk, butter, and cheese are high in saturated fat. Anything containing saturated fat should be consumed in moderation. If more is consumed than is needed for energy, the body stores the excess and one's weight will increase. The hardened fat will be tucked away in various places, potentially damaging your cells, heart, and arteries.

Unsaturated fat comes from vegetables. The fat from vegetable oil is in liquid form and remains that way at room temperature. It is smooth and pours easily. It is healthier for you than animal fat.

In 1910, hydrogenation was invented. Scientists discovered a way to heat liquid vegetable oil to high temperatures and pump hydrogen gas into its molecules until the oil hardened. To produce a semi-hard substance, they pumped less hydrogen into the molecules. They labeled that "partially hydrogenated."

The molecules in animal fat are solid. The spaces in the molecules are completely full of hydrogen atoms (saturated). In vegetable oil, however, the molecules are not all used up. They have gaps and spaces that do not have hydrogen atoms in them. *Mono-unsaturated* oil has one gap missing in its molecules. Olive and canola are two oils in that group. *Poly-unsaturated* oil has more than one gap missing in its molecules. Safflower and corn oil are in that group.

When hydrogen is pumped into those empty spaces of vegetable oil, the oil becomes solid. That creates a **man-made saturated fat,** called **trans fatty acid.** This new fat has had its molecular make-up drastically altered; therefore, it is abnormal. Our bodies cannot distinguish between animal saturated fats and man-made saturated fats. These trans fatty acids raise blood cholesterol in the same manner that animal saturated fats do. They may even be worse for your health than saturated fats. As our body builds new cells and receives these deformed, mis-fit, trans fats it does not know where to place them in the cell membrane. New research into the role fats and oil play in human health indicates that these trans fatty acids are associated with an increased incidence of cancer, heart disease, elevated cholesterol levels and a host of other health problems.

Crisco was America's first "hydrogenated" product. It was born in 1911. Before World War II, margarine was introduced. It wasn't until the 1950s, however, that hydrogenation "sprouted wings" and began to fly. This new process of turning vegetable oils into solid shortening was extremely beneficial to the budding fast food industry and the expanding baking and snack food industry. They now had a product that was more economical to produce and maintained a longer shelf life. When they turned corn oil into margarine it could be spread, piecrusts would be flakier, and puddings smoother and tastier.

Today, "hydrogenated" or "partially hydrogenated" oils are in most packaged and ready-to-eat food products. Most restaurants use it.

"Partially hydrogenated" vegetable oils cannot tolerate high temperatures, so, in order for the foods to cook, they must remain in the oil longer. This gives the oil plenty of time to be saturated into the food. French fries cooked in "partially hydrogenated" vegetable shortening can contain as high as 46 percent trans fatty acid!

It is interesting to note that French fries cooked in natural saturated fat, like lard (which tolerates very high temperatures), will cook fast and can be drawn out of the oil quickly. Fries cooked in this fashion have nearly zero percentage of fat saturation.

Check the ingredients on the packaged food in your kitchen and discover how many "hydrogenated" or "partially hydrogenated" (trans fatty acids) food you are feeding your family. Make a commitment to start reading food labels more carefully. Refrain from purchasing food containing "hydrogenated" or "partially hydrogenated" oils.

You may say, "I understand what you are saying, but a little bit of "hydrogenated" or "partially hydrogenated" fats will not hurt you will it?" The answer to that question is: A few termites gnawing on the foundation of your house may not quickly be noticed, but when "armies" of termites move in and start working, they will destroy your house.

The Heart Patients of 2020

Some who read Dr. Denmark's method of selecting and preparing food may conclude that it is far too much trouble and will consume too much time.

I remind you that open-heart surgery, chemotherapy, and insulin injections for diabetes take a lot of time and trouble as well as being extremely costly. Moreover, they are very uncomfortable.

If nourishing your family with wholesome food will help prevent or hinder any of these and many other painful ailments, you will be abundantly repaid for the efforts you make.

Dr. Charles Atwood, M.D., says in his *Dr. Atwood's Lowfat Prescription for Kids*, "Children eating the typical American diet today are going to be the heart patients of the year 2020." [11]

Chapter Six
Be Co-Workers

Now that I have described Daddy's and Mother's individual responsibilities, it is time to outline their work as partners together. The basic principles married couples must follow in their task of parenting are:

DADDY AND MOTHER		
I.	II.	III.
BE TOGETHER	*BE IN LOVE*	*BE STRICT*
1. In your teaching	1. Show it	1. Demand the best
2. In disciplining the children	2. Tell it	2. Your children will honor you
3. Alone	3. Stay in love	

Before I discuss each point of Daddy's and Mother's co-work together, notice that I have coined another memory phrase---*Together, in love, be strict*. If you will, commit it to memory. It will serve as an important, instant reminder for you later.

PART I - DADDY AND MOTHER, BE TOGETHER
In their book, *The Discipline of Well Adjusted Children*, Grace Langdon and Irving Stout relate their findings in a study they directed. They set out to discover special features of homes that produced well-adjusted children. They traveled into three states--Wisconsin, New York, and Illinois. With the help of cooperating principals and teachers, they were able to locate four hundred and fourteen children to research. Personal

contact was made with each set of parents, and extensive interviews were made with them in their homes.

After reviewing Mrs. Langdon's and Mr. Stout's study, I was impressed with at least seven features they singled out that were unrelated to the well-ordered lives of the children. And, I was very interested in their conclusions about the relationship that these children's parents had in their respective marriages. Since many parents use one of the seven unrelated features as their reason for lack of success with their children, let's notice them first.

(1) *The sex of the child.* Many people theorize that girls are easier to handle than boys. Others say the opposite. In this study, both boys and girls were represented.

(2) *The position of the child in the family.* There are those who declare that the middle child is the one who is left out; other parents believe that the first or last child has the advantage over the others. This group of children was composed of oldest, middle, in-between and youngest children from families.

(3) *The number of children in the family.* Some of the children chosen were the only children in the family. Others came from homes in which there were two to twelve siblings.

(4) *The age of the father and mother at the child's birth.* Some of the couples started parenting as early as sixteen and others as late as forty-six.

(5) *The education of the parents.* The mothers and fathers had a wide range of academic accomplishments. One set of parents had only a third-grade education. Other parents had earned master's degrees.

(6) *The occupation of the fathers.* The daddies held a wide variety of jobs.

(7) *The income of the family.* This study was conducted in the 1940s and the salaries ranged from two thousand to forty thousand dollars annually. This again proves that money, whether much or meager has little to do with the contentment and happiness of children.

Now that I have listed seven things that *did not* matter in the satisfactory adjustment of the children, let's give attention to a principle that did contribute to their well being. In their book Langdon and Stout concluded that one chief reason these children were well adjusted was that *the parents were able to maintain a harmonious relationship between themselves.* Statements such as "we show complete agreement on all essential matters" and "there are no differences as far as I know" were evidence of their cooperation and agreement. The positive impact on the children when their parents cooperated and worked together harmoniously was evident. 1

Even though the discovery by Mrs. Langdon and Mr. Stout is very exciting, it should not be judged as a new revelation. These families were simply practicing God's age-old principle of harmony and oneness. We learned earlier the importance of togetherness, when I emphasized that wives are to submit to their husbands' authority. God's purpose in this law is to unite a couple on a plane of agreement. Jesus cautioned families to practice unity when He said, "*Every kingdom divided against itself is brought to desolation; and every city or house divided against itself shall not stand.*" Matthew 12:25.

A *daddy and mother must learn to stand together*. It is imperative that they form a wall of unity so strong that no force can break it down. If each encourages and supports the other, they will be able to win any battle that comes their way. While they are rearing a family of children, their fortress may be assaulted, but if Daddy backs Mother and Mother backs Daddy, they will never go down in defeat. The little aggressors will be forced to surrender every time without exception.

No. 1 - Be Together in Your Teaching
First, *parents must stand together in their teaching*. Dr. William E. Homan says, "Parents who constantly disagree about the teaching of their children had better get help or match their child's college fund with a psychiatric fund." 2 Truly, parents have a great responsibility to teach their children. Teaching, as you recall, is the first step in training and is accomplished through the process of showing and telling. We reveal our characters, beliefs, and philosophies of life by the principles we teach, and our children reflect what they see and hear.

Teach the Same Things ♀
Each parent does his or her own individual teaching, but the more harmonious a couple's beliefs and behavior patterns are the better it will be. ⊿◯⊿   When children see and hear agreement, they are not confused with dual vision and conflicting values. When parents teach the same things, it is such a powerful influence that it makes deep impressions on their children.

Contrariwise, when one parent shows and tells one thing and the other parent exactly the opposite, that home is in trouble. Because of divisions between Mom and Dad, children are put in the unfortunate position of being forced to decide whose side they will choose. Frequently, they reject both.

Teach Good Things

We must never overlook the fact that *what* parents teach their children is important. They must be teachers of good things. If Daddy shoulders his responsibilities as spiritual leader of the family, the children will thrive in a Christian atmosphere. A submissive mother, standing by Daddy, keeping the home, and guiding the house, must also be a teacher of Christian principles.

The Most Convincing Translation

There is a story of four preachers who were discussing the various translations of the Bible. The first preacher said that, because of its simple beautiful English, he preferred the King James Version. The second minister favored the American Revised Version; because it is more literal and nearer to the original Hebrew and Greek languages. The third man liked Moffatt's translation; its up-to-date vocabulary had won favor with him. When it was time for the fourth clergyman to respond, he remained silent for a moment and then replied, "Well, gentlemen, the translation I like best was my parents. They translated the Bible into life, and it was the most convincing translation I ever read."

Teacher! True or False

To be effective teachers, we must bind together our two activities of showing and telling. The moment they disagree, we become false teachers and betray our principles.

John Balguy has said, "Whatever parent gives his children good instruction, and sets them at the same time a bad example, may be considered as bringing them food in one hand, and poison in the other." 3

There is an old adage that says, "I cannot hear what you are saying because what you are doing keeps ringing in my ears." If you smoke, drink, and play cards for prizes, do not reprimand your child when he smokes, pops pills, and plays marbles for keeps. When you cheat on your income tax, do not scold your son if he cheats on an exam at school. Scolding your children for being cruel to animals and using four-letter words is useless if you have the habit of kicking the cat, cursing, and swearing. Throwing pots and pans in anger will only pave the way for your young ones to hurl books, bats, and balls when they are frustrated.

"It's Hard for Me to Understand"

The following is a note that expresses the sentiments of a child:

"It's hard for me to understand why my dad threatens to whip me for smoking a cigarette butt he threw away. And why Mommy sometimes washes my mouth out with soap for saying a word that I learned from her. And how I should never tell a lie; but the other day Mom had me go to the door when the salesman came and tell him she was sick in bed, when she did not want to be bothered. And why I need to go to church on Sunday morning while Dad stays home and reads the paper. Wonder how long it will be till I can be like Mom and Dad?"

Set the Right Example or Keep Quiet

John, a young teenager, was walking down a busy city street with his counselor when he said, "See all of these strip joints up and down this street? This is where our fathers come for entertainment. Then they come home and lecture us about bad women. It takes a pretty stupid kid to fall for mockery like that. We've got eyes. Parents should set the right example or keep quiet." [4]

The National Conference on Juvenile Delinquency has listed fourteen points that contribute to making up a good home for a child. The fourteenth point is, "He has something to believe in and work for because *his parents* have lived their ideals and religious faith before him."

Engrave These Two Principles on Your Heart

We have learned two principles for parents to follow in their teaching. Engrave them on your heart and remember that (1) daddies and mothers must be sure they are teaching the same precepts, and that the content of their instruction is right and moral; (2) they must be true teachers and live their lessons in the manner they teach them.

An old saying is "practice what you preach." In order for parents to influence their children properly, they must be "parents who together are practicing what they preach."

No. 2 - Be Together in Disciplining the Children

Second, parents must be unified in disciplining their children. The Kentucky State seal, adopted in the year 1792, bears these words: "United We

Stand, Divided We Fall." If a couple stands united in their teaching yet fail to cooperate in discipline, they make a catastrophic mistake.

Remember that discipline is the last step in training.   While being taught, children are only spectators. When they are made to follow what their parents say and do, they become active participators. By exercising discipline, parents pass their beliefs, ideals, and skills on to the next generation. If they fail to discipline, their children will do as they please.

Conflict Over Discipline

Remember children sometimes exercise self-discipline? They willingly and enthusiastically follow their parents' instruction. At other times, they must have discipline imposed upon them to get them to obey you. The mistake young couples most often make are disagreeing about how and when to impose this discipline on their children.

Frequently, a mother will discipline her little one, and daddy will take the child's side. He may sympathize, take the little one into his arms, and soothe his hurt feelings. He may even go so far as to make derogatory remarks about his "mean Mommy." By doing this, he undermines his wife's authority with the children.

Even though daddies are often guilty of this foolish behavior, mothers are usually worse. For many women, the stern hand of a father's discipline is more than they can stand. She may confront the father, demand he retreat, and cuddle the child to her protective side. If she doesn't go to that extreme, she may run from the room crying, or display a fierce indignation and makes sure it is understood she disapproves of Daddy's stern discipline. The child immediately knows that Mother has taken his side against Daddy.

When this happens, the child sees the division and is delighted that Mother has taken his side. Constant occurrences of such unwise behavior cause the child to lose respect for Daddy. In time, he will lose respect for his mother as well. In the end, everyone is damaged. Daddy and Mother are defeated, and their child grows into adulthood expressing disrespect for both of them.

Stop At Once!

If you have dealt in this manner with your children, stop at once! From now on, when your husband exercises discipline or judges the children's behavior to be unacceptable, unfailingly back him. Even if you disagree, back him anyway! Later in privacy you may express your disapproval. If unjust discipline was administered, your husband should make it right with the child himself.

After daddy has disciplined your child and the little transgressor comes crying to you seeking refuge, sternly reprimand him! Respond by saying, "If you are in trouble with Daddy, you are in trouble with me. Straighten up and behave yourself!"

Leaving the child alone to accept fair discipline is wise. *God built within human nature two features that, when properly applied, work together to cause a child to comply with your commands.* These two characteristics are (1) the longing and craving for acceptance and (2) the intense desire not to be left out.

Once your child learns that you and your husband are always united, he will readily make the proper adjustment to win back your favor and be warmly accepted in the family fellowship.

If you have taken sides with your child in the past, it may take time to convince him that you and daddy are really on the same team. He will probably try waiting you out and attempt a number of tricks to test your sincerity and resolve. Once he learns that the two of you are really committed allies, he will make the necessary alterations to receive your approval and be united with the family.

In the Privacy of Your Bedroom

Even though parents must always stand together in their discipline, this does not imply there will never be differences of opinion. At times you will feel like jumping on one side of the scale   while your husband stands on the other. Ideas about exactly what Junior and Sister can or cannot do will not always be absolutely the same.

Remember that it is in privacy and out of hearing distance of the children that the two of you should discuss your differences. It is only then that you can frankly express your feelings and tell your husband why you felt that his discipline was unfair.

It is a different matter when the two of you have conflicting ideas about what style dining room set to purchase or what color carpet to buy. It will not be harmful, occasionally, for children to learn that their parents do not always have exactly the same tastes. However, it is when it comes to teaching values and discussing the children's behavior and in which activities they may appropriately participate that parents must be in harmony. When it comes to acceptable behavior, children always need to be presented with united facts.

When you and your husband conclude a conference, it is imperative that you be agreed. When you are before the children, you must stand united on the side of acceptance or non-acceptance of each issue.

Pause at this point and ask yourself. What are you going to do if you have a serious difference of opinion with your husband? You think something should be done one way. Your husband believes it must be accomplished another way. He listens to your point of view, but in his judgment it is not acceptable. To maintain order to the home, who relinquishes to whom? That is right! You will submit to your husband, and God will bless you for it.

In Essence

In essence, what I have said about Daddy and Mother being together in their discipline is this:

(1) When parents discipline their children and make them obey their teaching, they can pass their beliefs, ideals, and skills on to the next generation.

(2) *Do not ever* take your child's side after your spouse has administered discipline. If the child is left alone, human nature will lead him to repent and make the proper changes in order to be accepted back into warm family fellowship.

(3) Parents must remain united in matters that concern discipline of the children and never for a moment let them think you are in disagreement.

No. 3 - Be Together Alone

The third essential point for parents to remember is to make time to be alone together. Enjoying each other's company provides a couple the opportunities to strengthen their relationship and give support to each other. Throughout the day, Daddy may have taken blows from the public while Mother has been sheltered at home. At the close of a day, they can enjoy refuge in each other. Daddy brings strength and security to Mother, and she welcomes him with a loving and cheerful home.

Take Time and Be Alone

In the preceding chapter I mentioned the importance of a couple's being together and preferring each other's companionship. I said you should like being with each other more than with anyone else in the world. Spend recreation time together and share hobbies. And, as much as you love your children, never let them drive a wedge between you.

Another word of caution every couple needs to hear is --*Be very careful never to reveal your marriage confidences to others.* Spending time together is one of the best insurance policies you have against betraying the intimate secrets of husbands and wives to others.

Almost every young couple experiences moments of misunderstanding and conflict. Tempers will flare and tears may be shed. It is after these little conflicts that husbands or wives are tempted to reveal their marital misunderstandings to others. One or both may seek out neighbors, friends, or parents for sympathy. Once a couple reveals their petty conflicts, the information they share can never be retrieved. If couples carefully protect their privacy, remain united and accentuate the positive, time will heal most petty differences. Their trust will be strengthened and their reputations will be protected. Cherish your ability to display the image of a joyful, successful marriage, to your family, friends, and the church. Remember that the world desperately needs to see the beautiful images of happy Christian homes today.

I must share this word of caution. A couple that experiences serious marital problems should seek assistance from competent, experienced, professional, Christian counselors, but petty offenses and disagreements should be kept between husband and wife. A Christian counselor will keep the problems you share with him in confidence. Do not misunderstand, there is absolutely no excuse for a husband to abuse his wife physically or emotionally. If such abuse occurs, a professional counselor should be consulted immediately.

In the problems, challenges, sorrows, and hardships, which every couple eventually must encounter, the counsel of Scripture and prayer will prove more than sufficient to sustain you both.

My husband gives excellent counsel to young people anticipating marriage. He tells them to remember these two things: (1) Never share your marital misunderstandings with others within or without your house; and (2) All the days of your married life, speak only the positive and good things about your mate to others. If every couple would practice that advice, there would be far more lasting marriages and far fewer in-law problems.

Make Time to Be Alone

Make time to be alone together.   Since Mother may occasionally experience "house-bound blues" and Daddy needs to spend quality time at home, couples are far more content when they *make time* for each other. It is important for you to plan time to be together. Here are two suggestions that may help:

(1) *Plan a "Mother's Meal Out."* - In his book, *You Can Be a Great Parent*, Charlie Shedd promised his newborn son he would do two things for his mother to help keep her happy. He said, "Once a week, we'll go out together for dinner alone, and fifteen minutes a day we will visit in depth together." As Peter grew up, he learned to eat one meal a week without Daddy and Mother and to tiptoe away when he saw them sitting on the love seat together. 5 (Anytime you leave your child, *be extremely careful* with whom you leave him. A child can be scarred for life by one encounter with a sexual molester.)

(2) *Schedule early bedtimes for the children.* A child from birth through the fourth month is to have a 10:00 p.m. bedtime. Beginning at five months, his bedtime is to be immediately after dinner. (Read Chapter 6 in the Addendum) He will need from ten to twelve hours of sleep each night until adolescence. When after-dinner bedtime hours are maintained, it accomplishes a three-fold purpose. (a) The child's physical health and happiness are enhanced. (b) Your mental and emotional well-being is refreshed. (c) You and your husband have a peaceful, quiet time together.

Adults who think they are mistreating children by putting them to bed early fail to distinguish between adult privileges and what is good for children. By practicing the early bedtime plan, everyone benefits. Daddy and Mother receive the mental and emotional refreshment they need, and the children get the physical rest they require.

PART II - DADDY AND MOTHER, BE IN LOVE

No. 1 - Be in Love and Show It

Show small affections in front of the children.

Judge Philip Gilliam says, "The lack of affection between father and mother is the greatest source of delinquency I know." 6

Let your children see Daddy give you a good-bye kiss in the morning and you meet him at the door in the evening with your arms open wide for an embrace. One of my fondest memories of my childhood was seeing my big strong daddy hold my little mama on his lap. I never had to worry whether or not my parents loved each other. I knew they were in love because they openly expressed it.

Intimate Love in the Marriage Relationship
It has been said that if sex is as it should be, it is only ten percent of the marriage. If it isn't, it is ninety percent. God designed the sexual relationship between husbands and wives. It serves to procreate the human race, but it is more often a means by which a couple express their deepest feelings of love for each other. The time spent in sexual activity is short, but essential. It can be compared to the pilot light in the furnace. Just as the pilot light ignites the burners to heat the house, sex kindles the intimacy that strengthens a couple's love.

I mentioned earlier that the safest, most practical rule for a woman to follow is NEVER to reject her husband when he makes sexual overtures. With the numerous methods available to prevent conception, there is no excuse for frigidity. Coldness and sexual incompatibility often originate in the mind. When a woman is unresponsive sexually, it is because she chooses to be so.

A warm wife will obtain her greatest potential for happiness if she will follow the directions that often accompany a bottle of common cold medicine--"For best results, follow the instructions of the maker." [7] Remember that our Maker's instructions for husbands and wives is not to deprive each other of the privilege of sex. I Corinthians 7: 2-5

No. 2 - Be in Love and Tell It
Give your children the privilege of hearing you say to your mate, "I love you, honey." A Christian lady once told me that she had never heard her parents express their love to each other. How unfortunate!

One author has summed up love this way: "The most important of all is loving someone and letting him know it." We may love another deeply, but if we never tell him, it does little good.

Praise your husband to the children. Admire him in their presence, and always teach them a strong devotion to their father.

No. 3 - Be in Love and Stay in Love
Suppose we could give one gift to every child in the world. What should it be? Would it be education, enough to eat, freedom from fear, riches, or pleasure? As desirable as all of these things may be, there is

one thing better. According to those who know, it is a fact that the *most favored children in the world are the ones whose parents love each other.* The greatest thing you can do for your son or daughter is to love their father.

One psychologist has said that genuine parental love comes nearer to bringing a cure for all problems of child care than anything else. 8

There is evidence in every neighborhood that parents are not staying together. Separation and divorce are literally crushing our society. The Bible leaves no doubt that God wills that marriage be for life. (Matthew 19:4-6) Divorce has always been opposed to God's order. (Mark 10:4-12) Death or adultery is the only conditions under which a marriage can lawfully be dissolved. (I Corinthians 7:39 and Matthew 5:31-32)

In his book, *The Christian Family,* Larry Christenson writes, "Couples who come to the despairing conclusion that 'we just don't love each other any more' should be told quite simply: 'Well, start learning.' Love is far more subject to the will than we suppose. We help cultivate and develop love because we set our minds to do so. We are not the helpless pawns of love; rather, we train love to be the willing servant of our marriage." 9

The idea of learning to love each other is Biblical. Paul instructed the older women to *"Teach the younger women to love their husbands."* (Titus 2:4) I agree with Mr. Christenson. Any time a couple thinks they no longer love each other, they need to be told quite frankly, "Start learning."

PART III - DADDY AND MOTHER, BE STRICT

No. 1 - Be Strict and Demand the Best

If you assign your child the task of picking up his toys, making his bed, mowing the lawn, doing the dishes, or cleaning his room, and he does a sloppy job, make him do it over. Teach him the principle that *anything worth doing is worth doing well.*

J. H. Bruce Lockhart, a famous schoolmaster in England, was asked his formula for producing superior youngsters. "I demand," said the old headmaster. "And then when I have what I demanded, I demand still more. The more you demand, the more you get, and this is the secret of schoolmastering." 10

The whole object of demanding the best from your children is to bring the child to the point at which he will begin demanding the best of himself. 11 Emerson once said, *"Our chief want in life is someone who will make us do what we can."*

Jim Ryan was an accomplished track star. *Redbook* magazine published an article about him titled, "The Winner Who Can't Stop Losing." Here is a part of what it said:

"Running and competition dominated Jim's life. His family background is partly responsible. His father and mother brought him up strictly. As a young boy, Jim, the second son in his family, attended church three times a week and was not allowed to dance, smoke, or drink. *The discipline and regimentation of his religious upbringing became the discipline and regimentation he gave to track.*" 12

Do not misinterpret what I have said. Strictness does not mean being so overbearing that your children feel as if shackles bind them all the time. What I have said is that children are far more capable than they often are given credit for. You know your child! Be wise enough to determine his capabilities and strict enough to make him live up to them.

No. 2 - Be Strict and Your Children Will Honor You

Many parents are afraid to be strict with their children for fear they will lose their love. Nearsightedness causes them to make the serious mistake of failing to project their vision to positive results into the future.

Larry Christenson again says, "What your child may think about you in the immediate context of discipline is relatively unimportant. What your child will think about you twenty years from now is the thing to take more seriously." 13

The Meanest Mother

"I had the meanest mother in the world," writes a housewife, who is now raising a family of her own. "While other kids ate candy for breakfast, I had to have cereal, eggs or toast. When others had Cokes and candy for lunch, I had to eat a sandwich. As you can guess, my supper was different than the other kids' also.

"But, at least, I wasn't alone in my sufferings. My sister and two brothers had the same mean mother as I did.

"My mother insisted upon knowing where we were at all times. You'd think we were on a chain gang. She had to know who our friends were and what we were doing. She insisted if we said we'd be gone an hour, that we be gone one hour or less - - not one hour and one minute. I am nearly ashamed to admit it, but she actually struck us. Not once, but each time we had a mind of our own and did as we pleased. That poor belt was used more on our seats than it was to hold up Daddy's pants.

Can you imagine someone actually hitting a child just because he disobeyed? Now you can see how mean she really was.

"We had to wear clean clothes and take a bath. The other kids always wore their clothes for days. We reached the heights of insults because she made our clothes herself, just to save money. Why, oh why, did we have to have a mother who made us feel different from our friends?

"The worst is yet to come. We had to be in bed by nine each night and up at eight the next morning. We couldn't sleep till noon like our friends. So while they slept, my mother actually had the nerve to break the child-labor law. She made us work. We had to wash dishes, make beds, learn to cook and all sorts of cruel things.

"She always insisted upon our telling the truth, the whole truth, and nothing but the truth, even if it killed us - - and it nearly did.

"By the time we were teenagers, she was much wiser, and our lives became even more unbearable. None of this tooting the horn of a car for us to come running. She embarrassed us to no end by making our dates and friends come to the door to get us. If I spent the night with a girl friend, can you imagine she checked on me to see if I was really there? I never had the chance to elope to Mexico. That is, if I'd had a boy friend to elope with. I forgot to mention that while my friends were dating at the mature age of twelve and thirteen, my old-fashioned mother refused to let me date until the age of fifteen and sixteen. Fifteen, that is, if you dated only to go to a school function. And that was maybe twice a year.

"Through the years, things didn't improve a bit. We could not lie in bed, 'sick,' like our friends did, and miss school. If our friends had a toe-ache, a hangnail or other serious ailments, they could stay home from school. Our marks in school had to be up to par. Our friends' report cards had beautiful colors on them - - black for passing, red for failing. My mother, being as different as she was, would settle for nothing less than ugly black marks.

"As the years rolled by, first one and then the other of us was put to shame. We were graduated from high school. With our mother behind us, talking, hitting and demanding respect, none of us was allowed the pleasure of being a dropout.

"My mother was a complete failure as a mother. Out of four children, a couple of us attained some higher education. None of us has ever been arrested, divorced or beaten his mate. Each of my brothers served his time in the service of this country. And whom do we blame for the terrible way we turned out? You're right, our mean mother. Look at all the things we missed. We never got to march in a protest parade, nor to take part in a riot, burn draft cards, and a million-and-one other things that our friends did.   She forced us to grow up into God-fearing, educated, honest adults.

"Using this as a background, I am trying to raise my three children. I stand a little taller and I am filled with pride when my children call me mean.

"Because, you see, I thank God that He gave me the meanest mother in the world." 14

Summing It Up

Every building must begin with the laying of a foundation. In this section of Daddy and Mother, Behave in Your Beehive, we have laid the foundation.

Daddy must be the head, protector, physical provider, and spiritual leader of the family. Mother must be his helpmeet, in subjection, keeper of home, and guide of the house. As co-workers they must be united in teaching, disciplining and taking time to be alone. They must prove their devotion by showing, telling, and staying in love. And finally, they must have the strength of character to demand the best of their children for the sake of their children. If parents carefully practice these principles, they will reap honor in the end.

Couples who are following these principles con *sist'* ent ly are now ready to begin constructing a happy and responsible child.

ASSIGNMENT

1. Write a summary of all the areas in which you and your husband need to improve in organizing an autocratic home.

2. If the two of you have frequent disagreements about finances, try the two-separate-budgets idea. If your husband agrees to your having your personal household bank account, be thrifty and see how much you can save for additional investments.

3. Start today practicing the TUAC principle of, "Say what you have to say once, never more than twice, unless you are asked."

4. Start being a real HELPMEET and please your husband with: (1) Food the way he likes it, (2) sex and companionship when he desires them, plus (3) thirty seconds of admiration EVERY DAY.

5. Share the idea about the "Mother's Meal Out" with your husband. Perhaps he will agree to plan a special night out for just the two of you this week.

LOVE

Has Its Beginning

Chapter Seven
Love

Love is the third car on our little home express. Couples must learn how to love and be loved by their child. Success in this challenging assignment is vital for the remaining cars on our train to function properly.

Without the existence of a strong love bond between parent and child all other training will derail and cannot be accomplished satisfactorily. The expectations of obtaining *obedience*, granting *independence*, teaching *good habits*, creating the *work* ethic, establishing effective *communication* and creating a bond of *togetherness* will falter.

Each car on our home express must be coupled in proper order. Until you and your husband have learned and accept your "God Ordained" responsibilities in the home and how to work together, you have not laid the solid foundation necessary for you to successfully develop a child.

Once you each understand your unique roles, you are ready to start your family. However, no couple is forced to bring children into the world. A woman may choose to remain single or a couple may decide not to have children. The two of them together may still enjoy a rich and full life. God does not stipulate that parenting children is a prerequisite to inherit Heaven.

Nevertheless, the day you become parents, you must take seriously your obligations to your child for which God will hold you accountable. Parenting a child must take precedence over other activities in which you may like to be engaged.

A mother must always be on full-time duty. John Dresher says, "The average child asks 500,000 questions by the age of fifteen. That is half a million opportunities to teach. Many of these are 'why' and 'how' questions which take us right to the feet of God." A mother must be present to seize this irretrievable opportunity to train her little ones and lead them to Christ.

David Wilkerson observed, "If there is a thread that has run through my own experience with parents and children, it is the thread of love in homes that produced our 'goodniks' " [1]

Love Has Its Beginning

The theme of *Training Up a Child* suggests that your child must receive training beginning at birth. Early infancy is when the window of opportunity is opened for a child to fall in love with his parents. That impressionable period lasts from birth to twenty-four months. (Read Chapters 5 & 6 in the Addendum)

All a child requires during this "falling in love" period is that his needs be met. The one who meets the baby's needs is the one with whom the baby bonds. For the baby's security and stability that one must be his mother. She must play the dominant role during his first two years.

Love Has Two Sides

I have been a Christian since I was fifteen and a minister's wife since I was twenty-four. One truth I have learned is this: *There are always two sides to a story and I should never pass judgment until I have heard both sides.*

Mothers must also understand that love is two-sided. It is love when you express warmth and affection. I will call that--*tender love.* It is also love when you show firmness and need to chasten. That side of love I will refer to as--*strict love.*

Take a coin, for instance. There are a front side and a back. At athletic events referees toss coins into the air to make a decision. The visiting team captain will call either heads or tails. If he makes the call right, his team will have the advantage.

Likewise, a mother must make accurate calls when she skillfully exercises love. On some occasions the appropriate call is for kisses and hugs. Other times the proper choice will demand chastening.

I will share two stories from my earliest childhood memories to give you examples of how my mother knew exactly how to make these love calls. She exercised *tender love* and taught me compassion. At other times she was forced to use *strict love*, which taught me responsibility. I will also share how those early love lessons enabled me to help Mother later in her life.

Mother Must Be Her Child's First Love

My mother was my first love. She cared for me every minute of every hour of every day my first two years of life. My bonding and attachment to her became deep and abiding.

My Mother's Tender Love - When I was a small child, our family of eight lived in a very small house that contained approximately 800 square feet of living space. The house included a living room, kitchen, two bedrooms, and one small closet. My four older brothers shared one of the bedrooms and my baby sister and I slept in the other with Mother and Daddy.

My parents slept with their babies. Infants sleeping alone were known to freeze to death in those days. Families heated their homes with coal, but the fires in the "pot bellied" stoves always burned out before morning. When the fire went out, temperatures dropped sharply inside the house during the night. As a precaution against hypothermia, my parents put us in bed with them to sleep. Mother breast-fed us, so I am sure that was another incentive for letting us sleep with her.

When my baby sister was born, she slept in the bed with Mother and I slept in a separate bed with Daddy. My first memory of *tender love* was something that happened to me one night while I was sleeping with Daddy. During the night I became sick and vomited in the bed and all over my Daddy's back. I recall sitting up in the bed listening to my parent's search for the kerosene lamp. They groped in the dark until they found and lit the lamp. I remember as if it were yesterday watching them clean up the awful mess I made. I was the source of much trouble and discomfort for my parents that cold winter night so long ago.

We did not have electricity or indoor plumbing in our farmhouse. Water for cooking and cleaning had to be pumped from an outside well and carried in buckets into the house, then heated on the top of a kerosene stove. We did not have an inside bathroom. "Out houses" were the custom of the times and all families had one located in their back yard.

My parents did not scold or blame me for the terrible inconvenience I caused them that night. They worked together until everything was cleaned up and they were ready to blow out the light and go back to sleep. Their major concern during the whole ordeal was that I was cared for and comfortable and that there were no signs of a reoccurrence of my vomiting.

That is my first "baby memory" of receiving *tender love*.

My Mother's Strict Love -My world was very small living in that little frame house. In that familiar setting I felt snug and completely secure, but three of my brothers were rapidly becoming teenagers and our living conditions were too crowded. My father was a tenant farmer and he knew we needed a larger house.

My paternal grandparents' farm was located two miles from us. It was during this time that they both passed away. So Daddy purchased their land and farmhouse from his brothers and sisters. I shall never forget when Daddy moved our family from that little frame house where I had been born. I still remember the pots and pans stacked in the car as I rode in the front seat with Mother to our new home.

The house that my grandparents had built was a large house with seven rooms downstairs and three bedrooms upstairs. I perceived that our new house was the biggest, most mysterious house in the whole world. When my brothers were gone to school and Daddy was busy in the field, the house grew very scary to me. I imagined all manner of threats and dangers. The long flight of stars frightened me more than anything. I would gaze up those stairs and fanaticize that some "evil man" might be lurking at the top of that staircase waiting for an opportunity to snatch me away.

Mother's washday was always on Monday. She was required to go outside our house to a cinder block well house to do the laundry. She would go to the well house and start the gas motor on the washing machine to do our gigantic washing. Every Monday morning she had to replenish our family of eight with clean shirts, jeans, overalls, dresses, bedding, towels, and socks.

One washday morning mother went to the well house to start our washing. I did not hear or see her leave the house. When I realized Mother was gone, I was terrified and started crying and frantically calling for her. I quickly worked myself into a hysterical frenzy. That mysterious "old man" that might be upstairs was sure to descend and get me. My mother heard me screaming and rushed back into the house to see what was the matter. It was typical for my mother to show such loving concern. She calmed me down and assured me there was no one upstairs. Everything temporarily returned to normal.

Mother always had a heavy load of work to do and a great deal of her responsibilities had to be carried on outside the house. There were eggs to gather and chickens, turkeys, ducks, geese, and guineas to feed. The clean clothes had to be hung on clotheslines to dry in the sun. She planted a garden and it had to be cultivated. Vegetables had to be gathered, cleaned and canned.

Because of my fears of an imaginary "evil man" that waited at the top of the stairs, day after day I ran after her crying hysterically every time she left me to go outside. No matter how much she comforted me or assured me she would not be far away, my irritating fits of crying when mother walked outside continued.

After several of my crying tantrums, Mother convinced me of the practical benefits of practicing self-control. I shall never forget the little switching she gave me by the old cellar door. I wept as if my heart would break, but after that chastisement I did get the message that my mother was not going to desert me and that she would not tolerate my out-of-control behavior. I stopped the crying sprees and Mother never had to chasten me again for that aggravating behavior.

Often mothers hesitate to exercise *strict love* because they fear their children will cease to love them. That concern is completely groundless. *"No chastening for the present seemeth to be joyous, but grievous; nevertheless afterward it yieldeth the peaceable fruit of righteousness unto them which are exercised thereby."* Hebrews 12:11

On that day when I was a pre-school child, Mother taught me three important lessons about life. (1) My mother would never forsake me. (2) I must control my fears instead of allowing them to control me. (3) I must be brave. She insisted I be courageous, which in turn gave me confidence to face life bravely.

That is my first "childhood memory" of having *strict love* applied to me.

Alzheimer's Disease Strikes

Many years after I was married, Mother developed Alzheimer's Disease. She deteriorated mentally to the point that she was totally unable to care for herself and our roles were completely reversed. My husband and I took Mother into our home and I nursed her for twelve years. My mother became my baby. She lived with us until she passed away at ninety-three.

For months after she was gone I would be awakened by sounds in the night. My immediate impulse was to jump out of bed and look in on her to make sure she was resting comfortably. I would soon realize that she was no longer with us. I have told my brothers and sister that as long as

I live, when I look into the heavens at night and see the full moon, I will remember our precious mother.

The day she passed away my husband and I had to remain at the hospital until long after nightfall making arrangements for her to be transported from Oklahoma to Kansas for burial. I stood in that hospital emergency room crying and holding her hand for a long time. Those precious hands that I had gripped so tightly for so long when I was a child were now lifeless and could never again return my squeeze. It was so difficult to let them go. I bent down and kissed her sweet face. My heart was broken into a thousand pieces.

My husband and I drove home and parked in our drive. As I was walking into our house, I looked into the sky and the full moon was beaming through the trees. It shone in brilliant splendor on our front step. It seemed as if Mother was smiling down at me and saying, "Gwennie, don't cry! I am happy and free. I am in my permanent dwelling place that I lived all of my life to attain."

When I talk with people about the twelve years I took care of Mother, they inevitably will ask me, "How did you do it?" I wonder are they really asking, "Why did you do it?"

Why was I so determined to care for her? I was devoted to my mother. She had prepared me to face life's uncertainties and I was determined she would not be left neglected and abandoned in a nursing home. She had never abandoned me and I certainly was not going to forsake her. Personally caring for my mother was the right thing to do and I had faith that God would help me. And He did!

During the twelve years I cared for my mother I was never too sick to attend to her needs. Never once was she left in a bed that was not fresh and clean nor was she ever allowed to go hungry. I returned her *tender love* by caring for her as she had cared for me when I was a little child. Daily I gave her sweet face many kisses.

I did only for a little while what she spent a lifetime doing for all of our family.

How Does a Mother Get Love from Her Child?

A mother is smothered with love from her child by letting him understand that she belongs to him. I remind you that a newborn infant desires nothing more than his mother. God intends for him to have her and be with her. How else can you explain the Creator's elaborate provision of mothers' irreplaceable breast milk? There is no physical nourishment that can be adequately substituted for the milk from his mother's breast.   God in His infinite wisdom created this nursing dependency as a part of His miraculous bonding plan between mother and child.

Each mother should give her newborn exactly what he wants and needs--her complete attention and devotion! *No baby should ever be placed in the unpleasant circumstance in which he feels the need to cry for his mother.*

Mothers receive love from their children when they bestow the gift of sacrificial love on them.   When one becomes a mother, her child's needs must come first.

A baby begins bonding with his mother when he learns that he can always place his TRUST in her. Carrying out daily activities in a routine manner further enhances a child's confidence in his mother. A mother who adopts Dr. Denmark's schedules will discover that she will meet all her child's physical needs.   A Dr. Denmark baby will not need to cry because he is hungry or tired. He will be fed his meals on time and be put down for naps on a regular schedule. (Read Chapters 5 & 6 in the Addendum)

A baby will warmly attach to his mother when she expresses *AFFECTION* to him. When she cuddles, kisses, hugs, rocks, sings, bounces, embraces, and fondly talks "baby talk" (motherese, it is called) to her baby, a strong maternal connection begins to develop.

This process of bonding and attachment takes approximately twenty-four months to complete.

The Cycles That Develop Love

There are logical reasons for Dr. Denmark to teach mothers to stay home with their children, maintain regular schedules and eat meals at the same time. Keeping a consistent routine is necessary for a child to learn trust, enhance his health, and develop a sense of security and a general feeling of well being.

By working through the following cycles of development, a mother teaches her baby how to love:

First Month- In his first month an infant begins to discover how his world functions. "Am I in control or is Mother in control" is the first question for which he must learn the correct answer.   Mother must immediately teach him -- "Mommy is in control."

When a baby learns his food, his bath, his naps, and his play all come on a regular schedule, he discovers he can depend on his mother. He knows when his mother puts him to bed for the night that she intends for him to stay there and no amount of crying (unless for some legitimate reason) will change that plan. (Read Chapter 10 Gem # 3 in the Addendum)

2- 6 Months - *The child becomes united with mother.* During this five-month period, the baby begins trying to imitate his mother. He makes eye contact with her and smiles. This behavior will increase from a few seconds to several minutes. While he nurses, he becomes preoccupied with watching his mother's face. If she frowns or scolds, he may cry. If she smiles and laughs, her baby will be happy. *Wooing* begins during this cycle of development. The baby will make his first attempts at trying to please his mother. When mother makes various sounds, her baby listens attentively and may attempt to imitate them. These progressive actions indicate that he is making a wholesome bond with his mother. (Read Chapter 6 in the Addendum)

7- 9 Months - These months is the time when the baby begins to experience "*stranger anxiety.*" If the baby exhibits anxiety when he sees strangers, it is another indication that he is making normal attachment to his mother. If no one is a stranger to the baby, he may not be making a strong bond with his mother or anyone else. If a child behaves with the same familiarity toward everyone, this indicates he may have complications in developing strong, loyal attachments in the future.

"*Separation anxiety*" usually begins at nine to eleven months. It will reach its peak between twelve and fifteen months and can continue from sixteen to thirty-six months. When a child suffers anxiety when separated from his family, it is evidence that proper parental attachment has been made.

When separated from his parents he may protest by crying, attempting to cling to the parents, appear withdrawn or behave with anger or aggression until his parents return. When a child reacts in this fashion, it is an additional indication that attachment and bonding have been accomplished.

10-18 Months - This is the time a child begins his "love affair" with the world. He begins to explore and refine his motor skills. He will approach the end of his comfort zone and then check to see if Mother is still there before moving farther away.

"*Shadowing*" (following Mother around) begins in the crawling and walking stage.

"*Darting*" (moving away from Mother and then running back to her) commences during these months as well.

A child increases his attachments with Daddy and other members of the family, but he will always seek his mother's shelter when he is hurt, tired, or sick. Attachment to his mother is still clearly his dominant early relationship.

Summing Up Baby Love

Babies must be taught to love. As surprising as it may seem to some, love is not an inborn quality. A child is born into a hostile world in which his first conscious experience is discomfort. His initial response is to cry.

An infant's predicament is aggravated by the fact that he is totally helpless and dependent. It is only when his mother soothes and feeds him that he can relax into peaceful sleep. However, a baby's comfort is never permanent. He will soon become hungry and soiled again. His mother should always be close by to relieve him when he is in distress.

When the baby's cycles of discomfort are relieved in a timely manner, the baby learns trust and when he gazes into the loving, smiling face of his devoted mother he experiences both peace and joy.

A baby basks in the warmth of his mother's affection when she cuddles him. The tenderness of her voice when she talks to him, and sings to him, introduces him to love, which is the most fulfilling human emotion. He looks forward to the appearance of his mother's loving face and the touch of her gentle hands and develops a strong, absolutely essential emotional connection to her.

In His perfect design, God created this condition of total dependency, which lasts for many months. No other creatures require so much time before they can care for themselves as do human babies. This period of total dependency is a time for testing.

Mothers must meet the test by freely giving sacrificial love for the child's sake. If she stays with her baby, makes meeting his needs her priority, and always faithfully cares for him, she will enjoy her child's devotion. What a fabulous reward! What more could a mother ask?

How Vital Is It For a Child to Bond and Attach?

Dr. Lawrence Smith, a child, adolescent, and family therapist, explains, *"Bonding and attachment are both cornerstones of human development, essential to a child's stable functioning as he grows.*

"The quality of an infant's initial attachment is enormously important, for it influences all subsequent development. Bonding and attachment has been

identified as playing a vital role in all of the following: maintaining the bonds of trust, attaining full intellectual potential, acquiring a conscience, developing relationships with others, identity and self-esteem, learning to regulate feelings, language development, and brain structures and organization of the nervous system." 2

Baby's First Two Love Gifts

There are two love gifts that are essential for each new baby to receive. One gift is from Daddy and the other from Mother. One will cost money, the other saves money.

Before a new baby arrives, Daddy should take Mama shopping for a rocking chair. Before making her choice Mama should try out various sizes of rocking chairs. She must find the one that fits her body comfortably. Its armrests should be the proper height for mama to rest her arms easily. The rocker should come with a footrest or an ottoman. When the perfect rocking chair is found, Daddy should buy it for his first love gift to his baby!

Mamma's love gift will come when the baby is born and will spread over many months. *The first most valuable love gift mothers can give their baby is her breast milk!*

"How would you like to give your baby a gift that could raise his IQ by 10 points; cut medical bills; make your baby's eyes, heart, intestines, and nearly every other organ work better; reduce the risk of life-shortening, debilitating disease, such as diabetes; and help your baby avoid many of the common complaints of infancy, such as ear infections, tummy upsets, even diaper rash? What's the magic gift that can do all these things? Your milk," says Martha and William Sears, M.D.

"You can make your baby's life that much healthier and happier simply by choosing to breastfeed." 3

Dr. William Sears continues to explain, "By providing milk from your breasts, you are guaranteeing the best nourishment for your baby. But breastfeeding is healthier not just for babies. It is healthier for mothers, too. During breastfeeding, you give your baby ideal nourishment and nurturing, and as 'payback' your baby, in effect, gives something back to you. You tap into a formula for mothering and nurturing your baby that is tested and true--as old as time itself. Breastfeeding will make it easier to care for your baby, and it will make it easier for you to know and understand your baby. It will affect the way you listen to your child, the way you communicate, and the way you respond for many years to come. This will make disciplining your child easier as he grows, and it will help you feel good about parenting.

"Breastfeeding is, after all, more than a way of delivering food. When you breastfeed, you continue the oneness that you and your baby experienced during pregnancy. Your body continues to provide nourishment, a warm touch, comfort, and safety, just as it did when baby was inside you. This relationship is unique, a different journey for each mother and baby." 4

"The Greatest of These Is Love"

Beyond all reasonable doubt, love is the greatest need in the life of any child. I Corinthians 13, the love chapter of the Bible, teaches the greatest of all abiding virtues is LOVE.

Love is a unique human ingredient of which there can never be too much. Too much correction, work, or independence can be harmful, but with love, the more the merrier.

Love forms three essential qualities in a child. It builds acceptance, confidence, and compassion. Dr. Drieker, in his book *Logical Consequences* says, "The need to belong or to be accepted is the basic human motivation." 5 To be loved and to love gives a child the feeling of really belonging to someone. It brings the security, which is necessary to possess confidence.

"Subtract parental love from the parent-child relationship, and the child lacks the feeling of acceptance. He feels frustrated in his desire to belong." 6

Young people who engage in illicit sex generally give the same reasons for doing it. They do not feel loved and accepted at home; so they are on a perpetual search for acceptance. Every human being feels, "Someone has got to care about me. I must have an important place in someone's life."

Three Levels of Love

It may be impossible to crowd a full definition of love into one cluster of words, but it is within reason to attempt to explain different stages and growth of love evident in life. The following are three levels of love which I will describe.

THREE LEVELS OF LOVE [7]

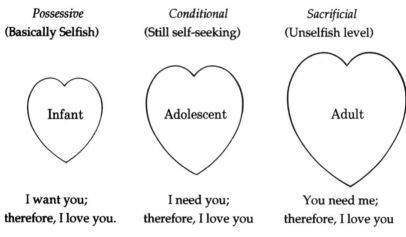

Possessive	*Conditional*	*Sacrificial*
(Basically Selfish)	(Still self-seeking)	(Unselfish level)
Infant	Adolescent	Adult
I want you; therefore, I love you.	I need you; therefore, I love you	You need me; therefore, I love you

POSSESSIVE LOVE

A possessive love is love in the infant stage. It says, "I want you, and that is why I love you." Possessive love is that which I have described as the emotional attitude of a baby during the first two years of his life. He is content possessing his mother and pleasantly basking in her attention. A little child is engrossed with this selfish degree of love when he clings to his mother, pushes his brothers and sisters away, and proclaims, "This is *my* Mommy, and you can't have her."

The possessive stage of love is also often recognized in a new romance. A young man may observe many young ladies on a college campus before a special one begins to consume his attention. He arranges to meet her, because she possesses all of the charms that are especially appealing to him. After developing a warm acquaintance, he decides she is exactly what he has always dreamed of in a wife. He begins to desire to possess all of her attention. He asks her to go steady with him and eventually slips an engagement ring on her finger.

As their relationship continues, their love will grow into a more mature reciprocal conditional affection; "I love you, because I need you." The couple realizes more and more that they need each other to make their lives complete.

Marriage usually takes place while both are in the conditional stage of love development. She concentrates on all that she believes he will do for her, and he thinks about the multitude of blessings she is going to bring him.

After they are married, in order to remain happy, it is necessary for them to continue to grow in their love. They must attain sacrificial love -- "You need me; therefore, I love you." The success of their marriage depends on a husband and wife achieving this level of love.

They must voluntarily begin to give of themselves for their partner's sake. A wife freely gives herself to her husband, not because she feels erotic, but to fulfill his sexual needs. She will prepare his favorite food for dinner just to please him. He will take her out for dinner or home to see her parents, not because he desires an evening out or enjoys a long journey, but because these are activities that especially please his wife.

Possessive love may be natural for children or new lovers, but parents must portray a higher form of love for their children.

A couple may want a baby very badly. After it is born they may cherish it like a new toy. But soon, the new fades away and they learn the immense amount of time and devotion rearing a child requires. If their love does not grow into the mature stages, the child's best interests will not be served. Parents who have a possessive love in which their first concern is to satisfy their own interest and goals will neglect and eventually harm a child.

"The child will be treated like a little sapling in the forest. By misfortune, it sprang up too close to a giant pine. It has to live in a cramped and unwanted position and is never allowed to extend its branches and grow. 8

CONDITIONAL LOVE

Conditional love is love in the adolescent stage. It is nobler than the possessive love, but it is still self-seeking. It carries with it the idea, "I'll love you as long as you please me," and "I'll love you as long as you meet my needs."

Dr. William E. Homan says, "It is far too common for young children to be given the impression that their parents love them because of what they do." 9 If you don't do that which pleases me, I won't love you. I won't love you unless you make the honor role, or I won't love you unless you are an outstanding football player. I insist that you be in the band and play the flute like I did when I was in school. I won the state spelling bee when I was in sixth grade; therefore, I insist you practice until you can compete and win.

Parents must not attempt to fulfill their frustrated dreams and ambitions through their children. Children should be free to develop into their own persons who pursue their own dreams and aspirations. The son, who has an ambition to be an airline pilot, should not be pressured by his father to take over and run the family grocery business.

Two Common Ways Parents Portray Conditional Love

There are two common mistakes that parents make which indicate to their children-- we extend our love as long as you meet all of our conditions.

(1) *By condemning their child as a person instead of disapproving of his wrong action.* "You clumsy kid! You're as awkward as an ox," may often be the reaction when a child spills a drink or breaks a dish. It would be much better to say, "Food is too expensive to waste like this." Or "Those are the best dishes we have. When they are all gone, it will be hard to replace them."

With these warnings, a child will learn, "The next time I pick up a glass or dish, I will be careful not to break it."

When I was teaching in public school, I remember a little girl in my class who misbehaved to the point that I had to speak to her after school about her conduct. I approached her, not by striking at her person, but at the wrong thing she had done. I said, "Janet, I love you, and there are so many good things about you. But you disrupt our class. Your talking out loud and giggling in class make me very unhappy. Do you think there is anything you could do about this?" She was impressed that I loved her but it was her talking out loud in class that I did not like. This little student went home and told her mother what I had said. At a parent-teacher conference her mother expressed appreciation to me for the kind and effective manner in which I had corrected her daughter.

Here are three examples of how we can express disapproval of a child's behavior without degrading him as a person:

Suppose A Child	DON'T SAY	DO SAY
(1) Is hitting another child	You are a bad boy and I know you will end up being a criminal.	Hitting and slapping other people is very unkind. I do not approve of those actions
(2) Tells a lie	You are a liar and I will probably visit you in prison some day.	Telling untrue things is very wrong. A lie cannot go uncorrected.
(3) Steals	Why, I didn't know I was rearing a thief.	Taking things that don't belong to you is stealing. God doesn't approve of that, and I don't either. It will have to be returned with an apology.

By aiming disapproval at the wrong action instead of at the personality, you convey to the child, "I correct your behavior because I love you."

(2) *When they show more approval for their child's achievements than for the child himself* is a second way we convey that our love is conditional.

"Parents generally react favorably to a good report card or to a kind and thoughtful act on a child's part. But it is even more important that children receive an abundant measure of praise and approval unrelated to their achievements and successes." 10

"A child should receive a word of praise, a hug and kiss, or a pat on the head when he brings home a good report. But he should be cuddled, kissed, admired, and told, 'I love you,' more often for doing absolutely nothing. He should receive the greater reward just because he is himself and you enjoy the privilege of his presence." 11 Your child must understand that you love him just for himself.

When parents only love conditionally, they will often make the following two additional mistakes:

(a) *They will compare their children unfavorably.* "Now just look at big brother. See how well he can read." Or, "You ought to be ashamed of yourself. Look how much better your little sister does that than you do." This mistake will cause jealousy and sibling rivalry that may endure throughout their lives.

(b) *They will play favorites.* One child may be more obedient and personable than the others. Favoring one child above his siblings is a sure way to hurt both children.

A conditional love is not the mature love that is necessary for building a well-rounded adult. We must upgrade to a higher level of love, in which the parents are wise enough to see beyond themselves and their interests to the well being of their children.

SACRIFICIAL LOVE

Sacrificial love is Christ-like agape love and the level of love we must seek to achieve for the fullest possible success as parents. One who possesses full-grown love asks, "What can I do to help make your life better?" This level of love will *seek the ultimate good of the loved one.* Once parents reach this level of love, they are ready to do whatever is necessary to bring about the best for their children.

Parental love must be a love for the child's sake. 12   Dr. William E. Homan says, "This love is most vital during the first twelve years of a child's life." 13

At the beginning of this chapter I explained sacrificial love exclusively. For two years you must perform a love for the child's sake but your love offerings will not stop there. Sacrificial love must continue throughout your child's lifetime.

Sacrificial Love on the Prairie

A pioneer woman was a living example of a mother who loved her children with a sacrificial love. This lady and her husband had settled on the prairie to scratch out a living and rear their family.

The Lord had blessed them with healthy children and they were anxiously awaiting the arrival of another little one. One day she gave birth to a beautiful baby girl. A neighbor lady had traveled in a covered wagon to assist with the birth and help in any other way she could. After the little girl was born, the helpful lady was cleaning the child when she noticed something was wrong with the baby's foot. One little foot was perfect, but the other was twisted in a horizontal position.

A few days later an old country doctor was traveling through the area. He knew this woman was expecting a baby; so he made a special stop to see how she was getting along. When she showed him her baby's foot, he told her that if she did not want the child to be a cripple, she must start giving her therapy treatments immediately. These were the instructions of the doctor: "Hold her in your lap and force her foot frontward one hundred times daily. Do this without fail."

While the little bones were pliable, that mother faithfully followed the doctor's instructions. The first time the foot was turned, the pain was so intense that the baby gave a piercing scream. Bravely, the mother turned the foot again and again and again, carefully counting each turn. At first the baby writhed in pain, tears streamed down that mother's cheeks, but she did not give up.   Day after day she administered this painful therapy. As the weeks and months passed by, she could gradually see the little foot beginning to straighten.

This mother's heart rejoiced when one day she looked out of her kitchen window and saw her child running and playing in the sunshine as normally as the other children.   Even though it had been heartbreaking for her to give the painful treatment, she patiently accomplished that which was for the best for her little girl's future life.

This is another example of *strict love* applied in a different fashion.

For the Good of--Not Goods For

The Nazi Germans initiated a project during World War ll.   They wanted to produce superior children and rear them away from any "weakening family influence."   Selected Nordic males and Aryan girls conceived these babies. They were then placed at the Lebensborn Baby Farm. After the war, Dr. Hellbruegge of the Munich University Pediatric Clinic examined a group of these Lebensborn babies before they were adopted.   He recalls: "They were blond and blue-eyed, but completely emaciated.   When you went close to them, they showed the empty stares of idiots."

These babies were mentally and physically backward because of lack of parental care. Professor Hellbruegge says a similar fate threatens many children today when both of their parents go to work.   He further contends, "Many modern mothers" think they have to go on working so they can make enough money to spend on the children, for better dresses and playrooms. They put the children into day schools – I think they should be called 'day orphanages' – and then they wonder why the children do not thrive." 14

Sacrificial love is not seeking the ultimate *goods for* the loved one, but it is seeking the ultimate *good of* the loved one. Far too often modern parents lavish material things on their children. In many homes lavish possessions are foolishly substituted for sacrificial love.

Ruth Bell Graham, the wife of Dr. Billy Graham relates this true story. 15

In a little town in Florida there was an unpretentious home for small, unwanted boys. Having little of this world's goods, the kindly matron made it up to them the best way she knew how.

She loved them, mothered them, fed them, spanked them, taught them to love God, to read their Bibles (those old enough to read, that is), to say their prayers. She laughed with them, listened sympathetically to their troubles (even while she stirred the soup), made her corrections few, her exhortations brief, and then she loved them some more.

One day a well-to-do lady from a distant city came to see about adopting a boy. Everyone was pleased and happy for the fortunate little boy who was going to have such a fine home - - such a successful man for a father and such a beautifully dressed, bejeweled and befurred lady for a mother.

The lady smiled down at the small boy and asked, "Do you have a bicycle?"

"No, ma'am."

"Well, she promised. "We will buy you one. And have you roller skates?"

"An old pair," he replied.

"We'll buy you a lovely new pair. And tell me, have you a transistor radio?"

The boy looked puzzled. "I haven't got any radio at all," he said.

"Well, never mind, we'll get you one."

Still puzzled, the small boy studied her solemnly - then blurted: "Please, ma'am, if that's all you're going to give me, I'd rather stay here."

How Can We Survive Financially?

During one of the many times I have accompanied my husband on one of his speaking engagements, I met two impressive teenage brothers. I thought these unusually handsome brothers were twins, but later learned that they were separated in age by eleven months. They stood out among the other teenagers present that day. They were well dressed, clean-cut, and appeared to have an abundance of self-confidence. It was easy to detect that they had been well trained. They were friendly and at ease talking with adults. They also took an active part in the worship service that morning. My husband and I commented to each other later how different the boys were in comparison with far too many unhappy young people we meet today.

During our short stay I had a wonderful opportunity to visit with these boys' mother. I complemented her fine sons and told her how much I was impressed by them. She voluntarily told me this story:

After I gave birth to the oldest of the boys I returned to my good government job and my mother took care of him for me. When he was three months old I discovered I was pregnant again. When I announced that I was pregnant and our second baby would arrive in eight months my mother said to me, "I love my grandchildren, but I will not take care of two babies for you. These are your babies and you should be the one taking care of them."

When my mother told me that, my husband and I wondered what we were going to do. I had a secure job that paid well. I had many extra benefits and a good retirement plan. Besides that we had grown accustom to two paychecks. By the time the second baby was ready to be born we had decided that our best choice was for me to stay home with our babies. We did not have a clue as to how we would survive financially. But do you know, after I quit working and was staying home with our babies we discovered that we were getting along fine financially. We always had all we needed and I put my time and energy into our two boys.

After observing her two courteous, well-adjusted sons, of whom any mother would be extremely proud, it was obvious that she had made the wisest decision when she chose to stay home with her children.

We need more grandmothers who will insist that their daughters stay home and mother their own children! It should be the goal of all parents to rear children who will accept their responsibilities for rearing their own children. Paul Lewis has said, "Remember, your basic assignment as a parent is to work yourself out of a job." (Read Chapter 4 in the Addendum)

More new mothers need to be convinced that it is possible to work as a wife and "domestic engineer" and still thrive financially.

I received a letter from a TUAC mother who shared with me the surprising discovery she and her husband had made about their budget. They both worked very hard at their jobs. One day they decided to sit down and do some detailed figuring. Here is what she said they discovered. "When we added up all our credits and debits, do you know how much money I was bringing home in actual profit each month? $5.00! I was furious to think how hard I worked for someone else and how chaotic our lives were because of it. And to think, it was profiting us nothing! I quit work and my husband is happy. I am peaceful and rested and the children are elated to have a home."

I am sure there are many competent financial advisers who could confirm this same conclusion for millions of American couples.

Love Is Like Electricity

One way to determine whether love is present in a family is by witnessing the results of its presence. Love reminds me of electricity. Just as it is difficult to explain love in a few words, I cannot completely explain electricity. I can't see electricity; but if it is present, I can surely observe its effects. If I stick a pin into a live plug-in, I immediately feel the shock of its presence.

Love is like electricity in that it is a living, active power. If it is present, our children will witness it in many ways. If we sacrificially love our children, it will shine forth in at least the following six ways:

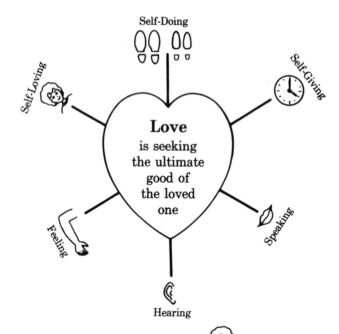

SELF-LOVING

The first important aspect to understand about love is that children will experience and receive no healthier love than the love that their parents have for themselves. R. Lofton Hudson said, "One of the most significant findings of modern psychology is that people cannot love others unless they first have a healthy self-love." [16]

Eric Fromm, in his book, *The Art of Loving*, writes, "The love for my own self is inseparably connected with the love for any other being." [17] Jesus said the second great commandment is, "*Thou shalt love thy neighbor as thyself.*" Matthew 22:29. How can one love his neighbor or his child as he should if he doesn't first love himself? The answer is obvious - - he can't.

Some sincere parents are hypercritical with their children. The basic cause lies in the fact that the parents do not have good self-images. Dr. Bruce Narramore says, "It takes about one hundred compliments to make up for one criticism." [18]

One schoolteacher had a student who was plagued by serious problems. The boy not only did not like himself, he hated himself. Every morning he practiced the same ritual of throwing his hat and coat on the floor. The teacher would say, "Pick up your coat and hat, Johnny." This went on for weeks. One morning the teacher was pleasantly surprised when Johnny came in and voluntarily hung up his coat and hat. He looked around to the teacher and said, "I like myself today."

Do you like yourself today and manifest it by a healthy self-love? If so, you can properly love your children.

SELF-DOING

The second manner in which we radiate our love is by working to provide the physical needs of our children. Daddy works daily in order to provide food, clothing, shelter, and the other necessities of life for his family.

Mother works at homemaking by shopping, preparing tasty, nutritious meals, sewing, cleaning and mending the clothes, decorating and keeping the house clean and attractive, taking care of the children when they are sick, teaching them not to leave their toys, clothes, and personal belongings scattered about and by performing other tasks too numerous to mention.

Always remember, while it is important to provide adequate physical necessities for children, there is far more to showing your children you love them than by showering them with material things.

SELF-GIVING

Third, our children will know that we love them by our willingness to give to them of ourselves. This self-giving is done through personal companionship. It is extremely vital that you work and play and especially listen to your children. All of this takes *TIME* and can only be accomplished by being present with your children.

Mothers sacrificially love their children by staying home and giving them their full time and attention. They will refuse to employ surrogates to perform their God-ordained parenting responsibilities.

Daddy will come directly home after a day's work to take special time to be with his family. As his wife and children settle down for the night, they feel the protective presence of a strong and loving father. Only loving daddies and mothers will take the time to demand the best from the children. They will not perform their children's chores and responsibilities for them, but will make sure the children do their chores for themselves.

"Switching Price Tags" [19]

There is a story of hoodlums who broke into a department store one night. They did not steal or destroy anything. They just had a wonderful time- - switching price tags. The next morning customers were puzzled and delighted to find fur coats selling for $15. Cold cream was priced at $450. A silver service was marked $5.25 and a pair of ladies' hose $390. There were umbrellas for $3,000 and diamond rings for $6.

Has someone invaded our lives and switched the price tags? Have 'things' become more valuable than spending time together? Are material gifts worth more than gifts of the spirit?

Do we place higher price tags on the community than on the family? On personal pleasures, rather than the needs of those we love? On a TV program, rather than family prayers?

When our children long for love and sympathy, do we give them a pair of roller skates instead?

SPEAKING, HEARING, AND FEELING

Last, our children will experience the reality of our love when we express it through the senses of speaking, hearing, and feeling. Reading and experience have taught me that these three areas of communicating love are often the most sadly neglected.

One young man said of his home: "One thing I regret about my home is the fact that love was very rarely expressed openly. I am certain that deep love was felt for the other family members, but somehow it was seldom put into words. I think this has stood in my way as I have tried to enter into deep personal relationships." [20]

A hug, a kiss, an arm around the shoulder, or being tucked in bed -- all are important ways parents can convey to a child that 'I care about you.' Children never outgrow the need for physical demonstration of love. The human touch is necessary for emotional development. Too much can never be said about the need for the human touch. [21]

Dr. Rene Spitz, a New York psychoanalyst, spent three months observing babies in a foundling home. The nursing staff was so busy that the babies had only one-tenth of a mother. Dr. Spitz estimated that thirty percent of the babies died before they were a year old. [22]

With the Lips, Ears, Arms, and Hands

We communicate love with our lips. We can (1) *Give affectionate kisses.* (2) *Say "I love you."* A dozen times a day will never be too many. George Eliot has said, "We need not only to be loved, but to be told we are loved. The realm of silence is large enough beyond the grave." A favorite phrase at our house has been, "I love you, and don't forget it." (3) *Give words of praise.* Praise is a confidence builder. It is a superior way to communicate love to a child. Praise your child before strangers, to relatives, and to your mate and let him hear you compliment him to others.

One who is praised and made to feel valuable when a child will become an adult who has confidence in himself and possesses healthy self-esteem. He will not constantly thirst for recognition and brag about his every small accomplishment. Self-praise, a weakness found in many adults, is condemned by the Bible. "*Let another man praise thee, and not thine own mouth; a stranger, and not thine own lips.*" Proverbs 27:2. We can immunize our children from feelings of inferiority in adulthood by furnishing them with ample positive, sincere praise while they are small.

Our ears receive love communication. It is pleasant to hear words of praise, and especially to hear others say three of the most treasured words in the English language, "I love you."

We express our love by the human touch through hugs, squeezes and love pats. Concerning the human touch I have two suggestions for new mothers: (1) If you must bottle feed your baby, always hold him close in your arms *each time* he is fed. Handle his feeding time in the same manner as a mother who nurses her baby from the breast. Never prop up his bottle with pillows on a bed for him to feed himself. (2) Use the rocking chair and rock your baby a lot. Rocking is essential when a child does not feel well. Rock your precious little one when it is story time, sleepy time, or anytime the two of you spend a quiet moment together.

And please do not forget *the time to communicate love to your child is when he is doing or producing nothing.*

Have an Affectionate Family

Expressing affection is consistently practiced in the homes of "the winners." I know from observation that an affectionate, love-communicating family is far too rare in our hectic world. I had the blessing of growing up in an affectionate family. I suppose we were one of the kissingest families in our community. We expressed our love for each other often and still do.

When I brought friend's home to meet my family, they often made comments about the love that they saw us openly express. Listening to comments from my friend such as "I have never seen my daddy and mother kiss each other, and they never kissed me;" or, "I never heard my parents tell each other, 'I love you,' " have taught me that coming from a family which openly expressed its love was tremendously valuable, but it is far too rare an experience.

Be the Generation That Breaks the Family Tradition

A story is told of two young boys who were walking home from school together. "I've carried her books twice and bought her ice cream once," the older boy said. "Do you think I ought to kiss her now?" After thinking a while, the younger boy replied, "No, I don't think you have to. I think you've done enough already!" [23]

Many parents are like that. They bring the hamburger home and cook it, but it is against their natures to be affectionate and complimentary to their children. They feel awkward about showing love and insincere when giving praise. Why? It is a result of their home backgrounds. Perhaps their parents were cold and unaffectionate; and because children are products of their environment, these traits of coldness are often passed on to another generation.

In his book, *Help! I'm a Parent!* Bruce Narramore says, "This cycle doesn't need to carry on! We can stop it now! We can become positive even though it runs against our grain." [24]

A few years ago I accompanied my husband to a large city. While we were there, I was invited to speak to a group of ladies. After I had encouraged the women to communicate their love to their children, a very pretty young mother approached me. She expressed her feeling that it would be almost impossible for her ever to take her five-year-old twins into her arms and caress and kiss them. Her reason was that she had never been treated that way when she was a child. Needless to say, I did all I could to encourage her to break that family tradition of coldness.

Showing Affection Is Biblical

The idea of being affectionate is Biblical. Remember the story of Jacob and Esau? They were twin brothers who had been separated for many years. When they were reunited, the Bible tells us, *"And Esau ran to meet him, and embraced him, and fell on his neck, and kissed him; and they wept."* Genesis 33:4.

Jacob and Joseph were father and son who tragically had been separated for years. When they were finally reunited, the Bible says, *"And Joseph made ready his chariot, and went up to meet Israel, his father, to Goshen, and presented himself unto him; and he fell on his neck, and wept on his neck a good while."* Geneses 46:29.

The Bible describes Paul's last meeting with the Ephesian elders on the isle of Miletus. They were telling him good-bye and knew they would never see his face again. Did they shake his hand and say, "Paul, it has really been nice to know you"? Of course they didn't! The Bible says, *"And they all wept sore, and fell on Paul's neck, and kissed him."* Acts 20:37.

Once Jesus was a guest in the house of Simon the Pharisee. A sinful woman approached Christ. She wept, washed Jesus' feet with her tears, kissed them, dried them with her hair, and anointed them with ointment. Simon the Pharisee was standing aloof from the scene, condemning Christ in his heart. He reasoned, *"This man, if he were a prophet, would have known who and what manner of woman this is that toucheth him; for she is a sinner."* Luke 7:39. Jesus, knowing Simon's thoughts, rebuked him. He said, " Simon, I came into your house, and you did not even give me water to wash my feet; furthermore, you gave me no kiss." Jesus indicated that, by failing to show him these outward expressions of affection, he had neglected being a truly warm, hospitable host.

Carpe Diem

Is your home one in which all the members of your family receive sacrificial love? Do you love and accept yourself so that you are capable of loving others? I am sure you provide the necessities of food, clothing, and shelter for your family, but are you freely giving of yourself and your time? And last, are you a love-communicating family?

If you do not shower your family with affection, I say to you, "Carpe diem." This is an old Roman phrase that means, "Seize the day." So seize this day and start expressing and communicating your love at the sacrificial, agape level. And remember that the remaining TUAC principles will not work effectively until you have accomplished the level of love that *seeks the ultimate good of the loved ones*, and give it Con sist' ent ly.

ASSIGNMENT

1. Take an empty medicine bottle, make a written copy of the following prescription and paste it on the bottle. Put it in the refrigerator and apply three times a day.

> AFFECTIONATE PHARMACY
> No. 322912   Dr. Dew Alittle Lovin
> For: Daddy Bee & Mother Bee
>
> Three times a day, apply an affectionate kiss,
> Hug, and squeeze to each child in the family.
> Accompany it with an "I Love You."

2. Write yourself this reminder on a piece of tape and wrap it around your lipstick tube: *Did I kiss them and say, "I love you," today?*

3. Write this note on your tube of toothpaste: *Have I squeezed them today?*

4. Prepare a "sweet treat" and have it ready to serve for dinner on Tuesday. Mix up some homemade lemonade and have it ready when the children come home from school.

5. Give praise to each of your children EVERY DAY.

OBEDIENCE

Must Be Taught Before
the ABC's and the 123's

Chapter Eight
Obedience

Obedience is the fourth car on our little train. If this car becomes inoperative, you do not need to stop your locomotive. Your training has already malfunctioned. You must get out your toolbox and quickly begin critical repairs. At the time your little passengers refuse to obey you, you are in serious trouble and they are in worse trouble. Furthermore, until your children mind you, neither independence, good habits, work, communication, nor togetherness will work for you either. Building an autocratic family will come to a dead stop if you do not have the obedience car operating efficiently.

Obedience builds three essential virtues in a child: trust, respect, and responsibility. Without these ingredients, your child will become a social cripple and be handicapped for life.

I compare this lesson about obedience to a race. A VIP will never win this race. I can assure you of this before you start. Because, you see, a VIP is a *Very Indolent Parent*, and a lazy parent will never exert the energy necessary to win respect and obedience from his children. It takes wisdom and a tremendous amount of skill and determination to win the obedience race. The little racers with whom you compete are full of energy; they are fast, cunning, and very intelligent. They are capable of out-foxing you again and again if you do not develop into a competent parent who demands and receives obedience from your children.

I am sure that as a parent you would like to win loving obedience from your children, but do you have it? If not, do you believe you can get it? This race is hard. It is tough. And to many parents, it seems impossible. But, if you think you can win, you can.

If you think you are beaten, you are;
If you think you dare not, you don't.
If you want to win but don't think you can,
It's almost a cinch you won't.

If you think you'll lose, you're lost;
For out in the world we find
Success begins with a fellow's will:
It's all in the state of mind.
If you think you're outclassed, you are;
You've got to think high to rise;
You've got to be sure of yourself before
You can ever win a prize.

Life's battles don't always go
To the stronger and faster man;
But sooner or later the man who wins
Is the man who thinks he can.

--Walter D. Wintle

Go Into Concentrated Training

In previous chapters you were cautioned that training involves teaching your children to follow your instructions. In order to proceed with the study, you must learn how to gain obedience.

To receive obedience from your children, you may need to enter into an intense training program yourself. You should choose a winning parent for a coach. Let the winning lady explain to you the rules of the obedience game and then follow her instructions.

I emphasize, be *sure* you pick a *winner*. And what is a winner? Winners are parents who have reared or are rearing obedient children. Their children respect and honor them, and they exhibit respect in their speech, manners, and actions.

"Boys, Shut the TV Off"

I have spent many years searching for winners. Claude was an elder in a congregation for which my husband once preached. Claude and his wife, Dorothy, were winning parents whom I had the opportunity to observe. They had three of the finest teenage boys I had ever known.

One night we drove out to their little farm. Their house was small, no big den or family room, and all three of the boys were stretched out on the living room floor deeply involved in a TV program. As my husband and I entered the room, each of the three boys acknowledged our arrival with a courteous greeting. Then they settled back to continue viewing their program.

We made ourselves comfortable and enjoyed visiting with Claude and Dorothy for a few minutes. Then the time arrived for us to get down to serious matters for which we had made the call. There were private subjects that needed to be discussed which Claude did not want his boys to hear. So, he said, to them, "Boys! Shut the TV off and go to your room."

Without hesitation, all three promptly got up and obeyed their father. There was absolutely no questioning, or back talk ("Oh, Dad! Can't we just finish this program?"), nor nasty attitudes involved. They said good night to us and went to their room immediately. (Incidentally, these three boys shared one small bedroom, even as teenagers.)

That was a demonstration of a winner at work. Claude had received obedience from his sons. True obedience is (1) immediate, (2) unquestioning, and (3) doing exactly as one is told—no substitutions, additions, or omissions.

In recent years, my husband and I had the privilege of attending the "Golden Wedding Anniversary" celebration which Claude and Dorothy's three sons gave in their honor. It was an elaborate event that took place in Branson, Missouri. The respect and tribute with which the boys honored their parents were delightfully memorable.

Much to everyone's sadness, Claude lived only two weeks after his Golden Wedding Anniversary. God was gracious to grant him the privilege of experiencing that celebration given by his sons as the last important event of his life. What an honor!

Do Not Listen to the Losers
In your parent-training program, whatever you do, never listen to the losers. Often the parents who have the most disobedient and disrespectful children are the ones most eager to tell you how to rear your children. Losers are the ones who will be your most vocal critics when you are strict and make your children behave.

If you meet a grandmother who shames you for "being too strict with your children," just take a look at her adult children. If they have disordered, unhappy, chaotic lives pay no attention to her advice. She is a loser, and you must follow a more successful pattern than hers.

The reason I caution you about this is that winning mothers have often told me that, in their earlier years when they disciplined their children, they had to contend with the problem of unfair criticism. Gaining obedience from children is sometimes an unpleasant task. So I encourage you. Be brave. Read Proverbs 29:17 and complete effective training by making your children follow your teaching. ❋

If your mother was a loser in getting obedience from you, do not adopt her unsuccessful practices for the obedience race with your children. Find a mother who was a winner and follow her example.

Watch Those Authors

Again may I caution you! Do not permit yourself to be influenced by the authors who advocate the democratic or laissez-faire method of child training. These authors make ridiculous statements, such as: "You cannot hope to get good results from children through corporal (physical) punishment." "Children have to be impressed with something other than yielding to the superior power of an adult." Or, "Children are their parents' equals when it comes to their right and ability to decide things for themselves."

Theories like these have been taught and advocated for too many years. From my study and experience, I have discovered that the majority of child rearing books that line library and bookstore shelves advocate liberalized, permissive, unworkable parenting theories.

Unique authors like David Wilkerson express the views of "the winners" when he writes:

> "Disciplining is out of style today. It is considered harmful to the child's development patterns. Disciplining is called 'child beating'; scolding is 'brow beating'; old fashioned discipline is called 'parental temper tantrums.' My parents had a different name for it - - they called it *woodshed therapy*. I believe it's time for a woodshed revival." [1]

I Want to Share

I have encouraged you to seek out your own winning parents to observe. You will learn a lot of helpful tips and get some excellent advice from couples who have parenting skills that are tried and proven. Again, I caution you these winners may be hard to find. You will need to search diligently to ferret them out. When I give this assignment to the ladies in my classes, they often come back the next week and say, "I can't find a winner." But I encourage them to keep looking. If you search long enough, you will find some successful parents who have reared admirable children.

The one thing I have always been cautious about in choosing winning parents is to make sure the advice I receive does not conflict with biblical teaching. I encourage you to do the same.

In the rest of this chapter, I will share with you what the Bible teaches about getting obedience, and combine it with the methods "the winners" have shared with me. There are ten basic facts I will present here, and after that, winning the obedience race is up to you.

1. TO LOVE AND TO DISCIPLINE DO NOT CONFLICT

The first fact you need to learn before you can win the obedience race is that to love *is* to discipline. A Los Angeles psychologist, in a keynote speech, said: "The greatest social disaster of this century is the belief that abundant love makes discipline unnecessary." [2]

From the previous chapter, you learned that the correct definition of love is "seeking the ultimate good of the loved one." It is for the good of every child to develop acceptable behavior and to learn to get along well in the family, in the neighborhood, and at school. Discipline is the ingredient that teaches a child how to behave properly in order to survive in society. A parent goes to the trouble to discipline, then, only if he loves the child.

Many sets of parents who are troubled by unruly, misbehaving children use the weak excuse, "I love my children too much to physically discipline them." Those who reason in this manner have failed to understand the definition of authentic love. God says, *"He that spareth his rod hateth his son: but he that loveth him chasteneth him betimes."* Proverbs 13:24.

To give a child his own foolish way is not a mark of love, but an indication of a VIP. This weakness of character on the part of the parent will in a short time harm the child.

Opposite Results

Love can produce results that are exactly opposite. It can cause excruciating pain, or it can bring exquisite joy.

Suppose a child has an abscess that is poisoning his system and threatens his life. The doctor prepares to lance the abscess. This procedure will cause terrific discomfort. What if a sentimental nurse grabs his hand and demands—"Don't you dare hurt that poor baby!" Which one expresses a true love for the well being of the patient, the doctor or the nurse? The answer is the doctor, of course. Even though his treatment resulted in pain, he did what was best for the child.

The pioneer woman who straightened her child's foot also experienced the two results of pain and joy that come from exercising strict love.

2. PUNISHMENT IS NOT ALWAYS DISCIPLINE, BUT IMPOSED DISCIPLINE IS ALWAYS PUNISHMENT [3]

The second thing an autocratic parent must understand is that there is a difference between pure punishment and true discipline. *Punishment is pain or discomfort inflicted upon another.* If pain or discomfort is imposed upon a child for his welfare and to make him a better and a more pleasant person, it is *discipline.* But if pain is inflicted on a child out of spite or when a parent is in a rage, it is *pure punishment.*

Historically, enemies of our country have punished United States prisoners of war. Often they were beaten until they were unconscious. The hostages' fingernails were sometimes pulled out by the roots, and they were tortured in many other cruel ways. These acts were done out of hatred and were not for the welfare of those who suffered. This was pure punishment and had no resemblance to corrective discipline.

I once was acquainted with a Christian couple who consistently punished their children. The father and mother would sandwich their three children between them on a pew during a church service. Each parent would periodically reach across and slap or cuff them during worship services. It was not unusual to witness them administer a dozen or more whacks to their children's upper torsos within thirty minutes. Needless to say, these children were very unruly, disobedient, and so extremely unhappy they cried a great deal of the time.

Because parents are human, there may be times they punish their children in anger. It may relieve them for the moment and may vent frustration, but mature, skillful parents should never behave in such a foolish manner. When your children are disobedient, you must make them follow your instructions by firmly directing them with a calm and loving spirit. Administered in this manner, discipline will be for the child's sake and not an outlet for your own pent up emotions.

3. A CHILD'S JUDGMENT TAKES YEARS TO DEVELOP

The third fact young parents must keep in mind is that children are children, and it takes months and years of living experience for them to develop sound judgment.

Dr. William E. Homan says: "On behalf of children everywhere, I beg of you, don't terrify them with explanations. Just support them with facts." He further says, "Don't force a child to make decisions before he has the facts upon which to decide and the self-confidence to do so." 4

The following are two examples of parents' failure to follow this sound advice:

Example 1

A mother takes her pre-schooler to the closet, opens the door, and says, "What do you want to wear today, sweetheart?" The child begins to study her choices, but does not know whether it is going to rain or the day will be warm and sunny. Neither does she have sufficient information about the events planned for the day. She does not know whether her mother is going to take her to play in the park or to church for worship. So the child's choice is, "I want to wear my long yellow dress today." "Oh, no, honey! We are going to work in the flower beds this morning. You can't wear that," is mother's response.

So the child tries again. "I want to wear my short red dress then." "Well, darling," Mother reminds her, "that dress has long sleeves and it is too hot to wear it." Before long, the child is frustrated, whining, and crying, and may throw herself on the floor in a tantrum. *Mother* is the one who knows the activities planned for the day. She should have made the choice and given the child the facts by selecting the appropriate apparel and saying: "This is the dress you will wear today."

Example 2

A couple takes their little one with them when they go out for the evening to have dinner in a restaurant. The child cannot read; he has no idea how much money Daddy wants to spend; in fact, he does not know how many pennies are in a dime. The family is seated in the restaurant and anticipating an enjoyable meal together when Mother spoils it by asking, "Freddie, what do you want to order?" Freddie, who is unable to read, replies, "I want a peanut butter and jelly sandwich." "Oh, honey, they do not have peanut butter and jelly sandwiches here." "I want a hot dog then." "Darling! This is the Chicken Palace and they do not serve hot dogs." By this time, Freddie is frustrated, angry, or sulking, and the meal is ruined. He tried twice to order what he wanted and failed each time. Mother had the knowledge and judgment to order for him. She knew what he liked and how much he was likely to eat. She should have made the decision and given Freddie the facts: "This is what you are having for dinner."

Parents who deal with their children in the fashion given in the above examples will ultimately have to contend with many unpleasant situations. I have witnessed children tearing through the house screaming, wallowing on the bed in a fit, and even diving under the table in a restaurant.

That kind of unnecessary scene can be avoided if the parents will furnish a child with the facts. This is the reason God gave children parents. It takes years for a child's judgment to mature. It is true that, as they become more responsible, children should be granted the privilege to make judgments. Dr. Haim G. Ginott's "Voice and Choice" activity is an excellent way to start a child in learning to make judgments. 5 (We will cover that subject in Chapter Nine.)

Often a child reasons like this, " Daddy could buy all of the bubble gum in the store, but he doesn't. If I had all of his money, I would. Grownups just sit around and talk. They never play tag or climb trees. My parents always walk to the car. I like to run. Mama doesn't go to bed right after dinner, and I have to." 6

Autocratic parents must remember to spare their children unnecessary worry by supporting them with facts until they are old enough to make sound judgments on their own.

4. YOUR CHILD MUST LEARN RESPECT FOR AUTHORITY

Knowing this fourth fact will give you relief.

"There is one, just one, basic lesson you will need to teach your child. And that is respect for authority. No matter what else you want your child to learn, he must learn this lesson first." 7 If he learns respect for authority, this is the basis by which all of the hundreds and thousands of other lessons will fall into place. Dr. William E. Homan says, "Whatever the

age of your child, if he has not learned this lesson, stop all other teaching and concentrate upon it." 8

You may ask, "When and how do I begin to teach authority? There are the school authorities, police authorities, and many other authorities." This brings us to the fifth fact you need to know.

5. YOU ARE YOUR CHILD'S FIRST AUTHORITY

An autocratic family is one in which the parents are the first authority.

You cannot be your child's first authority, however unless you are practicing a sacrificial love by being a full-time, on-duty mother. Any child who has to mix up Daddy's and Mother's orders with those of three or four ladies at the day care center, and who is handled in still different ways by baby-sitters a couple of nights a week, will be a confused child. He will not know his boundaries, what he can or cannot do, nor what or what not to expect. The need to build a secure one-on-one relationship and teach respect for parental authority is the major reason for mothers always to be present with their children.

God intends for parents to be their child's first authority, not to boost parental ego or exercise power, but, rather, to provide dependable guidance which will enable their child to develop respect for his family, himself, and others as well.

"The respect your child has for his first authority will determine how he will honor the authority of his Bible class teacher, his teacher at school, the policeman on the corner, the store manager, the baseball coach, the Cub Scout leader, and most of all, God and Christ. He will follow the instructions of others in authority in the same manner he has learned to follow yours." 9

What Is an Authority?

There are three steps in becoming an authority. They are:

AN AUTHORITY

Step 1. Knows the subject better than the person
he's addressing.

Step 2. Verbally gives his facts. (One time, never
more than twice, unless he's asked.)

Step 3. He then follows his facts with proof.

The following are examples of how easily this works for parents.

Example 1
You are the authority. It is time for you to put your eighteen-month-old daughter to bed for a nap.
Step 1. You know the subject better than your eighteen-month-old.
It is ten o'clock, and babies need extra rest.
Step 2. You verbally give the fact once - -
"Tammy, come to Mother. It is time for your nap now."
Step 3. You follow your fact with proof.
Tuck Tammy in her bed.

Example 2
You are the authority. It is a beautiful day and you want your three- and five-year-olds to play in the back yard.
Step 1. You know your subject.
You need to mop the floors, and your children need fresh air and sunshine.
Step 2. Verbally give the fact one time.
"Children, go outside and play in the back yard. I will call you when you can come in."
Step 3. Follow the fact with proof.
"You take them or make sure they go immediately to the back yard.

Example 3
You are the authority. Two-year-old Richard is climbing on a chair.
Step 1. You know more about the subject than Richard knows.
The chair is dangerous. He could get a splinter, or the chair might fall over on him.
Step 2. You give the fact one time.
"No, Richard! Come away from the chair."
Step 3. Follow the fact with proof.
Help Richard down, and steer him away from the chair.
Look what these children have learned. Their mother spoke with authority and they were aware that she knew her subject. She furnished immediate proof. Her children *trust* her and will show their *respect* by following her word. They will learn *responsibility* because they have been taught to obey a trusted parent.

Con sist' en cy

An authority must always be consistent with her knowledge, word, and proof. No reliable authority would tell Jim not to throw balls in the house, whistle at the dinner table, or slide down the banister, on Monday and overlook it if he disobeys her on Tuesday. If it is a fact that mother does not want balls thrown in the house, whistling during the meal time or reckless behavior on the stairs, those facts must be dependable. Changeable moods, good days, bad weather, sickness, headaches, grandmother's visit, nor any other circumstance should alter the facts.

A competent authority will teach consistent facts each day of the week. And remember, Daddy and Mother must be united, agreed on their facts, and be determined to back them with proof.

Be Sure You Know Your Subject

One is not, nor can be, a respected authority if her students know the subject better than she does. Often, parents entangle themselves in difficulty when they do not know the facts.

Sometimes children have a better knowledge of a subject than do their parents. A newborn baby is an example. He knows when he has had enough milk. If his mother tries to force him to continue nursing when he is full, he will resist. A mother may place a plate of food before her child and give the fact that he has to eat it all. The fact may be that the child is not hungry or his stomach cannot hold the amount of food that he has been given.

It is unreasonable to give a fact to which your child is mentally or physically unable to respond. *Before giving facts, be sure that you know the subject better than your child and can with confidence follow up with unquestionable proof if necessary.*

What Did I Hear You Say?

Isn't it easy to be an authority? Just look at the results when you follow the three simple steps of knowing your subject, giving the facts, and enforcing them with proof. Your child is happy and your home is peaceful.

Or did I hear you say, "Oh, yow! My eighteen-month-old will not stay in bed, and my Richard will climb right back on that chair." Did you say that? In that case, you need to learn another truth about winning the game of obedience.

6. TO IMPOSE DISCIPLINE YOU WILL NEED A ROD

If Tammy will not stay in bed and Richard refuses to leave the chair alone, you must enforce your facts by furnishing proof that they are reliable. You must impose discipline upon Tammy and Richard to *make them* stay in bed and away from the chair.

In order to insure your child obeys your spoken word, you will need to use a rod.

Who Says To Use a Rod?

How do I know you should use a rod? First, "the winners" said so; but more importantly, it is God's command. Read the following Scriptures carefully. Follow what our Creator teaches about using the rod to gain obedience.

Proverbs 13:24   – "He that spareth his *rod* hateth his son: but he that loveth him chasteneth him betimes."

Proverbs 22:15   – "Foolishness is bound in the heart of a child; but the *rod* of correction shall drive it far from him."

Proverbs 23:13-14   – "Withhold not correction from the child; for if thou beatest him with the *rod*, he shall not die. Thou shalt beat him with the *rod*, and shalt deliver his soul from hell."

Proverbs 29:15 & 17 – "The *rod* and reproof give wisdom: but a child left to himself bringeth his mother to shame."

           "Correct thy son, and he shall give thee rest; yea, he shall give delight unto thy soul."

What Is a Rod?

According to Webster's dictionary, a rod is "a straight slender stick growing on or cut from a tree or a bush." I use the word *switch* because it fits my train illustration. "A good father or mother who finds his son or daughter on the wrong track will provide switching facilities."

Two passages in the Bible specify that rods are cut from the branches that grow on trees, Genesis 30:37 - "*And Jacob took him rods of green poplar, and of the hazel and chestnut tree.*" Numbers 17:8 - "*And, behold, the rod of Aaron - - -was budded, and brought forth buds, and bloomed blossoms, and yielded almonds.*"

Oh, But Lord

"Oh, but Lord! You surely do not mean I should use a switch to make my child mind. I love him too much to hurt him."

Wait a minute! What did Proverbs 13:24 say? *"He that spareth (refrains from using) his rod hateth his son."*

"Well, just how do I administer this? Just how severe should I get?" Let us read it again. *"If thou beatest him . . ."* Proverbs 23:13.

"Well, Lord, if I do that I would feel so bad I could hardly live with myself." No! Let us see what it will do for you. *"Correct thy son, and he shall give thee rest; yea, he shall give delight unto thy soul."* Proverbs 29:17. The ultimate result of using the rod appropriately is that your child will give you peace.

Therefore, if eighteen-month-old Tammy and two-year-old Richard will not stay in bed or away from the chair how do you make sure they obey you? By using a little rod, of course.

Here is another important principle to remember: *"The rod is the first response and not the last resort."* 10 By understanding this principle, you will never tell your child, "You just wait until your Daddy gets home." There should be no waiting. If your child does not mind your spoken facts, then you should respond with the rod immediately.

Occasionally when you give your child a spoken fact, he will not immediately obey your word but will procrastinate. When he sees you approaching him with the rod in your hand, however, he will hasten to do what you told him to do. What should a mother's response be when this happens? If you go to the trouble to get a rod, you should use it. If you do not, your child will play a daring little game of "how far will she let me go" every time you tell him to do something, and you will always be the loser.

Three Good Reasons

When I teach new mothers God's rule of using a rod for the purpose of discipline, I try to make sure they understand that that is exactly the instrument He means. Belts, ropes, Ping-Pong paddles, fly swatters, wooden spoons, rulers, spatulas, or your hand are not proper substitutes for the rod. (Hands are to be used for the purpose of expressing love.)

There are at least three good reasons that God specified using a rod (switch) for discipline.

(1) *Discipline, rather than pure punishment, is more likely to be administered.* Many people struggle to keep a tight reign on their tempers. When your

child defies you, this can be very upsetting. However, by following God's plan you have time to gain control of your anger. Making a trip into the yard to get a rod from a tree will give you time to calm down. When you are calm you will be far better prepared to exercise effective, corrective discipline, rather than venting your anger by administering pure punishment.

(2) *Permanent damage is not inflicted.* When a rod (switch) is used for chastisement, it is very flexible. Therefore, it does not cause lasting physical harm to the child. *"If thou beatest him with the rod, he shall not die. Thou shalt beat him with the rod, and shalt deliver his soul from hell."* Proverbs 23:13 & 14

Even though this means that discipline will protect his spiritual welfare, in addition, it may save him from physical harm. If you tell your child not to play in the street and he disobeys you, he could be hit by a car and killed. If you teach him not to experiment with drugs and he disobeys you, he may become an addict or die from an overdose.

Furthermore, you will not endanger him physically by using a rod as your instrument for correction.

(3) *The sting of the rod (switch) is intense enough that it is unlikely that a child will want it repeated.* I have heard some parents say, "Well, we tried spanking, but it just didn't work for us." (I can understand why; slapping with your hands is not effective.) But when a rod is properly administered, a parent doesn't need to worry that it won't work. A child chastened with a rod will quickly respond to a command he initially ignored.

My Boys Laughed at Me

After teaching the principle of using a rod for correction to a group of new mothers I was sure that I had convinced them that it would quickly produce speedy compliance to commands. But the next week when we met, one mother was disturbed about her experience with using the rod.

She had failed in her effort to teach her boy's respect for her authority. She, like most mothers, had known her subject, but could not get past verbally giving her facts. She had explained to her boys five and seven that she had been wrong in nagging and shouting at them. "Now that will change. I am going to tell you what I want you to do one time; and if you do not mind me, I will discipline you."

Of course, children who have been scolded and nagged more than five years had acquired the habit of temporary deafness. Their mother's facts are much like the sound of the cuckoo clock - - they ignored her koos.

Breaking their habit of convenient deafness was enough challenge for her, but she made another mistake. When she attempted to discipline her boys with the rod, it did not work. She told us, "My boys stood there and laughed at me."

This seriously concerned me. I could not imagine children that were so tough that they were insensitive to the sting of a switch. So I asked her: "What was the size of the rod you used?" "From what kind of tree was it taken?" "How many times did you strike them?" She had answered everything correctly until I asked her, "Did you use the rod on the bare skin?" She replied, "No, I didn't. They had their Levis on."

I explained to her that the next time she imposed discipline, she should switch them on the bare bottoms. I assured her that her boys might dance, but they would not laugh at her.

The next week, when we met this young mother, her testimony proved to be a positive re-enforcement of the age-old remedy of "hickory tea" to cure disobedience and disrespect. When switched on their bare bottoms, her boys were not amused, and their hearing problems were cured without a single visit to an ear doctor.

7. START TEACHING OBEDIENCE EARLY

How early should one begin teaching obedience and respect for parental authority?   This is a question frequently asked by young parents. I once wondered about the answer to this question. Before I had experience with an infant, I had asked, "the winners," "At what age did you start imposing discipline?" I was surprised when they said, "You should begin when a child is five to six months old." "Why should one discipline a baby that early?" I inquired. The winning mothers assured me that when I cared for a baby I would learn differences in their cries. Babies cry because they are wet, hungry, sleepy, frightened, or in pain. Other times, they may only be angry and will express their tempers by stiffening, turning red in the face, and exhibit a loud scream. During these displays of anger "the winners" say you must give a firm swat on the legs or buttocks. When he refuses to lie still for diapering is another time to impose brief discipline to let your baby know that you are displeased.

"Child Proof" Your House

Babies normally begin crawling at around six months. After this age they become more mobile. Your baby may begin walking alone between nine and thirteen months. (Remember--discourage walking before twelve or thirteen months.) At these stages of your baby's development, you must carefully "child proof" your house.

When your baby starts crawling fast enough to get out of your sight quickly, go throughout your house and remove, cover up, or close up anything or place (use gates and latches when necessary) that might harm your little one. Your child is entering a stage of development in which he longs to explore his world. He will touch and handle everything that is within his reach. His curiosity is good! That is how he learns. You want this stage of development to be positive.

When he stands on his feet and balances and takes shaky steps around the furniture, "child proof" again. This time, remove dangers that are higher up. Remove everything that he can tear up, pull down or break.

A coffee table is perfect for your baby to hold onto as he takes his first steps. Remove everything from that table that he can damage or that may harm him. If you keep trinkets, albums, or candy dishes on the coffee table, put them out of his reach. In their place decorate with wicker or plastic baskets filled with articles, such as large plastic fruit, that have no parts that can break off if he puts them in his mouth. Let him handle and play with items that are safe. Go shopping and purchase articles that he can safely touch, feel, and put in his mouth. For a few months, remove all of your "pretty pretties," as I used to call them, from your curious little investigator's reach.

Prepare a bottom drawer or a lower space in your kitchen cabinet into which your baby can safely crawl to play and explore. Be absolutely sure he does not have access to any box or enclosure from which he cannot easily escape. This safety precaution should be taken for older children, too.

When you are in your kitchen, your toddler will want to be with you. Fill a drawer or cabinet space, with kitchen utensils with which he can safely play, like---rolling pins, wooden spoons, old pans, measuring cups, tea strainers, flour sifters, plastic funnels, basting tubes, potato mashers, metal spoons, pizza pans, wooden bowls, muffin tins, or colorful plastic glasses. You can leave the dishwasher lid down and give him a little water to pour in glasses. The dishwasher lid is a perfect height for a toddler to reach. In his curious exploratory activities, he is examining, learning, and loving the security of being with his Mother.

NO

The first spoken fact you should teach your baby to understand and obey is "No!" Another reason for making your house safe is so you will not need to use "No" very often. The use of the word "NO!" should be kept to a minimum.

Teach him "no" for objects that are dangerous. One enticing article to a baby is an electric cord. He often will be discontent until he successfully puts it in his mouth. Even after you have gone through the house and removed all other dangerous articles, there are times when you must run the vacuum sweeper or use the sewing machine. In order to use these appliances, an electric cord must be exposed.

When your baby attempts to grab the cord, shake your head, say "no," and take the cord away from him. If he persists, use a tiny rod from the tree and swat him on the buttocks or leg two or three times. Repeat your fact, "no!," and take the cord away again. Repeat this until he is willing to leave the dangerous object alone. It will not take many lessons like this for him to respond immediately to your "No!"

"Come to Mother!"

In the love chapter I mentioned that between six and eighteen months babies enter the "shadowing" and "darting" stages. Shadowing is the time of your little one's development when he stays so close to you that he becomes your shadow. He will cry when you get out of his sight. Soon, however, he will enter the bold, adventuresome "darting" stage when he will run away from you.

During this bold toddler period you must teach that he must obey the command, "Come to mother!" Teaching your toddler this lesson will save you thousands of steps and in dangerous circumstances could save your child's life. You begin this lesson by motioning with your hand and saying, " Come to mother!" Approach your baby extending your hands, showing him exactly what you mean. Take him by the hand and walk him back to where you were standing (your "home base") when you called.

When the time comes (and it will with every child) that your "little darter" runs the opposite direction when you say, "Come to mother!" get your rod and discipline him while walking him back to "home base" where you were standing when you called. Repeat this lesson from day to day until your little one learns to obey you each time you call, "Come to Mother!" Soon your toddler will come to you from any room in the house or even if he is in the yard when you call him.

You must remain at "home base." Call him no more than two times. He may not hear you the first time. But if he does not respond after your second call, go to the place where he is playing and switch him back to "home base." If he runs farther away after your initial call, then the switching will be more lengthy and painful and it will take him longer to reach "home base."

Too many new mothers miss this invaluable opportunity to teach this first lesson of obedience to their children. When you call your child and he refuses to come and starts playing the game of catch me if you can, he is playing a dangerous game. You must refuse to participate. At this crucial time, you must construct the Foundation Bridge of obedience over which your child must safely pass until he is grown. If you fail to lay this cornerstone, your obedience bridge will always be shaky and one day may completely collapse.

Create a Home for Your Switch

When your toddler disobeys, he must be disciplined on the spot or he will be unable to associate discipline with his transgression. For that reason you must have a handy place to keep your switch. Store it out of your child's reach on a high shelf. You may select a little animal figurine that will guard the switch to keep it from falling off the shelf. Your little one will quickly learn where the home is for your switches and will develop a wholesome respect for that location. He will learn to mind so that the rod will stay with "Myke the Mouse" (in our house it was Myrtle the Turtle) rather than in the hand of his mother.

8. CONQUER YOUR CHILD'S WILL AND DO IT EARLY

This eighth step in conquering your child's will and doing it early is a *must* for every new mother to learn and she must be ready to implement it when the proper time comes.

Susannah Wesley has been recorded as one of history's most successful women at the task of child rearing. She was a bonafide obedience winner. Susannah reared nineteen children, two of them were John and Charles, who were great religious leaders. Here is Mrs. Wesley's philosophy:

"When turned a year old (and some before), my children were taught to fear the rod and to cry softly. I insist upon conquering the will of children early. In order to form the minds of children, the first thing to be done is to conquer their wills and bring them to an obedient temper." 11

What she means by conquering the will is this. At some point, your child is going to stubbornly match his will against yours. This is a time when he wants his way badly enough that he is willing to test your word to prove if it is genuine or counterfeit. He will be willing to endure additional pain to see if he can win by being stronger and more determined than you. Your little one may already have a fair idea of whether or not you have the will to enforce your instructions.

A permissive mother once said: "I would not want to kill my child's will." But notice, Susannah did not say kill the will. She said conquer the will. There is a difference between killing and conquering a child's will. When you conquer your child's will, he readily and willingly submits to your facts when they are in conflict with his own. The child has a will, but he learns the will of his parent must take precedence.

Thank You, God, for a Mother Made of Pure Gold

My mother reared six children, and I have heard her say many times, "There is a conquering time in the life of every child," She clearly remembered the day she conquered my stubborn spirit.

I was in my early formative years. Our family was seated at the table for lunch. I accidentally or purposely, probably the latter, dropped a piece of bread on the floor. My mother knew her subject and stated her fact. She said, "You get down and pick the bread up." I just looked at her. Since I was so young, she repeated her fact again to be sure I understood. I looked at the bread and then at her, but I still refused to budge.

Observing my defiant attitude, she promptly removed me from the table and took me to the bedroom and disciplined me soundly.

We returned to the table, she put me in my chair and again stated her fact, "Now, you get down and pick the bread up." Through my tears, I still stubbornly refused.

She removed me from the table again and administered another dose of firm discipline. She brought me back to the table, put me on my chair and again said, "Now, you get down and pick the bread up." I still adamantly refused to mind her. In defiance, I looked at the bread and back at her and continued to challenge her authority.

By that time the majority of mothers would have surrendered, and said, "This is not going to work. I will have to accept this situation or try something else."

I have thanked the Lord many times that I had a mother made of pure gold. She was more determined than I was and was not going to allow her baby to dictate the facts to her.

We made a third, fourth, and possibly (she did not remember for sure) a fifth trip to the bedroom where I was disciplined. Later, when she described the conquering moment, she said it was such an unnerving experience that she was amazed to learn that I had no memory of it.

Mother finally won and conquered my will. She brought me back to the table, told me to pick the bread up, and I crawled down from my chair, picked it up and placed it in her hand. She said that from that moment she never had trouble getting me to mind her.

Of course, through the years I, like any child, needed occasional "reminders." But I knew when my mother said something, she meant it and she would not tolerate my ignoring her facts.

Like thousands of winners, my mother never earned an M.A. or Ph.D. degree. Neither was her house decorated with trophies and souvenirs that she won by doing other things. But, because she exercised a sacrificial, strict love, Mother left a positive, constructive influence on her children. Now, as adults all six of us "call her blessed." Proverbs 31:28

Would You Believe, Eighteen Months?

To illustrate how early this conquering time may come, one young mother relates this story about her eighteen-month-old son:

"I had just bathed our son. Bath time was always a playful and loving experience for him. He had been walking for several months; so after we finished his bath, I took him down from the dressing counter so he could roam while I completed some additional tasks. Instead of roaming, he decided to open the cabinet doors and examine the items under the sink. Our bathroom and his dressing area were in our basement and I was soon ready to take him upstairs to the main floor. When he started getting out sponges, towels, and bars of soap from under the sink, I told him, 'Put them back and shut the door.'

"He was not talking much at this age, but he understood what I meant. He hesitated momentarily but continued with his fascinating project. I told him a second time, but he paid no attention. By that time, I was finished with my work and was ready to go. After his refusal to follow my spoken fact, I lowered his pajamas, disciplined one side of his leg firmly, and repeated, 'Put those things back and shut the door.' He cried as if his heart were broken but made no move to do as he was told.

"I disciplined him again, and the second time he was chastised he cried even more loudly. This time, however, he braced his back and shook his head back and forth defiantly, meaning NO. The third time, I worked on his other leg, since the first one had already had a thorough going over. Again, he expressed extreme distress, but continued in his braced position and continued to shake his head back and forth NO. It took four sessions of very sound discipline to conquer his will. Finally, he got down, hurriedly put everything back in the cabinet, and shut the door.

"We then went upstairs. I rocked him, held him close, and told him that 'Mommy loves you, but you must mind me.' He sniffled a while and soon fell sound asleep.

"My husband had heard all of this commotion in the basement, but did not interfere. He asked me about it later, and fully supported me in teaching our son to obey me."

9. CHASTENING IS AN "EVENT"

For years I used the term "spank" or "spanking" to describe the act of chastening a child. I no longer use that term. The dictionary definition of "spank" or "spanking" is to slap or strike on the buttocks with the open hand as a punishment or a series of slaps on the buttocks given as punishment. Many people visualize a spanking as a scene in which an "out of control" adult strikes a child repeatedly with his hands.

In *Training Up a Child*, I do not recommend slapping or striking a child with your hands.   If a child is acting foolish or defiant, or refuses to follow your instructions, he should be *chastened* by God's method. *"Chasten they son while there is hope, and let not thy soul spare for his crying."* Proverbs19:18 *"Foolishness is bound in the heart of a child; but the rod of correction shall drive it far from him."* Proverbs 22:15 Notice, it is the rod that the Bible endorses.

The ninth fact that must be understood and practiced to gain obedience is that chastening is an "event."

"A young mother was ironing, and her little one kept getting too close around her feet. She knew her subject. He was not sleepy, hungry, or sick, but was behaving in an annoying manner to occupy his time. She swatted at him a few times and told him to leave her alone, but he refused to mind.

"Grandpa was sitting nearby in his rocking chair, reading the paper. He had indirectly been watching his daughter's ordeal. Finally, he lowered his glasses and said, 'Sandra, to chasten a child takes an "event." You are simply abusing that child." 12

The next time her child did not mind, she marched him to the bedroom and they had an "event" and the "event" worked.

Steps to Having an "Event"

The next time your child does not follow your spoken facts, have an "event." To impose discipline, here are the seven steps you will need to follow:

(1) *Get a rod.* Go to a tree and choose a rod that is fitting to the age and size of your child. A fresh one that is limber is far more effective than one that is old and brittle. When your children are older and need an occasional "reminder," make them get their own rod. If you do not have trees in your yard, go to a park and collect rods ahead of time and store them in your freezer. They will stay fresh and flexible for months.

(2) *Impose discipline inside your house in a private room.* A child's self-esteem is important and he should always be treated with respect. When he is disobedient this is a matter between the two of you, and discipline should not be administered before friends, or family. Never chasten a child in public! Regardless of whether or not an observer knows the details of your child's misconduct the human psyche generates sympathy for a child who is punished. There are adults who find it intolerable to witness a child being disciplined. Never chasten your child in the yard. Take him in the house and to a private room before you make corrections.

It is an axiom that "children act in public the way they are allowed to act at home." If you consistently administer "on the spot" discipline to your toddler, he will be well behaved and you will be proud of his conduct when he is in public.

Occasionally, when children are older, they are tempted to take advantage of their parents in the presence of company. They imagine that when company surrounds them, you will overlook mischief. On those rare occasions it may be necessary to postpone your child's "reminder" until you get home. If you do not forget to discipline him, he will exercise better judgment the next time he is with company.

(3) *Express disapproval of the action.* Say, "I love you too much to allow this kind of behavior. This will help you remember not to let this happen again."

(4) *Administer the rod thoroughly on the bottom and legs.* Always remember, "*to spare not for his crying.*" Proverbs 19:18. The child's age, attitude, and offense will determine the number of times you apply the rod. A good rule is to administer no more than a half-dozen imprints at each session.

Remember this warning. *Never* allow older siblings to discipline younger ones. It should be a firm rule that this is not allowed. All of your children must learn respect for the same authority - - yours. They are not authorities for one another.

(5) *Take the child back to finish your spoken word.* Never drop the subject or the switch until your child complies with your spoken word. If it takes two, three, or more of these switching sessions, stick with discipline until your child is ready to finish what you ordered him to do. If you do not give up, he will give in.

(6) *After sufficient time has elapsed and your child has a submissive spirit, take him into your arms and express your love.* In Chapter Six I stressed that you should not give sympathy to your child when your husband disciplines him. After you discipline your child, you allow time for his desire for acceptance to work. If you give immediate sympathy after correction, you may leave the notion that you were wrong instead of him.

Let your child warm up to you and then receive him again into your good graces. Go on with your work. If it takes him half a day to warm up to you, give him the time he needs. Once you see that he is repentant, express your love.

The question is often asked, "Should you allow children to comfort each other after discipline has been administered?" The answer is "No!" Children giving immediate love and sympathy to each other after discipline can become a problem, especially when there is a baby in the family. It is difficult for older children to see their little brother or sister receive correction.

As soon as Mother puts the rod down, their first inclination is to pick up the toddler and console him. This must not be allowed. The older children must be told they will be chastened themselves if they intervene by comforting a sibling who has been disciplined.

(7) *Forgive!* Once discipline is over, and the child has repented, do not bring up the transgression again. Return to your normal loving relationship.

What an "Event" Is Not

I remind you once more that hitting or slapping a child on the head or upper portions of his body is not an acceptable way to administer discipline. This sort of treatment will cause the child to disrespect your authority. It will anger him and may eventually cause him to strike you back.

If you have the foolish habit of banging and swinging sudden blows with your hand at your children, tie your hands. You and your children will be better off.

There are cases of adults who are deaf or have a hearing impairment because they were struck on the head when they were children. I have witnessed mothers slap their children in the mouth when they were sassy and say, "I believe in punishing the area from which the disrespect came."

The soundest advice for any young couple is to NEVER strike your children anywhere on the head or upper portion of their bodies. ALWAYS discipline with a rod on the buttocks or legs.

There is a small exception. Even though we should never slap or hit our children on the head or upper body, at times a firm hand swat on the bottom and a whispered warning are effective cautions and very much in order. If you are in worship, or in the store shopping, and your child is unimpressed with the importance of being quiet or exhibiting good manners, a firm swat will often be all that is necessary to remind him that if he does not settle down, he can expect an "event" when he gets home.

If you will curl up a little switch and place it inside your purse before you leave home, that will also encourage your little one to behave in public. Many children have been inspired to be reverent during worship when they knew their mother had instant access to a rod and would exit the services to a private place and use it if necessary.

A Word of Encouragement

Mothers, it is while you are on "watch" all day that most of this training must take place. You must be the one who is with your child to "nip in the bud" any acts of rebellion or wrongdoing. You must not allow disobedience to take root in your child. If you do a good job of nurturing and training while Daddy is away making the living, when he arrives home, the time spent with his child will be pleasant for all.

After a child is taught to be obedient from birth to six, his foundation is set. Having "events" after the "negative and disciplining" years will seldom be necessary. Explaining to a child what is proper and improper will be almost all that will be necessary during the "learning years" from six to twelve. (Read Chapters 7 & 8 in the Addendum)

It will encourage you to know that after an obedient child passes through his "learning years," his parents can look back and count on the fingers of one hand the times they ever had to have an "event" or give a "reminder."   Instead, they will have built mountains of glorious memories with their happy, well-behaved child.

When a child enters the adolescent years, you must let him take center stage.   You will still need to prompt and guide, but much of your guidance will be from behind the scenes. (Read Chapter 9 on Adolescence in the Addendum)

10. THE SWITCH ALSO SWEETENS SOUR ATTITUDES

If your child is older and you have just learned the TUAC principles and desire to practice them, your home will undergo a drastic change. But you follow the same steps of becoming an authority for an eight-year-old as you do for a two-year-old.

One of my former students studied TUAC when her youngest child was eleven years old. She told me that, in order to prepare her daughter, she explained the changes she was going to make. She told her about the class she was taking and confessed that she had been wrong about shouting at her daughter. She promised her child that she was going to change, and she did.

She started giving her facts once and following up with proof. Her child adjusted. One night their family had guests for dinner. When it was time for her eleven-year-old to go to bed, she told her once and her daughter immediately obeyed.   The company was impressed and commented, "You told her only one time and she obeyed you," as if it were unusual for them to see a child willingly cooperate and follow parents' instructions.

With children of any age you need to watch their attitudes. A child may physically yield to your requests but express resentment with a nasty attitude. He may pout, slam doors, go into seclusion, or exhibit some other subtle sign of defiance.

Never tolerate a defiant attitude. If your child goes out the door and slams it, call him back and make him close it, again and again if necessary until he can shut it softly.

There is nothing that will sweeten a sour attitude more quickly than a switch. Apply it the same as you did to gain initial compliance with your authority.

A Final Word About Excessive Crying

One last word about excessive crying. Now and then, after a child has been disciplined he will cry legitimately and then continue with forced, angry crying. This is another indication of an unsubmissive spirit. This sort of wailing is another avenue to express frustration or to gain your sympathy. If it is allowed to continue, the child will eventually develop an unpleasant whining disposition. After you have disciplined, the crying should subside. Do not permit prolonged crying. Simply state, "You HUSH that crying right now, or I will give you something more to cry about." And if he does not obey promptly, discipline him again.

The problem of unnecessary and excessive crying can begin early. An older mother in a TUAC class shared some very helpful advice that a doctor had given her. Her doctor's advice coincides with Dr. Denmark's counsel of putting a newborn to bed to sleep through the night. This mature mother said she felt sorry for new mothers who were constantly worn out from being kept up half the night with a crying baby.

She continued: "When my husband and I had our first child, I was worn out getting up and down with her all night. I would feed her, make sure she was warm and dry, but as soon as I put her in bed and turned out the lights, she would start to cry. Being a new mother, I was fearful that something was wrong. But as soon as I returned to her room, turned the light on, and picked her up, my baby would stop crying.

"On my next visit I told our doctor about my baby's puzzling behavior. He advised me that the next time this happened, to be sure to check the facts. Make certain the baby is not hurting, is fed, dry and warm, and after that, put her in bed and let her *'cry it out.' Don't go in and pick her up!*

"The first night we let our baby *'cry it out,'* my husband could not stand it. He had to leave the house, but I just plugged my ears. Our baby cried for forty-five minutes.

"The next night there was an encore performance, but this time the crying lasted only thirty minutes. The third night our newborn still had not given up, but she only cried about twenty minutes. By the fourth night her crying spell was down to ten minutes, and by the fifth night she had quit crying altogether.

"From that day forward, we were able to put our baby to bed, turn out the light, and enjoy a restful night's sleep."

My student suggested if a new mother would listen to that doctor's advice she would save herself from many sleepless nights, and prevent her child from developing a disagreeable and cranky disposition. (Read Chapter 10 in the Addendum, Gem #3)

Troubles With Junior

Junior bit the meter man;
   Junior kicked the cook.
Junior's anti-social now - -
   (according to the book)

Junior smashed the clock and lamp,
   Junior hacked the tree.
(Destructive trends are treated
   In chapters two and three!)
Junior threw his meat at Mom.
   Junior screamed for more.
(Notes on self-assertiveness
   Are found in chapter four.)

Junior tossed his shoes and socks
   Out into the rain.
(Negation, that, and normal - -
   Disregard the same.)

Junior set Dad's shirt afire,
   Salted Grandpop's tea;
(That's to gain attention.
   See page 163).

Grandpop seized a rod,

Yanked Junior across his knee!
(Grandpop hasn't read a book
Since 1893.)

--Author Unknown

ASSIGNMENT

1. Search for a winning mother this week. Ask her about the principles she followed in rearing her children. If you have a particular problem, ask her advice.
2. Open your Bible to the book of Proverbs. Take a pen and underline the following scriptures:
    Proverbs 13:24
    "   19:18
    "   20:11
    "   22:15
    "   23:13-14
    "   29:15 and 17
3. Start teaching your children respect for your authority immediately. If they are older, explain to them the change that you are going to make, and be sure to keep your word!
4. Make a fancy bookmarker for your Bible; write the words, Chastening is an "Event," and write the seven steps of discipline to help you remember.
5. Place a card on your kitchen windowsill that reads:

To Be My Child's Authority
1. I must *know* my subject.
2. I must *give* my facts (one time, never more than twice)
3. I must *prove* my facts.

Section II

Independence

and

Good Habits

Work

INDEPENDENCE

Fly the Flag After the Victory is Won

Chapter Nine
Independence

In the previous chapter I emphasized the importance of a child learning to follow his parent's instructions. In addition, you learned that discipline produces wisdom. (Proverbs 29:15). Wisdom, then, leads the child to obedience. Obedience is essential for children's protection, security, and well being. Equally important, when a child does as he has been told, his cooperation and pleasantness produce harmony in your home.

However, obedience alone will not produce a well-rounded and responsible child. If a child's instructions and orders must always be dictated to him, he will be helpless in situations in which initiative is needed to achieve success. Gradually, he must learn to be independent, to think for himself and to make judgments when Daddy and Mother are not present.

What Is Independence?

Independence is "freedom from the control, influence, support, or help of another." Birth is one's first step toward independence. When a baby's umbilical cord is cut, he is severed from the protection he received within his mother during the previous nine months. The newborn has entered into a vast world in which he is no longer physically tied to his mother.

In an autocratic family, the children will not achieve complete separation from their parents until they leave home and establish homes of their own. Even then they will not be completely independent of their parents. Remember, "freedom from influence" is part of independence, but the influence of one's parents will be with him as long as he lives.

Be Prepared

One of the most valuable gifts that parents can bestow is independence. When a child enrolls in college, enlists in the military, takes a job far from home, or leaves his father and mother to get married, parents want that child to be prepared. It is an honor to parents to produce a child who successfully becomes a responsible adult and becomes a valuable asset to his or her community. Independence is not achieved by accident. It is a goal that must be planned and worked for.

What can parents do to assure themselves that their child will grow up to be an independent, responsible citizen, employee, marriage partner, and one day a successful parent himself? I will suggest four ways you can gradually grant small amounts of freedom and help your child develop the self-reliance, which he must have to become a responsible adult.

I have titled this chapter, Independence, "Fly the flag after the victory is won."

1. LOVE HIM AND MAKE HIM OBEY

You will be relieved to know that you are already on your way to helping your child achieve independence if you are doing your homework, because the first steps are to love him and teach him to obey you.

I re-emphasize what it is to love. Often people erect a facade of sentimentality and call it love. Parents who accept this distorted view of love will permit a child to have his own foolish way, grant every whim within their power to give and excuse every form of their child's bad behavior. This permissiveness is not love. Permissiveness is not only destructive, but it will never produce healthy independence.

Autocratic parents must have sacrificial love. A sacrificial love takes much self-discipline on the parent's part. It requires an inward strength that will help them stick with what is right and insist their children do the same. A love that demands obedience will build a child who accepts responsibility for his behavior and actions. Sacrificial love will hold a child accountable for his actions day after day. Only parents who seek the best for their children will devote the time and effort necessary to guarantee that their children will develop self-reliance.

2. RETREAT! LET HIM OCCUPY HIS TERRITORY

The second step a parent must take to help his child obtain independence is to retreat and let him occupy territory he has conquered. The American flag reminds the world of the freedoms and independence we enjoy as American citizens. It is through many battles that have been fought and won that our freedoms have been protected. If we take our freedoms for granted or abuse them, Old Glory will eventually be torn down, and another flag will be hoisted in its place.

Likewise, our children fight the smaller battles of life and win worthy victories as they grow into well-balanced adults. When they master a skill, whether small or great, they deserve the right to proclaim their victory and exercise it freely on their journey to self-reliance. The following are five steps autocratic parents should remember in granting a portion of independence to their children.

When a Child conquers a Physical Skill of Life

1. Fly his flag.
2. Lavish the praise.
3. Have a celebration.
4. Parents, retreat.
5. Let the child occupy his new territory.

Three Examples

Let's consider three examples in which a child makes *physical* achievements. For months and years he has depended on his parents for help, but now he is capable of doing more things for himself.

Example 1 - Baby learns to walk! From birth to between nine and thirteen months, a child must depend on his parents to carry him everywhere he goes. Little by little, he begins to develop his strength and balance and finally attempts to walk on his own. In his first efforts, he will often stumble and fall. Soon the day arrives when he lets go of Mother's hand and toddles across the room by himself. When the baby wins this small battle, what should his parents do? They should grant him freedom to exercise his ability to walk. They should (a) *Fly his victory flag.* (b) *Praise the baby.* When you give praise or show attention, psychologists say, you reinforce the action. Baby will be eager to repeat the performance because of all the attention that is lavished upon him. (c) *Have a celebration.* Clapping, cheering, squeezing, and hugging will make the baby feel so important that he will love demonstrating his new skill. (d) *Parents, retreat.* No longer must Daddy and Mother carry baby everywhere he goes. (e) *Let him occupy his new territory.* The baby can now walk almost everywhere he needs to go.

Example 2 - Three-year-old James learns to put his shirt and pants on. For approximately forty-two months, Mother has dressed and undressed James two, three, or more times a day. For the past few weeks, he has been interested in learning which are the front and back of his shirt and pants, how zippers and buttons work, and which arm goes in which sleeve. Finally the day arrives when James is able to put it all together. He proudly tells Mommy what he can do, and shows her what a big boy he is getting to be. He can put his clothes on all by himself! What is his mother to do? She must (a) *Fly his victory flag.* (b) *Praise James.* Give him approval and attention. This will reinforce James's accomplishments and he will want to repeat it tomorrow. (c) *Have a celebration.* At dinnertime, Mother should tell Daddy and all the family what James did and what a big boy he is getting to be. She may fix his favorite dish of chicken and noodles to celebrate the event. (d) *Now, Mother must retreat.* No longer will she be required to help James put on his shirt and pants. He has proven that he is capable of doing it alone. (e) *Let James occupy his new territory.* Allow James to exercise his new skill freely.

Example 3 - Five-year-old Alicia learns to tie her shoes. For the past five years, it has been mother's job to tie Alicia's shoes. One day Alicia becomes interested in learning the art of tying shoes and starts practicing. Mother patiently demonstrates and explains each step in tying shoestrings. The morning arrives when Alicia squeals with delight, "Look! I tied my shoe all by myself!" What is Alicia's mother to do? She will (a) *Fly Alicia's flag.* (b) *Praise her* for this marvelous accomplishment. (That is reinforcing the action.) (c) *Celebrate! Hug, squeeze, and have a love feast for Alicia.* (d) *Mother must retreat.* (e) *Let Alicia occupy this territory.* Now Alicia must always tie her own shoes.

All of these children have learned responsibility, and are achieving small portions of independence. Now, "I do not need Mommy to carry me, dress me, and tie my shoes, because I can do it by myself."

3. INSIST! MAKE HIM OCCUPY HIS TERRITORY

Now that your child's flag is flying and he has had a victory celebration, you should step aside and insist that he take complete charge of his new territory. This step is essential in helping your child achieve greater independence.

I must caution you that children will be children. After the victory celebration is over and the new wears off, they have an annoying tendency to be lazy. It is much easier to let Mama help, and sometimes, I might add, it is much faster and easier on Mama to take charge again and perform tasks that should be done by her child. Do not do that! Instead of assuming your children's responsibilities for them, if necessary get your switch out and see to it that they occupy their own territory. Expect from your children the best performance they can give. They can perform the task. They have proved it. Do not permit your children to retreat. Never follow the path of least resistance by surrendering to them. Remind your children, "You cannot be an American and say I can't." Amer I Can!

Our Pattern Is Taking Shape

Observe how the TUAC pattern is taking shape. Remember what you have learned about how one achievement sets the stage for the next. Love comes before obedience, and obedience must be learned before independence can be fully attained.

If your children do not respect your authority, how are you going to get James to put his pants and shirt on if he happens not to want to put them on? Or how will you succeed in getting Alicia to tie her shoestrings if she is not in the mood?

Many times something like this happens - - James and Alicia know that Mommy is in a hurry and everyone is running late trying to get to worship on time. They reason, "If I stall long enough, Mother will do my job for me." And, sad to say, that is often what happens. Always remember that you are hurting your child's respect for authority and hindering him from developing independence when you give in and do his jobs for him.

Please, Daddy, Let Me Learn to Milk

How well I remember as a child watching my big brothers milk the cows. I wanted so much to learn how to milk. I could hardly wait until my daddy let me take a bucket and sit down on the milk stool. Finally, when I was old enough, he let me sit down close to our most gentle cow and he showed me how to milk.

My basic motivation for wanting to learn this skill was that I had seen my brothers squirt milk in a long stream across the barn to the place where the cats were lined up. They would stand on their hind legs and leap in the air to catch the flying milk. I loved cats and I wanted to feed the cats that way, too.

I worked and worked trying to squeeze a stream of milk. Pretty soon, I got the hang of it and that first stream of milk splashed in the bottom of the bucket. I could milk! My brothers really had a victory celebration. They raised my flag, praised me greatly, and they moved over. There was one more milker now!

It did not take me long to learn that it was not all play but that milking cows was time- consuming and hard work. Typical of all children, I grew tired of milking. It was not my favorite way of spending my time. But during the time I was in high school, my father made me occupy the territory of the milking barn when he needed me. My brothers did the majority of the milking, but in the summertime, when they were on tractors or bringing in the crops, my sister and I were the milkmaids. Because we had conquered this territory, our parents saw to it that we continued to occupy the space.

You Can't Make Me Do It!

Children often speak disrespectfully to their parents. It is not uncommon to hear a child obstinately tell a parent in response to a command, "*You can't make me do it!*" When a child is sassy, if parents administer *strict love*, the child can be made to do as he was told.

However, there are things you cannot make your child do. Your young child knows this is true and the more you try to force him, the more he will show you that he can win.

There are three functions of his body over which he has absolute control. *You cannot make your child eat, sleep, or eliminate.* You may put food before him, but you cannot force him to eat. Furthermore, he can lie awake and refuse to go to sleep and his bowel and bladder actions are completely under his control. Attempting to force a child to perform a task over which he has complete bodily control is the point at which a new mother must learn that her child knows the subject better than she does and that attempts to use force are futile.

Parents make a serious mistake if they do not stay a step ahead of their child in these three matters in which the child is born with independence.

You Can Help Him Want To Do It!

Dr. Denmark warns us about these three plagues of childhood independence. She also teaches parents how to take control. If you will follow her schedules, you will discover how you can help your child want to eat, sleep, and eliminate.

How can you help your child want to eat? Your child will eat if you will allow him to get hungry. And he will get hungry if you forbid him to eat snacks and drink juice between his three regular meals. You can also help him build his appetite by sending him outside to play. Study Dr. Denmark's schedules to learn the proper portions of food to give a child according to his age. And remember, if he will not eat, take his plate away and offer him food at the next meal. When you manage a child's nutrition in this fashion, you are the one in control.

How can you help your child want to sleep? Your child will want to sleep when he is tired. Awaken him early for breakfast and allow him to play hard all day. After his second birthday there should be no more daytime naps. Follow your schedule carefully and have dinner the same time each evening. Make sure your child is fed, bathed, and in bed by seven o'clock. He needs twelve hours of restful sleep. And then he will be ready to play the next day.

How can you help your child want to eliminate? If you feed your child a wholesome diet, he will form healthy bowel and bladder habits. If you serve him three meals a day, properly spaced, and he eats three proteins, starches (consisting of whole grains), fruits, vegetables, and water to drink, constipation and urinary infections will not be a problem. Eliminating cow's milk from your child's diet will help his digestive system and in multitudes of other ways. (Read Chapter 10, Gem #4 in the Addendum)

If you will follow Dr. Denmark's method of caring for your child, no battles should ever arise over your child's three independent territories of eating, sleeping, and eliminating.

Tell Us How To Potty Train

Since I am addressing the subject of a child's control of his bodily functions, I will briefly discuss toilet training. For many years I have searched for an effective method for potty training. But I have not discovered a "magic formula." If there were one, I should have learned about it by now.

The counsel I have received from Dr. Denmark, "the winners" and my personal experience about potty training is this--*exercise extreme patience regarding the potty.*

Before a child can be successfully potty-trained, his central nervous system must be mature. The average age for this maturity is about twenty-eight months. Little girls seem to mature faster than boys and are often potty-trained by age two. Little boys may not be completely trained before age three or later.

Mothers of earlier generations had greater incentive to remove their baby's diapers as soon as possible than mothers do today. Rinsing and cleaning dirty diapers without running water in the house was a difficult chore. Those mothers completely removed the cloth diaper, closely watched their child, and kept a potty close at hand. Pioneer women lived in smaller houses with wooden floors. These floors were much easier to wipe up than carpet. This made it easier while children were being potty- trained. Most babies do not like to be wet. When those mothers removed the diaper, the baby disliked the wetness they experienced when there was no diaper to catch the urine. The mother would talk kindly to them, and as quickly as possible set them on the potty. Soon the baby made the association of how to avoid getting wet. These wise mothers also kept a can close by for their little boys. They would let him urinate in the can and the little fellow liked the amusing sound he could make when voiding.

Bowel movements will come with regularity when one feeds a baby by Dr. Denmark's instructions. Mothers can learn the rhythm of their child's body and about when his bowels will move. The moment she sees her baby straining she should immediately set him on the potty.

Reading a book to your toddler on the subject of potty training is another good way to introduce him to the concept. There are many books from which to choose. Go to the library and pick the one you like best. Use that rocking chair! Put your "littlest angel" in your lap while you read the book. Begin talking to him or her about becoming a big boy or girl and how they need to stop wearing diapers and put on pretty panties or big boy underwear.

Bed-Wetting

Recently I picked up a brochure in a doctor's reception room on the subject of bed-wetting (enuresis). Families who have a child with enuresis try to deal silently with the problem. They believe their child will outgrow urinating in his sleep, and most do. Other, well meaning, parents become frustrated with the daily chore of cleaning up the child and the bed and use harsh discipline. I believe this is a serious mistake.

There is a range of suggestions to explain why some children suffer with enuresis. "Arousal dysfunction" (deep sleep) where the child does not wake up to normal stimuli is one plausible suggestion. Others believe being allergic to milk and milk products is another cause of this problem. Small bladders may also be to blame. Heredity fits into the list of culprits as well. If a child has one parent who was a bed- wetter, he has a 50% chance of being a bed-wetter. If both of his parents were bed-wetters, he has a 75% chance of being a bed-wetter.

Here is a profile of a child who may be a bed-wetter. He is extremely bright, is affectionate, and has a sensitive personality. Some tend to be overactive, unable to sit still, have a poor attention span or daydream. Teachers will sometimes say, "She's an extremely bright child, but doesn't work up to her potential. She could do better."

One group has studied the problem of bed-wetting for years. They found that children seldom know why they wet; they simply know they cannot help it and fear someone will find out about their problem. They say that bed-wetting is the result of a sleep disorder. The person who has this problem is sleeping incorrectly, and therefore cannot awaken to his bladder signal.

Parents should exercise patience with a child who is a bed-wetter. Avoid embarrassing him, and work patiently with the child to solve the problem. Work with your pediatrician and keep up on the latest developments that may help your child-overcome enuresis.

Let's Review

To this point, I have discussed children's ability to develop their physical skills. I have advised you not to push them, but to let them learn at their own pace. When they show an interest in developing a skill, encourage and praise the accomplishment made. Once children can do a chore themselves, the parents must retreat and let them exercise their independence. When they get lazy (and all children will) and do not enjoy making their beds, washing and drying the dishes, sweeping the garage, mowing the lawn, weeding the garden, folding the papers for the paper route, or hanging their clothes in the closet, parents must step in and strictly insist that they do their jobs. Never allow them to be quitters.

Again, I caution mothers never to allow a power struggle to begin over eating, sleeping, or eliminating. A child has command over his bodily functions, but his mother has control over his environment. By your following a regular schedule the child will be hungry enough to eat on time, and tired and sleepy enough to go to bed on time. When he is fed natural nutritious food, he will not need to be coerced to sit on the potty, or given harsh laxatives. Instead, his bowels will move naturally and with ease.

Helping children develop physical skills is relatively easy. They are, by nature, curious and want to try every new thing they see their parent do.

We are now ready, however, to launch into the area of teaching mental independence to our children. This is a much harder task. Even after children have conquered many physical feats, their mental judgments are still not mature. Now we must proceed to the next step in helping our children mature to greater independence.

4. USE YOUR HEAD TO HELP DEVELOP HIS HEAD

Apart from his being openly disobedient to your spoken word, there are many situations in which your child must function alone. He will be in positions where he will be by himself when he must make a decision. He may have fought, won, and have his flag flying as far as many physical skills are concerned, but, without further help, he still lacks the mental ability that he needs to make judgments about how to exercise those skills properly.

For Example

Physically, a Child Can	*Mentally, He Does Not Have the Judgment to Know*
1. Learn to walk.	1. Not to walk into the street.
2. Dress himself.	2. What apparel is proper to wear on all occasions.
3. Climb trees.	3. Not to climb in the neighbor's prized peach tree.
4. Ride a bike.	4. Where and how far he can ride his bike safely.

5. Take a bath.	5. When or how often to bathe.

Learning to be mentally responsible is a slower process than learning physical skills; and parents need to keep in mind that "a child's desire for freedom runs ahead of his capacity for freedom." [1]

Modern Philosophers versus God

In *Training Up a Child* you have been taught that parents should impose discipline on their children to punish them for disobedience and disrespect. In order to correct rebellious behavior "chastening is the first response and not the last resort." [2]   Imposing physical discipline teaches children respect for parental authority. To deny that God commands' parents to chasten a disobedient child is to deny the Bible. God knows this act of "strict love" works and when parents obey Him, their children will obey them.

However, many modern philosophers refuse to accept God's instructions to use a rod to correct a child. They label chastisement "child abuse." They have "sounded their trumpets" so loudly that many parents are afraid to use a rod to make their children mind. Instead of putting their trust in God they choose to be influenced by these misguided pedagogues of permissiveness.

In the remainder of this chapter I am going to introduce you to the use of environmental control, deprivation, isolation, natural and logical consequences as useful methods of discipline.

I emphasize that these are all effective means of discipline for children who make foolish mistakes due to their immature judgements.

Some modern child psychologists err by advocating these passive methods of discipline to the complete exclusion of the use of the rod. This is a tragic mistake and autocratic parents must not allow themselves to be influenced by them.

A. USE ENVIRONMENTAL CONTROL

Exercising environmental control is an example of the adage, "an ounce of prevention is worth a pound of cure." By careful planning, wise parents can remove dangerous objects before they cause harm to a child, or before the child breaks or damages some valuable trinket or decoration. Placing gates at the top of stairs, storing valuables, keeping guns and medicines out of a child's reach, and providing safe toys to occupy play time are methods that should be used to protect a child.

Earlier I emphasized the value of using environmental control with your crawler and toddler, but for emphasis I will stress it once more. I do not think it is necessary for a new mother to put everything out of her baby's reach and leave a bare living room. Neither is it wise for her to allow a beautiful delicate figurine, which has been in her family for four generations, to be left exposed on the coffee table to test Junior's obedience. A crawler or toddler is capable of learning that a few items (very few) are "pretty pretties" or "no-no's" and should be left alone. If, however, everything he can reach is censored because it is a "pretty pretty" or a "no-no," you will be scolding or chastening your baby constantly. He will be afraid and you will suppress his curious and adventuresome spirit that leads him to explore, examine, and learn. Remember the saying, "many temptations cause many transgressions." Teach your child that a few things are forbidden; then exercise environmental control and arrange everything else so that he can function freely and comfortably.

Substitute a "Yes" in Place of a "No"

Christian families should begin when their children are small to balance their "no-no's" with a "yes-yes." You begin practicing that concept when you say, "You may not play with the glass candy dish, but you may play with this plastic bowl." Or, "You may not get into these drawers and cabinets, but here are special trinkets in these other drawers and cabinets just for you to play with."

Distraction is a proven method to help a child forget his frustrations when he is told "no" or to leave an object alone. In a church assembly, a noisy and fretful baby can be quieted quickly if you whisper, "Look what I have in my purse!" Or, to stop a baby's crying, take him to the window and say, "Look at that pretty bird. Let's go outside and see if he will talk to us."

Stop and Evaluate

Autocratic parents should frequently evaluate their home environment. If you find yourself scolding your children for the same offenses, perhaps some changes in surroundings are needed. Perhaps your child continually comes to the table with dirty hands or he knocks his glass over at every meal. You may need to purchase a stepping stool for the bathroom sink so that it is easier for him to reach the soap and turn on the faucet to wash his hands. Or, choose a different size and shape of drinking glasses that are more difficult to tip over.

It is exasperating to find muddy footprints on a freshly mopped floor. Placing foot scrapers and throw rugs at the entrances of your house can save a lot of cleaning and correcting. If a child is developing fear of the dark and frequently awakens you in the night with his crying, place a night light in his bedroom. This often is all that is needed to relieve his fears and help him to rest peacefully.

One year I planned to cut down on back-to-school expenses; so I purchased a cheaper grade of underwear, pants, shirts, blouses, and dresses. That proved to be a frustrating experience! I was kept busy patching and sewing the cheaper clothing. I ended up buying another set of school clothes to finish out the school term. The next year I exercised better environmental control. I purchased the best grade of clothing and fabric I could afford. I double and triple-stitched all seams with my sewing machine. Little patching needed to be done that year, and some of the school clothes were in good enough condition after they were outgrown to pass on to smaller children.

Use your mature judgment and exercise good environmental control. Take an inventory, study problem areas, and see what changes you can put into effect to make your child's environment safe and comfortable.

B. DEPRIVE

Depriving is taking away a privilege when it is necessary.

If parents are con *sist'* ent with their spoken word and always back their facts with proof, they build their children's security and trust for their parents, and at the same time develop a character that their parents can trust. When a child tells his parents something and his information is always accurate, or when he makes promises and consistently caries them out, his parents will begin to have confidence in his word and actions. *When a child proves himself to be trustworthy, he should be fully trusted.*

Once your child proves that he is reliable, fly his flag of honor and trust. He has not only achieved physical independence but now is firmly on the path to the treasured prize of mental independence as well.

The following are five steps autocratic parents should take in relinquishing portions of mental independence to their children.

When a Child Proves That He is Trustworthy
1. Fly his flag.
2. Show confidence.
3. Trust the child's judgment.
4. Praise him.
5. Silently rejoice.

As long as your child exhibits good judgment, trust him in the area in which he has proved himself. Mentally fly his honor flag of trust. In case he should digress and prove himself unworthy, you must *deprive* him of his privilege and lower his flag of honor until his judgment matures. Later, give him another chance to prove himself.

Two Examples

Example 1 - Little Jeremy has physically learned to draw with crayons. His physical flag of skill is flying and, for his age, he can color skillfully. He has coloring books and drawing paper for drawing. For some time the crayons have been stored on a low shelf. He has access to them any time he wants to use them because he has used good judgment in exercising his artistic skills. One day, while playing alone, little Jeremy marks all over his bedroom walls. What is his mother to do? She has flown his flag, expressed trust in him by letting him color with crayons. Now, since Jeremy abused her trust, his flag of honor must be taken down and he should be deprived of his crayons until he has learned he must not abuse his privilege by using them improperly.

Mother must teach Jeremy that he must not scribble on the wall. She must further teach him that his transgression has caused unnecessary work and that the wall will have to be cleaned. Mother should gather cleaning materials and teach him (showing him how) to clean the wall. After he helps repair the damage, give him a few days to think about his transgression. After he has been deprived of his crayons for a reasonable time, give him another chance. Place the crayons back on the low shelf. As long as Jeremy uses good judgment, trust him with the crayons, praise him, and silently rejoice.

Example 2 - John has learned to ride a bike. In his efforts to accomplish this physical skill, he has suffered a few bumps and bruises. Now he can ride well, and his parents have tutored him on the safety rules and told him where he may and may not ride his bicycle. For a long time, John used his bicycle responsibly. One day, when some friends are watching, he gets an irresistible urge to show off for them. In careless exuberance, he rides in front of an oncoming car. The driver slams on his brakes, and the neighbor's rush to their windows to see what has happened. The car barely missed John! What should his parents do? They must take his flag of trust down, park the bicycle and deny him the privilege of its use. After giving John a reasonable time to think about what he has done, give him another chance to prove himself. As long as he uses good judgment, (a) fly his flag, (b) express confidence, (c) trust, (d) praise, and (e) silently rejoice.

Any time children behave in an irresponsible manner parents should make them accept the consequences so that they will be more reliable when their independence is restored. Children who are taught to handle their freedoms in a mature manner will develop into dependable young people who can be trusted to behave wisely when in difficult or challenging situations.

Make Depriving Relevant to the Misbehavior

When parents use deprivation of privileges as a means to help their child achieve more responsible and independent behavior, they should remember to make the deprivation relevant to the misbehavior. It would be foolish, when Jeremy scribbled on the walls with his crayons, to deprive him of his favorite food for dinner; or, when John rode his bicycle in front of a car, to deprive him of his baseball glove. The specific item or privilege a child misuses is the object or activity of which he should be deprived.

No TV for Three Days

One mother, who was faced with the task of keeping her children occupied with constructive projects during their summer vacation, came up with this plan. Her children loved television and, if allowed, would have spent most of their day watching every available program. She knew it was wise to limit children's TV viewing; so in their summer schedules she allowed only one hour of TV viewing a day. They could choose one one-hour show or two thirty-minute programs from a list she made up (censored) from the TV schedule. The rest of their day was occupied with gardening, cleaning, cooking, painting, letter writing, reading, Bible study, library visits, playing, and relaxation.

Their vacation was going smoothly. It was not long, however, until the children's love for TV got the best of them. One day their mother was working in the basement. When their program was over, they did not shut the TV off. When they finally did shut the TV off, they immediately went to explain to mother that the next program that came on was so good they just had to watch it. She listened quietly to their lengthy excuse. When they were finished, she responded, " I understand that it must have been very interesting to you, but the fact remains that you have abused your privilege. For the next three days, there will be no TV at all." The children shed tears of regret, but after they had been deprived of watching television for a reasonable time, they exercised responsibility with their TV viewing for the rest of the summer.

Try Depriving with Your Finicky Eater

Here is a hint to those of you who may have a child who is a finicky eater. This idea has worked for some mothers, and for others it has not. You may want to try it and see if it works for you.

The next time you introduce a different food, deprive your finicky one of his helping. Do not make a scene about it; in fact, do not even mention it. Just do not put any of the food you are introducing on his plate, but serve it to the rest of the family.

It will not take long for him to notice that he was not given his share of the new food. When he recognizes this oversight, he will bring it to your attention by saying, "Mama! You forgot me, I did not get any."

You respond, "Oh, no, honey, I did not forget. I was sure you would not like it; so I did not bother to give you a portion." The thoughts of being deprived of a new tasty food will often bring the rebuttal, "I would like it, Mama. I know I would." You can respond, "Well, all right. I will give you *one* taste and, if you like it, I will be sure to make enough for you next time." Most of the time a child will join the circle of fellowship and discover he really does like the new food.

C. ISOLATE

Children are very gregarious, and to be set apart from everyone else in the family is painful for them. They like to be in the center of the activity for fear they will miss out on something.

There may be other ways of isolating, but I suggest two ways you can temporarily isolate a child from the rest of the family. A child can (1) be sent to his room or (2) be set on a chair.

If your four-year-old is in the back yard and insists on disrupting the other children's play, you can bring him in the house and set him on a chair. Your explanation may be, "Now, when you think you can play nicely, you may go back out and show us." Most of the time, when this condition is given, the child will sit on the chair for about thirty seconds before he is absolutely sure that he is ready to do better. When he rejoins the other children's play, it is usually a repeat performance. If you must bring him in a second time, explain, "This time you must sit on the chair until *I tell you* when you may get up."

For children, a thirty-minute rest on a chair is equivalent to about three hours for an adult. It does give them time, however, to calm down, think, and determine to behave themselves when given their freedom to try again.

One of my older brothers, who is a wonderful Christian man today, laughs when he recalls his childhood. He says the thing he remembers most is the multitude of times he had to sit on a chair. If isolation will help one's son to become as fine a man as my brother, I highly recommend this practical form of correction.

If little brothers are not getting along, isolate them. Put one on a chair in one room and the other on a chair in another room. I did not mention this in my previous example, but if your children will not obey you, you will be helpless in trying to make isolation work. Multitudes of mothers try putting their children on a chair, but the children refuse to stay put. (Remember that obedience must be accomplished before independent responsibility can be achieved.)

D. LET NATURAL CONSEQUENCES WORK FOR YOU

In order for environmental control, depriving, and isolation to be used as effective methods of discipline, parents must be willing to do some careful planning. Exercising natural consequences is much different. There is nothing at all difficult about letting this law work for you. "Natural consequences" means just what the words imply. You have little, if anything to do. Nature takes over and demands that your child pay a price. The natural consequences of some forms of misbehavior are that your child will ultimately pay a very unpleasant price.

Children must learn some things the hard way. All the cautions and warnings in the world from one who is wiser and more experienced will simply be ignored. Unfortunately, many children must learn that a lighted stove is hot and fire burns by touching to see for themselves. Many children do not accept their parents' warning when they tell them, "The little green pepper will burn your mouth!" When the little one takes a bite, he learns more in two seconds than he will learn from repeated warnings. After gulping down a glass of water, he is not eager to try to eat another hot pepper.

Do Not Nag Children to Eat

One of the most common situations in which to use natural consequences is with children who have finicky appetites. Children with poor appetites often will not eat at mealtime.

This should no longer be a problem if you will let natural consequences work for you. Feed your child three well-balanced meals a day, properly spaced, and sitting with the family at the table. According to Dr. Denmark's' instructions, if your child will not eat at mealtime, you must believe that the natural consequences of hunger will not allow your child to starve. If he is hungry enough, he will eat when the next meal is introduced.

When the family sits down to the dinner table, carry on your regular conversations and enjoy the togetherness of the family. While everyone is enjoying the meal, there should be no nagging, "Junior, eat your dinner." When sufficient time has elapsed for dining, the family should excuse themselves from the dinner table. Even if Junior has not touched his meal, calmly remove his plate and dismiss him from the table.

Before bedtime, "natural consequences" will take over. Junior will appeal to your sympathy and start pulling at your heartstrings and plead; "I'm hungry, Mother. May I have something to eat?" When this happens, you must not give in! Explain to him, "I am sorry, but there will be no more eating until Mother fixes the next nutritious meal."

Give him a glass of warm water to drink. Drinking warm water cleanses our bodies as well as helps quench our appetite.

You must never allow eating snacks between meals! Do not even buy them! Save your money and preserve your family's good health!

A "No-Thank-You Helping, Please"

Many grandparents and great-grandparents remember the depression days when food was not plentiful. Others of us understand that it is wasteful to throw food away. Because of these strong beliefs, we may be overly strict and demand, "You must eat everything on your plate!" If a child chooses the size of his own helpings of food, he should not be allowed to waste it. If he consistently takes too much food, in time, natural consequences will teach him to take smaller portions.

If you have the custom of Mother serving the food, this tip may help. Before you dish the food onto the plates, let the children see what you have prepared for the meal. If there is a particular food that is not your child's favorite, he may ask for a "no-thank-you helping." A "no-thank-you helping" is only one scant tablespoonful.

A grandmother once shared this idea with us in a TUAC class. I thought it was such a good idea that I have used it and shared it with my students.

E. USE LOGICAL CONSEQUENCES

Logical consequences are altogether different from natural consequences. With natural consequences, nature leads to the desired results. "Logical consequences" ensue when a choice of outcomes is presented to a child.

Dr. Haim G. Ginott calls this a "Voice and Choice" activity. 3 You give the voice, and the child makes the choice. In Chapter Eight I referred to using logical consequences as a good way to teach little ones to make wise decisions. Give a child a choice between two facts. You might say, "Which of these two dresses would you like to wear today?" Freddie's mother may have inquired, "Which would you like to have for dinner, a hamburger or fried chicken?"

Other examples of the "voice and choice" activity are "Would you like a half slice of toast or a whole slice?" Or, "Would you like a half apple or a whole apple?" *The important thing to remember in using logical consequences is to hold the child responsible for the choice he makes.* If the child chooses a whole slice of bread or a whole apple, make sure he consumes all he asked for and that nothing is wasted. If he made an unwise choice and takes too much, he must suffer the natural consequences. The natural consequences of making a poor choice will help him to have better judgment the next time that he must make a decision.

Three Examples of How To Use Logical Consequences

(1) *Perhaps mealtime is always a headache.* It seems that every evening when dinner is served, some member of the household is absent. You must take time to scout the neighborhood to find a missing child and the family sits down to a cold dinner. It's time to create a logical consequence for the tardy member. Mothers may invent any number of ideas for giving the *Voice*. Here is an example of what you might say: "Greg, I do my best to serve dinner at six o'clock. We are not going to

wait for you, or hunt for you anymore. If you are not at the table on time, we will eat without you and you will miss your dinner." Greg now has a *Choice.* He can choose to be responsible and come to dinner on time, or he can continue in his late habit and miss his dinner.

When parents create logical consequences, it is imperative that they carry through with their word and see that the child reaps the consequence of his choice. If dinnertime is at six o'clock, be sure that it is promptly served at that time. On the days you know that dinner will be delayed or will be earlier, inform Greg ahead of time. The choice to be on time or miss dinner is then left up to Greg.

(2) *Getting off to school in the morning is a problem.* If you are in the habit of nagging and trying to rush your school children to get ready for school, ruining the morning, use logical consequences. *Voice!* "The bus comes at 8:30. From now on, if you are not ready in time to catch the bus, you will walk to school." The children's *Choice!* Be ready and at the bus stop by 8:30 or walk to school and face the principal and teacher if you are late. Mother's responsibility is to furnish a reliable alarm clock, have the children's clothes clean and ready to put on. Be sure to have a nutritious breakfast ready for them to eat, but meeting the school bus on time is strictly the children's responsibility.

One lady in a TUAC class described an older sister who had fallen into the late habit. Her mother decided to put a stop to it. She created a logical consequence that relieved her of bearing the total responsibility for rushing her daughter out the door to school every morning. My class member said, "Sure enough, the first day on the new plan, my sister missed the bus." She was not driven to school, and since it was too far for her to walk, she had to stay home all day. It was not an enjoyable and relaxing day, however. In addition to being assigned hard work to do, she was also ordered to sit down and write a report to her teacher explaining why she had missed school that day. The next morning her mother accompanied her to school and made sure the teacher got the note. The lady said her sister never missed the school bus again.

(3) *Your child is dependent on you to help with her homework.* Jennifer always expects you to sit down and help her with her homework. You made a mistake when she was in the first grade and thought helping her would make her feel more secure in school. Now that she is in the fourth grade, she still thinks her homework is part of your job. Use logical consequences. *Voice!* "I am not going to sit down and help you with your homework any longer. If you do not get it done, you will have to

explain why to your teacher." Her *Choice!* Either get her homework by herself, or face the teacher without it. Your responsibility is to provide a quiet place for her to study and respond by helping her a little if there is something that she does not understand. The rest is left up to her.

Any good instructor will have respect for a fellow instructor. If your child is in trouble with her teacher at school because of laziness or disobedience, you should back the teacher, not your child.

Often school discipline is lax and conditions are so chaotic that the children have little respect for their teachers. Their instructors shout and yell, but never follow up with action. Many school systems refuse to practice strictness and will not administer discipline because they fear reprisal from parents.

An autocratic family suffered this kind of unsatisfactory school situation for their children. One daughter was lazy with her homework and did not feel concerned at all about facing serious consequences from her teacher. It was mushrooming into a significant problem that was causing the girl to fall behind in her schoolwork. These parents insisted that the schoolteachers and authorities demand respect for their authority at school. They gave the principal and teacher written permission to chasten their child. Once the child was called into the office and saw that the school officials really did care enough to do something significant about her lazy study habits, chastening did not need to take place. She understood that they could be firm, and she accepted her responsibility to complete her schoolwork. Remember that children are always more comfortable and secure when they understand the boundaries and know that those boundaries will be enforced.

Alternative Methods of Educating Your Children

Many Christian families have given up on the hope that their children will get a satisfactory education from public schools.

Because of the tragic deterioration in America's public schools, thousands of families are homeschooling their children. They have learned that by orchestrating their efforts with other homeschooling parents they can provide a superior education for their children. These parents have formed sports teams and cooperate with each other by sharing their academic skills. My husband and I travel widely and we witness very favorable results from the children who are being homeschooled.

Homeschooled children are well mannered and are developing calm and peaceful spirits. They are capable of engaging themselves in individual research and study. They are not pressured to conform to silly clothing trends or goofy hairstyles in order to feel accepted. Homeschooled children avoid the daily peer pressure that children in public schools must endure. They are not upset by ridicule from some bully or dysfunctional child. Their minds are freed to learn in an orderly setting. The home schooled child can practice the Christian examples their parents teach without ridicule or scorn. While children in public schools are being bullied or suffering injuries on the playground, homeschooled children may be touring Washington D.C. with their parents or visiting an Amish community in the hills of Pennsylvania.

Homeschooled children in American are rising like cream to the top of the educational pyramid. Public school officials are being called on to explain why homeschooled children won the National Spelling Bee several years in a row. Colleges and universities are enthusiastically recruiting young men and women who have been homeschooled.

Many parents choose to search for reputable private schools in which to enroll their children and there are a growing number from which to choose. My husband and I made that choice and were extremely pleased with our experience. It was expensive, but well worth the money.

If I were starting over as a young parent, I would choose either homeschooling or the best private school in our area in which to educate our children.

Summing it up and Searching Our Souls

I call this lesson my soul-searching lesson. Independence needs to be handled as carefully as a prescription of medicine. If you give too much too fast, it can be harmful. If you give too little too slowly, it will not work. Parents need to measure out the proper dose of freedom at the proper time.

I have already given some helpful hints about knowing when to give a measure of independence. I have said that a child must develop physical and mental independence. The physical emerges more rapidly than the mental. This causes a child to desire more freedom than he is capable of handling.

When he masters a physical skill, fly his flag, praise, celebrate, retreat, and let him freely exercise his accomplishments. Then you should not only *let* him but, if you want him to develop a healthy independence, you must *make* him take over his new responsibilities. Never make a habit of doing your child's chores for him.

Apart from chastening for disrespect and disobedience, I mentioned other methods of discipline to help develop a child's mental ability and teach him to think for himself.

WHEEL OF CHOICES

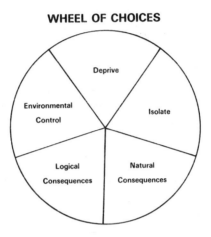

By con *sist'* ent ly using environmental control, depriving, isolating, natural and logical consequences over a period of years, you will help your child achieve responsible self-reliance. Later, when he leaves home he will be competent and survive and flourish on his own. His foundation will be solid, his principles firm, and his character developed.

Once a child has proved he is trustworthy by demonstrating that he can handle a situation, fly his flag, show confidence, trust, praise, and silently rejoice. Any time he digresses and displays irresponsibility in an area, take his flag down, give him time to think and grow, then let him try again. When he proves at a later time that he can handle the circumstance, restore your confidence in him.

I encourage you as autocratic parents, do not grant independence too slowly. Those who work with disturbed young people say the failure to let children mature is one of the greatest causes of teenage rebellion.

Avoid the other extreme. Dr. Max Rafferty addresses to parents who give too much independence too fast when he says, "Independence and self-reliance are the last things in the world our offspring need to learn." 4 To know what he is talking about, all you need to do is read newspapers and learn about the thousands of dollars it takes to repair school buildings and other facilities that have been vandalized by roaming, irresponsible youths who have been given undeserved independence.

These young people have their flags of freedom flying but have never been required to prove they are worthy of trust.

Make Your Children Walk, Not Ride

A psychologist once performed an experiment with two groups of white rats. The first group of rats was guided through a maze riding in a little rat wagon. The psychologist pulled the little wagon by a string through the many turns and paths. All the rats did was ride. At the end of the journey, their food was waiting for them to eat. This was repeated twenty times.

The second group of rats did not have it quite so easy. One at a time, they were turned loose at the entrance of the maze. Through trial and error they worked their way to the exit where the food was waiting. They also had to do this twenty times.

At the conclusion of the experiment, the psychologist took a rat from group one and a rat from group two. He put them together at the entrance of the maze to see which could most quickly find his way to the food at the end. Rat two won, paws down. Why? Because he was forced to use his head. Rat one had only gone along for the ride, and the psychologist had done his work and thinking for him. 5

Independence builds within a child self-respect, self-control, and courage. Let's help our children walk to a victory of independence by (1) loving and teaching them to obey, (2) retreating and letting them occupy their territory, (3) insisting that they occupy their new territory, and (4) using our heads to help develop their heads.

Joseph and Mary Our Example

By the time your child enters adolescence, you must have him so well prepared to make wise judgments that you are ready to "cut the apron strings." Teenagers simply must not be babied. They will resent it bitterly and will rebel. (Read Chapter 9 in the Addendum)

Joseph and Mary are an example of how we must not "smother love" a child who is reaching maturity. When Jesus was twelve, he accompanied Joseph and Mary on their annual pilgrimage from Nazareth to Jerusalem to attend the feast of the Passover. The following is the Biblical account of complete trust that Mary and Joseph placed in their son and the manner in which the child Jesus exercised his independence.

"And when they had fulfilled the days, as they returned, the child Jesus tarried behind in Jerusalem; and Joseph and his mother knew not

of it. But they, supposing him to have been in the company, went a day's journey; and they sought him among their kinsfolk and acquaintances. And when they found him not, they turned back again to Jerusalem, seeking him. And it came to pass, that after three days they found him in the temple, sitting in the midst of the doctors, both hearing them, and asking them questions. And all that heard him were astonished at his understanding and answers. And when they saw him, they were amazed; and his mother said unto him, Son, why hast thou thus dealt with us? Behold, thy father and I have sought thee sorrowing. And he said unto them, How is it that ye sought me? wist ye not that I must be about my Father's business? ...And he went down with them, and came to Nazareth, and was subject unto them (Luke 2:43-51)

My College Debut

Many who knew me as a child say I was a "Daddy's Girl." I loved my father very deeply and he loved me. I would come behind him in his rocking chair and throw my arms around him and give him a big hug and a kiss. If I accidentally knocked his newspaper out of his hands with my expressions of affection, he never seemed to mind. I always dreamed of marrying a kind man like my daddy. One day when I told a girl friend I knew in high school that I would like to marry a man like my daddy, I was mortified by her response. She said, "I'd rather kill myself than marry a man like my dad." There was no way that I could relate to that kind of tragic father-daughter relationship!

Perhaps Daddy had a special love for me because, after the birth of four sons, I was his first little girl. Besides that, I looked much like the other girl that was the love of his life, my mother. Patience is the word I use to describe my daddy. He was always patient with me.

I remember one day he was writing and dipping his pen in an opened bottle of ink. I was in the same room with him playing with a ball. He had just cautioned me, "Be careful where you throw that ball." He had barely spoken when, Crash! My ball hit the inkbottle and splashed ink all over the bedroom wallpaper. He remained calm. He knew it was a childish accident and there was little that could be done since in those days wallpaper was not washable.

I will forever remember the lesson of "thou shalt not steal" that Daddy taught me. I had accompanied Mother to visit an elderly lady in our community. While they were visiting, I noticed marbles among her grandchildren's playthings. My older brothers were my playmates and they always had beautiful marbles. I suppose I reasoned that they were so small that I could slip them into my pocket and no one would ever know. Of course, my vigilant mother discovered my stash of stolen marbles before we got home. It was late in the evening and she had to prepare dinner. I am sure she decided that this problem was one for Daddy to handle. So, as soon as Daddy came in from doing his chores, Mother told him about my theft of the pretty marbles. He expressed surprise and deep disappointment (I was only four) and immediately began to shame me. I remember sinking down by the wall and the "pot bellied" stove and hanging my head with remorse. I was extremely contrite and humiliated about disappointing my daddy. The next day, I was taken back to our neighbor's house, made to apologize, and return the marbles.

My parents always made me take responsibility for my actions and in turn expressed their love and approval when I lived up to their expectations. Whether I was playing a game on our girl's high school basketball team or singing in our high school trio, my parents were always supporting me.

Leaving home for college was the hardest thing I have done in my life. I made the decision that I was going to attend a Christian college that was located hundreds of miles from my home. I knew that was the only place I could find a preacher to marry, and being a preacher's wife was a dream I had prayed for since I was twelve years old.

Week's prior to leaving for my first semester, I was so upset that I could hardly eat. When I thought about how far away I was going to be from my family, I lost my appetite. I would say to myself, "You must be brave. You have talked about attending a Christian college for years and you have to stick to your plan."

Soon the day arrived that we packed my clothes, and my parents drove me to that far- away campus. When we arrived at the college that I had spent years dreaming about attending, my parents helped me unpack the car and move my belongings into my dormitory room. Mother put the beautiful white bedspread and pink pillow that she had filet-crocheted to read, "My darling daughter," on my bed. My room was accented in pink. Even my pink radio matched the curtains, throw rug, and towels. We hung the clothes that Mother had spent all summer sewing for me.

My heart was so heavy that the thought passed through my mind to tell Mother and Daddy that I wanted to go back home with them. I would go to the college where my two brothers had attended close to our home. Daddy and Mother had urged me for months to stay near home where the tuition was not so costly. But I stubbornly insisted, "I am going to a Christian college! I don't care how much it costs! I will work, take loans, and pay them back myself." (The latter is exactly what I ended up doing.)

While my parents were preparing to leave me on the college campus, I was brave on the outside but faint on the inside. When I kissed my parent's good-bye and they left me alone, I had absolutely no idea that their hearts were heavy too. Mother later told me how she had cried all summer as she sat at the sewing machine making my clothes. Daddy! He never cried! But on that day he did, although he was careful not to let me see his tears.

Years later Mother told me that when I waved good-bye they sat in the car and watched me until I was out of sight and that she had to console Daddy because he could not stop crying. I had no idea he was taking it so hard.

Independence! That is the status all parents must seek for their children. But, oh, how hard it is to give! We older parents can tell stories about the quiet tears we shed when we stood and waved as our children vanished into the distance to take their places in life.

As a young parent, you must understand that you, too, one day must tell your children good-bye. While they are with you, you must redeem each moment and prepare them for their day of departure.

Compare giving your children their independence to launching an ocean vessel. Every engine must be tuned, the hull sea-worthy and the deck polished. The ship is ready to pass easily through calm seas and endure the fiercest storms. It is now ready to serve the purpose for which it was created.

You should thoroughly train and educate your children. Give them every advantage you possibly can, so that when the time arrives to launch them into the sea of life they will be thoroughly prepared to seize successfully the opportunities with which they are presented and conquer the challenges they will face.

The day your child sets sail, you and your husband will stand with your arms around each other. You will watch your child's image grow dimmer and ultimately fade out of sight. In your heart of hearts, you need to know that you have done your best to prepare him for a life of independence.

ASSIGNMENT

1. Make a miniature Wheel of Choices and tape it on the inside of the most used door of your kitchen cabinet.

2. Sit down with pencil and paper and write your children's names. Make a list of as many ways as you can think of in which each has proved himself and you trust his judgment.

3. Take special notice this week of ways you can exercise environmental control to make life more comfortable for your family.

GOOD HABITS

Must Be Taught and Sought

Chapter Ten
Good Habits

If you were talking to a foreign exchange student who asked you the meaning of the English word "habits," this is the way you might explain it . . .

> *"Habits are practices that are enforced by repetition until they become a part of one's life. They are set ways a person has made for himself of acting and doing things."*

Everyone forms habits. My habits may be different from yours. Some have the habit of drinking herb tea or eating with chopsticks. My life style is one in which I drink plain hot water and eat with a fork. There is nothing wrong with our having different habits.

Habits are passive, positive, or negative. As long as my habits are passive and do not affect you in any direct way, or they are positive and influence your life for good, you should have no objections to my way of life. If, however, my activities interfere with your life and have a negative effect on your living conditions, you are within your rights to request that I make alterations.

Our habits are our business. They only become other people's business when they adversely affect their lives. You may say, "It is not anyone's business what I do." Two conditions must exist for that to be true. (1) You would have no authority greater than yourself; and (2) you would live isolated on a desert island.

Otherwise, our habits and manner of life are very much a part of other people's business.

Our Habits Become Our Influence

Jesus referred to our life styles as our influence. He compared this to leaven, to salt, and to light. Just as these items spread and influence other elements in a silent manner, one's habits influence the lives of others. Influence has been compared to throwing a rock into a pond. The water ripples in a widening circle. In a like manner, our habits affect ourselves, then our families, and eventually others.

Our Habits Influence

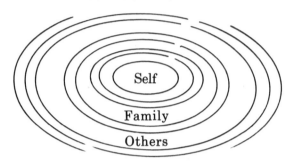

"For none of us liveth to himself, and no man dieth to himself." Romans 14:7 Therefore, our lives and behavior do matter to other people.

Jesus Increased in Favor With Man

Autocratic parents who are concerned about the development and welfare of their children want them to like themselves and be liked by others. This can be accomplished by training children to practice good habits. When they touch others' lives, they will have a positive influence.

When Jesus Christ was twelve, the Bible says, He *"increased. . . in favor with God and man."* Luke 2:52. From this passage we learn that Jesus' childhood behavior met with approval in the eyes of the adult world. Since there are few passages in the Bible that mention His childhood, the fact that God included this information is an indication He considers children's behavior very important. *"Even a child is known by his doings, whether his work be pure, and whether it be right."* Proverbs 20:11.

Good Influence versus Bad Influence

The following are two illustrations of how one's influence can spread until it touches hundreds and perhaps thousands of other lives.

Account 1 - Max Jukes was a Dutch settler in New York. He had two sons who married into the same family. These boys' wives came from a family of six daughters. Five of the girls, including the boys' wives, had bad characters. Mr. R. L. Dugdale, appointed to make an investigation of the New York prisons, ran on to this Jukes family. He traced their history for five generations. From these two sons' marriages, this is what he found.   Of seven hundred and nine descendants who were investigated, one-fifth of them were criminals, nearly one-fourth were paupers supported at government expense and about one-fourth of the children were illegitimate.   Of the women, one out of six was a prostitute.   Dealing with crimes committed by this family cost an estimated one billion three hundred million dollars. And, of course, no one knows the indirect moral and social evil that has sprung from this family's evil influence.

Account 2 - Jonathan Edwards was a minister and a strict disciplinarian in morals.   Tracing his genealogical tree, we find twelve college presidents, two hundred sixty-five college graduates, sixty-five military officers, sixty prominent authors, one hundred lawyers, thirty judges, eighty public officers such as governors, mayors, and state officials, three congressmen, two U.S. senators, and one vice-president of the United States. [1]

As autocratic parents, we want our children to exert a good influence. If we guide them into lives of good habits, they will like themselves, be a joy to the family, and meet with favor in society. Good habits will build self-approval, self-confidence, and pride (the kind that will help your child hold his chin up, not his nose up).

What We Do Is What We Are
From the beginning of this book, I have tried to impress the reader with the truth that a child's life is not shaped by mere chance.   Rearing children properly is work, and it calls for adults who are willing to concentrate on good parenting. This chapter title, "Good habits must be taught and sought," is another way of saying that children must be trained to exercise good habits. Parents must show and tell their lessons, and practice them daily in their own lives.   They must continue to exercise firm discipline and train their children to follow their good examples.

Parents may be early-morning risers, industrious, well groomed, and thrifty yet fail to instill these good habits in their children. If they allow the children to lie in bed till noon, refuse to work, be sloppy in their dress, and spend their money foolishly, parents' wholesome values will never be a part of their children's lives. What a parent permits his child to practice is what the child will become.

Trainer, Teacher, or Traitor

Educators estimate that one remembers 90% of what he does, 80% of what he sees, 70% of what he says, and 10% of what he hears. Using these figures, we can see how much more effective it is to train. If you add the 80% a child sees, the 10% that he hears, and 90% when he is made to do something himself, this adds up to a 180% influence.

When parents teach their children, but fail to make them follow, they may get 80% response for seeing and10% for hearing, but will make only half as much of an impression as a parent who trains his children.

Just being a *teacher* of good habits is not good enough for an autocratic parent who is working to *train* his children. Parents who do not set a proper example are *traitors* and destroy any good influence they may have had.   Jesus called people who say one thing and do another hypocrites. He said, *"But do not follow their practice; for they say one thing and do another."* 2 Matthew 23:3

You do not need to explain the word hypocrisy to a child. He can easily recognize it without a scholarly definition. Once a little girl arrived at home from school. She bounded up the steps of her house with a little friend right behind her. As they opened the door, they overheard a conversation. The little girl stopped, turned to her friend and said, "Mother has company. She is using her company voice."

Parents can preach to their child to be honest, but the child then observes that Mother did not return the sack of potatoes that accidentally was left on her grocery cart or the extra dollar of change the checker gave her at the store. He also sees Mother take grapes from the bunch on the counter in the supermarket and eat them without paying for them. The preaching he heard about being honest will not make much of an impression.

Empty threats are another means by which a parent practices hypocrisy. I have heard mothers threaten children by warning, "I'm going to spank you if you do that again!" The child does exactly the same thing again and again, but no chastening follows. The parent said, but she did not do.

Here is another example of a way a mother can threaten. "If you don't come on, I am going to leave you here." The child continues to run the other way or continues with his play. He does not come, and Mother does not leave him. That inconsistent mother said, but she did not do.

When a mother makes threats, she proposes a logical consequence. With her voice and choice activity, she is asking the child to make a decision. When a mother does this, she should always carry out the consequence and chasten the child, or never give him the warning in the first place. Being an authority and giving the facts is preferable. If a mother doesn't want her son to throw his ball in a neighbor's house, she should say, kindly but firmly, "Do not throw the ball in the house again," or "Come on, it is time to go home." If he disobeys her by throwing the ball in the house, she should consistently back her word with discipline.

Habits are formed only when one repeats an action over and over. How then must parents instill good habits in their children's lives? Is it by training, teaching, or by proving oneself a hypocrite? The answer is simple. It can best be done through training. When a child listens to his parents and follows their dependable example, he will be influenced to form noble habits. You must remember, for children to be trained in a skill, practice, or principle, the children themselves must be made to exercise these virtues in their personal lives.

Invest in the Bank of P's

What are some good personal habits that will help improve our children's lives?

I encourage autocratic parents to invest their time and energy in the Bank of P's. They will be paid rich dividends, not in penny profit, but in people approval. Their children will receive benefits far more valuable than anything money can buy.

The following are six areas of life in which parents can train good habits:

Train a Child to Have Good Habits Concerning His

erson
ossessions
astime
oliteness
eacefulness
ublic approval

1. TRAIN A CHILD GOOD HABITS FOR HIS PERSON

A child trained to take care of his physical person will be a healthier and happier child.

To train a child to take proper care of his body, we need to be sure that *he does* the following nine things:

(1) *Keeps a regular bedtime hour each night.* To maintain good health and a happy disposition a child needs ten to twelve hours of sleep a night. Dr. Denmark's instructions are to put a child to bed by 7 o'clock in the evening and get him up at 7 o'clock in the morning. This twelve-hour sleeping schedule should continue through the child's "negative and discipline" years. When a child enters the "learning years," parents must decide at what age he can stay up later and remain rested and healthy on less than twelve hours of sleep. Adolescents and adults should have eight hours of sleep.

(2) *Eats three well-balanced meals a day.* A young child needs twelve hours of sleep to *stay* healthy. That leaves Mother twelve waking hours to *get* him healthy. No longer must a TUAC mother search elsewhere for a formula of how to feed her family. Dr. Denmark's dietary instructions are given in this book. (Read Chapters 5, 6, & 10 in the Addendum)

In twenty-first century America, Dr. Denmark says her biggest problem is getting mothers to cook for their families. This unwholesome situation should not exist. As wives and mothers, how dare we not take the greatest care of the only bodies our family members will ever have?" God did not design the human body to be feeble and sick; rather, He made it resilient and robust. Even when we are sick our bodies have the capacity to heal themselves if properly nourished. Some busy mothers may object, "Even if I cook my family still likes to eat out." Contrariwise, over the years I have proved, "*If I cook, my family will come!*"

(3) *Bathes and puts on clean clothes.* Daily baths are always a good idea and essential in the summertime. Often children develop a perspiration problem. These children need special emphasis placed on keeping clean and changing their clothes daily.

(4) *Washes his hands and flushes the stool after using the toilet.* At school registration many kindergarten teachers will ask if a child has been trained to do these things. Spreading germs and sickness can be cut down immensely when children are taught these two good hygiene habits. Also, follow Dr. Denmark's counsel on teaching little girls how to clean themselves to avoid vaginal infections.

(5) *Brushes his teeth regularly.* Clean teeth will not only produce a pretty smile and freshen the breath but will eliminate much dental work and expense.

(6) *Dresses, washes his face, and combs his hair before play.* All one has to do is ask the UPS or mailman to learn how frequently they meet mothers who come to the door in their housecoats and slippers at noon. It builds

one's self-esteem to get out of bed, dress, and groom oneself the first thing in the morning. (It will help you be a 3A woman, too.) It gives you an incentive to accomplish more and is a sign of diligence. Children should not be allowed to run around the house for hours in their pajamas. They should be trained to wash their faces, comb their hair, and get dressed the first thing in the morning.

(7) *Keeps his body covered with modest apparel.* Modesty is a forgotten virtue in modern America. From the time a child is small, many mothers will strip him naked in the living room and in front of the family and sometimes in the presence of visitors. His modesty is further weakened when he is allowed to parade through the house naked or go about in scanty attire.

The best advice I can give Christian parents on choosing proper apparel for themselves and their children is to stay within God's guidance for adequate covering. If clothes cover your anatomy from shoulder to knee, do not fit too tightly or are not too transparent, then they should pass God's test for modesty.

(8) *Playes and exercises.* Children normally do not need to be coaxed to play, but the televisions and computers we have in our homes can be detrimental to children's play and exercise. Many children are content to be entertained all day by these devices and never create recreation activities for themselves.

Some children have trouble reading because their brains are not properly developed. Brain growth is associated with good coordination, and good coordination is a result of play and exercise. Daddy and Mother, you must insist that your children get out of the house to play in the fresh air and sunshine. Physical activity will develop good body balance, which will in turn enhance their mental alertness.

(9) *Washes hands before and after eating.* Washing hands before eating helps keep the food, dishes, and silverware sanitary. Washing hands after meals helps to maintain clean furniture, doors, and walls. Jelly may be smeared throughout the house if sticky little hands are not washed. Again, this one good habit can eliminate the spread of germs and some sicknesses.

2. TRAIN A CHILD GOOD HABITS FOR HIS POSSESSIONS

Training a child to take care of the things that belong to him will assist him in becoming thankful and appreciative. A child should express gratitude when he receives a gift, or is given a new possession. A child who is given too many things may lose his appreciative nature. A girl with three dresses often will take better care of them and appreciate a new dress more than a girl who has thirteen dresses she seldom wears. Children who have their rooms crammed with toys may care less for them than children who have only a few things with which to play. And remember that *children appreciate toys they make more than toys you buy.*

One key bit of wisdom for parents to remember about developing good habits in children concerning their possessions is to provide them with the essentials of life and conservatively give them some of the non-essentials.

(1) *Make his bed.* Some mothers begin training their child to make his bed as early as two years old. You may choose to wait a little longer. The important thing is not to forget your teaching program. You must not walk into your child's room on the morning of his fourth birthday and announce, "You are old enough now to make your own bed. Starting today, I will expect you to do that job!" A mother who starts to train her child to make his bed should be sure she is diligent in making her own bed and sets a good example by doing it the first thing every morning. Second, she will work with her little one, and teach him over a period of days each step in properly making a bed. As soon as he can do it by himself, Mother can fly his flag, celebrate, praise, retreat, and let him occupy the territory.

(2) *Hang up his clothes.* Hanging clothes is another thing a child can learn to do early. Install a closet-organizing kit in your child's closet. There are many different configurations. Install low-hanging rods your child can easily reach and have sliding drawers for toys and shoes.

When a child is old enough to remove his coat by himself, there should be a hanger low enough where he can go directly and hang his coat after entering the house.

(3) *Pick up his room and keep it orderly.* A special time of the day can be set aside for a child to practice good housekeeping inside his bedroom. In the morning before school is an ideal time for him to tidy his room.

(4) *Pick up and put away his toys.* Two years old is not too young to start training a child to place his toys in a toy box. And, may I remind you, the fewer toys (good, durable ones) a child has, the easier it will be for him to take care of them. Furthermore, when new toys are added at birthdays or Christmas, they will be more highly valued.

(5) *Feed and care for his pet.* My husband has a deep regard for helpless animals. When he was a boy, his mother trained him always to feed his

animals before he fed himself. He recalls occasions when he would sit down to the table to eat and would be excused to go feed a helpless animal.

(6) *Wake up to his alarm or get up promptly when Mother calls.* In some cases a mother will purchase a special alarm clock for her child when he starts school. She will make sure it has a pleasant sound and is loud enough to be easily heard. When the alarm sounds, the child knows he must get ready for school. This early training at age six can be very helpful in getting her child off to school on time. Personally, I preferred to tiptoe into the room, give a gentle shake, plant a sweet kiss on the forehead, and whisper "good morning." I enjoyed using this gentle loving approach when the children were small and the alarm, for the adolescence years.

Mother, if you will prepare breakfast and have it waiting prior to awakening the children, they will be less likely to loiter in bed. The aroma of good food cooking will draw a healthy child to the table eager for breakfast.

(7) *Respect others' possessions and property.* Train your children to respect each other's personal possessions. Before using another's toys, one should first receive permission from the owner. Mother's purse or Daddy's change spread out on the dresser is possessions that must be respected and a "hands off" policy established for them. Another area in which a child can be trained to respect the rights of others is at birthday parties. A child should learn to rejoice on these occasions. He must not be permitted to sulk or cry because he does not receive gifts when his brother or sister has a birthday.

There are few children who have not been guilty of stealing something at some time. When this happens, the theft should be corrected immediately and on the first offense. Take the child back to the store or from wherever the item was taken, and make him return it with an apology. Usually one experience like this, along with a little shaming, will prevent its ever happening again.

3. TRAIN A CHILD GOOD HABITS FOR HIS PASTIME

The story is told about an elderly woman who had spent the major portion of her life rearing five sons. Her hopes and dreams had always been that they would enter the ministry. Much to her disappointment, none of them became preachers. Each one went to sea. One day while she was entertaining a visitor and reminiscing about the past, she shared her disappointment with her guest. Later in the visit the guest observed several paintings of ocean scenes her hostess had hanging on her walls. Over the years the boys had been impressed with life near the sea by their mother's pictures.

Perhaps this story can be a lesson to us to be careful of the things to which we subject our children. The following are six suggestions about how to supervise a child's spare time:

(1) *Supervise his television and computer time.* The use of televisions and computers can be good or bad. It depends on parents. Some mothers allow the television to become a built-in baby sitter for their children. They place no restrictions on television viewing and allow it to run non-stop all day. Uncensored television viewing will not only infect their children with evil thoughts but rob them of creative play. Furthermore, it causes them to waste time.

When God created the world, after each day's accomplishment He said, " *it was good.*" After the sixth day of creation it is written, *"And God saw every thing that He had made, and, behold, it was very good."* Genesis 1:31

Christians should turn man's inventions of televisions and computers into tools that are *very good.* Our challenge is to use them for our advantage. We must be careful to filter out evil influences and expose our children to that which is advantageous for their development and learning.

Television has the potential to educate, relax, and produce wholesome laughter. We can shop, play games, or research many subjects by means of computers. They provide us with the ability to communicate with people all over the world at our fingertips.

Twenty-five years ago I wrote the first manuscript for TUAC on lined notebook paper. I then transcribed it onto plain white paper with the help of a small portable typewriter. Today, I have the convenience of doing the same work at my computer, which is a great blessing to me!

My advice to mothers is to forbid children selecting television programs without supervision. When the television is on, Daddy and Mother should monitor what their children watch. The same holds true with on-line computers. Computers accessed by children should be located in the central part of the house where parents can monitor every web site their children visit.

The majority of a child's twelve waking hours should be spent in creative play. They can be outside playing in a sand box, playing with the pets, climbing trees, running, making mud pies, playing house, skating, or riding bikes.

(2) *Supervise his CD's, radio, and reading material.* Music from CD's and radio sets the tone of a home. Parents have control over the choice of music and information that enters the house through the airwaves. Introduce your children to the pleasures of a quiet and peaceful atmosphere by selecting good music. Monitor CD's or reading material that your children may desire to purchase.

Mothers should start reading to their little ones early. A Bible story should be included in your daily reading schedule. *The Bible in Pictures for Little Eyes* by Kenneth N. Taylor is an excellent book to read to little ones. When the children learn to read for themselves, a Bible reading should be a daily requirement for their routine. Teaching children to memorize the Scriptures when they are young is the best way to implant the Word of God on their hearts, where it will live forever.

(3) *Invite your children's friends into your home for playtime and meals.* When the neighborhood children play in your yard or family room, you be there to supervise. You must know what goes on and to what your children are being exposed. If there were another autocratic mother on your block, it would be only fair to trust your children at her house part of the time.

Let Sunday be a special day when your children invite their church friend's home for lunch and an afternoon visit. These occasions will build lasting memories, and your children will be proud to prove that their mother really is the best cook in the world.

One tip to remember about helping children to play happily together is to divide them into pairs. Rarely, if ever, will three children play harmoniously together. Two will invariably team up against the one. If you have two sons, let each one invite a guest home for dinner.

(4) *Encourage doing homework at a designated time.* Children often develop the habit of procrastinating in doing their homework. Prevent that problem by establishing the time that homework must be finished is before dinner. Your child will learn promptness as well as good study habits.

(5) *Know where your children are at all times, and insist upon promptness.* If you allow your ten-year-old daughter to walk a few blocks to a girl friend's house, have her call you when she arrives. For safety, you may want to provide her with a cell phone to carry with her. Give her instructions as to how long she may stay and exactly what time you

expect her home. If she is home early, that is wonderful. If she is late, then depriving her of privileges for awhile will help her remember to be prompt the next time.

One family was having a problem with their children taking too long to walk home from school. Their loitering allowed them to get involved in quarrels and unnecessary confrontations with other children. The parents solved the problem by giving a fact that they had fifteen minutes from the time school was dismissed until they were to arrive at the front door. These children lived far enough away that it was necessary for them to run part of the way in order to make it home on time. It solved the loitering problem, and they did not come home again with torn coats or broken thermos bottles.

If parents expect their children to call and report their whereabouts, the parents should repay the thoughtfulness. If there is a delay or change in schedule, parents should understand that children get worried, too. A call or note explaining when Mother and Daddy will be home will relieve their children's worry.

(6) *Encourage your children to develop their talents.* Each child in a family may be endowed with different talents. Some are more gifted than others. No child should receive more lavish praise simply because he possesses greater talents than his siblings. As long as children are diligent in exercising their personal abilities, each should be equally honored and praised. If a child with superior talents is honored above others, it may cause the other family members to feel inferior and resent the gifted child. The tip that I gave to remember about husbands applies also to children. Every child is talented only in different areas. Discover the area in which each of your children expresses an interest and encourage him in those areas.

Every child is gifted in his head, hands, or feet. He may be educable, personable, mechanical, musical, or especially talented artistically, athletically, or domestically. Children under twelve can be encouraged to explore many new territories. They can be inspired to learn to paint, cook, embroider, crochet, knit, sew, sing, play musical instruments, build, garden, raise show animals, give magic or puppet shows, be an artist, author or authoress, poet or poetess, actor or actress, play ball, or run track. The list of potential interests is endless.

4. TRAIN A CHILD GOOD HABITS IN HIS POLITENESS

Polite children are loved and appreciated by everyone. If a child is to be courteous, however, he must learn from courteous parents. He will learn to be polite to others because his parents are polite to him. In order for a child to learn good manners, he must be taught to observe the following eleven acts of kindness:

(1) *Respect others' privacy by knocking on their doors before entering.* If Mother and Daddy expect the children to knock on their bedroom door, they must treat the children in the same way.

(2) *Say "please," "thank you," "you are welcome," and "pardon me, please."* Again, a child will use these expressions if his parents use them consistently. Nothing can tone down a parent's authoritative voice and cause a child to enjoy obeying spoken facts more quickly than a kind, "Honey, would you please?" After a child has promptly obeyed, he should hear a gracious, "Thank you, sweetheart; I appreciate that."

(3) *Address older people as "Mr." and "Mrs."* It will never be out of fashion to teach a child to address one older as "Mr." and "Mrs." Sometimes older people do not want to be addressed by their surnames and prefer that children call them by their given names like "Joe" or "Bernadine." If that is the case, respect the individual's choice. One lady said that, in these cases, her mother still insisted that she and her brothers and sisters express respect by addressing older persons as "Mr. Joe" and "Mrs. Bernadine."

(4) *Say "yes, ma'am," "no, ma'am," "yes, sir," and "no, sir."* A child can be taught to respond with a "yes, ma'am" when he is called, just as easily as he can learn to respond with "what?" And, of course, when children call Mother from another room in the house, she should also answer with respect.

(5) *Recognize a visiting guest or older person by speaking.* Many young people are so preoccupied with their peer group and personal interests that they show little respect or courtesy to older people. Children should be taught always to be polite, speak, and make friendly conversation with older persons or houseguests.

(6) *Do not interrupt when adults are speaking.* Waiting their turn to be heard is a courtesy that is difficult for children to learn. One way to remind a child to wait patiently when you are engaged in a conversation with another adult is to plan a hand signal with him. Children sometimes feel that adults do not notice them and therefore they must make their presence known. If a mother will tell her child to tap her

lightly on the arm, she will then clasp her hands on his, and will recognize him as soon as she can pause in her conversation without being rude.

(7) *Boys should open doors, help with chairs, and permit girls to go first.* It makes no difference how "hip" the modern age, it will never be out of style for a young man to behave like a gentleman. When he is older, girls who are interested in behaving like ladies will favor him.

(8) *Ask, "May I be excused, please?" before leaving the table.* A hostess will be delighted with a gracious child who is appreciative enough of her hospitality that he does not rudely jump up and leave the table when he has finished his dinner. Learning to sit quietly and listen to adult conversation is not only polite but also can be a valuable learning experience as well. Occasions such as this are excellent opportunities for children to learn how to participate in conversations and exchange thoughts with grown-ups.

(9) *Always serve your friends food before yourself.* Children can practice this graciousness with their special Sunday guests.

(10) *Bad or unpleasant attitudes are not allowed.* Disagreeable and ugly actions often begin when a child learns to walk, gets angry, and throws himself on the floor in a tantrum. Such an episode is commonly referred to as "throwing a fit." When things do not go his way, an out-of-control child may kick, scream, bang his head on the floor, and even hold his breath until his face turns blue.

Many child psychologists advise parents not to let these little incidents bother them, but ignore them and go about their work as if everything is normal. They further caution that, if you do make a big thing out of this kind of behavior, your expression of concern will reinforce the action and cause the child to repeat it over and over. They promise that, if the little actor or actress is unable to attract an audience, he will soon give up the performance. They further relieve parental concern by pointing out that it is impossible for a child to hold his breath until he dies. He may turn blue, but he will soon pass out and will naturally begin to breathe again.

Winning parents do not agree with those laissez-faire tactics. Some parents of an offending child may exercise a determination strong enough to ignore such shameful behavior, but it is certain that no one else will. Any observer will get an unpleasant opinion of any child who behaves in such an ugly fashion.

A wise autocratic mother will "nip in the bud" fit-throwing at the first episode. She should certainly notice it, remove the child from the floor, express emphatic disapproval of such actions, and chasten soundly with the rod. If the imposed discipline is properly administered, she can be assured that her child will not consider engaging in this sort of behavior again.

Some mothers ask, "What is an appropriate way for a child to be allowed to vent his anger?" Some educators suggest that, when a child is angry with Daddy or Mother, he should be given a doll representing Mother and allowed to poke it full of pins, or that a paper silhouette of Daddy should be tacked to the wall and the child permitted to throw darts at it. Such suggestions as these are absolutely absurd! *A child must be taught to control his temper.*

The Bible teaches that anger should be suppressed. *"Cease from anger, and forsake wrath."* Psalms 37:8. *"Be ye angry, and sin not."* Ephesians 4:26 Other Bible passages that command to restrain anger are Proverbs 14:17, 16:32, 19:11. It is not necessarily wrong to be angry, but it is wrong not to control that anger.

A child should never be allowed to slap, kick, or tell his parents, "I hate you," "I'll kill you," "I won't do it," or "No!" Neither should parents under any circumstance practice tit for tat with a child. If a child hits, pinches, pulls hair, scratches, or bites his parents; they should *never* hit, pinch, pull his hair, scratch, or hit him back. Children should be absolutely forbidden to say or do anything hateful or abusive to their parents. Swift chastening should follow any attempt a child makes to take revenge on either of his parents.

Any time a child exhibits a sullen attitude or does not control his behavior, he should be disciplined with a rod. Nothing can sweeten a sour attitude or straighten out uncontrolled behavior more quickly than a switch.

(11) *Write thank-you notes for gifts received.* A child should be trained, as soon as he has learned to write, to express gratitude for gifts by sending thank-you notes. If grandparents, older brothers and sisters, or aunts and uncles love a child enough to go to the time and expense of sending him a special gift, the child should be trained to have the courtesy to send a note of appreciation.

While writing about training a child to be grateful for presents he receives, I am reminded of a problem area that is frequently mentioned in TUAC classes. Many new mothers have asked me to say something about problems with grandparents. Before writing anything negative, I must express something positive. I personally believe that every little boy and girl should experience the joys that accompany a warm relationship with grandparents. Granddaddy and Grandmother often have a lot of time to give for individual attention.

However, over-indulgence with lavish gifts is often resented by young parents. Some grandparents provide a never-ending supply of toys and clothes for their grandchildren. It is difficult to know exactly what to give children for Christmas or birthdays because Granddaddy or Grandmother has already showered them with so many things.

When grandparents live close to their children, this can pose added problems. How does a young mother limit the time Junior and Sis spend at Grandmother's house without hurting her feelings? The only suggestion I know to give new mothers with the problem of over-indulgence of things from grandparents or children who beg to stay with grandparents much of the time is to talk frankly with the grandparents about it. Preferably, the spouse whose parents are being overly generous is the one who should have a friendly conference about the problem. The principle of giving too many material possessions is as unwise for grandparents as it is for parents. Often, the more material things a child receives, the less he appreciates them.

Chapter four in Dr. Denmark's Addendum is dedicated to grandparents. If you have a grandparent problem, ask the grandparents to please read that chapter.

5. TRAIN A CHILD GOOD HABITS IN HIS PEACEFULNESS

In the seventh beatitude Jesus commends peacemakers. As we look at the condition of the world, it is evident that there are far too few peacemakers and far too many peace breakers. *"But the fruit of the Spirit is love, joy, PEACE, longsuffering, gentleness, goodness, faith, meekness, temperance: against such there is no law."* Galatians 5:22 and 23

Before a child can become a peaceful person, he must be trained to exercise self-control and to practice ruling his spirit. Parents can promote peacefulness by insisting on the following seven guidelines:

(1) *No fighting is allowed in our family.* Fist-to-fist confrontations, kicking, slapping, biting, or any other kind of physical combat should not be permitted among children in a family. Brothers and sisters may playfully scuffle and test each other's strength, but anger should never be permitted as a part of their game. If warlike conditions arise, autocratic

parents should let it be known at once that such behavior will not be tolerated. And, if necessary, parents may have to use the rod of reproof.

Parents should not, however, think one session of discipline will forever solve the fighting problem of sibling rivalry. It probably will not! Children will be children and they will occasionally attempt to settle their differences behind the barn or in the alley, but if Daddy and Mother ever hear of it, or see battle scars, the children must know beyond any doubt that they are in serious trouble.

Ugly and unkind exchanges of words should also be curbed. If the harsh verbal confrontations are not halted quickly, they also should result in some form of discipline from Daddy or Mother.

How many families do you know who are at peace and have strong loving bonds? Sadly, it is not uncommon to observe families that are constantly involved in some sort of a running family feud. There are sisters who have not spoken to each other in years, and brothers who live in the same town and never visit each other. When such children's mother and father pass away and the family estate must be settled, a bitter battle over the inheritance usually ensues.

Brothers and sisters must be taught to love and care for each other. Eliminating fighting and fussing among children will strengthen their bonds of love. And, Mothers, the fighting problem is another reason you should stay in the home.

A young mother in one TUAC class told how her mother handled the fussing problem when she was a girl. She and her brother were often assigned to do the dishes together. It seemed that every time they started their project, they managed to get a verbal battle going. She said, "One day Mother finally had had all of it that she could stand." When her children's words were getting heated, she made them stop washing dishes, dry their hands, and come with her. She took them into the living room, sat them on the couch and made them start hugging and kissing each other. They were extremely angry, but their mother insisted that their expressions of "I love you" be in a warm and sincere manner. After thirty minutes of genuine expression of love for each other, they were allowed to return to their dishes.

She said she did not remember ever quarreling with her brother again, and as adults, she and that brother were closer than any of the four children in their family.

(2) *Always tell the truth.* The best way to teach a child to be honest is to avoid setting up opportunities for him to be dishonest. When you notice

that the new book you bought Sally last week is torn and the pages are scribbled on, you should not say, "Did you tear and write in your new book?" If a parent knows the answer, he should not ask the question. And if he has no evidence of wrongdoing, one should never make false accusations. When you are sure that Sally is guilty of wrongdoing, then you can approach her by saying, "I see that you mistreated your new book. I would like you to tell me about it."

(3) *Ask permission before using another's property.* This gesture of thoughtfulness will also reduce the number of sibling misunderstandings. A headstrong child whose bike has a flat tire may not take "no" for an answer when his brother tells him he cannot ride his bike. He may continue to pester and behave in an obnoxious manner until he causes strife. It should be explained to this child that he might ask his brother once and never more than twice to use his things. Any time he does not abide by that policy he will be disciplined.

(4) *Forgive and ask for forgiveness.* The art of not bearing grudges seems to be natural with children. As they get older, however, it does not hurt for them to express forgiveness verbally.

(5) *Say, "I am sorry," and "I was wrong."* There are multitudes of husbands and wives, who would give a sizable sum if their spouses had learned as a child to admit wrong and say, "I am sorry." Some people are always right, even when proved wrong, and will refuse to humble themselves and express regret over wrong actions or unkind words they have spoken. Training children in these human kindnesses will help them solve misunderstandings and be loved abundantly by those who know them best.

(6) *Talk to God in prayer.* An inner peace will rest with a child when he is taught to pray to God and ask for His forgiveness. (More will be said about prayer in Chapters Thirteen and Fourteen.)

(7) *Brothers and sisters should be content to play together or alone.* Children living in towns and cities often think they must be in the street, or have neighborhood children at their house playing, constantly. Children who are allowed to do this without limitations may grow up being discontent to stay home. When they become teenagers, they feel that home is boring and that they must be going somewhere all the time.

An autocratic mother should limit the time her children spend with other children. One to two hours in the morning or afternoon on designated days are plenty of time for them to be influenced by children from other families. Brothers and sisters should learn to be content playing and working together. When they tire of each other's company, quiet time alone is in order.

6. TRAIN A CHILD GOOD HABITS FOR HIS PUBLIC APPROVAL

Parents are often embarrassed and make excuses for their children's bad behavior in public. The truth is that children will behave away from home in the manner they are allowed to act at home. It will not be difficult to get them to obey your spoken facts in public if obedience is their daily custom at home.

Every good habit that I have listed thus far will improve a child's life, make family living delightful, and leave a favorable impression on others. To assist your child in gaining favor with the outside world, you can train him to:

(1) *Be prompt for appointments.* Making sure that your child keeps appointments with you is an excellent way to prepare him for the future. Being responsible for getting to school on time and to bed at a certain time each night, and for returning home on time after playing with a friend, will help him be responsible in getting to his job punctually when he is a teenager.

(2) *Have good telephone manners.* It is never a good idea to permit preschoolers to have unrestricted telephone privileges. Most of us have had the experience of placing a long distance call and paying for time talking to an unresponsive child. When a school-age child is allowed to start making occasional phone calls, his calls should be rehearsed with Mother ahead of time. Mother can pretend to be the party who is going to be called and see if her child is capable of adequately delivering the message. This is fun for a child and keeps a call from being wasted.

(3) *Do not stare and point at people.* Gazing at people, gesturing, and making comments about them is an honest and natural reaction for children. You can train them to be more graceful socially by reminding them that they should be careful not to hurt the feelings of others. Talking with a child is usually all it will take to help him avoid being rude.

(4) *Let older folks have his seat.* Any time a child is occupying a seat on a bus, train, or in a crowded room or assembly, and an older person is standing, your child should be trained to relinquish his seat to the elderly.

(5) *Never yell or run in public buildings.* Injuries to other people and to the child himself can be avoided when running in public buildings is

prohibited.   This, like everything else with a child, takes constant training. How marvelous it would be to tell him one time not to run in public buildings and never need to remind him again, but it does not work that way with children. The temptation to run is always present, and he must be reminded each time that the temptation presents itself.

(6) *Cover his mouth when coughing and sneezing*. This is a polite thing to do, and it is one more way to eliminate spreading germs and diseases.

As I close this chapter about training in good habits, I remind new mothers of one last thing. *Always remember that you are building that little boy or girl who one-day, must be accepted as they are by their spouses.*

ASSIGNMENT

1. Read a "good manners" book to your child and yourself this week. Visit your local library and choose a book that fits your child's age.

2. Explain these two statements to your husband by using the knowledge you have of training.

    Sentence 1 - You cannot train a child to practice a good habit by being a poor teacher.
    Sentence 2 - You can train a child to practice a bad habit by being A Good teacher.

3. Encourage your child to invite a guest home with him from worship service this week. Fix a special lunch, and help your children concentrate on all the good habits that apply to this occasion.

WORK

A Priceless Heritage

Chapter Eleven
Work

Once upon a time there were three men who were engaged in the same employment. Each was asked this question: "What are you doing?" The first man replied, "I am making five dollars a day." The second man said, "I am cutting stone." The third answered, "I am building a cathedral." All of these men were stonecutters, and all made the same wage. 1

From this story we learn two all-important laws that govern work. I will hang them as clouds over our heads in this chapter.

Law No. 1

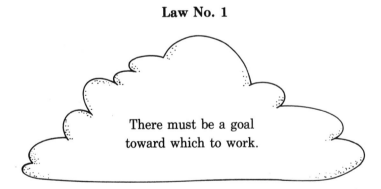

There must be a goal
toward which to work.

The men who were stonecutters had a purpose for getting up every morning. Awaiting them at their place of work were slabs of stone ready to be carved. They never had to sit idly by and wonder what to do next.

Law No. 2

One must see and enjoy
the fruits of his labor.

For one to work, he must have an incentive or reason for doing the job. No human being is going to exert himself and produce a lot of effort if there isn't a purpose in it. Time is too valuable to spend on something you feel is futile or without aim.

What incentives did the stonecutters have that caused them to put forth so much effort? One expressed by his answer that his motivation was to get the five dollars at the end of the working day. From the second man's statement, we understand that he received his greatest reward from simply enjoying what he was doing. He, in addition to his wage, received a deep personal satisfaction from exercising his skills. As for the third man, it was sheer pleasure for him to visualize the mighty building that he was helping to build.

God instituted the best and only methods for motivating one to work. They are happiness and reward if you do, and unhappiness and punishment if you don't. *"This we commanded you, that if any would not work, neither should he eat."* II Thessalonians 3:10 (Read Matthew 25:30 and Revelation 2:10.)

These two laws, of a work to do, and reward or satisfaction when you've finished, motivate children as well as adults. The key to success in getting children to exert energy is knowing how to put the two laws that govern work into effect.

Parents who do not know how to institute a working program will usually make two serious mistakes. (1) They will relieve their children of responsibility and will do everything themselves, or (2) they will allow their children to get away with shoddy or half-finished work and never correct them. Neither approach is good for the children they love.

As autocratic parents, let's analyze the subject of work while keeping in mind the two laws that govern it.

Word Is Spelled WORK

From the four letters W-O-R-K we can outline our subject. In order to train a child and instill within him the desire to work, it will take:

Wise

Organization

Regular

Keeping

I will take these four components and elaborate about each. Since the parents, are the trainers, I will talk first about your need to become *Wise;* second, how to institute proper *Organization;* and last, the importance of your children's *Regular Keeping* of their WORK.

I. WISE

Work is like a play in a football game. It has a goal in mind. In order to achieve your goal of training a child to work, there are five all-important plays to remember in the game. You will be *Wise* to tie a string around five fingers to remember each one.

Play No. 1 - *Children Play by Nature; They Work by Nurture*

The first rule parents must be wise to remember is that children must be nurtured to work. The Mother Goose nursery rhyme, "Little Boy Blue" well describes a child's view of work and a parent's challenge to inspire him to work.

"Little Boy Blue, come, blow your horn,

The sheep are in the meadow, the cow's in the corn;

But where is the little boy tending the sheep?

He's under the haystack fast asleep.

Will you wake him? No, not I!

For if I do, he's sure to cry."

Little Boy Blue was not doing his work, but no one was willing to awaken him to his responsibilities because they feared the results. Autocratic parent! Crying or no crying, you must awaken your child to do his work. You must nurture (that means bring up or train) him to be reliable.

If your child does not volunteer to do the many tasks that obviously need to be done, don't be surprised. He is only being normal. (In Chapter Nine you learned that sometimes you must make your child do what he is capable of doing.)

Play No. 2 - *Children Feel Useless If They Aren't Made To Be Useful*
The fact that children feel useless unless they are made to become useful may sound contradictory to what I just said about a child's nature. How is it possible for a child to dislike work but be happier when he has work to do? I don't know that I can give a satisfactory answer to that question, but it is a fact of human nature that we all need to feel we are capable of producing and are good for something. "Our chief want in life," said Emerson, "is someone who will make us do what we can."

"Do-With" Toys Superior to Mechanical Toys
Even when children play, they like to feel useful. In the early 1900s, Caroline Burrell compared mechanical toys to children's self-organized play. She was of the opinion that, since a child has an instinct for doing something himself, the "do-with" toys are far superior. They help develop the power in boys and girls to depend upon themselves for amusement, whereas the mechanical toys leave little for the child to do. 2

Have you had the experience of buying your boy a battery-run car and your little girl a pull-string doll? They were amused for a time, but it was not long until you heard "booden booden" and "wa wa" as they were playing about the house. They had discarded the use of the mechanical movements in favor of making their toys run with their own power and creativity.

The Lego Company has built an empire on the principle that children prefer creating their own toys. In our home, I have saved hundreds of Lego pieces and treasure the many pictures I have of incredible Lego creations. Legoland, near Carlsbad, California, is becoming the favorite place of many young families to vacation with their children. On the Internet, Lego advertises their amusement park of fifty rides and attractions as the Land of Creativity.

Teenagers Must Feel They Are Needed
In her book, *Faith in* Families, Evelyn Duvall writes that teenagers must feel they are needed. Fathers and mothers tend to do the important jobs around the house and assign adolescents the less important and more disagreeable chores. 3

Mother's preparation of delicious meals is an example. She plans and prepares the food for her family, and everyone praises her for it. After the meal is over, as Mother leaves the kitchen, she will say, "All right, girls, you do the dishes and clean up the kitchen."

Of course, the dishes have to be washed, but mothers should let her girls be creative, too. If young people are permitted to occupy positions in which their efforts receive praise and recognition, their desire to be useful is satisfied and they are more willing to volunteer their services.

Once you understand that a child wants to be useful, you will be alert to arrange jobs to encourage "mother's little helpers."

Play No. 3 - *Children Will Tag Along With a Tactful Trainer*

It is my prayer during this study that you will never lose sight of the fact that you are a trainer. You *show* and *tell*, and your children *follow* your example. Children are tag-alongs and, as the saying goes, are as "curious as a cat" when it comes to grown-up affairs. They will pursue you and want to try every new thing they see you do.

If you are a tactful trainer, you will take advantage of the times when your children want to help. If you are washing windows or polishing silver, and they want to help, move over and welcome their assistance.

As an autocratic parent, learn to work along with your little tagalongs.

Today Is Mother's Day

Once I had a marvelous opportunity to witness in action children whose mother had practiced the tagalong principle. My husband was preaching a weeklong meeting at a neighboring congregation, and our family had the privilege of accompanying him to the services each night.

After one of the mid-week gatherings, the local preacher and his wife invited our family to have lunch with them the following Sunday. We appreciated their thoughtfulness and gratefully accepted the invitation.

The preacher's house was next door to the church building; so, following the morning service, we walked to their house for lunch.

When we arrived, Roy and Norma met us at the door and cordially invited us in. They offered us a seat in the living room. After a few minutes I became puzzled about why Norma was not rushing to prepare lunch. When I asked if I could help her in the kitchen, she replied, "Oh, no! This is Mother's Day, and the children are doing all the work. They came to my bedroom early this morning, served me breakfast, and told me they didn't want me to work in the kitchen all day. I reminded them that we were having guests for lunch, but they volunteered to prepare everything."

I had brought a change of clothes for our family and asked Norma where we could change. She took us to a room close to the kitchen. As we approached the kitchen, the three girls (late grade school, junior high, and high school) reminded me that it was Mother's Day for me, too, and I was not to help, either.

Soon we were called to the dining room. The table was beautifully decorated and the meal was superb. We were served ham with pineapple glaze, hot rolls, and fresh berry pie, all made by the girls. They waited on us during the meal, cleared the table, and cleaned the kitchen without their mother's help.

The experience impressed me so much that I learned Norma's secret. I asked, "What have you done right with your girls that they were capable of preparing such a delicious meal?" She humbly replied, "I don't know, unless it is because all of their lives I have let them help me in the kitchen. Any time they want to assist, I never shoo them away. Since they were little, I have always tried to give them something to do that made them feel useful, even if it was nothing more than slicing the cheese or grating the carrots."

Blueberries For Sale

Since parents are the trainers, they must set an example of being industrious. A lazy father and mother cannot reasonably expect to produce hard-working sons or daughters.

One summer our family was informed about an abandoned blueberry field located in a valley near where we lived. The highway department had purchased the land, and the public was welcome to pick the blueberry crop before the bushes were destroyed.

My husband and I felt that it was a shame to let the blueberries go to waste. We also knew that it was an excellent opportunity to introduce the "little girls" to picking berries.

Several mornings we got up early, drove to the field and picked blueberries for a couple of hours. Some days we picked after lunch and then returned to the field again in the cool of the evening. My husband and I always kept the children with us as we worked our way through the rows of berry bushes.

Each day after returning from the field, we divided the berries into pint boxes. After we had stored a winter supply for ourselves, the children loaded the rest into a little wagon and sold them to people throughout our neighborhood. We also sold some of the berries to businesses.

Over a period of six weeks enough blueberries were sold to pay for some of their school clothes and shoes. The children were pleased to say they had helped to purchase their new school clothes.

After we bought school clothes for the children, my husband insisted that I buy a new dress with a portion of our profit. I purchased a floor-length black jumper and a white lace blouse. For years I called it my "blueberry dress" and enjoyed wearing it to the TUAC classes on the days I taught my lesson about work.

The third point we must remember about getting children to work is that we the parents must first show the way by being industrious ourselves and letting our children work alongside us. We should never make a practice of sitting down to relax and assigning them a difficult task to accomplish while we sit idly by.

Play No. 4 - *Children's Perspiration Adds to Their Appreciation*

The fourth fact wise parents need to know in the game of work is a hidden truth that lies in the heart and mind of every child. That secret is the fact that children always appreciate what they are able to do for themselves more than what is done for them by someone else. You learned in the independence chapter that teaching children to do for themselves is what we want to achieve. As your child develops independence, he will think, "Just leave me alone, and I will prove to you that I can do it without your help."

If your twelve-year-old wants a motor bike, let him mow lawns, throw papers, raise and sell an animal, or save his working allowance to pay for it himself. He will take care of that bike better than he did any of the trikes or bikes you bought him in his early childhood.

Too Much Salt

One day the older of the "little girls" came home from school and asked if she could bake something. I agreed, because I needed food items to put in their lunch boxes. She did not know what to bake, so I suggested cupcakes. That was agreeable with her, so I helped her select a recipe and gather the necessary utensils. She had already done some baking by herself, so I left the kitchen and let her work alone. (This is a tip I learned from an older mother. I will tell you about it next.)

Everything seemed to be going well, because she had not asked for any help. She appeared to be doing an excellent job, and the cupcakes began to send a delicious aroma through the house. Soon she removed them from the oven, and they were beautiful. She was very proud of herself and, of course, wanted to be first to sample one.

When she took the first bite, her enthusiasm disappeared. Too much salt had ruined the taste of the cupcakes. When she read the recipe again, she discovered her mistake. Instead of putting one teaspoon of salt in the batter, she had added a tablespoon of salt!

That evening at dinner, no one uttered a word of criticism about her cupcakes. Needless to say, however, the cupcakes were not the most popular item on the table. Did she refuse to eat them? Certainly not! She packed them in her lunch, and not one was thrown away. Why? Because she was the one who had baked them. She appreciated them far more than if someone else had done the work.

Advice from an Older Christian Mother

Once your daughter is familiar with the kitchen and has watched and worked with you awhile, the time will come when you should retreat, get out of her way, and let her occupy the territory by herself.

An older Christian mother taught me the importance of leaving the kitchen and letting girls cook by themselves. What girl appreciates baking a pie and having to give credit to her mother for making the crust? She wants to serve a pie that she made *ALL by herself.*

My sister in Christ had a teenage daughter who was an outstanding cook. At the age of sixteen she was capable of preparing a banquet for fifty people and doing an excellent job. Years ago she gave me a recipe that has been a family favorite.

When I asked my friend, Katharyn, how she taught her daughter, Jeannie, to be such a great cook, here is the formula she shared:

"When Jeannie was younger, I learned it worked better, when she entered into the kitchen, for me to get out. Someone else's mess always bothered me, and when she did not do things as I thought they ought to be done, it worried me. The most logical solution for the happiness and welfare of both of us was for me to leave the kitchen and do something else. If she needed help, she would ask for it. I avoided hovering over her and offering constant suggestions."

Any time one begins to exercise a new skill, he does not feel comfortable having an expert "breathing down his neck." Also he likes to try a little experimentation on his own. A girl may reason, "I know Mother does it this way, but I believe I will try it another way." And, believe it or not, children can come up with excellent ideas that are far more creative than anything we may ever have thought about.

Try letting your young children put a fruit or vegetable salad together *all by themselves*. It is fun to watch how they do it, and I assure you it will be delicious and you will not have to beg them to eat a bite.

Birthdays and Christmas

As I discuss the wisdom of letting children work, earn money, and accomplish things by themselves, I am not advocating that you should never buy your children presents for their enjoyment. I am suggesting, however, that you keep the extras to a minimum.   Birthdays and Christmas are special times in the year for parents to give gifts to their children.

It is a fact of human life (and we should face it in times of prosperity as well as times of poverty) that every human soul attains real happiness when he is able to achieve for himself. A child will grow up feeling worthless if he has parents or relatives who do everything for him and give him everything he wants. His maturity will be hindered because he never had an opportunity to sacrifice, plan, and save for dreams of his own.

I believe that early childhood is when parents begin making poor judgments in the matter of buying unnecessary extras for children. Babies are so precious, and they are especially adorable when they start expressing themselves verbally.

At this stage of a child's life Mother will take him shopping with her. During the course of the ride through the store, his little pointer finger starts selecting items that catch his eye. In his baby language, he will start asking for them. If mother doesn't readily respond by letting him have what he wants, he will start demanding it. When mother says "No!" he may respond with crying and ugly behavior. In order to prevent a scene in public, Mother may give in, and say, "All right, honey. I guess you can have it this time."

What has the baby learned? He has learned that, because Mother will not stick to her "no" and be willing to discipline, all he has to do is make a demand, become obnoxious, and he will get his way. Baby may reach the point that every time he is taken to the store, he feels he should be endowed with a new toy.

Children who are permitted to manipulate their parents in this manner will grow up to be selfish and demanding adults. It will become almost impossible to excite them with a gift of any kind.

Autocratic parents will be wise to remember that children need to dream, plan, and save for the extras they want.

Play No. 5 - *Children Readily Respond to Reason and Reward*

So far you have learned these truths about the game of work: (1) Children must be taught to work. (2) Children are happier if they are productive. (3) Parents must set the example of being industrious and let their children work alongside them (4) Children have a greater appreciation for things that they accomplish *all by themselves.*

We have one finger left to tie a string around. The last play we must remember in the game of work is (5) Children will readily respond to *Reason and Reward.*

You may ask, "Do you mean that if I expect to get any work out of my child, I must give him an explanation and furnish a reward every time there is something that needs to be done?" That is exactly what I mean! But don't worry about providing a payroll yet.

If you teach your child OBEDIENCE, he has built-in *Reasons* and *Rewards* for doing the work you assign.

It works magnificently! *An obedient child's Reason for working is that his parents told him what to do.* The healthy respect he has learned through their discipline will inspire him to perform his tasks immediately. *What are his Rewards?* Since fear of chastisement is an incentive for a child to work, it must also be pointed out that God does not motivate by fear alone. When a child obeys his parents, he receives, first, an inward peace and feeling of love and acceptance as a result of his parent's approval. Through his cooperation he also helps maintain a peaceful home atmosphere, which is priceless.

Second, his obedience and respect for authority result in receiving a reward that is above all other rewards. That gift is from God. God's marvelous promises of abundant protective care grace the obedient child who honors his parents. "*Children, obey your parents in the Lord: for this is right. Honour thy father and mother; which is the first commandment with promise; That it may be well with thee, and thou mayest live long on the earth.*" Ephesians 6:1-3

Isn't it fantastic that simply teaching a child to obey works to achieve so many benefits? I have wondered why God did not give a more detailed list of dos and don'ts to parents about rearing children.   When God decreed that parent's train, love and use the rod to teach a child to obey, He knew that would be sufficient.   When autocratic parents follow those simple instructions, a child's life falls into place.

Free Rewards

Parents should amply supply the free rewards of a smile, kiss, hug, pat, a word of praise, a comment of "I appreciate that" or "I am proud of you." These gifts of the spirit are reflexes that should naturally accompany parental approval.

If a parent has a poor self-image, is cold and unaffectionate, the gifts of affection, compliments, and acceptance will be withheld from the child. When this happens, he will be deprived of the warm and delightful feeling that obedience should bring.   This is why I emphasized earlier that parents must convey affectionate love for obedience to work effectively.

These free gifts of the spirit are the most enduring and satisfying rewards one can receive.   A woman who is consecrated to her husband and children thrives on them. On the other hand, if she works her heart out, yet never receives approval from the man she loves, it will kill her spirits and cause her to give up.

Children, like mothers, do not seek a weekly paycheck for the efforts they put forth.   They will thrive if they are given the intangible gifts that express that "you are great, and we cannot live without you."

We can therefore conclude that the rewards of tenderness, politeness, embraces, and commendations should be given and are to be expected from autocratic parents. They should automatically accompany the parental approval shown for a child's obedience.

"I Never Took My Eyes Off the Furrow"

Praise should not be overdone, but should be used enough to keep a child well-balanced. Undeserved praise can cause one to become egotistical and develop an arrogant personality.   If a child is starved for appreciation, he may be withdrawn and lack a feeling of self-worth.

My youngest brother tells how words of praise from our father made a lasting impression on his life.   His determination to strive for excellence was, more than likely, awakened by early experiences such as this.

All my brothers worked with Daddy. Our dry-land farm did not yield enough income to make us wealthy, but with each of us doing our part we never were hungry or without adequate clothing and shelter.

One day my youngest brother and my father were in the small town near our farm. After they had taken care of some business transactions, they stopped by the local grain elevator. Since our town was small, there were only a few places for the farmers to gather to visit and keep abreast of the latest community news.

Several farmers were assembled at the elevator that day. During the conversation, my father pointed to my brother and said, "Do you see my boy? I am really proud of him! He can plant a straighter row of crop than anyone in this country."

My brother said, "After Daddy praised me before that crowd of men, I never took my eyes off the furrow when I drove the tractor through the field." He was dedicated to living up to the praise he received and determined that none of those men would ever pass our father's fields and see a crooked row. He lived up to that compliment, too! I remember riding along the fields in the spring and fall and seeing the row crops he had planted. They were always perfectly straight.

Can There Be Other Rewards?

After a child experiences heavenly approval and receives the free gifts of warmness, affection, and praise from his parents, are there other rewards he can receive for work well done? Yes, there are! Parents can, if they wish, give material things as added compensation for good work.

Any and all added rewards, however, are optional and should be left up to the discretion of parents. As long as they remember to teach a child to produce, any added compensation is up to them. The extra rewards parents may give are numerous. The following are only a few suggestions that may serve as special rewards for work well done: Extra money, added TV time, special family nights, a night to stay up late, watch a special movie, eating out, a trip to the circus, a trip to the mountains, inviting a guest for dinner or to spend the night, a special pizza dinner, the privilege of sleeping in a tent in the back yard, or spending a night with grandparents or a friend.

Personally, I think it is an encouraging incentive to receive tangible things. I enjoy the luxuries of life enough myself to understand how exciting it can be to look forward to receiving something for which you have worked.

My Wise Fourth Grade Teacher

My fourth-grade teacher had much to do with developing my ability to spell. Her rewards motivated me to study hard to learn spelling. Her rule was that if we made a perfect score on our weekly spelling tests for a month, we would get a prize. I won her prize several times.

The reward I remember most was a large chocolate bar. It was the biggest bar Hershey made at that time and cost all of twenty-five cents. Candy was not an item that my parents kept around the house, so it was truly a prize for me.

II. ORGANIZATION

Your next challenge in training your child to work is to learn how to make the daily chores around the house run more smoothly. Since children almost never see anything that needs to be done, how can parents relieve themselves of being foremen giving constant orders to each child? Is it possible for children to be taught to perform their chores consistently, thoroughly, and spontaneously? Is it possible for parents to eliminate constant reminders to "empty the trash, make your bed, hang your clothes, walk the dog, dry the dishes, gather the eggs, feed the chickens, set the table, clean your room, do your homework"?

Wouldn't it be a blessing to assign jobs once and be done with it? The answer to these questions is absolutely *"yes."* It is possible to get children to do their chores without constant reminders every day. It can be accomplished simply and peacefully through *Organization*.

Here's How to Start

When organization is mentioned, many people throw up their hands and declare, "I am one of the world's most unorganized persons. I can't organize my own work, much less my children's."

If that expresses your reaction, permit me to show you how easily organization works and how to start. All you need to start an organized work program for your children is an hour of your time, a pencil and paper. Here is how it is done. Sit down with each child, take a sheet of paper, write his or her name across the top of the page, and number one to ten.

Start out with early morning and mentally go through a day. The age, sex, and abilities of each child should to be taken into consideration when making your work list. Make a list of all chores your little worker needs to accomplish from the time he rises in the morning till bedtime. Let your child express his opinion about his jobs and how he would like for them to be listed.

The first hour and a half of a seven-to-twelve-year-old's schedule might look this way: He must get out of bed when awakened (or his alarm goes off), wash his face, comb his hair, get dressed, put his pajamas away, make his bed, straighten his bedroom, set the table for breakfast, feed his pet, eat breakfast, brush his teeth, participate in family devotions, and be on his way to school by 8:30 A.M.

Continue to work through the day mentally. After your child arrives home from school he must change his school clothes, do his homework, feed his pet, play, do additional chores, eat dinner, have a time of sharing with the family, take a bath, brush his teeth, and off to bed.

Many parents of children aged four to twelve scold and prod, then give up and finally perform most of the work themselves. This is ridiculous and totally unnecessary! The frustrating process of getting a child to perform his chores can be achieved by sitting down with him twice a year (once at the beginning of school and once at the beginning of summer) and organizing his duties on a chart.

Figures 1, 2, and 3 are suggestions of how children's work lists can be organized. The following is the key to the symbols that precede each number: O=Jobs that must be done prior to breakfast or before school. □=Jobs that must be done after school and before dinner. ✱ = After-dinner jobs.

Figure 1
(Ages 4 - 6)

Since children this age cannot read, pictures are all that are necessary on their organized work list. Comments in parentheses are for the parents to use in explaining the chores to the child.

O   1.   (Get dressed.) You lay out his clothes.

O   2.   (Comb your hair and wash your face.)

O   3.   (Make your bed.)

O   4.   (Hang up your clothes and arrange your room.)

□   5.   (Feed the fish.)

□   6.   (Pick up and stack Daddy's paper in the garage.)

☐   7. ⬜   (Empty the bathroom trash.)

✱   8. ▭▭ (Take your bath and brush your teeth.)

✱   9. TOYS   (Pick up and put away all your toys.)

✱   10 🕐   (Go to bed at 7:00.)

Figure 2
(Ages 7-9)

The chores at this age will vary according to whether the child is a boy or girl, and whether you live in the city or country.

O   1. Make your bed.

O   2. Clean up your room.

O   3. Set the table and count out the vitamins for breakfast.

O   4. Help with breakfast clean-up.

☐   5. Feed and water the cat.

☐   6. Keep napkin holder, sugar bowl, and salt and pepper shakers filled.

☐   7. Set the table, and prepare the glasses of water for dinner.

✱   8. Bathe and brush your teeth.

✱   9. Empty the kitchen trash.

✱   10. Pick up and put away the baby's toys.

✱   11. Go to bed between 7-9. (Parent's choice)

✱   12. Read the Bible or a Bible story book before "lights out."

Figure 3
(Ages 10 - 12)

Notice that by this age some previous chores can be dropped from the chart. Hopefully they will have become habits by this time. If a child occasionally omits making his bed, brushing his teeth, or hanging up his clothes, a warning can correct the situation.

Some of the items listed may not appear to be work, but they are responsibilities that children need to assume instead of the parents. Such things as watching the clock for school or bedtime and remembering to brush teeth should be a child's responsibilities instead of mothers. Listing these on the work sheet will help him remember them so that they will eventually become habits.

○   1. Practice your musical instrument.
○   2. Clean and fill the pet's bowl.
○   3. Prepare the water and toast for breakfast.
☐   4. Do your homework.
☐   5. Clean the garage.
☐   6. Walk the dog.
✳   7. Help with the clean-up after dinner.
✳   8. Sweep the kitchen, and dining area.
✳   9. Prepare tomorrow's school lunch.
✳   10. Take a bath and brush your teeth.
✳   11. Go to bed between 7-9. (Parent's choice)
✳   12. Read your Bible and "lights out."

Step Two

After you and your child have worked on the list, go to the store and purchase a bulletin board. Type or write your chore lists that will be tacked on the bulletin board. Plan a method of how each chore can be marked as it is accomplished each day. You can use colored peg pins, magnets, paste-on stars, a marker, or pencil.

Remember two things: (1) Place your bulletin board low enough on the wall so *the child* can do the marking, pasting on stars, or moving peg pins or magnets. (2) Display several copies of the children's chore lists at different locations in the house. Put them on their bedroom or closet doors, their bedroom or bathroom mirrors, on the refrigerator, near the breakfast table and on the entrance door. On these copies, remind them to go to the bulletin board and make their entry when each chore is done. At the bottom of each note, sign your name. On my notes I have written through the years I established my own trademark by turning the "O" in the words Love and Mother into a heart as I made my signature.

Here is an example of what your bulletin board with peg pins will look like:

NAME

1 2 3 4 5 6 7 8 9 10 11 12

O O O O □ □ □ ✳ ✳ ✳ ✳ ✳

O   1
O   2
O   3
O   4
□   5   JOBS
□   6
□   7   ASSIGNED
✳   8
✳   9
✳ 10
✳ 11
✳ 12

Three colors of peg pins should be used. Blue could be for before-school jobs (O), yellow for after-school and chores to be done before dinner (□, and red for after-dinner jobs (✳). Line these twelve peg pins vertically along the left side of the numbers 1-12 of the assigned jobs.

Explain to the children that, as they do each assigned job, they should remove the peg pin on the left and place it in its corresponding number at the top of the page. At the end of the day, all you will need to do is glance at their charts; and if all twelve peg pins are horizontal across the top numbers, you know the jobs were done. Mother, you should put the peg pins in their original vertical positions. The next morning the children will know that you are diligently watching to see that their chores are completed.

Step Three

Parents often make the mistake of setting goals that will take a child six months or a year to attain. If a child is told he can spend the summer at his grandparents' farm if he makes A's in school all year, it is too overwhelming and will destroy his enthusiasm. The goal is simply too remote and hard to attain. The child will give up in discouragement.

Notice that you must be wise in assigning your children's jobs and goals. Just as children take short steps and have short attention spans, you should give goals that can be reached in a day.

At the end of each day when your child finishes his goals, what can he look forward to as a reward? The answer to that question depends on you. If you want to praise him and let his breakfast, lunch, dinner, and occasional new clothes be his daily reward, that is your prerogative. You do not *have to do anything more.*

If you would like to see your child's eyes brighten with joy and enthusiasm, give tangible rewards for a day's work. *After you have completed steps one and two by making and posting a work list, step three is to plan the tangible reward you will offer your child at the end of each day or week.* Once you have your work program organized, you may choose a variety of rewards. But, to get started, here are some simple suggestions.

Children four to six love coins. Before you start them with their work, go to the bank and buy several rolls of coins (I would use pennies to start little ones and, as they grow older, increase to coins of larger denominations) and place them in a jar. At the end of the day, give a coin for each job done. To eliminate the temptation for a child to deliberately omit one or two of his least favorite chores, establish a rule that all peg pins must be posted across the top of the chart or no coins will be given.

Valuable lessons can be taught with a coin chart. Go to a store and purchase three little coin purses and attach them to your child's bulletin board. On one write *God's,* on another *Savings,* and on the last *Mine.* As you give your child his coins each night, divide the coins among the three purses. Start with God's purse. This will teach him that from his earnings he always gives to God first. Each Lord's Day before he goes to worship, he will open God's purse and take that part of his weekly earnings and place them in the offering plate.

The *Savings* purse gets every second coin. A child can learn at an early age the value of saving some of his earnings to help him attain a worthwhile goal in the future. When the *Savings* purse is full, let your child empty it, take the money to the bank to deposit in a savings account you help him open.

Every third coin can go into the purse labeled *Mine.* These are the coins that your child may use to buy things for himself. Give him the liberty to spend these coins as he chooses.

When children are old enough to figure percentages, you can begin preparing them for the future when they will receive a weekly paycheck. *Teach them the wise principle of giving God ten percent, saving twenty percent, and living on seventy percent.*

Giving money for work completed can be used for children of any age. The philosophy of a child's working for an allowance is superior to the idea that, whether a child produces or not, he should be given money simply because he is a member of the family.   Remember-- a child always has greater appreciation for what he does for himself.

If you choose to give coins, remember to give the coins at the end of each day, instead of at the end of a week or month. Your bulletin board will now look like this:

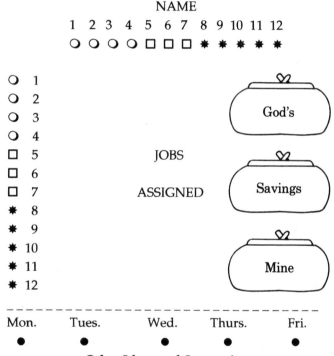

Other Ideas and Suggestions

Notice five days of the week have been added at the bottom of the chart. This is for the purpose of establishing an additional weekly goal. As the jobs are completed each day, an additional peg pin can be posted for that day. If there are five peg pins going across the bottom of the work chart at the end of the week, grant a special weekend reward. In addition to earning an allowance, a child can spend a day with a friend, go skating, attend a sports event, or do some other activity.

Over the years, my husband and I varied our work lists and rewards in many ways. During some periods we would give money or allow viewing a favorite TV show to be the daily reward for good work. But our special family night was the all-time favorite reward. I give my husband the credit for making these nights so exciting and enjoyable.

When Friday night rolled around and the peg pins stretched across the chart for the week, our family did something special together. We would all load into our car and go to a restaurant or to a hamburger stand to eat, then to a good movie, or some other enjoyable entertainment. We often visited the local marina to watch the boats coming and going or we would take a bike ride on the bike paths in the city or mount our bikes on the car and go to the country for a ride. Miniature golf or a drive in the mountains was fun in the summer. Whatever we did, we enjoyed it together, and the children were allowed to stay up late.

When we stayed home on family night, we played games like Risk, Monopoly, Mouse Trap, Wah-Hoo, or dominoes in front of our fireplace. We usually popped popcorn, made candy, or enjoyed some other special sweet treat. We topped off the reward for the week by promising a Saturday morning of cartoons.

If the Work Chart Is Not Working

This organized work program captures new mothers' interest and enthusiasm when I present it. They go home and immediately set it up and try it with their children.

After a few weeks' trial, however, a few will say, "My children were excited about the work idea for a while, but now it is not working." (Remember that children play by nature, but they work by nurture.)

If the work chart is not working, there is a reason. The following are three reasons that a child may not follow his written work assignments:

(1) *He may lack respect for parental authority.* Lack of respect for parental authority is the first reason that a child may refuse to do his work. Before a child will work, it is imperative that he respects his parents' authority. *"Foolishness is bound in the heart of a child; but the rod of reproof will drive it far from him."* Proverbs 22:15.

The work chart is simply a beneficial tool that parents can use to eliminate giving daily facts. By this means they write their facts once, instead of speaking them every day. Until the written facts are changed, the child must understand he is expected to obey. If parents choose to give a material reward, it is an additional kindness from Daddy and Mother.

An occasional honest omission of a chore should be forgiven, but the child will not receive his reward. But when the dog consistently goes unfed, the trash is never emptied, or the napkins are never folded in the napkin holder, parents must mete out appropriate discipline.

(2) *Failure of parents to be consistent* is the second reason the written work assignments are ignored. Mother must be as diligent to check her written word as she does her spoken facts.

She must be diligent to make sure all chores are done. If one child has neglected his work and his brothers and sisters have been diligent, the negligent one will be required to remain home with a baby-sitter on family night, in addition to missing his allowance. If the parents are inconsistent and let the indifferent child have his allowance and participate in family night, do not expect him to improve next week.

(3) *Rewards are not meaningful rewards.* This will cause a child to be disillusioned with the work chart. If he works diligently and is never commended or praised for work well done, he will be discouraged.

Furthermore, if a child is jaded because he has everything he wants and already enjoys adult privileges; he comes and goes when and wherever he chooses, and is permitted to stay up as late as he pleases, Daddy's and Mother's rewards will mean little or nothing to him.

To be effective, rewards must be meaningful. They must be something a child can be excited about and will work to obtain. If every day is Christmas and he already has anything and everything he wants without exerting effort, then it is almost impossible to motivate a child with the promise of a reward.

My great uncle was an insurance salesman who made house calls on clients and used to tell this story. After completing a call, he walked to his car to leave. He thought he would be nice to the family's smallest boy. He reached in his pocket, pulled out a nickel, and gave it to the child.

The lad took the nickel, without a thank-you, and drew his arm back and threw it into a patch of weeds. He said to my uncle, "What's a nickel? We have a lot of those around here!"

If a child has too much, a reward will fail to impress him.

The Summertime Work Schedule

It is good for a child to have a summertime work schedule. When school is dismissed in the spring, it causes a major headache for some mothers. What do you do with your children when they are home seven extra hours during the day?

The best way to solve that problem and to experience a peaceful and happy summer is to *Organize!* Sit down with your child and write things that must be done throughout the day.

Summertime is an excellent time for children to learn new skills like painting, cooking, gardening, sewing, ceramics, wood-working, horseback riding, swimming, and attend Christian camps.

Out To Breakfast

I always looked forward to having the children home in the summer. Good organization and planning helped us enjoy each other and at the same time accomplish worthwhile goals.

The first morning after school was out in the spring, I made a date with the children to visit a restaurant for breakfast. While we ate, we worked out our summertime schedule. If one happened to have a weakness in a particular school subject such as math or reading, we planned to spend some time each day strengthening that area. Band instruments were not stored for the summer. They were practiced daily.

The summer months are an ideal time for children to learn various kinds of creative handwork. After we finished our breakfast, we went directly to an arts and crafts store. I explained that each one could choose two projects. It had to be something they could sew, paint, or build. On the first day after school was dismissed they were involved in a creative project.

During the summer vacation, there is time to teach your children to perform charitable deeds for others. There are plenty of opportunities to do acts of kindness. Assign children the tasks of writing a letter, making a telephone call to one who is sick or lonely, call on a neighbor and offer to do a small chore, or read a story to baby brother or sister; these are good ways to develop Christian character. Take the children with you to deliver a loaf of homemade bread or share produce from your garden with a lonely widow.

On our summer morning restaurant trip, we stopped by the neighborhood library and checked out several interesting and informative books. We signed up to do volunteer service, too. Children ten and older are sometimes welcome to go to the library on designated days to learn how to do library work.

By the time we had finished breakfast, all of the following responsibilities were listed on individual summertime schedules: clean my room, make my bed, and groom myself for the day; set the table for breakfast; set out vitamins; help with breakfast clean-up; care for the pets; work on a piece of creative handwork; do a kind deed; help with garden work; help with lunch; help with lunch clean-up; read a chapter from a library book; practice my musical instrument; work on math; set the table for dinner; help with dinner clean-up; bathe, brush my teeth, and put on clean clothes; empty the trash; go to bed at (7 to 9); read the Bible.

Garden work and cleaning duties were assigned daily. A garden can be kept free of weeds, and walls throughout the house kept cleaned, simply by assigning *small* chores to your children each day.

Following an organized schedule helps to make your summers more enjoyable, and you and your children will build happy memories.

I Remember

I am reminded often of the summertime work schedule I used to keep with the "little girls" while they were in their "learning years." Hanging on my bedroom wall is a beautiful needlepoint flowered picture done in pastel pinks and blues. The youngest of the "little girls" made that for me after she was married and expecting her third child.

I remember the summer that she learned to do needlepoint. We had enjoyed breakfast together in a little shop and then stopped at the hobby store to choose our crafts. She showed me a needlepoint kit that contained two small pictures that when finished, would be pretty decorations for her bedroom wall. I was slightly apprehensive about buying the kit because I thought it might be too difficult for her. I knew how to crochet but had never done needlepoint. She insisted she wanted to learn, so we bought the kit. As I suspected, she could not do it without help; but we located a lady who was skilled at needlepoint who helped her learn. She not only finished both pictures, but became very skilled doing needlepoint.

The Saturday and Spur-of-the-Moment Jobs

Now that I have given a detailed description of how to organize routine chores, let's consider spur-of-the-moment jobs and Saturday clean-up. How can Mother get Melvin to clean out his cluttered closet and the shelves in the garage that have not been touched for six months? How can Mary be motivated to plunge into Saturday morning vacuuming, dusting, and cleaning of the bedrooms?

The question is not whether Melvin and Mary agree to do the jobs. The question is how long before they will be finished? Since children will be children, if Melvin and Mary are left unsupervised, they may make an all-day project out of an hour's job. Mother has two choices of how to handle this problem.

(1) She can permit Melvin and Mary to take as long as they please. Or (2) she can create a logical consequence involving various rewards or consequences.

When I was a girl, our family's Saturday afternoon trip to town was a real treat for me. We drove thirteen miles into town to shop for the weekly groceries and household supplies. My Saturday morning chores were often done quickly and quietly because I did not want to miss the trip and stay home. The reward of going to town on Saturday served as a special incentive for me to get my work done.

Do's and Don'ts of Special Job Assignments

Here is a word of caution about jobs that you have not included on your daily work list. Do not say, "Girls (boys, or children) go do a certain job!" There is an old saying that a girl is a girl; two girls are half a girl, and three girls are no girl at all.

You should assign specific tasks to each child. *Do not leave organizing up to the children.* It is also a good idea to separate the children, so that each is left alone to do his tasks. When children work separately, the temptation to play and quarrel is removed.

A fair way to make job assignments is to draw straws or flip a coin. If two sisters are assigned to clean the house, divide the house between them equally by rooms. Take a broomstraw and break it into short and long straws. The one who draws the short straw will be assigned to clean certain rooms and the one who draws the long straw cleans the other rooms.

Making Major Adjustments

Before leaving the subject of organizing children's work, I suggest that you may need to make major adjustments in your living conditions if you are really serious about training your children to work. This is especially true, as they grow older. You may be required to relocate completely in order to provide your children with the best employment opportunities.

One minister tells an impressive story of how his father taught him to work. This man's father wanted his son to learn the lesson of *hard* work, so he approached a farmer friend. His father told the farmer, "If you let my boy work on your farm, it will be free labor for you. I will pay his wages. I just want you to teach him to work."

It wasn't until the minister was a grown man that he learned the sacrifice his father had made in order to teach him the principle of hard work.

Books on Korea

My husband and I once used this idea of paying the wages for the older of the "little girls" to work. She went to the library and checked out three books. It was the beginning of the school year, and a new Korean student had enrolled in her class. The children were so exuberant over the experience that she and some friends wanted to check out library books to read all they could about Korea. Of course, like many childhood thrills, it wasn't long before her enthusiasm faded. She put the books in a drawer and forgot them.

Six weeks had passed before I remembered those library books. I asked her about them and, sure enough, they were still tucked away in the drawer and long overdue. From the librarian we learned the fine had grown to more than two dollars. I knew she didn't have enough money to pay her debt and didn't believe there were enough unassigned chores around the house to give her the extra work needed to earn enough to pay her fine.

To solve our problem, we worked out an agreement with the librarian. We would pay her fine if they would let her work thirty minutes a day at the library for two weeks. This arrangement worked smoothly and she learned a valuable lesson. We were grateful to have had a means by which we could teach her responsibility, and the library benefited from her free services.

III. REGULAR KEEPING

The last major consideration in the game of work is to stress the importance of your children's *Regular Keeping* of their work. Just as Daddy goes to work on time and Mother feeds the family on a regular schedule, children should be expected to do their chores regularly. They will feel useful and have a much deeper appreciation for their home and family if they are busily involved in helping the family affairs operate smoothly.

Children's work must be kept three ways:

(1) *Kept by the children* - We must never give our children jobs unless we know they are capable of performing them. If they are capable, then the jobs are theirs to do, not ours.

(2) *Kept separate from play* - Work and play don't mix. Work mixed with play is like water mixed with oil. It doesn't come out on top. We need to remind our children,

"Work while you work, and play while you play;

This is how you stay happy, throughout the day."

A Basketball Made From a Tea Towel!

During my "learning years" I needed to have an occasional "reminder." Most of those incidents were brought about because I did not separate my work from my play.

My evening assignment was to help Mother with the dishes. She washed the dishes and I was to dry them and put them away. One evening Mother was diligently washing and stacking the dishes for me to dry. While they were piling higher and higher, I was running through the house pretending to play basketball throwing a tea towel. I would wad the towel into a ball and throw it at the door facings. I loved basketball and pretended that I was engaged in a game, shooting the ball to score.

Soon, Mother had no room left to stack the dishes and they began cascading back into the sink. I knew I was in trouble when she dried her hands on her apron and went out the door to the nearest tree. Even though I worked as fast as I could to dry those dishes and catch up, Mother returned to the house with her switch. She didn't "monkey around." When her patience wore thin, our bottoms were worn out. I always knew, if she went to get a switch, it would be used.

The rod is the best remedy if play becomes a deterrent to work. *"Foolishness is bound in the heart of a child; but the rod of correction shall drive it far from him."* Proverbs 22:15

(3) *Kept well* - Do not accept children's work that is only half done. Make them repeat it again and again until it is done thoroughly and correctly. Our children are too valuable to permit them to get away with inferior work habits.

An article titled "Slipshod Methods" appeared in a young people's weekly paper. Here is a portion of what it said:

"Do your best, not because your work is worth it, but because you are. Whatever you are doing, you are making manhood. Half-hearted work makes only half a man. Slipshod methods mean loose principles. The only way to keep character up to the standard is by continually living up to the highest standard in all that you do."

--from Young People's *Weekly*,
as quoted in *Leaves of God*. 4

Start a Hock Shop

If you expect your children to do their work well, you must be a good example and do your work in an efficient manner, too. Often, when mothers are admonished that they should be more diligent about keeping their house in order, some are quick to retort, "If I only had to pick up after myself, my house would be immaculate! When you have five or six throwing clothes and other items around, it is an impossible mission to keep the house neat."

If you are a mother who is tired of picking up your family's clutter of coats, shoes, schoolbooks, purses, and hats that have been thrown across the chairs, on the table, or left in the middle of the floor, your life will be much easier if you break your children's habit of throwing things down and leaving them for you to pick up.

If you are convinced that you have done more than your share of picking up after your family and are ready to put a halt to it, here is how you can solve the problem. *Start a Hock Shop*.

Choose a special drawer or closet where there is plenty of room to store all of the misplaced items you collect throughout the house. If David's baseball glove is cluttering your coffee table after yesterday's baseball game, pick it up, put a price tag on it (whatever would be fair for David to pay from his allowance), and put it in your Hock Shop.

The next time David is ready to go out to play ball, the question will ring out, "Mom! Have you seen my baseball mitt?" Graciously reply, "Yes, sweetheart, it's in my Hock Shop for sale."

Explain to your children that when you must go through the house picking up their things, the articles are going to be put in your Hock Shop. Set a deadline when everything must be put away. Automatically confiscate anything that is left out after bedtime. You may put a low price on a treasured possession for the first offense. If the same item appears a second or third time, raise the price each time. If the child has no money and needs his only pair of shoes to wear to school the next morning, get him up early and let him do a special job in order to get his shoes out of the Hock Shop.

Prepare a special jar or piggy bank in which to deposit your Hock Shop money. It will not be many days until you will have enough saved to give to a charitable cause or purchase a pretty item for the house.

A Christian who reared four outstanding children gave me this idea, and it has worked marvels for me. If you have the same experience I had, your Hock Shop will thrive for a while, but your children will become so careful about putting away their things it will soon go out of business.

A Christmas Special

Mothers aren't the only ones who have difficulty maintaining neat quarters. Daddies do, too. They often wish they could mow the lawn or work in the garage without stepping over numerous toys. What can daddies do to solve this problem?

A TUAC student once told a class how her husband handled the matter. She said he decided to hide a large box in the rafters of the garage. Every time he had to pick up forgotten toys, he would toss them into his secret box. The children were puzzled and commented about their playthings that had disappeared, but her husband never revealed where they were.

At Christmas he took the box down, wrapped it, and put it under the Christmas tree. On Christmas morning, she said, the children were as excited about retrieving their lost items as they were over the new toys they received.

The Best Inheritance

A child's ability to work will build in him feelings of self-assurance, self-acceptance, and personal worth.

In closing this chapter, I pass on a message from "the winners." It was their conviction that children must be kept busy. They agreed that, whatever else you do for your children,

> "The best inheritance a parent can leave
> a child is a will to work."

ASSIGNMENT

1. Draw a picture of your hand on construction paper. Cut it out and write on each finger one of the five rules to remember in training your child to work. Display it somewhere to refresh your memory this week.

2. Sit down with your child and organize a work chart for him. Listen to his wishes and work with him until you have a satisfactory schedule. Buy a bulletin board and display the schedule on the wall. Be sure it is in a convenient location and low enough for him to reach. Remember to write extra copies of the chore lists, sign them, and place them throughout the house.

3. Start a Hock Shop.

Section III

Communicating

Together

we

Pray and Worship

COMMUNICATING

Takes Your Time and Tests Your Temperature

Chapter Twelve
Communicating

Some years ago Hollywood lost one of its famous stars when she committed suicide. The actress who took her life had won both fame and fortune, and was admired by hundreds of thousands. Because of her outstanding popularity and great achievements, a movie was produced in her memory. In the production a childhood scene revealed a great void in the young woman's life. The following is a brief description of that scene:

School had been dismissed one day, and the future actress was excited about being promoted. She knew her mother would not be home; so she ran down the street in her small home town to the store where her mother worked.

When she rushed into the store, the manager told her, "Your mother is in the back working." She walked hurriedly to the rear of the store and found her mother knee-deep in boxes. With bubbling excitement she started sharing the news of her eventful day. But, before she could finish her story, her mother angrily shouted, "Can't you see that I am busy?"

The teenage girl turned slowly, left the store with her head bowed and walked slowly toward home. Her footsteps quickened when she thought about going to her friends' house to share her news with them. When she arrived, she skipped up their steps and rang the doorbell. She rang it again and again, but no one was home.

With a sad face and dejected spirit she trudged home, throwing a few rocks along the way. When she turned the doorknob and walked into their lonely, dark house, no one was there to greet her but the family cat. She went to the refrigerator, got some milk, and poured some of it into the cat's bowl. As her pet eagerly lapped up his treat, the future movie queen lay down beside him on the kitchen floor. She stroked his fur and looked into his face and quietly said, "I got promoted today."

Emotional Versus Physical Neglect

This girl who would eventually become a Hollywood star was emotionally neglected as a child. She lived an unhappy and lonely life. Whatever the reason for her mother's working, the repercussions were devastating to the child. Her mother was obviously too tired and busy to give her the time and attention she longed for and needed.

Physically neglected children are easily identified. They are seen in ragged clothes, and go about with holes in their shoes. Their bodies may be thin, drawn, and perhaps even bruised and scarred. In the wintertime they may arrive at school without a coat, and day after day no provisions are made for their lunch. A child who is not sufficiently fed and clothed will usually draw immediate attention and sympathy from society. If the parents of such a child do not make improvements in their living conditions, they may lose their child to the juvenile authorities.

Unfortunately, the emotionally neglected child is not so easily detected. Many children grow up in financially privileged homes but are emotionally destitute. A child's emotional bruises and scars may not surface until years later. The frustrations he endures may be kept inside during his childhood. The troubles that deeply disturb him may lie dormant and unnoticed. When they finally surface in the teenage or early adult years, they are devastating. The time that parents of troubled children are awakened to their child's emotional disorder may be when he is arrested for stealing a car, their daughter is pregnant out of wedlock, or their son or daughter is on drugs or has run away from home.

Let's Immunize Our Children Against Emotional Neglect

As autocratic parents, immunize your children against emotional neglect. In addition to providing a properly ordered parental relationship, love and affection, firm discipline, independence, good habits and constructive work, you can help them by developing a strong bond of communication.

God created language as a superior means by which humans express their inward feelings of joy, excitement, disappointment, grief, fear, or anger. God confused the tongues of men to stop the building of the tower of Babel. All that was needed to frustrate the men of Babel and force them to desert their project was to confuse their tongues so that it was impossible for them to understand each other.

In a similar manner, deficient communication is harmful to children. The events of life naturally produce a mixture of feelings and reactions. A child must have a confidant with whom he can talk freely and openly. If no one is there to understand or care, his frustrations will mount. He can tolerate inattention or neglect for a while, but eventually he must have someone to care and listen or he may vent his feelings in a destructive way. In the case of the Hollywood star, her method of escaping her misery was to commit suicide.

Nine Communication Necessities

What are the skills parents need to achieve open lines of communication with their children? Before answering that question let's first consider things that are not essential. Many people have the mistaken idea that, in order to communicate effectively, they must practice good grammar, master clear pronunciation, possess a large vocabulary, and acquire a wide range of knowledge on a variety of subjects. If you were competing for a position as a television commentator, it would help to be skilled in those areas. However, you are a down-to-earth parent attempting to do a good job rearing your children. It is great to have an excellent command of the English language and a vast storehouse of knowledge, but these are not prerequisites to good communication with your children.

There are nine requirements for good parental communication.

No. 1 - GOOD COMMUNICATION
REQUIRES GOOD LISTENING

Napoleon, the famous leader of France, was asked what he felt was the greatest need of his nation. He replied, "What France needs most is mothers! Mothers! Mothers!" If that same question were asked of an American, an additional word could be included. America needs *listening* mothers! *Listening* mothers! *Listening* mothers!

The first talent you must master as a parent who is a skilled communicator with your children is to become a good listener. When I teach this lesson about the importance of communication, I have fun checking new mothers' communication equipment. Since ears are for listening, I give a test to see how well mothers hear. They must listen to a clock tick for a minute and then tell me how many ticks they heard. If they get within ten of the number on the recording, I give them a point. Very few pass the test. The purpose of the exercise is not to discover defects in the physical hearing of class members, but to impress the lesson that it takes concentration to be a good listener.

Hearing is one of the five senses, but *listening* is an *art*.

No. 2 - GOOD COMMUNICATION REQUIRES GOOD EYE CONTACT

Your eyes make up the second important piece of communication equipment with which you are blessed. It is through vision that many non-verbal messages are passed and received. Facial expressions, posture, smiles or even tears are ways we send messages that are received by the eye. Of the many women whom I have the privilege of teaching, I can with amazing accuracy select the ones who agree or disagree with what I teach. Without speaking a word, they often convey their approval or disapproval.

One of my brothers is a successful businessman and civic leader in his community. Because of positions he holds, he and his wife have had many opportunities to travel. One of the outstanding characteristics about them is that they always exert their Christian influence during their journeys. They do not mind being different even when it is not popular.

From Seattle, Washington, to Miami, Florida, they can *visually* be identified in a large convention crowd. When the bands play for the dances and alcohol flows freely and goes down smoothly, they remain in their seats and say, "No, thank you, we do not care for any." No sermon is necessary. Without speaking a word, they are recognized as Christians by many of their business associates. They communicate their faith through their behavior. They have made friends with other Christians whom they pick from a crowd who also refuse to partake in worldly entertainment.

Communicate Eye to Eye

The ability to look into the eyes of the one with whom you are attempting to communicate also is an aid to establishing rapport. It signals the one to whom you are speaking that you are interested enough in him to give your full attention to what he is saying (more important still, that the person himself is important to you.)

Eyes are the windows of the soul. I have heard my father say; "There is something wrong with a man who cannot look you in the eye." We have all had the experience of attempting to converse with another that would not look at us. His glances from ceiling to floor or around the room make it difficult to carry on a conversation. When this happens, we get the impression the individual feels uneasy with us.

How steady is your eye contact? The second test I give my students is to see how well they can fix their eyes on an object without being distracted. They are asked to follow the second hand of a clock for one minute without diverting or blinking their eyes. This little drill is not easy to master and requires strict concentration. When the test is completed, I remind the mothers that they do not need to stare at their children. I hasten to add, however, that if they were able to pass the test, they have the ability to maintain eye contact and convey the feeling that what their child says is important to them.

To listen well and establish eye contact with her child, a mother may need to stop the sewing machine, mixer, or vacuum cleaner many times in a day. It may also require sitting down or kneeling down in order for a five-foot five-inch mother to have eye level contact with her thirty-six-inch-tall pre-schooler. *It is great exercise, and every mother should remember that it makes for more effective communication, to kneel to be on the same eye level as her child when they converse.*

No. 3 - GOOD COMMUNICATION REQUIRES SIMPLE WORD RESPONSE

As I come to the third point in our communication lesson, I test the last major instrument of communication - - our tongues. As ears may become rusty from lack of use, tongues are often in danger of overuse.

To test your tongue and its ability to use simple word responses, practice the role of the *receiver* and view your child as the *sender*. Pretend that your little one has entered the house joyfully to share an exciting experience or event with you. After stopping your work, making eye contact, and listening intently, what response is necessary with your tongue? Actually, very little! It is so simple to be a good listener and let your child express his thoughts and feelings that no parent should fail this test. It only takes a few simple words and phrases to encourage your little *sender* to continue talking until he "tells all." A formal education is not a prerequisite to play the part of a good receiver.

Are you ready to learn if you can pass this final test? If you can utter the following simple words, you can clear the path to superb communication with your child when he comes to share his experiences with you:

Oh!	That's interesting!
Is that right?	You don't say?
How about that!	Terrific!
Really?	I see!
Uh-huh	Great!

How well did you do? Could you read those words and phrases with enthusiasm and zeal? If you did, you are in great shape. *As long as you look and act interested, listen carefully, and give simple and short responses, your child will continue to send you messages until he has told you everything he has to tell.*

NO. 4 - GOOD COMMUNICATION REQUIRES MUCH, MUCH TIME

Good communication takes time and tests your temperature. As I teach points four through eight of good communication, I use a clock to teach lessons we can learn from its features.

Communicating with children is *TIME* consuming. As a clock is made to keep time, we must be devoted to taking time to listen to our children.

The need to develop good communication is one of the chief reasons that it is vitally important for mothers to stay home with their children. The mother of the Hollywood star made a critical mistake in not sharing her daughter's world by taking time to listen. A baby-sitter or day-care worker is unlikely to take your "little angel's" dreams, fantasized stories, hurts, real or imagined, seriously in her heart. She simply does not have the time or concerns you have to give the invaluable gift of personal attention to your child

Psychologists are frustrated by the growing mental health problems in our society. They tell us the family is failing in its task of communication. The most effective solution they have discovered for helping those who are mentally deranged is small-group therapy. If patients who are emotionally troubled can sit down with two or three others and share their problems, it is tremendously helpful.

Mother, spend plenty of *TIME listening* to your little ones. You will be a great sounding board for your child, and help to prevent him from developing future mental or emotional distress.

Two Special TIMES
There are two special times in a day that parents can use to advantage in communicating with their children.

(1) *Mealtime* - Historically, it has been recognized that Chinese Americans have few children who become delinquents.   When the president of the Chinese Consolidate Benevolent Society of Chicago was asked why their children maintained such clean records of good behavior, he revealed a simple formula. He said, "Our children are always home at mealtime."

To the Chinese, mealtime is a ceremonious affair, which must be attended by every member of the family. As autocratic parents, you would do well to apply this lesson in your home. Use family mealtime to sit around the dining table and visit with your children.

(2) *Bedtime* - Lovingly tucking your children into bed at night is a delightful way to end the day and will build memories that last a lifetime. A friend of mine once told me of a practice she had started with her first child. Her husband worked at night, and she was left alone in the evening with their little girl. My friend was so lonesome that, when she put her daughter in bed, she would sit on the edge of her bed and they would talk. This became such a special time that the child would save her day's experiences to talk over at bedtime. As each of their three children came along, she did the same with them.   When they were older, the children kept no secrets from their mother. During their special time together (bedtime), they shared their thoughts and deepest feelings. They enjoyed the rich blessing of a mother who was a good listener.

*No. 5 - GOOD COMMUNICATION REQUIRES SENDING
WORDS THAT ARE NUMBERED*
As you think about the next four communication lessons, assume the role of the *sender*. This is when you have a message for your child. A clock has only a few numbers, and good communication requires sending words that are few.

Dr. Montessori, the Italian educator, had this motto on her school-room wall: *"Let Your Words Be Numbered."* It is a fact that the more you say, the less people remember. I have covered the concept of limiting your amount of talking. In the obedience chapter, you learned   (and I encourage you to practice) that an authority tells her fact once, never more than twice; and, if need be, she will follow her fact with further proof.

"No" Means "No"

I remember learning two important lessons from a Canadian missionary and his wife. For a week my husband and I had close association with them and their six children. The love and closeness radiated by their well-behaved children was impressive.

I asked them this question, "What is your secret in training your children to be so pleasant and well mannered? Without hesitation, they both responded with the same answer. "We have two rules that guide the way we handle our children. *The two of us are always united with regard to the rules we give our children; and "No" means "no."*

Four Important Rules About Using the Word "No"

There are four important rules for parents to remember about using the little word "no."

Rule 1 - *Don't say "NO" if you can possibly say "Yes."* If you have a tendency to be negative and pull the "NO" lever too quickly when asked for your permission to do something, write this rule on a slip of paper and paste it on a nearby cabinet or mirror.

In learning to obey, a child must be taught to respond quickly to his authority's spoken facts. Do you not agree that it is only fair for a mother to reciprocate with that same kind of honor and respect to her children? For example, when a child requests a drink of water or an object that is too high for him to reach, a mother should promptly respond to his needs. Delay in receiving assistance can be frustrating to one who is unable to help himself.

We often hear a little one described as a good-natured child. To some degree patience may be an inborn quality. But lovingly meeting a child's physical and emotional needs on schedule from early infancy will help him develop into a contented and happy child.

(This concept of tending to your child's needs first is Dr. Denmark's theme throughout her addendum.)

Rule 2 - *Reduce your "No's" to a minimum during the years from one-and-one-half to three years old and from thirteen to fifteen.* [1] You have previously learned about the shadowing and darting period and the "negative and discipline" years which begin at two. These transition periods bring about great changes in a child's development. The same is true when a child leaves his "learning years" and enters adolescence. It is during these intervals that a child experiences spurts of emotional and physical growth. He is, in a sense, experiencing new worlds. For this reason it is good for parents to be wise in giving their facts during these stages of growth.

Rule 3 - *Say "NO" to things that REALLY matter.* Make sure that the things you refuse your child are of real significance and beyond doubt would be damaging to the physical, spiritual, mental, or social well-being and safety of your child.

I once knew a man who was forbidden as a child to play at all on Sunday. He remembered with bitterness his parents' refusal to let him play ball when he was a boy. As an adult, he experienced serious emotional disturbance, left the church, and abandoned his wife and children.

Rule 4 - *Substitute a "YES YES" in place of your "NO NO."* This rule applies not only to the busy and inquisitive hands of a baby, but to older children, too. If you tell your child he may not read a certain comic book, choose one for him to read that is entertaining and harmless. Choose the "yes yes" movies, computer sites, videos, CD's, and television programs that your children can enjoy rather than saying "no no" and labeling all entertainment evil.

Unwholesome, immoral activities are strictly taboo for Christians. Any devoted Christian, young or old, understands he is different from the world. A boy or girl who is sincerely committed to Christ must resolve in his or her heart that he or she must at times stand alone on principles. Some of the world's fashion, parties, and speech simply cannot be integrated into a Christian's life.

The advice I give is that, when you restrict your children from engaging in an indecent or offensive activity, replace it with one that is both fun and appropriate. It is damaging if a child is made to constantly feel that he is a social outcast. Autocratic parents need to get aboard the bandwagon of being positive and provide wholesome recreation for their children to enjoy.

A Runaway Horse

I believe women have more of a tendency than men not to know when to hush once we begin talking, especially when we are angry or upset. We can be like a runaway horse.

I do not believe that, when being corrected, a child hears more than the first few words. When a rebuke turns into a long lecture, a child seems to have an automatic switch he turns off. It is usually wise for mothers especially to remember to let your words be numbered.

NO. 6 - GOOD COMMUNICATION REQUIRES SENDING WORDS THAT ARE TRUE

Everyone wants a clock that is an accurate timepiece. It is disappointing to view the beautiful face and hands of what appears to be a clock and then discover that it is a facade with no mechanism inside. A counterfeit clock reminds me of a dishonest parent. They may look good on the outside, but you can't depend on them from the inside.

If you have failed in some way to understand that honesty is indispensable, you have missed a vital part of the lesson of how to be an autocratic parent. In so many ways I have emphasized the importance of being truthful with your children. Be consistent. Give a command *once* and mean it. If you threaten or create a logical consequence, carry it out. If you say "no," mean "no." These principles of honesty are essential, but, if you would like to increase your children's respect for you immensely, learn to say the words *"I was wrong" and "I don't know."* If you make a mistake with your child, admit it to him and graciously apologize.

A needed apology may be extremely difficult for some parents to offer. They feel that to maintain respect for their authority, they must never confess any wrong. They believe that it reveals weakness to admit a mistake.

That simply is not so! Children admire honesty and will respect you far more if you possess that quality. If you attempt to appear infallible and refuse to admit it when you have made a mistake, your children will see through your hypocrisy. *The moment a parent loses the quality of truthfulness, he becomes transparent and his children can see through him.*

I believe it is possible to reveal honesty through actions as well as through words. To treat spilled cereal as if it were as serious a matter as a kitchen curtain being on fire is unfair. It isn't as serious a matter and should not be treated as such. If we treat an outright lie as if it were a genuine mistake, that, too, is not honest. A premeditated falsehood is an offense far more serious and had better be dealt with accordingly. Be determined as a Christian parent to be truthful both in your words and actions.

Are You My Real Mother?

There are few children who never wonder if they really belong to the parents who are rearing them. They may muse, "Perhaps they got me mixed up in the hospital, or maybe my real mother left me on these people's doorstep."

However, an adopted child, once he learns that he is adopted, knows that he has parents somewhere else in the world. If his adoptive parents do not give him truthful answers, his concerns can grow into a serious problem.

Occasionally young adoptive mothers will ask me what is the proper thing to tell an adopted child. My reply is this: "*tell him the truth.*" In the case of an adopted child, the truth is that his biological parents could not or would not keep him. Whatever the situation may be, a child can truthfully be told, "Everybody in the world has to have love, food to eat, clothes to wear, and a place to live. Your parents weren't able to give you those things, and they cared enough to arrange for you to be loved and cared for. Daddy and I wanted a little boy (or girl) to love. We had this nice house and enough money to buy food and clothes, so the adoption agency helped us find each other.

"That makes us very special people. We needed a little boy and you needed a daddy and mommy. I am so glad God helped us find each other."

It is my personal faith that, if an adopted child is taken at birth and is truly loved and reared the autocratic way, adoption will seldom amount to anything more than a passing fact of the child's life. The adoptive parents will always be his "real parents."

No. 7 - GOOD COMMUNICATION REQUIRES SENDING WORDS THAT ARE ON TIME

In the introduction I said that whatever you want your child to be as a teenager, you must start teaching him now. It is a mistake to believe you can give your eighteen-year-old son a two-hour lecture on the importance of marrying a Christian, after he has given a non-Christian girl an engagement ring. It is obviously too late. The time that the concept of Christians marrying Christians should have been implanted was by eight instead of eighteen.

Dr. Fitzhugh Dodson says, "It is important to answer all of your child's questions; and the brighter the child, the more questions he will ask." [2] (Remember that you have one-half million questions to answer from each of your children from birth to fifteen.)

You have enough practical experience to answer most questions asked by children twelve and younger. If you do not know the right answer to a question, no harm will be done if you are honest. Admit , "I don't know, but we can find the right answer." *If a child asks a legitimate question, the thing to remember is that he is entitled to a prompt and honest answer.*

There may be times you will feel like a computer that has had its buttons punched all day. I encourage you not to grow weary in the well-doing of answering your little ones' questions.

A kind and patient matron once helped a young mother who was going through the "learning years." After losing her patience, the mother told her son, "Please, *please* stop talking for a little while." The more mature woman quietly advised, "Just listen to him, Mother." The young mother never forgot that phrase, "Just listen to him, Mother." It helped her through many years to be a better Listening Mother. [3]

One Exception

There is one exception, when you do not need to pacify a child by answering all his questions. You should ignore questions that are foolish or when you are sure he already knows the answer. Occasionally, because of boredom, a child will ask silly questions. The best way to discourage this is to follow Jesus' example. Do not give an answer, but challenge him to do the thinking. Ask a good question in response and let the child answer his own question.

Help! What Do I Say?

Many parents feel uncomfortable about answering their children's questions in the area of sex. It is reported that ninety-five percent of American parents fail to give adequate, *on-time*, information to their children about sex. That means only a meager five-percent answer their children's questions about the sexual functions of male and female.

God designed sex to play such an important part in the world that it is impossible to ignore the subject. A family cannot drive down a city street, listen to the evening news, or read the Bible without the relation of the sexes being brought to their attention.

School systems have assumed the responsibility of informing young people about sex. This is a shame. *Autocratic parents should remember that it is their job, not the school's, to teach sex education to their children.* The reason many young people will go to a teacher or another individual to learn the meaning of words such as rape, homosexual, virgin, adultery, harlot, eunuch, incest, fornication or circumcision (all Bible subjects) is that somewhere along the way their parents cut the communication lines about this subject.

The first rule young parents need to know about teaching their child about sex is to be honest and on time with their information. It may be a crucial moment when a child asks his mother what his sex organs are called, or where do babies come from. Her reaction and truthfulness to these questions can either make or break future communication about such intimate subjects. I always encourage young mothers to remember that, if a child is mature enough to ask the questions, he is entitled to a simple and factual answer.

If you feel it will make you uncomfortable when your child asks, "Mommy, where do babies come from," let me help. First of all, I assure you that it is unnecessary to worry about what to say. When the unexpected moment occurs (and, believe me, you will not know when or where it will be asked), follow these rules:

(1) *Do not act embarrassed.*

(2) *Use a short, simple word response. Say, "That is an interesting question."*

(3) Further say to your child, "*I have a special book that I have been saving to read to you when you were old enough to ask that question.*"

(4) *Act immediately. Get the book and sit down and read it to your child.*

You must prepare in advance to answer your child's first questions about sex. Visit a Christian bookstore and purchase a beginner book that is written to children. Make sure the author has written the information to teach that sex is a part of God's marvelous plan. As your child matures, continue to buy books written by Christian authors that offer more advanced information. Your family pediatrician is another good source for suggestions about where to obtain helpful material about sex education.

A well-written book will answer your child's question in the most precise way. If you still feel uneasy about explaining the matter in your own words, read again any portions of the book about which you feel uneasy.

Keep the book special. It should not be kept with other books, but should be kept in a special place.

Once you have given your child accurate information about sexual functions, you will feel comfortable that you have given important information that your child should know. You will be able to communicate freely on any aspect of the subject of sex as your child grows to maturity. In addition to giving your child honest answers, you have opened the door for future communication on other important subjects. He will feel free to come to you instead of his peers for moral instruction.

No. 8 - GOOD COMMUNICATION REQUIRES SENDING WORDS THAT ARE SOFT AND BEAUTIFUL

The last lesson we can learn from a clock is to send words that are soft and beautiful. Everyone admires a clock with a soft tick and a beautiful chime.

I am reminded of the little poem that cautions us about our speech.

> I'm careful of the words I say,
>
> To keep them soft and sweet.
>
> I never know from day to day
>
> Which ones I'll have to eat.

The wisdom of the Bible informs us: "*A soft answer turneth away wrath.*" Proverbs 15:1

"*A soft tongue breaketh the bone.*"   Proverbs 25:15

The only occasion when a mother should shout is if the house is on fire or to warn about some other impending tragedy. Do you know that the more loudly one talks, the louder children become? I have quieted a classroom full of children many times by lowering my voice to almost a whisper.

In one school at which I taught, there was another Christian lady who worked with me in the same wing of the building. She could not muster a great deal of volume with her voice. One who walked past her classroom would hardly have known that it was full of children. Her softness and tenderness had a positive, quieting influence on her classes' behavior.

Try lowering your voice when talking with one or more children. As long as you keep your voice low, they must be quiet to hear you.

Beauty More Than Softness

Even more important than softness is the graciousness of our words. You can maintain beautiful speech when speaking about others. Mention the good you find in others and not their faults.

A child reared in an autocratic environment will at times be appalled by the atrocious behavior of other children. He may come home and describe all the bad things Jimmy did today. Take care that this does not develop into the undesirable habit of fault-finding

A Professor's Findings

Don't forget that mealtime is an excellent time to communicate. While you sit around the table and visit, you not only have an opportunity to influence the tone of your home, but you can teach your children many valuable lessons.

A professor at the University of Pennsylvania once did a study about the content of dinner-table conversations. He concealed microphones in two hundred homes. Upon completion of his study, he divided the conversations he recorded into five categories.

Some contained only monosyllabic terseness. All there was to these conversations was "more," "yes," "salt," "pepper," "please," and "thanks." In the second type, the conversation was centered on the faults found in family members. A third group conversed about the evils of people outside the family.

Only a select few were in group four. They conversed about the positive side of people and things. Group five was the smallest and had the most unique conversations. These few families discussed political and social issues. 4

One of the assignments at the end of this chapter is to hang a sign over your dining table. Hang it by a thin thread so that it will turn with the circulation of air. On one side write: *No bad talk about people.* On the other side write: *We talk about things, events, and ideas.*

Don't Bring Mud in on Your Feet

Keep your words positive, and avoid slang and profanity. Much teaching needs to be done about the New Testament command. *"Let no corrupt communication proceed out of your mouth, but that which is good to the use of edifying, that it may minister grace unto the hearers."* Ephesians 4:29

Slang and cursing are like mud on our shoes. We can teach our children they may not be able to avoid being where it is used, but we must not bring it into our homes. Keep profanity out of your hearts and keep your family's words soft and beautiful.

No. 9 - GOOD COMMUNICATION REQUIRES A MOTHER WHO IS HAPPY AND CHEERFUL

Good communication not only takes your time but it also tests your temperature. As I teach this final point of good communication, I use a thermometer as a visual aid. I employ it to remind mothers that, just as a thermometer measures the temperature of the atmosphere, children measure the emotional temperatures of their homes. They usually do this by estimating their mother's temperament.

What Do We Mean by Temperament?

One's temperament is his moods. It is how he feels at a given time. Is he happy and are events of his life going well? Is he sad and are things going badly? Is he depressed or elated? The way a person feels within determines the degree of his temperament temperature.

Mother, the Thermostat

Every home has its own emotional temperature. Whether that emotional atmosphere is warm, cold, or lukewarm is usually evident. The home atmosphere may be so hot or so cold that it is unbearable, or it may be warm, comfortable and very pleasant.

Mothers, usually, are the emotional thermostats that control the household comfort zone. Daddy is present fewer hours; therefore, he influences the family atmosphere less. He may occasionally cause the household temperature to plunge sharply or skyrocket, but as soon as he departs, Mother can regulate the emotional temperature again.

From Frozen Eggs to Hot Biscuits

In chapter seven I described the large two-story farmhouse in which my family of eight lived when I was a child. It was located in the middle of the Oklahoma panhandle, which was once called No Man's Land. The terrain is so flat that one can see for miles in every direction. In the winter, the old timers used to say, "There isn't anything between us and the North Pole but a barbed wire fence."

The temperature sometimes dropped to twenty degrees below zero at night. I remember seeing my father come into the house with snow and ice covering his face after braving a winter storm. Following sandstorms, my mother scooped dirt out of our farmhouse with a shovel. Life was very hard at times, but my parents always worked on.

When I was older, a floor furnace was used to warm the ground floor, but there was no source of heat upstairs. In the winter it was so cold where we slept that we sometimes put eggs or a glass of water on the inside windowsill to see if they would freeze. By morning the eggs had burst and the water had frozen solid.

On those cold winter nights my mother would pile the blankets and heavy comforters on our beds. My sister and I would snuggle down and soon be toasty warm and fall sound asleep.

In the mornings we welcomed the sunlight when it beamed through our east windows. We dressed as fast as we could while trying to avoid putting our feet on the freezing floor.

Then we ran downstairs and huddled around the warm furnace, and relished the aroma of hot biscuits floating from the kitchen. The thought of Mother's fresh-churned butter and homemade marmalade spread on hot biscuits was sufficient to coax us out of our warm beds on those frigid mornings.

Those are wonderful memories. I don't resent (and didn't at the time) sleeping in that cold bedroom upstairs, because the physical temperature of our home was not what mattered the most. My mother made up for such discomforts by warming the temperament temperature of our family. Her sweet songs that drifted out of the kitchen, and loving arms that hugged me each morning, made up for any physical discomfort I experienced in the winter cold or the summer heat.

It Is True

Yes, Mother, it is true that your temperament sets the temperature that really matters in your home. It is far more important than physical temperature measured by the mercury in a glass thermometer. If you have a cold and icy disposition, your children will huddle together in fear and dread. A mother who is hot and steaming with anger and frustration will cause her children to flee to more pleasant surroundings. But a mother who is soft with her voice, has a smile on her lips and a song in her heart will gather her children around her as a crowd gathers around a glowing fireplace on a cold winter evening.

Good communication demands good listening, eye contact, simple word response, much time, and an economy of words. Mothers, let your words be true, on time, soft and beautiful, and work to set your emotional climate with a cheerful and happy spirit. All this will help enhance your children's self-esteem, understanding, and knowledge.

A Happy Mother Must Be a Healthy Mother

As I write about the importance of a mother's being happy, I am reminded of a letter I have kept in my files. In my TUAC classes, I had never taken the time to dwell on the importance of mothers maintaining good health. Its importance was brought to my attention when I received the following letter from a former student:

Dear Gwen,

I just wanted to take a minute to write you. Perhaps my experience could help someone else. I took *Training Up a Child* last fall. You may not remember my name and face, but I must share this.

I was thrilled with the course. I had prayed for some time for guidance in raising our children (boys two and four). I went home optimistic that now I would do better. I did a little better, but not much. So I prayed and reviewed the lessons. And prayed some more. But I still failed repeatedly. I felt guilty and that my character was poor. The first part of March, we moved to a small town. I then got sick enough to go to the doctor, and he put me on antibiotics. I got better. I finished unpacking, trying to rest, too. I wasn't consistent and I'd lose control and yell. I'd be sorry and think I wouldn't do it again, but in a few days, I would. There were some good days, like the day I gave each boy a mixing bowl and we made two separate batches of cookies.

But in a while, I was sick again. I went to a different doctor and he put me on antibiotics, but in ten days I was worse. He put me in the hospital and scheduled exploratory surgery to find out what the problem was. He had to call in a surgeon, who described me as a "disaster area" (he said I would have been a fatality in one more week). My small intestine was infected and had formed an abscess which was leaking into my body cavity. They removed two feet of my small intestine, a half-foot of large intestine, and my appendix. There was a place on my colon which had been eaten through by the infected part, and gangrene had set in there. They repaired it and left it outside my body to heal for ten days. On May fifth, they replaced my colon. They couldn't suture my incision because of all the infection. I had to heal from inside out. I came home May ninth, and I praise and thank the Lord for my life.

I realize this is extreme.   The final diagnosis was Crohn's Disease. They said I've had it ten years.   No wonder I was struggling so.

Perhaps you could suggest to your ladies that if they try so hard and struggle so without much success, maybe they should see a doctor. Things will be better.

In Christ,
A TUAC Student

Letter From a Boy

Here is another letter I will share with you.   It appeared in a paper several years ago and carries with it my message of *Take Time and Communicate.*

LETTER FROM A BOY 5

"It is too late for us because the damage has already been done. Our child has a record, and no one forgets about a thing like that. But maybe if we share this letter, it will help other parents. Thank you very, very much.

Parents of a child who 'went wrong'

Dear Folks,

Thank you for everything, but I am going to Chicago and try to start some kind of new life.

You asked me why I did those things and why I gave you so much trouble.   The answer is easy for me to give you, but I am wondering if you will understand.

Remember when I was about six or seven and I used to want you to just listen to me?   I remember all the nice things you gave me for Christmas and my birthday.   I was real happy with them for about a week, but the rest of the year I really didn't want presents.   I just wanted you to *listen* to me like I was somebody who felt things, too.   I remember even when I was young I felt things, but you said you were busy.

Mom, you are a wonderful cook. You had everything so clean, but you were tired so much doing all those things that made you busy. You know something, Mom? I would have liked crackers and peanut butter just as well- - if you had only sat down with me a little while during the day and said to me, "Tell me all about it so I can maybe help you understand."

And when Donna came, I couldn't understand why everyone made so much fuss. I didn't think it was my fault that her hair is curly and her teeth so white, and she doesn't have to wear glasses with such thick lenses. Her grades were better. too, weren't they?

If Donna ever has any children, I hope you tell her to just pay some attention to the one that doesn't smile very much. That one will really be crying inside. And when she's about to bake six dozen cookies, tell her to make sure first that the kids don't want to tell her about a dream or a hope. To small kids, thoughts are important, too, and they don't have so many words to use when they tell about what they have inside them.

I think that all the kids who are doing so many things that grownups are tearing their hair out worrying about are really looking for somebody that will have time to listen a few minutes and who really and truly will treat them as they would a grownup who might be useful to them. You know - - polite to them. If you folks had ever said to me, "Pardon me" when you interrupted me, I'd have dropped dead. If anybody asks you where I am, tell them *I have gone looking for somebody with time, because I've got a lot of things I want to talk about.*

"Love to all"

It's Later Than It's Ever Been Before

One morning a little boy got up before the rest of his family. Soon after he was up and around, the family clock began to chime. It was eight o'clock, but sometime in the night a spring had broken in the clock. The little boy counted - - "eight, nine, ten, eleven, twelve, thirteen" chimes, and the strikes continued on and on. He became so excited over the mechanical failure of the clock that he began to run from one bedroom to another waking all the family. He shouted, "Wake up! Wake up! It's later than it's ever been before." 6

That is the way it is with communication. If you haven't started good communication with your children, it's later than it has ever been before. Set your clock, adjust your temperature, and remember - - *A family that talks together, walks together.* 7

ASSIGNMENT

1. Really concentrate on being a Listening Mother this week. Use these three steps:

    a. Listen

    b. Look your child in the eye as he talks.

    c. Use one of the short word responses.

2. Create a real conversation piece for your house. Paste a fancy little sign above your thermostat that reads: *Let's Be Partners.*

3. Hang a sign by a thin thread above your kitchen table. On one side write: *No bad talk about people.* On the other side write: *We talk about things, events, and ideas.*

TOGETHER

United We Stand or Divided We Fall

Chapter Thirteen
Together

The Gluecks were a husband-and-wife team, who conducted a thirty-year study for the Harvard Law School. They were assigned to go into a large eastern city and find the determining factors as to whether or not a boy would become a delinquent. Over many years of concentrated study, they isolated five critical factors in a child's home environment that would make the difference. They concluded that, if a boy had the following ingredients in his life, they would provide a protective shield from delinquency:

(1) The boy must receive discipline from his father.

(2) His mother must supervise him.

(3) The father must show him affection.

(4) The mother must show him affection.

(5) There must be cohesiveness in the family.

I have already thoroughly covered the Gluecks' first four points, which are the importance of the father and mother, love, discipline, and a mother who stays home and supervises her children. Their last finding was that a family must stick together. The importance of family togetherness is the subject of this chapter.

Before addressing the things a family should do together, I suggest you answer the following yes or no questions:

Do you want your daughters to follow your:

Yes No 1. Moral Standards

Yes No 2. Personal Habits

Yes No 3. Religious Convictions

Yes No 4. Example of being a wife, mother, and homemaker?

Do you want your sons to follow your husband's:

Yes No 5. Moral standards

Yes No 6. Personal habits

Yes No 7. Religious convictions

Yes No 8. Example of being a husband, father, and provider?

United We *Stand*

I have chosen *United We Stand or Divided We Fall* as the theme for this chapter. A very important word in this title is *Stand*. Every parent *stands* for something. Just as a merchant selects and sells his products, parents display the moral standards they keep, personal habits they practice, religion they embrace, and the manner in which they perform as mates and parents. The question is, "Are their products worth selling?"

If you were able to answer *yes* to the previous eight questions, you are displaying products that you believe are worth buying. You must gather your children close to you and expose them to your standards as much as possible.

Human beings are gregarious. Therefore, we want to be with other human beings. Family is the place in which the feelings of belonging, closeness, and companionship are learned. This human longing for fellowship is the reason parents must arrange their lives so that they will be their children's closest companions and draw them into a tight unit of togetherness. Parents must use their love and influence to deeply impress their children with their family values.

United Means Unified

Another important word in my title is *United*. I addressed this in Chapter Six, but because of its vital importance, it must be mentioned again.

Daddy and Mother must, above all else, present a united stand. No force is strong enough to break down the family walls IF Daddy and Mother are united. It is when one parent teams up with the children against the other parent that a home and what it stands for is seriously weakened. It is no longer united, but divided.

The children are put into positions where they must choose which standard they will buy, Daddy's or Mother's. They are neither wise nor mature enough to know what is best for them. When parents are divided, it leaves their children confused, and in a serious dilemma.

Parents must never forget that any time there is an area about which they do not agree, they weaken the foundation of their home. That weakness can be the beginning of problems that may eventually cause their home and everything they have stood for to come crashing down.

She Turned Her Back on Everything and Everybody

A minister tells the tragic story of his younger sister. When she reached the teen years, he said, she completely turned her back on their family. After she graduated from high school, she left their home in the South, traveled to the West Coast and joined a hippie colony.

When the minister was asked how this happened to his sister, he replied, "It was the way my parents handled her. Daddy was strict with us boys, and when our little sister came along, he didn't change. But Mother didn't agree with his strictness in handling our sister. Daddy would take a strict stand, and Mother would revoke it. She always took our sister's side against daddy. The only way I can explain why my sister has gone so wrong is that Daddy and Mother never agreed on how to handle her."

A Frequent Question

Each time I speak about the need for parents to be united, I am asked this question, "What is a Christian woman to do if she is married to a non-Christian husband and their values are sometimes poles apart?"

I must admit that I don't have answers to all the questions that may arise from such a union. One thing I do know, however, is that a woman in that position must always remember she is there because of her own choice. There was a time when she bought her husband heart and soul. If he was that attractive, there surely must be something about him worth selling to his children.

There are three reminders I like to give a Christian woman married to a non-Christian man.

(1) *Never forget God's command for a wife to be obedient to her husband.* I was acquainted with a Christian woman who submitted to the wishes of a non-Christian husband for many years. He demanded that his lunch be served and on the table at twelve o'clock and Sunday was no exception. She had to leave the morning worship service early in order to comply with his wishes. Because of her submission to him, as well as her consecrated service to God, he was won to Christ and later served as an elder in the church.

The scriptures teach that we must obey God rather than man. *"Then Peter and the other apostles answered and said, We ought to obey God rather than men."* Acts 5:29

A wife who refuses to obey her husband, in the first place, is not in obedience to God. If a situation exists in which a woman is unequally yoked in marriage to an evil and ungodly husband, who constantly pressures her to engage in sinful behavior, God does not expect her to engage in behavior that would destroy her soul. She can if necessary withdraw from his leadership and live alone. Any time conditions are so hopeless that a husband constantly jeopardizes his wife's spiritual welfare, she should arrange her life so that she can above all else, serve the Lord.

(2) *Work at being a superb helpmeet.* A second rule for a Christian wife to remember is to work at attracting, adapting to, and appeasing her non-Christian husband. This is a second key to winning him to Christ. When he witnesses daily his wife's gifts of admiration, sexual compatibility, companionship, and preparing meals that suit his taste, he will often become more receptive to spiritual instruction.

(3) *Let your Christian light shine to others.* After you have attended to the needs of your husband and children, do good deeds for others. As you have opportunity, help the sick, elderly, lonely, grief-stricken, shut-in, and orphans in any way you can.

Ten Building Blocks

When teaching this lesson, I use ten building blocks and construct a house. For the remainder of the chapter, I will emphasize the ten things a family can do in order to unify and strengthen its home.

NO. 1 - *A FAMILY CAN WORSHIP TOGETHER*

Worshiping God is the spiritual mortar that holds a home together. The reverence a family gives to God keeps everyone in a proper perspective. In Chapter Fourteen, I will list the acts of public worship, but first, think about the value of daily private worship that a family shares together.

Richard Baxter was a minister who lived in England many years ago. For three years he preached his heart out and had no visible response. "Finally one day," he wrote, "I threw myself across the floor in my study and cried out to God: 'God, you must do something with these people or I'll die.' " He said it seemed that God said, "Baxter, you are working in the wrong place. You are expecting revival to come through the church. Try the home."

Mr. Baxter then began to work at getting families to start daily worship in their homes. His congregation sprang to life and grew to be exceptionally large. 1

Nothing can start or end a day better than for a family to bow their hearts together before God's throne. God told His people of old:

> *Hear, O Israel: the Lord our God is one Lord: And thou shalt love the Lord thy God with all thine heart, and with all thy soul, and with all thy might. And these words, which I command thee this day, shall be in thine heart: And thou shalt teach them diligently unto thy children, and shalt talk of them when thou sittest in thine house, and when thou walkest by the way, and when thou liest down, and when thou risest up. And thou shalt bind them for a sign upon thine hand, and they shall be as frontlets between thine eyes.. And thou shalt write them upon the posts of thy house, and on thy gates."* Deuteronomy 6:4-9

A family worship should include these four ingredients:

(1) *Every member of the family should be in attendance.* The time of day when all family members can gather together for worship will vary. Early morning is the best time for some families, whereas late evening is better for others.

(2) *The devotion should be brief,* but not rushed. The time spent in worship will depend a great deal on the variation of ages of those attending. Usually from ten to twenty minutes is sufficient.

(3) *There should be variety.* Every day's devotional should not follow the same routine. There can be Bible reading; story telling; listening to tapes or CD's; sentence, silent, or individual prayers; singing; memory work; questions-and-answers discussion time; or simply silent meditation.

(4) *It should be understandable.* Everyone in attendance should be enriched. If Daddy reads Scriptures that are difficult to comprehend, he should stop periodically and explain the passage in simple words. If your children are small, choose one or two songs that are simple enough for a three-year-old to participate in and understand.

Whether a family's worship is private or public, they should all assemble together. Parents should not send their children to worship services, but take them. This is training. It is not only "doing as I say" but "doing as I do."

NO. 2 - A FAMILY CAN WORK TOGETHER

I have already addressed the subject of work, so my additional remarks will be brief. There is one more question I am often asked in TUAC classes.

Many mothers wonder, "Is it all right to teach boys homemaking chores?" The answer is yes. There will be occasions in the life of every young man when it would be helpful for him to know something about cooking and house cleaning. Contrary to the thinking of some, a boy is not a sissy because he knows how to use a broom or fry a hamburger.

Effeminacy in a young man is caused by factors that have nothing to do with learning domestic chores. An extremely cruel and unjust father or an overprotective mother often produces a boy deprived of masculinity. Mothers sometimes smother their sons with pampering and over-protection to such an extent that he identifies with the feminine gender. Mother becomes his constant refuge and defender. This boy is not taught to exercise masculine instincts of strength and bearing responsibility. He becomes a defenseless, self-indulgent weakling.

Children are never confused about identifying with the proper gender if Daddy and Mother accept their own God-given roles. When I was in my formative years, the roles of men and women were never confusing to me. My father's and mother's word was law, and they backed each other without variation. Daddy provided our living, and Mother's department was to be the homemaker. My brothers naturally identified with Daddy, and my sister and I with Mother.

Outdoor projects provide an excellent opportunity for all the family to work together. Gardening, keeping lawns and flowerbeds, picking fruit or setting up and keeping a campsite are things a family can work at together.

If you choose to homeschool your children, you will have to learn to work together efficiently.

Don't Expect More From the Oldest

I will at this point share with young mothers a common regret among older mothers. After their children are grown, many mothers may think back over the years and say, "I was so much harder on our oldest child. I expected more of him than I did of the younger ones. I wish I had that period of my life to live over."

Parents who are overly eager for a child to grow up may cause this mistake. They are overly anxious for their children to advance rapidly.

This develops into a pushy situation in which parents begin to expect children to develop adult skills quickly instead of letting them come naturally.

Learn a lesson from experienced mothers and do not expect your older children to achieve faster or work harder because they are the first born. Each child has his own capabilities, and we must be wise enough to determine accurately what they are.

NO. 3 - A FAMILY CAN TALK TOGETHER

The subject of talking together has also been covered thoroughly. However, there is one remaining facet about communication in a family that often causes problems.

Many times Daddy and Mother may, without knowing it, give contradictory permissions or facts. A child may approach his mother and ask for her consent to do something. Perhaps the time is not right, and it will upset her daily schedule, so she says *no*. The child then quietly slips around to Daddy and asks him permission to do the same thing. Daddy does not know about Mother's negative response, and his child's request does not interfere with his plans, so he says *yes*.

What is Junior to do? Daddy and Mother are divided. Children are smart as little foxes. Junior may have planned to have Mother overruled. This works especially well for children if Daddy gives the answer they want. A child immediately reasons that Daddy is the boss, so his positive reply should automatically overrule Mother's negative response.

Parents absolutely must not tolerate this sort of conniving. *A child needs to understand that if he is told NO by either parent, he is not to go to the other to attempt to get the no changed to yes.* Parents should also have another understanding. If a particular action is all right with one but there hasn't been an opportunity to talk it over with the other parent, the proper response is, "It is all right with me IF it is all right with your daddy (or mother)."

I remember how efficient my father and mother were at sticking together on permissions. They were as competent as private investigators. After worship on Sunday morning, a friend would often ask me to go home with her for lunch and to spend the afternoon. I would ask for the permission from whomever of my parents was closer. If it were Daddy, I would ask, "Daddy, is it all right if I go home with Phyllis today?" He would never give a direct answer. He always asked,

"Is it all right with your mother?" If I said, "I don't know. I haven't asked her." He always replied, "Well, you go ask your mother."

Away I would go to look for Mother. When I approached her with the same question, she never gave a hasty answer. She always inquired, "Have you asked your dad?" I would tell her, "Yes, but he told me to ask you." Her usual reply was, "If it is all right with your Daddy, it is all right with me."

Off I would go to find Daddy again. I would locate him once more and say, "Daddy, Mother said, if it is all right with you, it is all right with her for me to go home with Phyllis." Permission would finally be given when he said, "If it's all right with your mother, it is all right with me."

At the time I didn't understand the reason for all the red tape. But now as an adult I understand perfectly. My parents had a private communication system that permitted no misunderstandings.

Keep a Proud Family Name

Another important subject families need to discuss is the need to preserve a good family name. "*A good name is better than precious ointment.*" Ecclesiastes 7:1.

Many young men and women have refrained from indulging in activities that could eventually lead to disgrace, because they did not want to tarnish their family's name.

A young man once told his father after he was married, " Dad, many times as a boy, when I was tempted to engage in a questionable activity, your words, Son, don't forget you're a Harrison,' would go through my mind. You will never know how many sins those words kept me from committing."

YOUR NAME 2

You got it from your father; 'twas the best he had to give,
And right gladly he bestowed it; it is yours the while you live.
You may lose the knife he gave you and another you may claim,
But you'll never hurt your father if you're careful with his name.
It was fair the day you got it and a worthy name to wear;
When he got it from his father, there was no dishonor there.
Through the years he wore it proudly; to his father he was true,
And the name was pure and spotless when he passed it on to you.
Oh, there's much that he has given that he values not at all;

He has watched you break your playthings in the days
    when you were small.
You have lost the watch he gave you and you've scattered
    many a game,
But be careful when you're tempted to be careless with his name.
It is yours to keep forever, yours to wear the while you live,
Yours perhaps at some time distant . . to another boy to give.
And you'll smile as did your Father smile upon his baby fair,
If a clean name and a good name you are giving him to wear.

A TUAC student gave this poem to me, and shared with me this
beautiful family story.

    "My grandmother gave birth to fifteen children. Three died
before they were grown, but with the help of God and a
wonderful husband she reared twelve. Seven of the twelve were
sons. Most of them grew up in the days of cardboard suitcases
during the depression.

    "The story goes that, as each grew old enough to leave home to
seek his fortune or go off to war, Grandma wrote this poem on
paper and pasted it inside the lid of his suitcase. His instructions
were to 'live out of the suitcase' until he married.

    "My uncles tell me they revered their mother and did as they
were told. They say that each time they opened their suitcases,
they could not help seeing this poem written in her own
handwriting. They say it was reminder enough to keep them out
of plenty of trouble. I guess it was, because one now serves as an
elder in the church and two are deacons.

    "They were all raised in the church, and I heard Grandma say
many times, 'I raised them good, I raised them right, and I raised
them often.'"

NO. 4 - A FAMILY CAN TRAVEL TOGETHER

When traveling is mentioned, we tend to think of going on a long
journey to a faraway place. If you can afford to tour the world, that is an
excellent way to help educate your children. But not many of us can
visit the catacombs in Rome or the Eiffel Tower in Paris. If you are one
of the fortunate few who can afford long-distance trips, that is an
excellent way for a family to spend its time together.

But it is the short trips, like going across town to youngest son's soccer game, or six blocks to the school for the children's Christmas program, that are so important. *Any time a member of the family participates in a performance every family member who is able should travel together to attend the event.* An audience of a thousand people may be present, but, to a child, his parents and family are the most important ones there.

Should I Leave the Children?

Speedy air travel and international business affairs of large corporations have involved more and more men in much travel. It is a unique experience for many of us when we have an opportunity to go to the airport and board a plane for a long trip. But to the one who travels, it often becomes a real grind and lonesome routine. Many daddies who must travel a great deal are pleased when it is possible to take their wives with them on a trip. Consequently, this question frequently arises, "Should I leave the children at home to travel with my husband?"

The answer is yes! *A wife must always remember her husband comes first.* If you refuse to be a good helpmeet and your husband is unhappy, everyone suffers. Children will be happier to be left with grandparents or other responsible adults occasionally than for their mother to refuse to accompany their daddy to the regional convention or special conference.

It is possible for this practice to be carried to an extreme. You learned from previous chapters that I do not advocate that parents leave their children too frequently. Common sense tells us that, if a mother is absent four days out of every two weeks, it is far too much. But, if she travels with Daddy four days out of four months and the children are left with responsible people, it is not harmful.

The Ideal Trip

The ideal trip is not when Daddy travels alone. The ideal trip is not when Daddy and Mother travel alone. *The ideal trip is when all the family goes together.*

When I was a single schoolteacher, it upset me greatly for parents to allow their children to be absent from school for a family trip. My concern was focused on the instruction they were missing.

Now that I am a parent, I do not discourage parents from taking their children out of school for a short trip. I would far rather deal with a little one who feels deeply loved in his family relationship than one who is emotionally disturbed because he feels abandoned by his parents.

I encourage young couples to plan your trips with your children in mind. Build a family tradition of taking them wherever you go. Be aware that if you push them into the background when they are little, they will push you into the background when they are older.

NO. 5 - A FAMILY CAN PLAY TOGETHER

A family that has fun together will be one together. [3] A young autocratic family should concentrate on playing together and making recreation a family affair.

Many mothers are little more than full-time chauffeurs for Junior and Sis. On Monday they must be taken to their swimming lesson at 4:30. Tuesday is the Cub Scout meeting at 4:15. Music lessons are at 5:00 on Wednesday and baseball practice at 5:15 on Thursday. Friday evening the arts and crafts class meets at 6:00 at the park in the recreation building, and then they must be rushed to the Ice Palace for skating lessons at 9:30 on Saturday morning. There isn't even a break on Sunday, because Junior's baseball game is played that afternoon.

All of these out-of-the-home activities impress a child under twelve with one basic lesson: Fun is found away from home and in the company of other people.

One TUAC student testified about her disgust with the hectic schedule that she kept with her children when they were small. She said she was a Girl Scout leader and spent hours of her time working on demonstrations, crafts, and lessons. "One day," she said," it just dawned on me what I was doing. I was taking it upon myself to teach those little girls what they should have been learning from their mothers at home. I will never spend my time that way again, but will devote those invaluable hours to my own children."

The junior and senior high school years will provide ample time for engaging in out-of-the-home activities. The "negative and discipline" years and the "learning years" need to be used to teach your children the basic lessons of life. In the teenage years, when young people find jobs and begin to contribute to society, their schedules will be too packed full for very much work and activity at home.

Stay Home and Play With the Family

Children from birth to twelve should stay at home and play with their own family. It may sound strange to some to hear that a child needs to be taught to stay home, but he does. *"Withdraw thy foot from they neighbor's house; lest he be weary of thee, and so hate thee."* Proverbs 25:17.

A young autocratic family can, in addition to games and activities within the four walls of home, ski, camp, skate, bike, fish, bowl, attend the theater (when a decent movie can be found), swim, boat, and dine out together. The important principle to remember is *Do It Together.*

IF the Child Has a Special Interest

I do not wish to leave the impression that not one outside activity should be permitted for a pre-adolescent. Developing such skills as playing musical instruments and being involved in sports may require special tutoring and coaching. One such activity may be beneficial, IF the child displays a special interest for the activity; but let most of his activities be things the family and the church does together.

Yes, autocratic parents, it takes time and may require that you become young at heart. But, for the sake of building a closely- knit family, it will be worth everything you put into it. Have at least one special family night a week and keep your family together.

What Will My Boys Remember? 4
What will my boys remember
  When they've grown old and gray?
The pants knees oft were full of holes?
  Or the trout we caught that day?
Just what will they remember most?
  Two little beds unmade?
Or the fun they had at hide-and-seek
  The days that Mother played?
What matter if my ironing waits
  While I smooth out their troubles,
Take time to kiss those briar-scratched hands,
  And start them blowing bubbles?
Will they remember mud-tracked floors
  When they've grown old and gray?
What care they if each room is dusted,
  If I'm too tired to play?
                        —Phyllis C. Michael

NO. 6 - A FAMILY CAN PLAN TOGETHER

Allow your children to plan some activities in which all the family can participate. To many people, the thought of an autocratic home conjures up images of generals shouting orders at helpless little buck privates who must jump or cow-tow on command.

Once a potential student got up and walked out of my class during the first session. She said she would not be back. When I introduce a new TUAC session I always outline for my new students what they can expect to learn throughout the series. I explain that we will be learning how to establish an autocratic home. In her mind I was advocating "authoritarianism" (in which the children have absolutely no voice about anything and are treated with harshness.) This dissatisfied student complained, "I came from that kind of a home and I am not about to raise my children the way I was raised."

Since that experience I am careful to spend an extra amount of time explaining the difference between an autocratic home guided by loving Christian parents and a worldly authoritarian order in which the parents exhibit no love or mercy.

In an autocratic home the children should have a large part in planning activities for the family to do together. Family worship can be planned and conducted by the children on designated days. They should take turns planning the Friday family-night recreation. Arranging a special camping trip can be one of their projects. Planning where to go, what food to take, and what games to play around the campfire can be their responsibility.

Let your children plan as many things as they can, while you relax.

NO. 7 - A FAMILY CAN PRAY TOGETHER

The family that prays together stays together. 5 Teach your children to pray from their hearts rather than reciting repetitious prayers.

Personally, I wish the following children's prayers had not been written:

(1)   God is great! God is good!
        Let us thank Him for our food!

(2)   Now I lay me down to sleep.
        I pray the Lord my soul to keep!
        If I should die before I wake
        I pray the Lord my soul to take!

A child who has been taught memorized prayers has a more difficult time developing sincere communication with God.   His memorized prayers become only a quick formal ritual to hurry through. This leaves the impression that I know God is great, but He can wait. I've gotta hurry, or I'll be late.

Talking to God is like talking with a close friend. Prayer should be a sincere and relaxing time. A child will learn how to talk to God best by hearing his parents talk to Him.

As soon as a baby starts learning to form words, he should begin learning to pray. As he sits in his high chair at each meal, Mother can fold her hands, bow her head, and pray in short phrases and allow the baby to repeat what she says. Soon the baby will be putting his own words together. If you want to experience a little bit of heaven, just listen to the prayers of a two-year-old. There is nothing fake or insincere about them. He tells God exactly what is on his heart and is thankful for every toy in his toy box.

Every family should pray together. Family worship, mealtime, and bedtime are excellent times for this spiritual activity. As all of the family clasps their hands together, they can approach God's throne united in reverence and prayer.

NO. 8 - A FAMILY CAN SHARE TOGETHER

Nothing will bring about selfishness in a child more quickly and pave the way for him to be an uncongenial spouse than for his parents to give him his own private everything. The telephone, television, computer, radio, stereo, piano, desk, and automobiles are all things a family should share.

If an adolescent wants his own private communication equipment and buys it, pays for the installation, and makes the monthly payments, that young man or lady deserves praise. Wise parents know that these material items can be the prized possessions that are shared by the family in a circle of togetherness.

A young lady whose parents limit her to ten-minute telephone conversations quickly learns to consider the needs of her family. There are other members of the family who may be waiting to make or receive a call on the family phone. In the process of learning to be aware of the needs of others, she is also taught not to gossip or waste time in idle chatter.

If all the family shares the same television, there has to be give and take. Even more important, Daddy and Mother can oversee what is fed into the minds of their little ones when they view one television set. *A family that shares together cares together.*

NO. 9 - A FAMILY CAN SACRIFICE TOGETHER

Whatever the urgent need of any member of the family, the remaining members should rally to help meet that need. Jerry's broken leg may mean that Sam and John will do his chores and carry him up and down the stairs for a few weeks. Michael's careless baseball pitch may call for Dad to go half-way to pay for repairing Mrs. Smith's shattered picture window. Or, the family may have to forego repairing the television in order to pay for Amy's new braces.

Mama, Aren't You Going To Leave Me?

The youngest of the "little girls" suffered severe emotional damage when her biological mother deserted her. She was not quite three when her parents destroyed their home. Her bonding and attachment to them was strong.

Once when her mother came to visit her, they slept together in the same bed. By the time she woke up the next morning, her mother was gone again. She was so distraught that she went to the side of the bed where she had last seen her mother lying and cried and repeatedly called her name. She continued to cry and pat the pillow while calling for her mother to come back.

She was such a beautiful little girl. She had huge blue eyes, long auburn hair, and a tiny frame. My husband and I always thought she looked very much like her biological mother.

After we had cared for her for about three years, she awakened me in the middle of the night. Her temperature was high, and she was suffering terrible abdominal pain. I gave her some medication, and she relaxed enough to go back to sleep.

When morning came, she was no better. The medicine had worn off, and she was writhing in pain. We quickly took her to a doctor, who immediately determined she needed an emergency appendectomy.

We rushed her to the hospital, the surgical team was summoned, and she was whisked into surgery. After we spent two hours in the waiting room, the doctor came in to tell the results of the surgery. He said that her appendix had burst and peritonitis had set in. How quickly and unexpectedly misfortune can overtake us!

Of course, I stayed at the hospital with her while my husband went back to work. When she was wheeled out of the recovery room and taken to her room, she was pleased that I was there waiting for her. When I walked over to her bed and took her tiny hand in mine, the first thing she asked was, "Mama, aren't you going to leave me?" I assured her I would not leave her, and she would soon be well and home again.

The reason she asked if I were going to leave her was that my husband and I had planned a trip to California. The car was ready, and we had made arrangements for a Christian family to keep the children while we were away. If her sickness had been discovered twenty-four hours later, it would have been difficult to contact us because we would have been on our way to California.

It means something very special for a child when she learns that her family will make sacrifices to be near her, especially when she is sick and needs them.

NO. 10 - A FAMILY CAN CHOOSE COMPANIONS TOGETHER

At the beginning of David Wilkerson's book, *Parents On Trial*, he explained his purpose in writing the book. His original aim was to attempt to find first-hand information proving why some children become delinquents. He felt he would find the correct answers if he could interview the parents of juvenile delinquents. As he talked to each set of parents, he was amazed by what he learned. When he asked them what they felt they had done wrong with their children, they acted surprised and naive. From their viewpoint, they had done no wrong. They placed the blame for their children's downfall strictly at the door of bad companionship.

Mr. Wilkerson concluded in his book that parents are the ones who are at fault. Their failure to love, discipline, supervise, keep their home together, and hold their children responsible for their misbehavior is the real reason children become delinquents. But as far as the parents of delinquents were concerned, it was someone else's fault and they were completely innocent. 6

Bad companions are certainly an influence that is capable of tearing down good character. "*Do not be deceived: Bad company ruins good morals.*" I Corinthians 15:33 7

Parents should associate with Christian couples and teach their children the importance of choosing wholesome friends and later choosing a Christian mate.

"Son, I Don't Want You Dating Her"

My mother described an instance when she intervened in one of my brother's choices of a companion. She had developed good rapport with him over the years, and one day in a conversation he told Mother he was attracted to a certain girl in the community. He went on to tell her that he planned to ask the girl for a date. My mother was not happy about this, because she knew the girl and her family did not have good reputations. All she remembered telling my brother, that prevented him from pursuing the friendship, was, "Son, that girl does not have the reputation for good character, and I do not want you to date her."

He respected Mother's advice and never asked the girl for a date. Perhaps his willingness to respect his mother's judgment is one reason that he is a responsible family man today.

One Teenager Who Dared To Be Different

My sweet Christian mother had a saying about the importance of choosing good company that impressed all of us. I remember her telling us, "If you run with the goats, you are going to smell like them." That was her way of saying that if you associate with people who have bad characters, you will become like them.

My younger sister was also influenced by this truth she learned at my mother's knee. I have always loved and admired her for holding strong Christian convictions. When she was a teenager (the age when most young people think they have to copy their peer group), she wasn't afraid to be different or to stand-alone. She always chose her companions with a great deal of care. When it was time to attend worship, she refused to go somewhere else with her friends. She always insisted that they attend worship services with her.

Because of her decision to be a teenager who dared to be different and because she loved Christ enough to make Him Lord of her life, she was able to lead one of her best friends to become a Christian. This high school girl friend married a Christian man and has a Christian home today because of my sister's influence. Unlike most high school relationships, their companionship endures today because becoming sisters in Christ bonded them.

Resolve to teach your children to dare to be different, stand alone if necessary, and choose their companions with care.

"I Live Because She Passed This Way"

Family togetherness will build a sense of devotion and a spirit of loyalty within a child.

At the close of my life, when my family lays me to rest, I hope I shall have influenced them to the point that this poem will speak their sentiments about me:

ROADSIDE MEETINGS

A little more tired at close of day,
A little less anxious to have our way;
A little less ready to scold and blame;
A little more care for a brother's name - -
And so we are nearing the journey's end,
Where time and eternity meet and blend.
The book is closed and the prayers are said,
And we are a part of the countless dead.
Thrice happy then if some soul can say,
"I live because she passed this way."

—Stephen Crane 8

ASSIGNMENT

1. Let your children help plan a special togetherness activity for the entire family this week.

2. Go as a family to worship.

3. Start a daily family worship. Let your children pray and Daddy read from the Bible.

4. Choose the lesson that has helped you most. Write a short report on how that lesson helped your children, and give it to your teacher.

PRAY and WORSHIP

In Spirit and In Truth

Chapter Fourteen
Pray and Worship

"Except the Lord build the house, they labour in vain that build it."

Psalms 127:1

Dear Daddy and Mother,

You have been very busy every day getting me ready for school. You say that it is very important that I get an education. That is why you see the TV is not turned on until I have prepared my lessons for the coming school day. That is why you see that I get to bed early to prepare my body for the physical strain of school.

Yes, getting an education is a must to prepare one for the social demands of this life; but tonight, Daddy and Mother, when I am asleep, won't the two of you tip-toe into my room and steal a look at my sleeping face? There may still be a tear on my cheek, though my cares of the departed day have gotten lost somewhere in dreamland. Look at me, and ask yourselves how much spiritual education you are giving me. . .Is it more important to be a doctor than to be a Christian? . . .Is it more important to be a nurse than an angel of God? . . .What kind of person do you really want me to be? Now is the time to educate me spiritually. After I have opened the door of adulthood, it may be too late.

Please, Daddy and Mother, I need "Spiritual Education," too! Won't you please take me regularly to Bible Study and Worship - -on both Sundays and Wednesdays?

Lovingly, Your irreplaceable child
Author Unknown

Salvation Is What It's All About

I wish I could personally visit your home and sit with you around your table so that we could study this chapter together. I would ask you in all sincerity, "Is God really the builder of your home? And is Christ truly the Lord of your life?"

Basically, eternal salvation is what *Training Up a Child* is about. Why should we be seriously concerned with trying to rear our children properly if heaven is not the prize that we are striving to obtain for them and ourselves?

Build a Living Faith

Perhaps you may wonder why I left this lesson about "pray and worship" until last. If I were to list the topics in order of importance, should not this one have been first?

To answer that question, I must take you back to the time when I decided to use the little train as a visual aid. I visited a library and studied the features of an old-fashioned locomotive. It was interesting to me to learn that the most important car on a train is the caboose. It is there the conductor rides. It is there he maintains his office and keeps all records, including information about the contents of each car, and all communication lines are centered in the last car of the train. The caboose is the operation center of the train.

God is the conductor of our lives, and we must consult Him for direction. I could think of no more excellent way to conclude my class (and now a book) than to end it by giving further spiritual instruction.

This lesson is separated from the others because it leads us into the realm of our spiritual existence. Prayer and worship are vital spiritual activities. Any autocratic family, which prays and worships God, will build within its children a *living faith*. The children's souls will be awakened to spiritual values. A child whose parents teach him to pray and worship will not only receive direction from God while on earth, but will have a chance to live eternally with Him in heaven.

PRAY

If you chasten a child, you can change his actions. If you pray for him, God can change his heart. *Daily prayer is the hidden key that winning mothers have found to unlock the secret chambers of their children's hearts.* We can love, chasten, talk, and cry; but we fail if we neglect prayer.

We have spent hours studying how to organize an autocratic home. But because we are subject to human weaknesses, there will always be times when we fail to express tender love when we should, or when we administer strict love when we shouldn't. We can do our best to lay the bricks of our children's foundation for life as skillfully as possible, but only God can supply the divine mortar that will smooth out our imperfections as parents.

The Unveiling of a Secret

There was once a mother who spent thirty-six years of her life rearing a family of children. With the exception of the youngest, they were all grown and married or away from home.

One day, when she was in town shopping with her daughter, she revealed her secret of successful motherhood. She said, "Darling, there has never been a day of your life that I have not prayed for you. Many times I felt inadequate as a mother, but I always tried to do the best I knew how and leave the rest to God. At night I would lay my head on my pillow and call each of your names before God's throne. It has always been my prayer that He would give you a special blessing and use you in His service."

PRAY EVERY DAY FOR EACH CHILD

THIS SECTION IS PRINTED IN CAPITALS BECAUSE OF MY INTENSE DESIRE TO IMPRESS EACH NEW MOTHER WITH THE IMPORTANCE OF PRAYING EVERY DAY FOR HER CHILDREN.

WE HAVE LEARNED IN TRAINING UP A CHILD THAT WE MUST DO OUR UTMOST TO APPLY "CON SIST' ENT LY" EVERY PRINCIPLE WE HAVE LEARNED. AFTER THAT, OUR FINAL STEP IS TO KNEEL BEFORE GOD IN PRAYER. WE MUST ASK HIM TO TAKE EACH LITTLE LIFE FOR WHICH WE ARE RESPONSIBLE AND MOLD IT INTO AN ACCEPTABLE STEWARD FOR HIM.

I HAVE NEVER MET A WINNING PARENT WHO TOOK THE CREDIT FOR THE HAPPINESS OR WELL-BEING OF HER CHILDREN. ALL THE WINNERS SAY, "I GIVE GOD FULL CREDIT FOR ANY ACCOMPLISHMENTS OR OUTSTANDING CHARACTERISTICS OUR CHILDREN POSSESS."

GOD IS SO GREAT THAT HE FILLS THE UNIVERSE, AND YET HE IS SO SMALL HE CAN LIVE WITHIN MY HEART. DO YOU PRAY EVERY DAY FOR EACH CHILD THAT GOD WILL ABIDE IN HIS HEART?

WORSHIP

The important thing to remember in worshiping God is to make sure that your worship is acceptable to Him. It is vitally important to worship God EXACTLY in harmony with His divine specifications.

If Nadab and Abihu could speak to us today, they would warn us to worship God EXACTLY as He has commanded. These two priests must have reasoned that their act of bringing strange fire before the Lord was harmless. God, however, did not think so. Because He had not commanded their act of worship, these two men were immediately devoured by fire from the Lord. " *And Nadab and Abihu, the sons of Aaron, took either of them his censer, and put fire therein, and put incense thereon, and offered strange fire before the Lord, which he commanded them not. And there went out fire from the Lord, and devoured them, and they died before the Lord.*" (Leviticus 10:1-2)

Jesus said, "*...true worshippers shall worship the Father in spirit and in truth . . *" John 4:23. He explains in John 17:17 that MY *WORD IS TRUTH*. To worship *IN TRUTH*, then, is to worship according to the New Testament.

Simplicity, Simplicity, Simplicity

If the five acts of worship are performed as God has directed, your devotion will be free of pomp, ritual, or glitzy performances. In His wisdom, God made plans for Christians to be able to worship regardless of their circumstances or location.

While in the ancient city of Philippi, Paul and Silas were locked in prison and their feet fastened in stocks, but even under those wretched conditions, they were able to worship God. "*And at midnight Paul and Silas prayed, and sang praises unto God: and the prisoners heard them.*" (Acts 16:23-25)

Christian acts of worship are so simple Columbus could have practiced them while making his voyage across the Atlantic, or the pioneers could have practiced them as they traveled by covered wagon over the Rocky Mountains. Any Christian today can worship God, even when he is flying thirty thousand feet above the earth in the most modern jet, or is submerged in a submarine beneath the ocean's waves. No matter where Christians are, they can worship by (1) praying, (2) singing, (3) studying God's Word, (4) giving, and (5) partaking of the Lord's Supper.

Praying

According to *Acts 2:42, 12:5 and 12, 16:25, 20:36, Romans 8:26, I Thessalonians 5:17 and I Timothy 2:1-3,* we are to petition our Heavenly Father actively.

When we pray, Christ intercedes for us to the Heavenly Father. As a telephone carries our message across country, Jesus takes our requests and expressions of thanksgiving to God. (I Timothy 2:5) For this reason, we must be IN CHRIST before we have access to God's spiritual blessings. Since we pray through Christ, our prayers must be in His name. (John 14:13)

Singing

The Bible teaches that Christians' bodies are God's temples on earth. (I Corinthians 6:19) God built within each normal body the ability to make melody by singing. The human voice is *the only instrument* God instructed us to use in expressing adoration and singing praise to His name. (Ephesians 5:19 and Colossians 3:16)

We are further instructed to sing with the spirit and with the understanding. (I Corinthians 14:15)

Studying God's Word

We can study the Bible by reading or hearing it preached. The Bible is God's way of speaking to man today. (I Corinthians 14:37) Prayer is our means of talking to God - - He is the receiver; we are the sender. Bible Study is our way of *hearing* God - - He is the sender and we are the receivers.

A blind college professor made a lasting impression upon me of the importance of showing respect for God's Word. One day, led by his seeing-eye dog, he walked sternly to face our fifty-member a cappella chorus. Prior to his entrance, there had been a Scripture reading in the assembly, and he had heard a member of the chorus whispering during the reading.

We received a rebuke that I'm sure none of us has forgotten. He told us he did not care if we chose to whisper and talk during a prayer, but " **WHEN GOD IS TALKING TO YOU,** you had better be quiet and listen." You may be sure we did get quiet, and I try to share that lesson with as many people as possible.

Giving

The Bible states in I Corinthians 16:1-2 that Christians gathered on the first day of the week and contributed to God as they had been prospered.

Contrary to the Old Testament law, in which the people were told exactly how much to give, Christ's law states: *"Every man according as he purposeth in his heart, so let him give; not grudgingly, or of necessity; for God loveth a cheerful giver."* II Corinthians 9:7.

New Testament Christians, therefore, are to give free will offerings. They will naturally give to God according to the amount of faith, love, and appreciation they have in their hearts. Their contribution is then distributed to help those in need and to spread the good news of Christ's life, death, burial, and resurrection to those who are lost.

The Lord's Supper

Christ instituted the Lord's Supper Himself. (Luke 22:14-20) It is a wonderful privilege to remember the Lord's death by partaking of the emblems that represent the body and blood of Christ on each first day of the week. Jesus said of the unleavened bread, *"This is my body which is given for you: this do in remembrance of me."* and of the fruit of the vine, " . *"this cup is the new testament in my blood, which is shed for you."* ..."*this do ye, as oft as ye drink it, in remembrance of me."* Luke 22:19-20 and I Corinthians 11:24-25.

Paul told the Christians at Corinth: *"For as often as ye eat this bread, and drink this cup, ye do shew the Lord's death till he come."* I Corinthians 11:26. Early Christians gave the world an example of gratitude and thanksgiving for Christ's marvelous sacrifice by observing the Lord's Supper. How often did they observe the Lord's Supper? *Upon THE first day of the week, WHEN the disciples came together to break bread* .. Acts 20:7.

Even though it is not specifically stated that the early disciples took the Lord's Supper *every* first day of the week, we know they did. God's command to the Israelites was, *"Remember THE Sabbath day to keep it holy."* Exodus 20:8. They didn't argue, "God didn't say to remember *every* Sabbath," but common judgment dictated to the Jews that every week had a Sabbath day. Therefore, every Sabbath was a holy day to be respected by them. Since the disciples came together on the first day of the week to break bread, and every week has a first day, it is logical to conclude that we, like the early church, should partake of the Lord's Supper every first day of the week.

All Over the World

New Testament Christians all over the world assemble to worship every First Day of the week. Their worship is simple, just as Christ designed it to be. They pray, sing, study God's Word, give, and partake of the Lord's Supper to remember His death till He comes again.

With this discussion of the importance of taking our children to worship and teaching them reverence for God, I conclude my *Training Up a Child* study. It is my prayer that you have greatly benefited by reading this book and will experience many happy days of parenting.

ADDENDUM

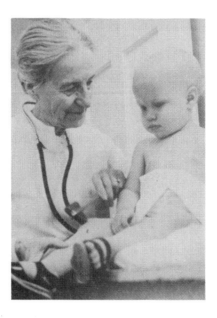

Dr. Leila Denmark

Dr. Leila Denmark is America's most experienced pediatrician. She graduated from the Medical College of Georgia, and has practiced medicine for more than seventy years. Every child in America can thank her for their DPT shots which immunize them against the dreadful disease of whooping cough. She worked over an eleven-year period on the vaccine for pertussis. She does not believe in day care for children, but teaches mothers to care for their own babies. She describes how God designed our bodies to work and how to follow a daily regimen. She informs you when and what to eat to keep your body fit and well nourished. She will share with you her secrets how she has lived to be among America's centenarians. What she has done for herself for more than a century, you will learn to do for yourself and your family.

Dr. Denmark Speaks

This portion of *Training Up a Child* is a collection of quotations taken from Dr. Leila Daughtry-Denmark's book *Every Child Should Have a Chance.* Dr. Denmark's altruistic motto with which she endorses her book is "Do what you can to help."

I express my gratitude to Dr. Denmark for granting permission to share with my readers a small portion of the wisdom and counsel she has amassed over her seventy-plus years as a practicing pediatrician.

I have profound respect for her as a humanitarian and physician. She has devoted her entire life to caring for the needs of children and helping them have a better chance in life.

A sincere word of thanks also goes to Madia L. Bowman for granting the permission to use extensive quotes and stories from her book, Dr. Denmark Said It! The quotations and material from Madia L.Bowman are indented and printed in this type setting.

Gwendolyn M. Webb

CONTENTS

Introduction

The thoughts and suggestions expressed in the following chapters are based entirely on my observations and experiences covering some seventy years in the practice of medicine, dealing with thousands of children in all walks of life...the poor and the wealthy, the weak and the strong, the loved and the unloved, the privileged and the underprivileged.

Primarily this writing should be of interest to parents and prospective parents. It should be to them in a general sort of way simply preventive medicine, helping them to avoid some of the mistakes and pitfalls many parents encounter in rearing their children.

What do I mean when I say that every child should have a chance? In the broadest sense, the opportunity to grow and develop in keeping with physical and mental capacity, to be healthy in body and soul, so as to enjoy a full, happy and useful life.

It means, among other things, that a child should be conceived by parents who have kept their bodies as perfect as possible, should be nurtured in the womb by a mother who will do those things that are good for her unborn child and avoid those things that may be harmful, and, after birth, loved and trained by parents who are willing to put the welfare of the child first in their daily lives.

Perhaps I should also explain dissipation. The word *dissipate* as defined by Webster means to scatter, to break up and drive off, disperse, dispel, dissolve. To scatter aimlessly or foolishly, as, to dissipate one's energies. To squander. To separate into parts and disappear, to waste away, vanish. To be wasteful or dissolute in the pursuit of pleasure.

Thus, we see that the word *dissipate* does not apply solely to the drinking of alcoholic beverages or the pursuit of other types of so-called pleasure. It includes everything on earth that destroys a child's chance and opportunity in life.

The greatest need on earth today is parents--parents who want to and will give their children a chance.

Today, when the "wise" leaders in the so-called psychiatric world teach casual living, they are preparing a race of people for a great deal of unhappiness. A baby who is not taught from birth a system and that man cannot live alone in this world, which was made to operate on exacting precision, has a hard time. When a child is taught he can have his own demand feeding, demand sleeping, demand dressing, demand keeping of his room visits in his playmate's home where there is a mother who believes her home came with a price and must be orderly and well kept, he soon finds that he is a misfit and is not wanted.

Then comes school. He has done everything on a demand basis, and now he meets a teacher who is trying to help forty children and she must have a system and rules. He must keep his desk neat, he has to stay in a chair, he has to wait his turn to speak. Now this poor little self-demand child is really in a tough spot.

After many years in the practice of medicine and having the mothers of these children coming to me for help, I can say that self-demand living has been the downfall for what could have been many fine people.

We should never teach our child a self-demand way of life and expect him to be accepted in a world that is governed by precision methods. A self-demand person would have to be alone--a hermit--to be happy because people will not tolerate a person who cannot conform to the golden rule that we should do unto others as we would have them do unto us. A child who is taught that it is right to satisfy his own desires and never take into account how much he is hurting someone else has a poor chance in life.

I teach fathers and mothers that their child must be trained into a system and that system must be kept with consistency. If they were building an important business, they'd have a system.

My philosophy is that if a mother runs her house the way a man runs a good business, it will be a success. Building a child is the biggest business on earth.

Chapter One
The Unborn Child
(Papa and Mama, Don't Dissipate)

After many years in the practice of medicine, I have seen a great change in the problems that come to doctors. The tears that were shed for little children in the early part of the twentieth century were brought on principally by the ravages of disease-causing organisms that killed or left the children handicapped. Medical science has made great progress in conquering and reducing disease but the mothers still come with their tears. Now they are shed over the child who is a product of dissipation, born to parents who did not care enough to give the child the best possible prenatal start, and then the best possible environment that would make for as perfect a life as possible.

The sad realization that comes to a baby doctor is that the little cuddly, well-born babies are decreasing in number. More of the dissipated types come to me each year.

Little babies from the dissipated mother and father are brought into my office and this is about what I find: First, a nervous, upset mother and father who feel that they have been dealt a very unjust blow to have had a baby who has not been any pleasure, who has made them lose sleep, and who has made a complete wreck out of them.

"Doctor, this baby has wrecked us!"

At this point it breaks my heart to think that they put the blame on this little baby they created, not willing to say, "Doctor, we have wrecked a child's life, and will you help us to take what we have and make the best of it?" No, I have never heard the parent take the blame. It is always the child who is running them crazy and yet that child was made by them.

When the mother and father enter the office, the baby is always crying. She puts him down on the table as if she would just like to walk out and leave the thing that has caused her so much trouble. Then I get the history and it is always the same, "Doctor, I did not know the things that went into my body would go into my baby. My doctor should have told me."

Then, if I look her right in the eyes and say, "Now, Mother, tell me the truth and put the blame in the right place," she will always say, "Sure, Doctor, I knew it was wrong."

On physical examination the first thing you see is a baby who seems to be in pain. When I stand him up, he is so stiff he can almost stand alone and every muscle is hard, seeming to be in tonic contraction. The expression on the face is one of great fear and pain. When you hold this baby, he pulls back and stiffens up and will not cuddle and fall to the body like a normal baby. (A normal baby, for the first three months, is so cuddly and relaxed he is like a little kitten when picked up.) The reflexes are exaggerated to the point that the legs, arms, and chin go into a convulsive state when disturbed. The feet and hands are cold, wet, blue, and the cry is loud and shrill. The baby jumps at the slightest noise or motion. As a rule, he is spitting up his milk and nothing seems to stay down, not even water. He seems to be nauseated.

This baby is the result of two people who did not care enough to give him a chance. The mother made this baby smoke, drink, and do without the proper food for nine months of pregnancy. Papa did not care enough about himself to keep his own body in as good health as possible. He drank, smoked, and did not eat a balanced diet, did not give his body proper exercise or proper amount of rest. The sperm that fertilized the ovum that made this little body was no better than the body that produced it.

Recently, one of these mothers came in with a three-week-old baby whom I heard crying before they reached the office. The maternal grandmother was with them. Although I was very busy, the child was crying so loud and hard, I asked my secretary to bring the baby right in. At a glance I knew what the trouble was. So I had the mother wrap the child tightly and place him on his abdomen. The baby continued to cry. As soon as I could get the table cleared, I had these people brought into the examining room. The young mother was in tears and the grandmother had tried all she knew to get the baby quiet and relaxed but she had failed. The formula had been changed several times; they had tried a little sedation, but the baby continued to jump at the least noise and to scream out when he was moved. His face showed that he was in severe pain; he was stiff as a board, cyanotic, feet and hands cold, and with the least motion I could feel his muscles go into a tonic contraction that must have been very painful.

After finishing the examination, I explained to the mother that it would take a while to get this baby off nicotine and that Vitamin B with C always seemed to help relax such a baby. So the baby was given one cc. Betalin Complex with Vitamin C in the muscle. The mother was instructed to wrap the child tightly, keep him on his abdomen, and put him on a schedule.

The grandmother spoke up and said, "Now I have learned something. My other daughter had a baby about the same time this baby was born, and that baby is as soft and relaxed as a little bunny; they have never had a minute's trouble. That daughter has never used tobacco or coffee."

I remember a little baby who was brought to my office late one night by a foster mother. He was about one week old. She said he had "cried solid" for one week, which I am sure was an exaggeration for the child had to have some sleep. He had a severe tremor, very stiff hands, and feet cold and blue. His liver was down to the crest of the ileum. His spleen was enlarged. He looked like a case of tetany. I had never seen a baby in that condition before. After I got the history, the cause was quite evident. The mother was an alcoholic who had been drunk most of the time for nine months. By depriving the baby of the large amounts of alcohol he had been receiving, he had developed all the after effects of an alcoholic deprived of alcohol. At the end of one year this child walked, talked, and had developed, but was not a normal child, although he had been cared for and trained by a foster mother who made every effort to give him the best food and training a child could get.

We are certain to get increasing numbers of neurologically damaged children. A child of this type has been deprived of his birthright, the right to be born under the most favorable circumstances possible with a chance to develop to highest capacity.

Mothers come in to me and say, "Doctor, Johnny could pass his work if he would put his mind to it." But poor little Johnny is not to blame for this inability to learn; he was once a real nicotine or alcoholic addict, and not by choice.

I remember one mother who brought two sons in for me to talk to about smoking. One was ten, the other nine, and I had had these children as patients from birth. They had started smoking and the mother was all upset. When I first saw the older boy, he was one week old. He had cried and spit for three days, or since he had left the hospital. This little fellow was stiff, cyanotic, and could not be cuddled. The mother had smoked, drunk alcohol, and consumed great quantities of coffee during the entire pregnancy and she did not want to nurse the baby. So he had to suffer the shock of giving up all of it all at once. We worked with this child and, as time went on, he became more relaxed and the mother showed a little love for him. It is hard to make a mother feel good toward a little baby who cries all the time, cannot be cuddled or comforted, refuses food, spits up and has frequent stools. The mother-child relationship reaches low ebb, and the child feels it. I have had mother after mother say to me, "This is it; I never want another child; I am a nervous wreck!"

After one and a half years another boy was born to this family and he was worse than the first. He had severe tremor and was tested for everything. All reports came back normal. We really worked on this little baby, trying to get a formula to stay down but it was four months before he began to relax and keep his food. Then any food seemed to be all right, for the trouble was not in the food. Allergy is often blamed for many of these unhappy babies.

These two boys did not do well in school. They were the types who could not sit still or be quiet and could not stay on one subject or project long enough to finish. As I have said before, the mothers always say, "Doctor, he could get his work as well as any other child if he would put his mind on it." But I say these children cannot put their minds on their work like a normal child. Something happened to these little boys that made them different.

Another interesting case was that of a mother from the Central Presbyterian Church clinic. Her mouth was always filled with snuff or tobacco. She brought her baby in because she could not retain her food and had diarrhoea. The little girl looked terrible. We worked with this child for fourteen years. She was just one of the hundreds of these children who did not look as if they were worth saving.

At sixteen she got married. She could not do well in school. The boy she married was a fine young man from the country who had never dissipated, and she had done the best she could with the body she had.

When their baby was born, he was perfect. She nursed him and kept him on a good schedule. At six years this boy has a good mind and body and is as well adjusted as any child could be. It seems that the sperm and ovum that originate in clean bodies, even though those bodies have been handicapped by their parents, can produce a perfect child.

Thousands of years ago, Samson's mother and Samuel's mother knew that a pregnant woman should not take wine or dissipate. Yet when we speak to a young mother about her dissipation during pregnancy, she will say that she had no idea her baby would get any of the nicotine, alcohol, or other drugs that she took. A mother must know that all of the drugs that she takes will have their effects upon her baby.

Some days, after working the usual long hours without stopping, trying to help these mothers get their babies straightened out so they can be the pleasure they should be, I look out into the deep forest back of my office and think: How are mother rabbits and the mother birds going about their job? With no bother, they seem to know just what to do. We may say that is instinct; but as the animal has instinct, mankind has knowledge, wisdom and understanding. If the rabbit with only instinct can bring into life a normal, happy baby, then woman with all her superiority in knowledge, wisdom, and understanding should do a much better job if she but uses these God-given abilities.

This is the day of the greatest dissipation by women since the beginning of time. There are more things now for a person to take that are harmful to the body than ever before. Each year the number of maladjusted, abnormal children is increasing by leaps and bounds.

A psychiatrist made a statement recently to the effect that more children classed as juvenile delinquents were being born to professional women than to any other known group of people.

It is hard to believe that such a statement could be true. But if we think this thing through, we will see that the professional women have gone into a man's world in a big way. They were the first women in the so-called better class to start dissipating. It was not true of all professional women, but those who did were bold enough to go all the way and really do a thorough job, not only smoking and drinking and carrying a cup of black coffee all day, but really showing the world they would not be bound down just because they had been born female.

Having to carry on their work in the role of both man and woman, some of them, I am sure, had to have something to quiet their nerves after a long, busy day that such a professional woman of this type must have. A woman who tries to have a family life and a professional life at the same time is tackling a job that has always been big enough to require two people to do it well. So it is easy to see the psychiatrist may be right. A child who is born to a woman who has consumed great quantities of alcohol, caffeine, nicotine, and sleeping pills, who has had two jobs and not time enough to eat a balanced diet could be a very upset individual. I am sure one could not expect a normal child out of that background.

Every girl should be taught from the time she can learn that the purpose of her body is to bring forth another body and it should be more perfect than her own, for she has the knowledge of the past. She should also look over her prospective mate and his parents before getting married and ask herself this most important question: "Will I be willing to accept a child of as good or as bad quality as that stored in the cell that will make my child?"

My suggestion to every woman who finds herself pregnant is that she have a frank talk with her obstetrician and get his/her advice as to how she should conduct herself during her pregnancy. I sincerely believe that every normal woman deep down in her heart wants her baby to be normal and, if properly advised, will give up during pregnancy any bad habits she may have formed, such as smoking, drinking, and using drugs. We can not over-emphasize the importance of a good start in the life of a baby and that start begins at conception.

In the two-room country school I attended as a child (my husband attended the same school) one of the subjects we studied was physiology. In this study we learned that some substances taken into our bodies were harmful and should be avoided. Among these were alcohol, tobacco, and some drugs. The older I get and the more experience I have as a physician the more conscious I am of the truth contained in the little physiology book we used as a text.

It is a scientific, proven fact that everything a mother takes into the body while pregnant, the baby also gets. I have given mothers whooping cough vaccine and, when their babies were born, they had as many antibodies in their blood as their mothers. There is not one atom in the baby that did not come by way of the mother except the sperm that was united to the ovum that made the first cell. After that, what the mother ate, drank, or absorbed through the skin or lungs made the baby, and nature is not able to separate the good from the bad.

One could never believe that the baby who has been forced to smoke, chew, or dip tobacco from the time it was two microscopic cells until it was nine months old could be the baby it would have been without this nicotine. Nicotine is classed with cyanide in the pharmacopoeia, yet thousands of babies are forced to consume this toxic drug at the most important time of life.

The sperm and ovum have certain innate characteristics that cannot be changed, such as color, mental powers, stature, number of teeth, color of hair, number of toes, color of eyes, and hundreds of other things produced when these cells combine. What everyone should be taught is that, above all, these cells should be nourished and protected from anything that is harmful to living protoplasm so that the innate characteristics in them can develop and go into the making of a body and mind that can function at maximum capacity and efficiency.

When a pregnancy is diagnosed, the mother should be given a thorough examination to be sure she is in good physical condition. She should then be instructed to eat a balanced diet and to be sure not to breathe, rub on her skin, or otherwise consume anything that she would not want her baby to get. No medicine is needed if the woman is in good health, nor is a special diet required. She should be told that, if she dissipates, her baby will suffer.

Chapter Two
Mothers of America
(Motherhood First--Career Last)

We who practice medicine hear the sad stories of mother after mother who has missed the opportunity of teaching her child a way of life until it is too late. This statement I hear day in and day out, "Doctor, I don't want to leave my child and neglect his training but I do want my child to have a better chance than I had." What is she saying? Does she mean she wants her child to have a better chance to have things? Things are important but things cannot bring happiness unless the child has been taught the use and value of things.

I see parents who are slaves to their children when it comes to getting them things, clothes, cars, trips, parties, things in general, and many of these young people are unhappy because they have never been taught how to appreciate and to be thankful for things. Children who have the most things seem to be the most dissatisfied, because the parents have neglected the most important thing on earth: preparing their children to live with people and things.

A child has to be taught everything. He has to be taught fear, love, hate, personal rights, security, honesty, truth, race customs, family customs, respect, language, and many, many other things. There is not a particular day for us to say, "This is the day to teach my son not to be afraid." This is a process of continuous teaching.

From birth to the grave, life is built of precept after precept and line after line. There is no way to live yesterday over. The opportunity to teach the things we should have taught our child yesterday is gone. Every day has its own problems, and these must be solved when they present themselves.

Today many children are not taught by their mothers day after day the manners and customs of their family and race. This job is often turned over to a babysitter, day care or to a nursery school while the mother is out working for some other person, in an office, school, church, child guidance organizations, child health organizations, doing P.T.A. or club work, or engaging in many other endeavors. She is giving her time and thoughts trying to make a better world for her child to live in, but is missing the only chance she will ever have to mold her child who is to live in the world she is trying to make. It is like a hen that would leave her little chicks out in the cold while she goes off to build a nest and finds, after the nest is built, her chicks have died from neglect. No, a hen would care for her chicks and pull the grass in and build the nest while she protected the chicks.

This is an era that will go down in history as a time when children were the most neglected in true mother care and home ties and the most indulged in gifts and money to soothe the parents' consciences, a period when children were the least trained by their own parents.

Surely, woman has a right to do as she pleases in the United States today, but, if she does not have the desire to love and train the child she brings into the world, she should not have the child. She can keep from having children in two ways. The first is, by not getting married to a man who wants a home and children and thus spoil his life and bring into the world children who know and feel they are not wanted. The unwanted children are one of the doctor's big problems. A mother with a guilt complex about her unwanted child is always overly anxious and indulgent, and the child can never feel secure. The second is, she should not get married at all.

One may say that many women are not capable of or don't want to be bothered with this job, and unfortunately there are a good many of this type in our country today. We read in the magazines and papers articles about a woman's rights and how she should not be tied down in a home with a husband and children to look after when she has the education and the mental ability to do great things instead of spending her life doing a job a maid could do just as well.

Then the great and profound question comes up. Is a life spent making a better gadget greater and more important than a life spent making a child into a man or woman? This question should be discussed before a couple gets married and again before a child is conceived. No woman who really thinks this question through and who truly loves her child and husband would give up by choice the job of making her child into an adult in order to go out and work for some other man or woman or somebody else's child. To work for somebody you love above all other people on earth should be the height of every person's ambition.

This is an example of the way thousands of little children are treated today by mothers who think homemaking is menial. Mama and papa, up at six o'clock, must get the children up, get breakfast, and be at the office or other place of business by eight-thirty. They get up unhappy because they did not get enough sleep. Breakfast is rushed and forced on the children, who will not eat fast or maybe not at all. Time is passing fast, and they must get to work; papa and mama get angry, talk loudly, and blame each other for not getting the children to eat. The children are too upset to eat or use the bathroom. At seven-thirty the children are rushed off without breakfast or a good elimination.

Mama and papa rush off to their separate jobs. Mama works for a handsome man who seems always to be in a good humor; his clothes are neat, and she becomes dissatisfied as she compares her husband with the man for whom she works. This man she works for has a good wife at home who looks after his children and his clothes and has time to see that he has good food served well. He feels that the money he makes is spent for a good cause and he is a happy man. The man she is married to could be happy if he had a wife who would make a home for him even though they would not be able to buy as many gadgets as they can buy with both working. Occasionally the woman actually falls in love with the handsome boss because he seems so perfect but, if she were the boss's wife, he would not be that perfect. A dissatisfied man is not a good person to work for or live with and a good wife is the best tonic to make a happy man. The working woman who falls in love with the boss will find him to be just like the one she is married to after she becomes his wife.

Papa rushes out and to the office and he may become attracted to a beautiful girl working for him. She has attractive clothes, pretty hands; she has no children or home to keep, no clothes to wash, pots to scrub, dishes to do. So he may compare his wife who is trying to carry two full-time jobs with this girl who works for him. She is happy and not too tired, has all the money she makes to buy clothes, has money to take trips and broaden her topics of conversation. She has time to read and keep up with the times, she is entertaining to be with, and it might put papa to thinking, "If I were married to a girl like that, I would be happy." But that girl would be just like the tired wife he has if she had him and his children and held down a full-time job away from home.

Both mama and papa spend a day at hard work they are being paid to do, and they may be unhappy because they are comparing the people they work with to the people they live with.

Little Johnny has been in day care or nursery school all day among people with whom he would not dare be his normal self, for no child will act for anybody except his own mother or father. The teacher will say, "Mrs. Jones, Johnny is the best little boy I ever had." But when mama and papa show up, he starts whining and showing his temper. Johnny's routine at nursery runs like this: He gets there at seven-thirty to eight; at ten o'clock a morning snack. (He did eat a few mouthfuls of food at breakfast.) Lunch at twelve o'clock which he eats because he is afraid not to eat, and there is not present anybody he loves to whom he can voice his objection to food. So he eats it all. Nap time at two o'clock, sleeps two hours, up at four, has a glass of milk and some cookies. At six o'clock, back in the car and taken home.

Mama and papa have just arrived, papa tired and remembering how kind and nice the office girl had been to him and how good she looked when she left the office; mama tired and conscience stricken about her neglected child, but remembering how kind the boss talked and how patient he was. Johnny was fed four times during the day and since his stomach did not have a chance to empty, he has the stomach ache from constant eating, and he is not hungry. He has slept all afternoon and is not sleepy.

Now supper has to be fixed, clothes washed and ironed for tomorrow, baths taken, apartment cleaned, as they did not have time to clean the apartment or wash dishes before going to work. Now mama says to papa, "I'm just as tired as you are, I have worked all day in the office, so put that paper down and give Johnny his bath while I cook supper." Johnny objects. He has not had a chance all day to show his will power, for he could not do this to a person who is not a good audience. So the show starts. Johnny will not take off his clothes. Papa tries first to persuade, then to bribe, then to tease. When all that fails, he uses a loud voice and then the belt. That makes mama angry so she comes in and finishes up the bath, and the little fellow finds out he doesn't have to mind papa when mama is around.

Supper is on the table, and it is a job to get Johnny in his chair. He had food just two hours ago, and his stomach is full of food that cannot leave until it has been digested. Papa serves his plate, and Johnny pushes it back and says, "I don't want to eat." Mama tries a little game to get him to eat, but he is not hungry. Papa tries to feed him and both mama and papa try all the tricks in the book to get him to eat, but it does not work. Then they speak in cross-tones to each other, and Johnny is spanked and put down. Mama and papa don't talk any more until they have swallowed what food they have on their plates.

They would like to get Johnny to bed, for the house work would be much easier if he were out of the way and not turning over chairs, turning up the television too loud, jumping off the best sofa, slamming the doors, and putting in a good amount of crying. All this he does to get attention and to show papa that he can't do much about Johnny's conduct while mama is around. (If the child is a girl, she shows mama up, for papa will be sorry for her.) Mama is conscience stricken about poor Johnny because she knows she is neglecting him, and she cannot stand to see him spanked by his father. She knows she needs the spanking herself.

So they try to get Johnny to bed. He is not sleepy, for he has slept all afternoon (although no child needs a nap in the daytime after he is two years old). He is undressed by force and put to bed but he will not stay, calls for water time and again, then eventually just crawls out. They give up and let him have his way until they get all the work done, which is about eleven-thirty. So they all go to bed and sleep for six hours, provided Johnny will quit calling out, "Mama, don't leave me; Mama, I don't want to go to sleep."

How can we teach our children a good way of life when we live like this? How can we have patience to teach our children manners and customs when our bodies are constantly in a state of tension and each little cry or question seems to be the spark that sets off an explosion of temper with maybe a slap or a brutal scream? I see the little children of such parents in my office and they are a sad lot. They have never had the chance to learn a quiet, peaceful way of life. All they have known is rushing, loud talking, snapping, and slapping parents. There is no way to help a child in a home like that.

A child is like any other live being--the mother must train him until he is ready to get out and think for himself. There are thousands of questions that must or should be answered by mama and papa, questions a child would not ask anybody else. These questions children ask over and over, and the parents should answer in simple terms at first and gradually more technical terms until the child learns this special family's way of life. He learns to be a Jones or a Smith. He learns to talk, walk, sleep, eat, behave like a Jones or Smith. I hear this so often, "Doctor, this child just doesn't do at all like I did when I was a child." This is so true. He has been trained by someone else and he acts like his trainer.

My child always played under my office window (my office was in our home). When I was examining a child, I could hear her and it was very revealing to listen as she played out the role of my conduct in the home. Sometimes I could see where I could improve my way of life. She would use the same phrases to her doll that I had used to her, the same form of discipline, and the same methods I carried out in the home. I learned much listening to her play.

Recently a mother came into my office with a little girl eight months old. The mother said, "Doctor, this baby has cried for eight months and we have not had a full night's sleep since we brought her home from the hospital. I tell you, Doctor, I don't know a thing about babies and for eight months this child has had a cold, will not eat, and will not sleep. I am a medical secretary and I have two college degrees. I liked my work and did a good job but at this job of being a mother I have failed."

I said to the mother, "Man is a funny animal. The things he wants to do are never hard, and he never finds obstacles in the path of a real desire. You were happy working with the doctors; you could dress beautifully and have people tell you how well you were doing your job. This job of being a mother you did not want."

"Yes, that is true. With all my education this looks like I am throwing my life away."

"What is the most important job on earth?"

"I don't know."

"The greatest job on earth is to build a man or woman. Any woman might do the job of a medical secretary but there is only one person on earth who can be a mother to your child. These people who make you feel great in the business world will soon pass on and you will be forgotten, but this child will be what you make her and pass that on to another generation. You could start a trend of neglect that might go on indefinitely. What you are saying in truth is you don't want this job and your baby knows it. Let's change that statement from 'I don't know' to 'I don't want to do.' "

The baby was examined; it was pot-bellied, pale, nose running, both ears abscessed.

"How do you feed this baby?"

"On demand." (Meaning, I allow her to tell me what to do.)

"How do you sleep this baby?"

"On demand."

"Do you get her outside?"

"No, I don't have time; I don't have time for anything since she came."

A good schedule was worked out: breakfast at seven consisting of a protein, starch, cooked fruit, a banana, and a cup of water; nap at ten; lunch at twelve-thirty consisting of a protein, starch, vegetables, cooked fruit, a banana, and a cup of water; out in the open until six when she has dinner consisting of the same foods as at lunch; a bath and to bed. Penicillin 200,000 units every three hours night and day for seventy-two hours for the abscessed ears. (See Chapter 10–Gem #7)

She was sent home with this statement, "Go home and feel that you are blessed above so many other women. You are a queen in your home and you have the greatest job on earth, that of building a human being, and it may be that this little girl you are blessed to have may be the mother of another great human builder. You should do all you can to make her life as perfect as possible."

One month later this mother came back and the baby was happy, they had not missed any more sleep, and the mother was so grateful that she had learned the true value of things.

When I was a child, I lived on a farm in South Georgia. My father was the head of our house. But my mother was the neck, and the neck was the thing that turned the head. Men ran our county, but women were exercising their greatest constructive influence. Men respected women. Men tipped their hats to a woman, opened and closed doors and gates, and offered her a seat when she entered a room. Women were queens in their homes in those days. No man would tell an off-color story or use profane language before a lady. Women had a tremendous influence in the home, and, although they were not heard in public, they were the secret influence that made or destroyed the home.

One day my father came home with two tickets to a tent show that was to be there just one night. He did not ask my mother to go with him to a show in a tent and at night. Women just did not do those things and, too, my mother had little children and a good mother wouldn't have thought of leaving her children at night. So, as I was ten years old, I was not old enough to be disgraced by going with my father to a performance of that type. That was a great night. I am sure it was the first night I had been out to anything, for there was never any place to go at night except to visit a neighbor.

To me, that was a big tent. There must have been a hundred seats, all filled with men, boys, and a few girls my age or younger. The show went on. The man in charge announced the program: "Our show tonight is 'Ten Nights in a Bar Room.'"

There was never such drama put on the stage! By the time the show was over everybody inside the tent was in tears. My big 225-pound papa had tears rolling down his tanned cheeks. I did not go prepared to cry so I had to use my petticoat to wipe away the tears.

Suddenly, the show was over, the stage was cleared, the lanterns were turned up and out came a tall, pompous lady dressed in a black silk voile skirt over a taffeta petticoat, a white blouse with a high collar, watch on one shoulder, and glasses on the other. She really looked important, a woman making a speech in that tent full of men. You could hear the taffeta swish before you could see her. That was music to my ears, as I had an old maid cousin who had a skirt like that and one of my desires was to have an outfit like it when I was old enough. She was the most important-looking woman I had ever seen. As she walked on the stage, everybody tried to dry his eyes.

Three statements she made that night made a lasting impression on my mind. They went something like this: "You people see what has happened here tonight. You are sad and I am sad, but this kind of conduct in our country is not necessary and should not be allowed. When the women of this country are permitted to vote with the good men of this country, we can stop all this tragedy."

The second point she made was, "When the women in these United States of America are permitted to vote with the good men of these United States, we can clean up politics."

The third point was, "When the women of this country are permitted to vote with the good men of this country, we can stop the tobacco habit that is getting a good hold on our young boys. You see all these young boys smoking these 'coffin tacks'? It stunts their growth and injures their mental and physical development."

As a child, these statements sounded good to me, and in my childish mind I felt that the whole country should fall in and do its part to give every little child a chance. I did not know anything about politics, but if she said it needed to be made better, she was probably right as she looked like a person who knew what she was talking about. So, I was all for making politics better. The so-called bad boys in our community had started the tobacco habit by smoking cigarettes, and I was sure that was not for the best. I left that show with a great dream of a better United States of America and I am sure that suffragette was just as sincere in what she was talking about as any reformer who ever lived.

Woman suffrage in 1906 sounded like a good idea. Some men and women were afraid of the idea, and there was a great fight. One of the strongest arguments against it was that a woman's place was in the home. There must be a foundation for any nation, and woman has always been that. If she left the home, the foundation would crumble and the country would go down. Another argument was that a home without a mother is not a home. We must not kill the goose that lays the golden eggs. When the trainer quits, we lose the race.

Yet in spite of all these arguments, women did win the right to vote, which was proper, since women should have the right to vote and to be free to do the things they want to on an equal basis with men.

Women are now engaged in every type of business, every profession, and they go as far as they please. We have them in the United Nations, in Congress, in medicine, law, and diplomatic service, as heads of schools, bartenders, cab drivers. Name the job and she is there. Women have conquered a man's world, and have the right to do anything a man does. No one would dare question that.

That suffragette was fighting a battle she was sure to win, but I wonder what she would now think her victory has meant in true value to little children. Women were queens in their so-called slavery and they ran the country but did not know it. Each home was a kingdom of its own and out of that kingdom came the great mothers and fathers, and out of that kingdom on the side of the hill or the flat lands came the great leaders of our country.

Has our emancipation brought man up to a higher level of right living and better health, or has woman lowered her standards and lost all she has been fighting for? Has the emancipation of women really made a happier world for little children? Have women used this great blessing of freedom to give little children a better chance of health and happiness?

I can't help thinking that perhaps freedom for women has been a little too much for us and that maybe, after women have shown men that they can do everything a man can do, we will come to ourselves and realize that the only way for this country of ours to go up instead of down will be for every woman in America to take her freedom and make of herself a true example of what she wants her child to be.

Women make or break a home, a nation, or a world, and we must come back to the importance of the individual if we are to save America. She should look around and see what she is doing to the child she has been blessed to have. The greatest happiness that ever comes to a human being is to see a job well done and the job of rearing a child, if it is well done, brings the most lasting happiness.

I heard a person say recently, "There is a tremendous waste of brainpower by women." He was talking about building gadgets. I say the greatest job on earth is to build a man or woman and that is where the best female brainpower can do the most good.

Chapter Three
Papa & Mama
(Papa is King, Mama is Queen)

A child needs two loving and dedicated parents to teach him the way he should go and this is vital up to the age of twelve. When a child is reared in an environment of confusion and uncertainty--without system and good planning--the chances that he will find a happy, meaningful, and productive way of life are lessened.

In some instances children are shuttled from one caretaker to another, with a minimum of parental love and attention, and trained during the crucial early years by people who are doing the job only for the money they get out of it. What a great mistake this can be! Every child deserves a mama and a papa and if both leave him, he is surely handicapped.

Mama, your child needs you to stay with him

Nobody can care for a new baby the way his own mother can, and no mother can be pleased with the way other people care for her baby. These two--mama and baby--should be permitted to live together quietly and have a chance to get acquainted before either has time to get upset.

A newborn child is perhaps the most helpless of all creatures. He or she is the best example I know of total dependency. Our Creator instilled into the breast of woman what we refer to as "mother love" and this comes to a climax in the birth of a child. It is natural that her child should come first with her and the child is fortunate when this is the case. I have strong feelings on the importance of close mother-child relationships during the formative or early years of a child's life. A child should be trained by his mother and father, a job that cannot be delegated to others except at the child's loss.

We must teach mothers that they are the most important persons on earth to their children and that their job should be met with joy and not with a feeling of punishment, that it is a privilege to be a mother, not a task. Little children can be salvaged before it is too late if mothers can be shown how they are destroying their lives. A mother has no way to know who this child is whom she has been privileged to feed and train and prepare to run the race of life.

Somebody might suggest that laws should be passed to make mothers look after their children. I say that would be the worst thing that could happen. You can't fool a child and, if a mother were forced to stay with a child with whom she didn't want to stay, the child would know it, and the reaction would be worse than if it were the nursery or foster home.

When a child has a mother who goes out to work because she thinks the job brings her more honor and happiness than rearing a child, this mother will not let a day go by that she does not bring the child something. This child is not fooled, for he knows his mother is trying to buy his love with things, and he knows this gift comes because she knows she is neglecting him. He would be much happier if she would help him make a toy with some spools or a box. You can't buy a child's love any more than you can buy a wife's or husband's love.

This matter of rearing children is the most tedious, demanding job on earth and there is no substitute for a mother.

You are to be the boss

Parents must remember that their little baby has come to live with them--not they with him; and they must understand that they are to be the boss. They have been here for twenty or more years, they know the way, and must show this little baby the way. The father is king, the mother is queen, and this little baby is their subject; and as long as he lives in their house, the child must be made to feel that they can protect and supply all his needs and meet any problems that come up. This training has to start the day a baby is born if it is to work out.

This job of rearing children presents a thrill every day if we accept it as the most important job on earth, and the one that brings the most happiness to a parent.

Be brave and lead your child in the right way

Parents are the first guides a child has to put him on the right trail and make him feel secure, and they must be sure they know the way. Life is one short day and for that day to be happy we must teach our children a way of life that is right for us and for our neighbors.

We don't have to be a tyrant, or carry a bull whip, but should be a parent who will take a child by the hand and lead him into a way of life that will prepare him to make a better world. Our child wants a master, not a brother or sister. He wants somebody to look up to, somebody to brag about. He wants somebody to help him over the rough places in life. Somebody to carry him when he cannot make it.

We hear so much today about parents getting down on a level with their children. Our children don't want us parents to get down on their level. They want us to be adults and somebody they can look up to. A child has other children his age to play the game of life with and wants his parents to be examples of perfect adults.

The training of a child for a good way of life must be started by the parents at birth. They must set a standard for their lives and live up to it and never let this standard down. The home is a wonderful kingdom if it is blessed with a beautiful mother for a queen and a kind, firm, loving father for a king; and the subjects know that the king and queen stand for rules and regulations that parents and children must live by--with no double standards.

A child must not see his parents shake, cry, and tremble when they have to face a problem. He should see and hear them say, "There is one way and only one way and that is the right way," never seeing them do wrong because that seems to be the easier way out; never hearing them say, "I know this is wrong but this is all I can do this time."

To be in my office for a day and see how these little frightened, insecure children suffer because they have never been taught that they can trust, believe, or be sure of anything, is a distressing experience. They were not born that way, but were born to parents of that type, and they had to be taught. In order for the child to be secure, the parent must have a definite belief and must live it every day.

You must not dwell on your past

A parent with a past has destroyed many wonderful children. We hear these statements over and over again: "My parents were too rich. They did not teach me how to cook or sew, how to spend money, and my child has got to learn these things." "My parents both worked, and I had no home life. I am going to see to it that my child has a mother who knows what is going on." "My mother drank, smoked, was divorced, and I did not have a good example, but my child is going to have a perfect home." "My parents cared nothing about education, but I am going to see to it that my child gets an education." "My parents were over religious and I am not going to force my child into church." "My parents were very wicked and never took us to church and one thing my children will have to do is go to church."

Parents must forget their past and live the present as they would like their children to live. They should set up a standard and never break it, learn to say "no" when it is no and "yes" when it is yes, never causing their child to doubt them, never recalling their past as a reason for their demands but letting the reason be that it is the right way. They should teach their child that the past is no excuse for the present, that man is made with a mind and he is judged by his acts and not by the acts of his parents or friends.

Never use the words "I can't" with your child

The words, "I can't," have ruined thousands of children when said by their superiors.

I have mothers come in and say, "I can't get my baby to take his bottle." The first two words in that statement should never be used before your child no matter how small or how weak he is.

Never say before him that you can't make him drink his water, you can't make him eat his food, you can't make him stop whining, you can't make him go to the bathroom, for as you say these things before him he knows that he has grown up and now his parents are his subjects.

From the cradle to the grave we like people who are strong enough to stand up for what is right and we have no respect for a weakling. Your son is no exception. When a child finds that his parents are not big and strong enough to guide, he becomes disturbed and insecure.

Practice what you preach

When I started the practice of medicine, I set up one standard. I would never do anything to a child that I would not do to my daughter, Mary. I never would send a bill I would not like to receive. It is hard to practice what we preach, for we are so likely to have two standards: one the way we want to live, and another the way we want our children to live.

Preaching without practicing has a great deal to do with our juvenile delinquent problems. No parent should ever try to teach something he doesn't believe or practice. Preacher and teacher should never try to teach children to follow the moral and civil laws if they themselves are not willing to live up to these laws.

I have young people come to me who almost hate themselves for feeling about their parents as they do because they have been taught that it is a sin not to honor one's parents. But how can they honor somebody who is not honorable? The parents tell the adolescent that it is wrong to drive too fast, smoke, drink, stay out all night, wear clothes that are too revealing, waste time, waste money, talk too loud, lose one's temper, and otherwise break the laws of life.

Papa eats with his hand, brother must use his fork; papa blasphemes, but little brother gets a spanking if he uses the same language; papa smokes, but little brother gets the strap if he is found smoking; mother gives a party and all those present drink, smoke, and talk about the neighbors; but if the children do any of these things, they are punished. Parents who do these things while telling their children not to do them make their children sin. It is difficult to counsel a young person, who says, "I am ashamed of my parents," when you know you would be ashamed of them if they were your parents.

A child can't help being confused if he has parents who teach him to do what they say to do and not what they do. If we could only practice what we preach and never demand more of our children than we demand of ourselves, we could be a happy people. I would say that any young person would rather have parents that he could brag about than any other thing.

Always be truthful

We must teach a child faith from the day he is born. If we lose faith in our parents, then lack of faith begins, like the proverbial snowball, to grow bigger fast. It is sad to see a mother come in with a spastic or an abnormal child but to see a child that has lost faith in his parents is far worse. You can hear them crying before they come near the office, "Mama, will Dr. Denmark stick me?" The answer is often, "No"; and then comes another loud cry, "Mama, will Dr. Denmark stick me?" then another, "No, Dr. Denmark will not stick you." On and on this will go until they leave the office.

The child continues to cry and ask the same question over and over. The mother has never told the child the truth and he can't believe her now. The mother will say, "I can't understand why he is so bad and why he is so afraid of doctors; all children are not that way."

He had to be taught to be afraid of doctors. This little child was started wrong. He had never learned to have faith in what his mother says. She did not carry through with what she said and made promise after promise that was false. He was frightened because he did not know what to believe, and he continued to ask the question over and over again until he had nightmares.

There is no way ever to make this child as secure as he should be for he has lost faith in the greatest teachers on earth, his parents. This same child, when he starts to school, is afraid of the teacher and will not trust his playmates. When taken to church, he cannot be sure the things his mother tells him about the church are true. When he enters college, he still carries with him this lack of faith in people, and eventually he loses faith in business, government, and country.

It is easy to teach a child to tell an untruth. A mother will say, "I am not going to town," and will slip out the back door and go to town. She will say to her child, "If you cross the street, I will whip you," but he crosses the street and she does not whip him; "If you do that, I will tell your daddy," and she does not tell him; "If you don't eat your vegetables, you can't have the cake," yet he does not eat the vegetables but he gets the cake. Day in and day out children learn they can't trust their parents to tell the truth.

We must watch what we say and be sure we tell the truth if we are to teach our children to tell the truth. A little false witnessing, like a little child, grows bigger each day.

Carry through on every command you give

There are three very important things in our lives we have to do. They are eating, sleeping, and eliminating.   These three necessities have a great part to play in the negative period (ages 2-6) of a child's life. A child soon learns that his parents can't make him do any one of these vital things. You can put him to bed, but you can't make him go to sleep; you can take him to the bathroom, but you cannot make him have a stool or urinate; you can take him to the table, but you cannot make him eat, or, if you do, he can vomit. Never make any one of these things an issue, for, if you give a direct command, he can show you that you are not adequate or big enough to handle him.

Every command parents give a child must be carried through or the child loses respect for them. They should never give a command in a manner they would not want to be commanded.

Be consistent

Parents should write the word "Consistency" on every wall in the house if they are to develop a happy, secure child. Children are not frustrated with definite acts or orders. The children that are upset are those who never know what to expect of their parents. The parents will let them act one way today and nothing is said or done, but tomorrow they object or inhibit.

If a child does not know how his parents are going to respond to his acts, he lives in constant fear; but, if he knows that a certain act will always bring out a certain response, he is a happy child even though his parents may use a very painful method of punishment. It is the breaking of a child when he finds that he can't depend on his parents at all times.

Punish your child for his wrongdoings and he will learn LOVE.

We punish a child because we love him and want him to have the right training. He must be punished when breaking the laws and rules of the home, school, or state.

Each day as a little child follows his mother while she does her work, he learns a little more until he soon wants to help with the dishes and other chores. Now, when this time comes and he drops his mother's choice cup, she should not raise her voice or punish him but tell him that was mama's best cup, and now it is gone, and we can't have it any more. She should tell him when he helps her to hold things tight so they will not drop. He learns a lesson and will not be discouraged in his efforts to learn.

If this same little boy picked up a cup in a temper and threw it across the room, the good old tried-and-proven method of discipline should be used. A little switch to the legs is the best method and his mother should not say she is sorry she switched him for then he will know she was wrong.

Deprive your child of things harmful to him and he also learns LOVE

Children learn about love when they see their parents deprive them of something they want that would not be good for them. From the time a child is born, he must be taught that he can't have everything he wants. He must know that his parents love him enough to hear him cry if he is crying for something that will harm him, and a mother who really loves her child would not do anything to that child that would harm him.

If a child is given things to hush him up, he knows it and knows that his parents are not interested in making a good life for him, but their interest is to hush him up so they will not be bothered. This is not a good feeling for one to have.

In the case of many neglected children, the parents try to show they love them by showering them with gifts, never coming home without bringing something.

A child who is permitted to want because his papa can't afford to buy has the utmost respect for that parent, because he knows that his father loves him enough to see him do without if it is best for the child and the family. Love never gives over to persuasion if it is not good for the child.

The insecure child is that child who knows he can get what he wants by a cry or a temper tantrum at times. When his parents are not the only persons he has to depend on for his happiness, his cry and temper tantrums will not work any longer. These children grow up to be insecure, immature, and it is too late to change them. They have been taught one way and society demands that they live another way, and they cannot adjust.

Know your child's stages of development

From birth to two a child wants to be held, protected, and loved. From two to six, a child wants to do it himself and finds out the things his parents stand for and learns a way of life. From six to adolescence, children are anxious to learn. They want a leader, they ask for a leader, they ask for and take advice, they believe and admire their parents and teachers; they like to help and be helped. Parents have complete control.

From adolescence on, parents find themselves unable to dominate as they have for the past twelve years. The adolescent feels a great urge to be free and run his own life; he has the desires of an adult but the judgment of a child. The adolescent wants the perfect parents as much as the parents want the perfect child. This is the time when right and wrong seem to be in a furious battle over which force will dominate. It is a time when self-discipline is put into play to decide which will control the adolescent--right or wrong.

A good relationship with your son or daughter must be formed by 12

A mother-daughter, mother-son, father-daughter, father-son relationship must be formed by the age of 12 or it cannot be made at all. Mother and daughter should have a great deal of time together. The same is true of mother and son, father and son, father and daughter. We cannot stress this relationship too much.

If the parent and child have not established the right relationship from six to twelve, there is always trouble from that point on. There is no period so important as this to save the adolescent.

Know how to feed your family

It seems that the human race has lost its knowledge and wisdom about how to take care of the human body, what it should eat and drink, when it should eat and drink, how much it should eat and drink, and how the food and drinks should be prepared. So a large portion of the doctor's time is spent trying to teach people what to eat or drink, when to eat or drink and to patch up the bodies that have been damaged by dissipation and by improper feeding.

One of the first things I am interested in when a new patient comes into my office is how the members of the family eat, when they eat, and what they eat. The body cannot protect itself against disease unless it is fed right. Unless our eating habits are proper, our health cannot be good and if our health is not good, we are not happy.

I talk to mother after mother about the way she feeds her family and so many times it goes like this: "My husband gets up at 6:30, makes himself a cup of coffee, and goes to work; I get up about 8:30 and fix a bite for the children that go to school and after they are gone, I get up the smaller children and fix them what they want."

I always say to them that, when a man goes to work without breakfast prepared by his wife and does not have his children eat with him and tell him good-by before he goes to work, he has a wife who is not worthy of the money he makes. A man who is willing to go out and put in a day of hard work to make a home and provide food for his family surely deserves a good breakfast and word of thanks before leaving each morning.

A child should get up in the morning when Papa and Mama get up. Mama should prepare a good breakfast of protein, starch, raw or cooked fruit, and water to drink.

This meal is to be at seven o'clock. The meal should be served with all members of the family at the table at the same time. There should be a blessing. There should be no talk about food and no suggestion made as to eating the food. As soon as Papa finishes, clear the table.

The child is to have no food or drink except water until twelve-thirty. If Papa is not home for this meal, serve what was left from the previous evening meal. Mama should cook with this in mind, so there will be enough to serve herself and the child a meal at twelve-thirty. Give no drinks with this meal except water.

There should be no food or drinks except water until six o'clock. This meal should consist of a protein, starch, vegetables, fruit, and water to drink.

Our stomachs digest food in a certain way and have been doing it a certain way since man was created, and we cannot change this at all. The stomach retains food for a certain length of time until it has finished the gastric digestion and additional food should not be added during this process.

A mother should be advised that feeding between meals will cause a delayed emptying of the stomach and a child if fed between meals or closer than five and one-half hours, will become pot-bellied, be a feeding problem, and perhaps develop anemia.

Some families spend large amounts of money for all kinds of sweet drinks, milk, dry cereal, cookies, and many other things that cost money that could be spent for good meat, vegetables, fruit, and starches composed of whole grain breads and potatoes. There are many products on the market today to make somebody rich and to destroy the person that is foolish enough to buy them. I hear parents in my office and in the clinic talking about how expensive it is to live and how little they have and, as a rule, if they will go over the budget, they will find they are spending more to destroy their bodies than they are spending to build them up.

The question about juices always come up. When and how much should a child have? Really, a child doesn't need anything to drink except water. All kinds of drinks are on the market to buy, but a child doesn't need that extra sugar. If given between meals, the drinks cause a feeding problem, and the money spent on them should be put on good food.

As to carbonated drinks, the mother should be advised very early about this. Carbonated drinks etch the teeth, causing decay and no child should have such drinks at all. There are too many things sold today that will destroy little children, while making somebody rich.

Only recently I had a fifteen-year old boy in my office. He was tall, flabby, every tooth in his head rotted off, skin covered with pustules, sad face, long hair combed like a misfit's. The mother said he would not eat, and from birth had literally lived on carbonated drinks, at least four a day. I thought to myself, how could a parent destroy a child so completely? What was this child the day he was conceived? What were his possibilities? We just cannot afford to do one thing that will destroy a child's chance in life. In this most wonderful country of ours what a great waste of human potential we see!

This is a day of casual living. We have casual clothes, casual houses, and casual everything; and casual means without care. We cannot rear a family that way and make it happy. If we are casual eaters, we help buy doctors and undertakers casual cars. Life is exacting and there is nothing about it that can be casual. Our children should be taught that way if they are to be happy.

So, the person who says, "I will be casual with my eating and will eat when I please and what I please," soon ends up with poor health and a doctor's bill. We cannot change nature and anybody who breaks the physical, chemical, or moral laws always has to pay the price. We should give our child a chance by teaching him when to eat, what to eat, and to be grateful for what he has to eat. (See Chapter 10—Gem #2)

Teach your child how to dress properly

Parents should be careful about how they dress their children and, more important, how they dress themselves as an example of a good way of life. Clothes play such a big part in man's behavior that proper dress should be one of the major teaching problems of every mother and father from the day a child is born until he is grown.

We must teach our children that the minute we meet a person, that person cannot help passing judgment on us. The first impression of a person is made on how he or she is dressed and, unless this person has been taught the importance of being properly dressed, he may be judged wrong. This happens every day in the business world as well as in the social world. If we are to get the most out of life, we must present ourselves in the way we would like to be judged.

We may say, "What does it matter how I dress at home before my children?" Children are passing judgment on us just the way we pass judgment on other people. Our little son and daughter would like to remember their parents as the perfect mother and father, parents they can be proud to show off. A woman may dress up for a guest, but for her children and husband she may decide that anything will do. Which is most important--our children's and husband's judgment or what our guest will think?

Every man should dress himself in such a manner as to make his sons and daughters proud of him. To see a father going around with his body naked to the waist is not a beautiful sight. I am sure no wife or daughter could consider such a man attractive nor would she be proud to have her friends drop in and see him dressed that way. A well-dressed man is always handsome, but a man with a bare chest is not very attractive.

The body is the temple of the soul, and it should be adorned as the most beautiful temple on earth so our children can use it as an example and a model to build upon. A great builder would not start a house without a model, and children must have a model. This model should be the parents, the teacher, the doctor, the minister, as well as all grown-ups. Children should be taught as they grow to take all these models and use them to build for themselves the kind of temple they would like best to live in.

By the age of twelve or thirteen boys and girls should have been trained in the art of dressing to the extent that it should not be a problem, but with the many outside influences such as movies, television, clothing advertisements, and all kind of books and magazines, the young people are so confused that they don't know what to do. The parental influence will have to be stronger than ever and more exacting if we are to give our children a chance to make the best out of their lives.

Many of these outside influences teach them that the only way to attract the opposite sex is by exposing their bodies in a way that will gain attention. So girls think they must dress to have sex appeal.

We must teach our daughters that to be beautiful is a gift of God, but to be vulgar is destruction. A girl should be taught that the body should be dressed as beautifully as possible, but she must not accentuate the parts that would tempt a man beyond his self-control.

She should be taught not to wear dresses that are cut too low, or are too short, too tight, or too thin. The same is true with pants. Any form of pants that are worn too short or too tight detracts from a girl's chance to win the man who would love and respect her. No matter how much a woman would like to change her sex, she has to remain a woman, and the more she tries to dress like a man and act like a man, the farther she drives a real man away. Man, no matter how low he goes or how high he goes, always likes to say, "I have the finest mother on earth." He would like to say the same about his wife, and the way she dresses has much to do with his judgment of how good or how bad she is.

Let us teach our children that "life is real and life is earnest and the grave is not its goal," and that this little house we are living in is just as beautiful as we make it; and it should be kept as a temple of God.

Maintain a well-kept home

A child must be taught the way to keep house and the way to make a home. We cannot walk through a flour mill without getting a little flour on us, and a child cannot live in a well-kept house without learning that this kind of house means less work and more efficiency.

When my child was small, she played with a little girl down the street. After one visit she said, "Mama, Mary's house looks like they closed the doors and shook it up." The way a house is kept makes a lasting impression on a child's life.

Keeping house is a wonderful school in which to teach the child that there is a time and place for everything and that for things to be of value, they must be in the right place at the right time. A toy in the wrong place may mean a visit to the hospital or doctor, or possible death. Medicine in the wrong place costs the lives of many children.

I have seen family after family in my years of trying to help in giving children a better chance where their home looked like a jumble and the children looked like the home. I have had one of these mothers come in for help, and I would give her a good outline on how she could make her den of confusion into a home if she would only try. First, put the house in order, make it neat and clean with the help of her children. Second, serve her meals at normal intervals regularly spaced and see that everybody eats at the same time, with a word of thanks given for the food. Third, keep in effect a regular bedtime, a getting up time, and a playtime.

A child who is reared in a jumble cannot think as clearly as a child who is reared in a home where there are order, cleanliness, and a good system. The habit of putting the toys up, cleaning his feet before coming into the house, washing hands before handling food, hanging up clothes, keeping shoes polished, and keeping things in the right place, will determine to a large extent the kind of life the child will live as an adult. We cannot stress enough the value of a well-kept house in the rearing of a child; the keeping of the house means the keeping of a life.

Chapter Four
Grandparents
(You are the Supreme Court)

We as grandparents have a great influence over our grandchildren. As a rule, a person who is old enough to be a grandparent has found a definite way of life and has smoothed out the rough places and given up the things that a parent would not want his child or grandchild to do. As grandparents we are capable and sufficiently experienced to teach our grandchildren how to live. We know the road, we have seen and felt the pitfalls, and we should be the perfect teachers. For some reason that I do not know, these little people love us and believe in us no matter what we do.

In a child's life, for the first twelve years, grandparents are the supreme court; they are the perfect pattern. In a child's mind grandma and grandpa have the last word and they can go to them when all other help has failed.

As grandparents we should take stock of our lives and see if we are the kind of people we would want our grandchildren to be. We get apples off apple trees, and the same is true of people. I have tried to tell a child that what he is doing is wrong but, if grandma or grandpa does it, it is almost impossible to make him see that it is wrong. "It were better for him that a millstone were hanged about his neck, and be cast into the sea, than that he should offend one of these little ones." Matthew 18:6 This judgment makes the job of being grandparents one of the most important challenges of our lives. With our influence we can make or destroy many little people.

Almost daily I hear these statements from a young mother or father: "We know this child does not eat right, but we cannot do anything about the grandparents. We try to train him one way and our parents will let him do as he pleases. Doctor, if we ever do anything with this child, we will have to move so the grandparents can't see him."

Why would grandparents ever do anything that would cause their own children to make the statement that, because of the grandparents, they could not train their child and develop him as he should be trained and developed?

It is difficult to conceive of a grandparent ever doing anything to injure a little grandchild's life. But during my many years of trying to help to give little children a better chance, I have seen homes and children destroyed by grandparents. Why should this be true? The grandparents should be a big help and they need the children to keep them young and interested in life.

A grandmother will call me and say, "Doctor, I have the best daughter-in-law in the world, but she is young and doesn't know anything about rearing children. I try to help her but she wants to do it her way." I say to her, "Twenty-five years ago you were young and did not know anything about rearing children. Did you want your mother-in-law to run your life? Your daughter-in-law is as old as you were when your son was born and at that time you were sure you could run your house. Why do you not let your daughter-in-law have the same privilege you wanted?

When you got married and started your family, you were the queen in your house, your husband was the king, and your son was your subject. He did as you and your husband commanded until he became an adult. Now that he is married, he is a king and his wife is a queen. Their little boy is their subject, and they have a right to reign supreme in their home. You did not want your mother-in-law to teach your child that you were not capable."

Children must be taught to believe in their parents if they are to feel secure and they can never have this feeling if the grandparents teach them by word and acts that their parents are young and incapable. For a child to be secure, he must know that his mother and father are capable of protecting and teaching him. I have seen this feeling destroyed by grandparents many times.

A mother will say that her child is not to eat between meals and destroy his health. Grandma or grandpa will say that a little bit will not hurt and will feed the child out of schedule. The child knows that somebody has told him an untruth; mama said it was wrong but grandma said it was right; grandma is older than mama, so mama must be wrong; if mama is wrong about this, she is probably wrong about many other things because grandma is older and wiser.

With this, something gets started that may never end, for the child doubts his parents' ability and can never feel secure with them. If one could be in my office for a few days, he could see just what I am talking about...children who do not trust their parents at all and much of it caused by grandparents who let the grandchild do things that they know the parents are teaching him not to do.

We grandparents have no right to go into the home of our child and try to impose our way of life, but we must make our lives as perfect as possible. We must teach the grandchildren to love their parents and obey their will because they are their subjects.

What are grandparents to do when they see their grandchildren being trained by parents who are vulgar, immoral, cruel, and selfish? Should these children be taught to hate and distrust their parents? This is a big question and I hear it often.

One might say that somebody should come in and take these children and give them a normal chance. As a rule, the grandparents are too old to be just and willing to discipline a child as he should be, and it is just as bad to destroy a child with over-indulgence as to destroy him by deprivation. To take the children away and teach them to hate their parents would create something in them that could never be cured, a mistrust that would go into every walk of life. If we doubt our parents, this distrust seems to go out to everybody and everything.

One of the heaviest crosses for grandparents to bear is to see a grandchild mistreated by poor parents, but the best way to completely destroy the child's chance in life is to go into that home and try to change it. They are out of bounds, they are aggressors, and they would not have wanted their parents to come in and try to reform their home. We grandparents should let our children work out their own problems and be willing to see them do without or even go hungry if they are not willing to help themselves.

If grandparents are wise and willing to be examples and not would-be dictators, they can save many homes. The child learns right from wrong and, with his belief in grandparents, he may suffer the curse of poor parents and follow the example of grandparents.

At night when I turn out my light and crawl into a clean snow-white bed, soft and smooth, in a room warm or cool just to my liking, free from odors or insects, I call it a little heaven. Then all of a sudden I become sick and heavy of heart when I think of the millions of little children in this world who are going to bed in filthy, tobacco smoke-filled, insect-infested rooms, in the slums, sick, hungry, pot-bellied, anemic, child and parent filled with hate and fear, with harsh talk from drunk demon-possessed parents, or parents who are so mentally retarded they cannot do any better.

I sometimes hear people say, "Oh well, it takes all that to make up a world, and we must accept this for there is no way to change a world; it was planned that way." The people who say that are those like myself who have the good things of life. God never planned anything to destroy a child. Man and the devil are the planners that create the conditions to cause death and destruction, and to say every evil and vulgar act is God's will comes from the devil. We mustn't ever say to our child that these conditions are God's planning, for it will teach him to hate a God of love.

Why was I not born in the slums? I had a grandmother who was left with two little girls to rear and she was willing to work for fifty cents a week, plow and hoe a garden, make the food they had to eat, and sell eggs to buy the clothes she did not weave from the cotton she grew, and she saved the fifty cents she made each week to pay for an acre of land that was to be cleared by hand. She continued to work and buy land until she had four hundred acres and a good home for my mother and aunt.

She taught my mother and aunt that it was a sin not to work and a sin not to give thanks for work; that a person must be willing to work for what he can get, and not put a price on his worth, but do every job as though he were working for the Giver of all things. I was saved the tragedies that have befallen so many children because of a grandmother and a mother who believed in God and work.

I have worked with many unfortunate children through the years and most of these would not have been so if the grandparents and parents had lived according to the laws of God. We can keep and feed our bodies on very little of this world's goods and teach our children a good way of life. Some of the finest and happiest children I have ever known were children with parents who lived by the laws of God and worked by the laws of God. A person can't fail if he lives this life.

We grandparents have an important place in the lives of all young people in providing an example of how a life should be lived; but to our own grandchildren we owe a special debt of right living, for we are responsible for bringing them into this world and should do all in our power to give them an opportunity to develop lives that will be happy and fruitful.

Chapter Five
The Newborn Baby
(Time of Total Dependency)

Many times when I meet parents who are in tears with their first baby, I say to them, "You see that little squirrel out there in that tree; she has babies and she has never read a book or been to a doctor--yet she knows just what to do for them. If you will just settle down and think for yourselves, you will find that these problems are not half as big as they seem. All that little squirrel does for her babies is to feed them, keep them clean, warm or cool, and away from people. Maybe it is not quite that simple, but it is not half as complicated as the books, neighbors, grandparents, and doctors would make you think it is."

Just mother and baby

When a baby is born, he is cuddly and fits the outside of the mother's body as well as he did the inside of her body. When she holds him on her chest, his little body fits her chest and his head finds a perfect contour pillow made by her neck and clavicle. At nursing time her arm makes a hammock that is secure and this little newborn is satisfied with only two things--his mother and his food.

A pat from the mother, or a song, or some bouncing on her knee, or a few rocks by her in an old-fashioned rocking chair can quiet this little life quicker and better than any sedative or narcotic that has ever been made. It is a case of mother needs baby and baby needs mother, and one can't be happy without the other. This mother-baby relationship is one life, and there has never been a love on earth to compare with it.

Having a baby is not a sickness, and it is not necessary for a mother to be treated as a sick person just because she has had a baby. She is not sick although she is tired from carrying extra weight for six months. She has lost some sleep during the last few weeks of her pregnancy, and she should have the right to rest for at least two weeks before going back to keeping house and making the meals. After such a rest she is able to care for the baby.

Quiet please

Too much company and too much talk have been the downfall of many little helpless babies. Mrs. Jones calls, talks for two hours, wears the mother and father out, and just as she leaves she says, "I should not have come over today with this bad cold but I just had to see the new baby." In seventy-two hours the baby has a cold, the mother is so worried she can't eat, the milk is gone...and papa loses his temper. This is such a common occurrence that it seems to me people who are sick would learn never to go near a new baby. New babies should not have company, but should be kept quiet and away from unnecessary people until they get a good start.

The quiet simplicity of rearing a baby cannot be stressed enough in this age of television, radio, telephone and noise from the street and the sky. A little baby should have the right to a quiet life for the first six months until his body can get adjusted gradually to a noisy world.

I hear parents say they are not going to make any effort to keep noises down, for the baby has to learn to live with them. That sounds good, but they would see the situation differently if they could only know how loud these noises are to that delicate little eardrum, and how frightened-- after having been in a quiet place for nine months--the baby becomes by having these noises appear all of a sudden.

This little life that is starting should be permitted to take the shocks gradually. So it is all-important the baby should be treated as the Indians used to treat their babies, or as the cat treats her kittens--he should be hidden away for the first few weeks of life until he can get a good start.

Doing a thing three times can start a habit

It is so much better to start a child off right than to have to backtrack and correct something that has started wrong. A habit can be formed in a little baby after three experiences of doing the same thing three days. If a baby is walked three nights at the same time, he has it fixed; and the parents must continue to walk him or expect to hear him cry. If we start a baby out on a routine we are not willing to follow, the baby suffers and the parents suffer.

Swaddle the baby

When a baby is born, he should be clothed, according to the temperature, in soft cotton or linen that is sufficient to keep him warm enough or cool enough. He should never wear clothes that do not absorb moisture or do not fit close to the body. Closeness is very important, for the baby has been held tight for nine months and he is much happier if he is swaddled.

How will the baby sleep?

The first question to answer in the care of a newborn baby is, "How will the baby sleep and how should the bed be made?" The bed or bassinet has a water-proof cover over the mattress and, if it is water-proof, it is also air-proof and would not be comfortable; so four towels should be placed over the mattress, and then covered by a sheet stretched skin tight so it cannot be pulled out. The baby should be placed on his abdomen; then he can breathe through the towels if he sleeps on his face and the air can get to the skin and prevent rashes and overheating.

There should never be free objects like pillows or big stuffed dolls left in the bed, for these might cause the baby to be smothered. The cover should be tight at the foot but not tucked on the sides as a normal baby can make his way over the bed as soon as he is born. As a rule he will move forward until he can touch the head of the bed before he goes to sleep. There is no way of knowing, but perhaps it is because the baby wants to cuddle up to mama and feel secure that he seeks a stable object. Anyhow, it is obvious that he wants to be in contact with something.

The second question to be answered is, "How should the baby be placed in the bed?" There have been many papers published in medical journals on this subject. Some say on the back, some say on the side, and some say on the abdomen. Here again the mother must think a little for herself.

All the talk about how a baby should sleep has been by good medical men and which one is she to follow? She can follow but one, so she should go to the lower creation and see what the cat, the squirrel, the cow, the horse do with their young, for them there is no trouble deciding how to place their babies. There is no animal on earth dumb enough to place newborns on their backs.

This little baby has been held tight for nine months and, when he is placed on his back, his hands and feet go free and he feels as if he is falling. He will grab for help that is not there and become startled. With this shock he takes in a deep breath, swallows air, then has the colic and cries--causing more air to be swallowed--and more colic. When he starts to fall asleep, his arm or foot drops and he is frightened again.

I have been called to see a newborn because he continued to cry and would find the baby flat on his back, so frightened that he would be in a tremor. I would turn him on his abdomen, and by the time I could be seated and obtain a history, the baby would be asleep. On his back he reacts like a bug on its back. He is frightened until he learns that when his legs and arms drop, there is something to catch them.

Nine reasons a newborn should be placed on his abdomen

1 - On his abdomen a baby is secure since his hands and feet are always in contact with the bed. This means much in teaching him to be a secure person. If placed on his back, he is helpless since he cannot move around over the bed as he does on his abdomen.

2 - On his back he cannot use his neck as he can on his abdomen. On the abdomen he will raise his head and turn it from side to side as soon as he is born if he is normal; and in this way he exercises the muscles in the neck and back and can hold his head up much quicker. If a baby does not hold his head up by the time he is two or three months old, a mother will start worrying. I have seen many babies that had been kept on their backs who could not hold their heads at the normal time, and the only reason was that they had not been allowed to exercise their necks and back muscles as they should have.

3 - If a baby is on his back and spits up, he could strangle as he cannot turn over to spit out the food. If on his abdomen, the food goes out on the cover and is soaked up.

4 - If a baby is on his back, the colic is much worse. All babies swallow air the first three months of life and this air causes colic. Anyone who has ever had colic knows the relief he gets when he rests on his abdomen.

5 - When the baby is on his abdomen, it is much easier to pass gas. During the first three months babies will pass gas through the mouth and anus all day, and they do not need medicine for this normal condition. When they stop swallowing air, they will stop passing gas if the baby is on his abdomen.

6 - If the baby is kept on his abdomen, his head will always have a good shape. The occipital bone in the back of a little baby's head is not united with the other skull bones yet--and if the baby sleeps on his back, this bone will be forced in and his head will become flat in the back. This will make the child look dumb, but it will not affect him mentally; however, it is a source of embarrassment, as he grows older. This may sound minor, but it can be major in the long run. Anything that may influence a child and be a source of embarrassment to him is major and should be avoided.

7 - On the abdomen the mucus that accumulates in the nose and throat comes out on the covers and he will not strangle, as would be the case if the baby were on his back.

8 - Every organ in the human anatomy works better in the prone position. The heart beats more normally in this position. Everything works right on the abdomen and nothing works right on the back. A newborn baby should be on his abdomen all the time except when he is nursing.

9 - On the abdomen the baby will sleep on his knees and if the feet tend to turn out, this position will help to turn them in. Will sleeping on his abdomen make him have flat feet or clubbed feet? If we examine a baby's feet the minute he is born, we will find that the shape is determined by the way he was held inside the mother. The shape of the feet is determined before the baby is born and no matter how the baby is placed in his bed, the feet will not be made worse. In most cases the feet straighten up with time. (See Chapter 10--Gem #6)

Should baby sleep in Mother's room?

I am sure babies have slept with their mothers from the beginning of time and I am sure a baby loves to sleep close to his mother's warm body. But mothers of today would be afraid of rolling on the baby, and she would not sleep if the baby were in her bed. It is best to have a separate bed for the baby near the mother's so she can see and touch the baby without getting out of bed. It makes the mother and baby feel more secure if they are close together for the first three months. Then the baby and mother are ready for expansion, and some mothers are ready for the baby to be put in his own room if there is an open door between them.

What about the room temperature in baby's room?

For the first three weeks, if it is wintertime, the room should be kept at sixty degrees or above so that if the mother has to get up, the room will not be too cold.

After three weeks, it is best for the baby to be out in the open a portion of the day. For this, the baby should be dressed according to the temperature. If the baby is kept in the house and the temperature is seventy degrees as it should be, never warmer, the baby should not wear a heavy shirt but should be dressed in a cotton sweater which should be removed as the house warms up.

A mother should always dress her baby a little cooler than she is dressed. It is easy to keep a baby too hot. If a baby perspires at all, he is too hot and will not be as happy as he should be. An overheated or overdressed baby as a rule is a sick baby.

Lighting in baby's room

If the baby is on his abdomen, the light will not bother much, but a young baby seems to object to a bright light. The light seems to hurt the baby's eyes and it is best to keep the bright lights shaded for at least the first three months, after which the baby will take the light the same as the parents. If the light is kept on at night for many nights, the baby learns to sleep in the light and objects to the dark. So it is best not to start keeping the light on unless it is planned to be continued.

Bathing and dressing the baby

A mother should place her newborn baby on his abdomen on a table covered with a thick towel for bathing. She will need two wash cloths, a tub of warm water, soap, and a soft towel. With the baby on his abdomen, she should go over the entire body with a damp, soapy cloth, lifting up arms and legs one at a time, turning the head from side to side to wash face and head, lifting head up a little to wash the neck, always keeping the baby on his abdomen.

All the soap should be washed off with a clean cloth and the baby should be dried with a soft warm towel using a patting motion--never rubbing, as this could injure the skin.

After the baby is washed and dried, no oil or cream should be put on the clean skin. If oil is put on the skin, the baby will perspire and the perspiration cannot evaporate as it is covered with oil; so the baby will become chilled and cannot feel warm. This would be like letting the baby sleep in wet clothes, which would be uncomfortable and would cause skin rashes.   Also, the chilling effect of the greased body causes a lowering of the white cells in the blood, and that makes the baby more susceptible to infections.   A baby's skin is naturally clean and frequent washing is not necessary, except the diaper area.

The eyes and ears do not need any cleaning other than with the wash cloth. Sometimes there is a little mucus that can be seen in the nose that is causing an obstruction, and a small twist of cotton wet in sterile water may be used to get the mucus out; but care should be exercised not to insert the cotton too far.   We should do as little to a baby's nose as possible, for crying cleans it out if the baby is on his abdomen.

The baby's head is washed every time the baby is washed, and oil should never be used on the head.   The important thing is to keep the baby's body clean and put nothing on the body unless something abnormal shows up.

The baby should be kept on his abdomen while being dressed.   All baby clothes for the first three months should be fastened in the back.

Diaper changes and diaper rash

While the baby is lying on his abdomen, fold the diaper in an oblong manner so that it can be fastened well on both sides; then fold it back to make it short enough to cover the buttocks. Lift up the baby's legs and slip the diaper under the body to reach just below the unbilicus, using the thick or folded part of the diaper under the body, then pull the diaper between the legs and over the buttocks and pin on each side. When we change a baby this way, he will not object, but on his back he will continue to jump and grab for help.

If a baby is sleeping well and he is wet or even has a stool, he should not be disturbed until he wakes or at feeding time.   Babies develop bad habits by being disturbed too much.   Unless a baby is getting something he is allergic to, being wet or having a stool that is not removed immediately will not make the diaper area red or sore; but if the baby is allergic to something he is getting or to the cleaning product in the diaper, even though the diaper is changed often, he will still have trouble with so-called diaper rash.

Diaper rash is not necessarily caused by dirty diapers or too little changing, but is caused by some allergy.   The urine and stool act as irritants and we get Monilia, staphylococci infection, or many other kinds of infections in the eczema caused by the allergy.

A baby should be kept clean and if the baby is awake, a wet or dirty diaper should be changed. Nothing should ever be put on the diaper area unless it is being treated for something. We do much harm to babies by putting on all kinds of oil, cream, and powder. Sterile water seems to be the best treatment to keep the diaper area well.

A baby's stools

How many stools should a baby have a day? That depends on the milk or milk substitute the baby gets--if the baby is not sick. If the baby is on breast milk, there may be two extremes. If the mother's milk is low in butter fat and she is not eating anything the baby is allergic to, the baby may not have a stool each day, but, in many cases, only every third or fourth day. Then when the stool comes, it will be a mustard yellow, thin, not formed, very smooth with no white particles or mucus, and thin enough to soak up in the diaper. A baby of this type gains fast and is happy, but this is the baby that is sometimes subjected to all kinds of treatment that makes him sick--enemas, suppositories, laxatives, catnip tea, too much prune juice, and many other things that upset him.

If the baby is on the breast and is happy, the parents should not worry if there are no stools for three to four days. If the mother eats nuts, chocolate, cream, dressing, or any other very rich food, the baby may have six to eight stools a day that will be green or greenish yellow, very thin with a large amount of mucus and strings, filled with white lumps that look like curds, and the baby's anus will get red and may bleed.

The large amount of fat acts as a laxative, which increases peristalsis, and the stool is expelled before the normal reaction of the stool contents is reached, blistering the skin of the buttocks. This is a condition that is often treated as diarrhoea with all kinds of medicines being given that make the baby sick. If the mother leaves off the rich food, the condition clears up. A mother taking food the baby is allergic to may cause a similar condition, but the stools in this case will be yellow and thin but too frequent; and also the anus may get red and bleed.

If the baby is on a formula of cow's milk, goat's milk, or some milk substitute, the baby should have at least one stool a day and not more than three. They should be yellow, soft, formed stools that will shake off the diaper. If they are light yellow and foamy, the formula contains too much fat. If they are thin, watery and yellow, or green, the food is wrong or the baby is sick. If a mother is in doubt about the type of stools the baby is having, she should let the doctor see the stools before treating the baby for a sickness.

Vitamins and sun baths

A mother may ask, "What about vitamins?" I say, "I would keep the baby out in the open as much as possible and, when the sun is out, I would give him a sun bath. Then you could give him one of the many vitamins in a small amount with the ten o'clock morning feeding. Breast-fed babies need no extra vitamins."

By the time the baby is two weeks old, you can take him outside and lift his shirt up and let the sun shine on his back for about five minutes. It will satisfy his requirement for vitamin D.

How to carry the baby

A newborn baby should be kept on his abdomen all the time. He should be picked up holding his arms tight to his body and placed on the arm of his mother, on his abdomen, as if riding her arm with his head at the angle of her elbow. (In this position her hand will firmly grasp the baby's lower torso and his face will rest comfortably on her forearm.) He should be held close to her body to make him feel secure. In this position there is no glare in his eyes and he can see from the right angle. This is the way to carry a baby if we want him to feel secure.

A mother will say, "Doctor, we have one of those seat baby carriers. What do you think of that?" To me the use of one of those boards gives the impression of a rejected child. A baby likes to be cuddled and held tight. The warmth of the parent's body is soothing and acts like a sedative to a child's body, and no child should be deprived of this wonderful feeling of security. On this board the baby has to be on his back and that gives him a very insecure feeling.

How much should I hold the baby?

How much should the baby be held? Rocking, singing, holding cannot hurt if it is done consistently and with love. Where the trouble comes with so many babies is that the parents are willing to start a habit with a baby and then get angry with the baby if he demands the rocking, holding, or singing when the parents are tired or have something they would rather do than to continue the little established habit the child has learned to love.

My own child had thirteen rocks* every night before going to bed with a few lines of a song sung in a monotone way. We started this as soon as we left the hospital and she always loved that time of day and we loved it more. It was a good time to cuddle her and get her in a good mood for a night's sleep. She always expected to have this little period and experience before getting off to bed for the night. It is the breaking of a child when he finds that he can't depend on his parents at all times. If we start a habit, we must not get angry if the child demands that we keep it up.

*Rocking thirteen rocks was the habit Dr. Denmark established for her child at bedtime. Her instruction for you is to establish your own routine of rocking and holding your baby. Once you introduce your pattern to your precious one, however, always be consistent to carry it out. Some mothers may rock and sing two lullabies before bedtime and then she will stop. Other mothers prefer to rock and sing until their baby falls asleep in their arms. The idea is to establish your own pattern of rocking and holding and stick to the routine you set.

Crying

Babies must cry and cry hard to open up their lungs to full capacity. I say to mothers, "If you don't let this baby cry today, he may make you cry tomorrow." A normal baby should cry from three to four hours out of the twenty-four hours in the day for the first three months of his life.

The baby can't sleep all the time, and during the hours he is awake he starts fussing. When he fusses, he swallows air and gets the colic; and then he cries and swallows more air and has more colic--a vicious circle but a very normal condition and a very healthful condition.

This crying should not be stopped by giving sedatives. Walking and rocking will not stop the occurrence of this normal crying, but walking or rocking will help the baby to form a habit that the parents will not like. Parents must learn that the crying of a baby is his way of telling them that he is unhappy, and the child must learn at an early age that his crying cannot get for him things that are not good for his physical or mental development. So the baby should be expected to cry some every day for the first three months because he has swallowed air and has developed colic to make him hurt enough to make him cry enough to open his lungs and give him the required amount of exercise.

If parents cannot stand to hear the normal baby cry, it would be better for them to take something to put themselves to sleep than to give the medicine to the baby and make him sick. We must know well that babies cannot sleep all the time; and we must love them enough to hear them cry if it is necessary for their normal development and training. (See Chapter 10–Gem #3)

How to change middle of the night crying

If your baby cries every night after the ten o'clock feeding until two in the morning, then falls asleep, eats well at each four-hour interval, sleeps until the next night at ten o'clock and then cries until two, the parents can rest assured that the crying is not from some abnormal cause but is the crying every normal baby should do.

Sedatives will make the baby sick, so the best thing to do is to keep the baby awake from two o'clock until six o'clock in the afternoon for three days, and the crying period can be changed to the daytime hours when crying doesn't sound half so bad as at night.

Thumb sucking vs. a pacifier

Thumb sucking has caused a great deal of controversy, as well as anxiety, among mothers, fathers, grandmothers, and even grandfathers. This act keeps family and friends in constant conversation when they see a baby enjoying his thumb.

The young mother and father should just settle down and do a little thinking for themselves. What happens to a little puppy when you step on his tail? He runs to his mother to nurse. He thinks sucking will stop the pain. He has been hurt, he has pain, and he thinks sucking will stop the pain. He wants comfort. He knows this act of sucking works when he has a hunger pain and he thinks it will work with all pain.

The same is true of a little baby. As soon as he is born, he starts swallowing air, and when his stomach fills with air, it hurts. Instinctively he thinks sucking will stop the pain, not knowing that every time he sucks, he swallows more air, which causes more pain. Thus, it is easy and natural for him to find his thumb or perhaps the pacifier in some of the more "modern" cases where the mother is afraid the baby will suffer from a frustration predicted by somebody if he does not get in a certain quota of sucking. Or she may give him the pacifier to shut him up.

If a person would think, he would not agree with the idea of a pacifier at all. A pacifier is made of rubber and is hard in comparison with the human nipple, which is the softest part of the body so it will not irritate the baby's tongue and mouth.

The skin on the baby's thumb is soft and could not harm the baby's tongue and mouth. The friction between the rubber pacifier and the baby's tongue takes all the epithelial cells off the tongue and the tongue gets a smooth, red appearance; the taste buds are flat and the tongue is sore. Then thrush begins to develop, which makes the baby more uncomfortable and he sucks more and more, thinking that the sucking will stop the pain. So he keeps the pacifier in his mouth all the time and continues to rub his tongue on the hard rubber.

A baby was in my office recently who had been on a pacifier all his life and his mouth was raw inside. Also the buttocks and all the fingernails were infected from Monilia (thrush) caused by the pacifier. This condition can cause death in a baby and it is so unnecessary. Thumb-sucking could not cause this.

I have seen a mother spend hours working so her baby will not get an infection, but take a pacifier out of her pocket or pocketbook and put it in the baby's mouth. Then I have seen her take the pacifier out of the baby's mouth and put it in her pocketbook or place it on the table, never washing it at all. Many of these pacifier babies have diarrhoea, which the mother cannot understand because she tries to keep everything clean, but she never thinks of how nasty the pacifier is. The pacifier is a troublemaker. In the skin of the thumb there are anti-bodies that kill microbes and the thumb is attached to the arm that can remove it at will, whereas in the case of a newborn the pacifier has to remain in his mouth until the mother removes it.

The "pacifier" mothers all seem to follow the same pattern. They are not problem solvers. They stick a pacifier in the baby's mouth to shut him up. They let him have papa's best tools. They let him stay home from school because he cries. This type mother has destroyed many children. Mothers should never pacify but love their children enough to help them solve their problems.

So the best way to stop this awful thing is to throw the pacifier in the trash and let the baby cry for a while. Every baby who sucks his thumb starts it because he is hungry or uncomfortable. With a correct diet and the elimination of other things that cause discomfort, the thumb sucking will less likely become a habit.

Breast-feed your baby

There is only one normal food to give a newborn baby and that is his own mother's milk nursed from the breast. The security, the antibodies, the mother-child relationship, the human protein cannot be created in a laboratory.   These things count most in a child's life and cannot be obtained from any other source; so the breast milk makes the best method and is far superior to other foods in developing a child to his normal capacity.

If a pregnant woman would eat a balanced diet, get the normal amount of sleep, continue to do her work, be happy in the prospect of becoming a mother, and refrain from taking anything into her body that she would not want her baby to take, she should in almost all cases be able to nurse her baby. With the periodic supervision of a good obstetrician to detect any complications that might occur, pregnancy should not cause any anxiety; and the mother-to-be should not go through that feeling, "I want to nurse my baby, but I am just sure I will not be able to do so."

I often think about the vast amount of happiness that is lost by both mother and child when a mother does not nurse her baby. This lost art has robbed the human race of something that cannot be replaced, for nursing results in a mother-child relationship that cannot be explained. This relationship is the nearest thing to heaven I know of and I speak from experience.

Don't give up on breast-feeding

The mothers who breast-feed their babies often call and say, "My breast milk is nothing but water." This is the reason that large numbers of babies are taken off the breast-- the conclusion that the breast milk was either too weak or too rich. All milk looks the same the first few weeks of lactation. The milk has very little butterfat and that gives the bluish transparent color that is normal. The reason the baby cries is that there is not enough milk or he is being fed too frequently or he is allergic to something the mother is taking in the way of food or drink, or tobacco, or some drug. You could never make me believe that the human mother is not able to furnish her baby breast milk if she is willing to do her part. (See Chapter 10-- Gem #5 Supplementing Mothers Breast Milk)

How can a baby be nourished without mother's milk?

Without the mother's milk, a doctor must instruct the mother how to feed the baby so he will grow up to be as normal as possible. The first thing the doctor and mother must know is that the milk the baby should be getting is very low in butterfat and ash. The lower the fat, the better the appetite. The formula should simulate human milk as nearly as possible.

Each baby has to be tried on the formula the doctor and mother think is best and if the baby spits, does not gain, develops a rash, is constipated or has too frequent stools, can't sleep, and shows other abnormal symptoms, there is something wrong with the baby or the food, and not a single one of these abnormal symptoms should be neglected, leaving the baby to suffer.

It is better to start a baby on a weak formula and gradually strengthen it as the digestive tract matures, which has to grow up just like the baby has to develop. A baby started on a strong formula may start spitting or having frequent fatty stools, may seem hungry and want to eat often because his stomach is hurting, or he may lose his appetite from nausea caused by the fat.

The market is flooded with all kinds of milk preparations and milk substitutes, but no one food is the answer for all babies. It takes an interested doctor and a patient mother to work these problems out. There is always a way to feed a baby, but it may take time and patience to determine the proper way. I always tell a mother if a food comes up, it should not have gone down.

A baby at the breast or bottle learns the importance of mother and this should be the happiest time of the day for mother and baby; it should always be quiet--never in a rush. (See Chapter 10--Gem #5)

How the human digestive system works

The human stomach is a small sack. Food taken into the stomach has to remain there where it is mixed with the hydrochloric acid and pepsin and digested before it is expelled into the gut to be mixed with the bile and pancreatic juices. After this process of digestion, the food is absorbed to supply the needs of the body.

If we continue to add milk to the stomach without giving the milk that is in the stomach time to be digested and expelled, the stomach has to expand more and more because the stomach does not expel milk into the gut until it has been digested in the stomach.

With the constant adding of milk, there would never be a time when all the milk in the stomach would have gone through the process of digestion; but the old would be mixed with the new. The only thing that could happen would be for the stomach to expand to accommodate all that was put in, or the undigested milk would have to be passed into the gut, or the baby would have to spit up to get relief.

The stomach retains food in the same place longer than at any other step in the entire digestive tract, and it must have time to digest the proteins before they leave the stomach.   A baby that is fed too often develops a pot belly; and his stomach gets much larger than it should be just because it never has a chance to empty one meal before another is added. The baby's distended stomach causes colic all the time, so the baby is a constant care.

After studying the emptying time of the stomach through X-ray, we see that the baby taking cow's milk empties its stomach at four-hour intervals, but for the baby taking human milk alone three hours seems to be the perfect emptying time.

Put your baby on a schedule

Many complaints start with a casual method of feeding.   The baby never knows when he will eat and the same is true of his father.   Papa late for work, mama over-worked, and the thing that should bring the greatest happiness on earth--a baby in the home--brings unhappiness and conflicts between the parents.

Feeding a child every time he cries creates a serious problem. I have found that demand feedings are very bad.   The advocates of demand feeding are trying to simulate the mother of early times who did not watch a clock in the care of her child.   In order to simulate that mother, we would also have to simulate her way of life.   A mother of that day had to have a system.   She cooked on a stove that had to be fired, she had to make the clothes for the family, do all their baking, get the food and prepare it.   Women were too busy to stop every time the baby cried and nurse the baby.

These people had a perfect schedule and they did not need to look at the clock to see when to feed the baby.   They had to get up early to get all their day's work done so they were up before the sun and they nursed or fed the baby before preparing breakfast.   After fixing the family breakfast and cleaning up the kitchen, the mother nursed the baby. Then after fixing lunch and doing the house work she nursed the baby and then again at bedtime.   This schedule was determined by circumstance, not by choice.   The baby was happy because he knew this schedule and he expected to eat at a given time.   The only way for any animal or man to be happy and secure is to know, and unless there is a schedule, neither man nor animal can know. Security comes only with knowing.

The advocates of demand feeding argue that if a child is inhibited, he may develop a complex and that the lower animals are not inhibited and they are a happy lot. I am sure that the person who started the story about the lower animals not being inhibited never lived on a farm or observed animals closely. This word "inhibit" may be called instinct in the lower animals but the animal has a definite way of life and does not vary. Animals have a time to eat. Hogs in a peanut patch will eat for awhile, then they will go get a drink of water and find a mud hole and sleep until the food is digested. No matter how much you wake them up, they will not go back to eating until their stomachs are empty. The same is true of all animals. A bird feeds her young at the same time each day. We need not go fishing just any time of the day and expect the fish to bite, for they have a certain time to feed.

How much should you feed the baby?

How much food should the baby take? The amount of food taken and digested is just as varied in babies as the amount of sleep needed. It is not the amount they take, but it is how they digest what they take that matters. One newborn baby may take one ounce and be happy; another may take four ounces and be happy; and both babies may gain the same amount of weight. The manner in which their food is metabolized and assimilated determines how they will gain and be satisfied.

It does not matter how much babies take at the time if it is human milk, so long as they make the proper gains in weight and are happy. On the breast the average baby gets all there is in one breast in about seven minutes.

With cow's milk, goat's milk or milk substitutes, as long as the dilution is right, they can take as much as they want; and, unless the baby is sick, he seems to know just how much to take. The baby should have as much as he will take in fifteen to twenty minutes. The feeding should be four hours apart as long as the baby is on milk alone.

The longer the baby nurses, the more air he swallows, and the more air he swallows, the more colic he has. He swallows air through his nose every time he sucks and soon he is so distended he will bring the air up and also the formula or cry from the colic. No matter how little or how much the baby takes, the spacing should be maintained.

Burping the baby

After the baby is fed, you should hold him up in front of you with his back to your abdomen, in a standing position with his head straight up, holding his hands with one hand, and placing the other hand over his abdomen. Press a little on his abdomen and he will bring up the air he has swallowed while nursing.

Don't force a baby to eat

The baby should never be forced to eat and never fed a formula that is too concentrated or fed too frequently just because he will not take much at the time and does not gain weight. Two wrongs will not make a right but may make a sick baby. Forced feeding creates one of the biggest problems in pediatrics today. We should never try to force our children to eat, sleep, or eliminate, but they should be taught from birth that these acts are a privilege and not a task.

The feeding should never be forced and the mother should not be over-anxious.

If the baby is well, he might refuse a complete feeding at times or take a small amount, which does not matter for he can wait until the next feeding when he will take enough. So it all comes down to this: maintain a good schedule, have the food prepared properly, be happy at feeding time, and have patience.

What is a proper weight gain for a newborn baby?

How much should the baby gain each day or week? It is not best to weigh the baby each day, for the gain is not a regular daily gain, but he should be weighed at the end of each week. The average baby will gain seven ounces a week. Some breast-fed babies will gain much more than that and some will not gain that much. The thing to watch for is a gradual gain and a happy baby. This one-ounce-a-day gain will continue for three months and then the gaining is not so fast--about one-half ounce a day until the baby is six months old.

If the baby does not gain gradually, there is something wrong with the food or the baby, and this problem should be solved as soon as possible. Just because a baby does not cry when he does not gain is no reason for a parent not to be concerned. A baby can be sick and not cry. If a baby does not gain, there is something wrong with the formula or something wrong with the baby's capacity to digest or assimilate the food, and this should be worked out.

The fat baby is not always the healthy or happy baby, so parents should not want their baby to be fat but just to make a gradual gain.

A word about allergies

The mother of long ago did not know the word "allergy," but she knew that certain foods she ate and things she drank upset the baby so she left them off and did not take the baby off the breast.

A nursing mother should eat her regular diet until symptoms appear, and then she should work out her problem by the process of elimination, leaving off the most common offenders one at a time. Chocolate would be first, cow's milk next, tomatoes next--on and on she should go leaving off one food for two weeks. If there is no improvement she should leave off another and go back on the food that did not seem to be the offender. This method has saved breast-feeding many times.

Before a person can be allergic to a food or anything else, there must be some direct contact with that substance. I am of the opinion that if those women who are not planning to breast-feed their babies would not drink cow's milk during pregnancy, they would not have a great deal of trouble getting the baby started on a cow's milk formula; and cow's milk seems to be our best and cheapest method of feeding these babies whom the mother cannot or will not nurse. To leave off cow's milk and milk products during her pregnancy would not be too much to ask a mother to do if she does not plan to nurse her baby.

The power to build up an allergic reaction to any substance differs with each individual. Some individuals seem to be able to develop an allergy to almost any food or substance they come in contact with; others seem to be allergic to nothing and have no trouble. The woman who has a tendency to develop different kinds of allergies should be the one to take no cow's milk during pregnancy if she is not going to nurse her baby...for her baby may have these allergic tendencies.

If a baby is on breast milk and has become allergic to cow's milk by the mother's constant consumption of milk for nine months before the baby was born, the mother must leave off the cow's milk in her diet while she nurses the baby. The spitting, crying, frequent stools, eczema, or other abnormal symptoms that are caused by the milk the baby is allergic to will disappear, and the mother can continue to nurse the baby.

Some doctors and medical books suggest cow's milk to a mother who is nursing her baby as a way to make more milk and better milk. I have never been able to figure that out. If milk is such a good milk maker, why don't we feed it to the cow? She makes it, and she nurses her baby without drinking a drop herself. No other animal except man takes milk during the period of pregnancy or lactation to make milk for a finer baby, and all members of the animal kingdom seem to do a good job. The anemia of pregnancy continues to develop as the consumption of cow's milk increases. Any animal consuming great quantities of milk after the sucking period develops anemia. (See Chapter 10--Gem #4)

Mother, do what you know is best

When a child is born, he is endowed with a certain amount of talent and ability, and it is my belief that there is a plan for his or her life. Each person has a certain number of brain cells and they have a certain innate ability, We cannot add one more to the lot and we cannot make them any better, but we can make them worse by not feeding and training them.

When a child is born, his size, his hearing, seeing, and every part of his body have all the possibilities stored up in that body; and it is the responsibility of the child's parents, the teacher, preacher, and all of those who make up his or her environment, to develop them. The challenge is to take this child as he is and the brain he has and develop both to greatest capacity.

A mother must think for herself and build the type child she wants. This is her chance and she should have free rein and not be dominated by parents or in-laws. She should listen to all the advice of family and neighbors and then do, as she knows best.

Summing up the life of a newborn baby

The mother should be assured that having a baby is not a sickness; that she is able to handle the baby and look after him, and the help she needs is for the housework, laundry and food preparation. The mother should live close to the baby and know what is going on at all times. She should cuddle the baby and keep him swaddled and on his abdomen until he gets adjusted to having his hands and legs free. She should feed the baby on a good schedule; keep the environment quiet without too much light; never let anyone with a cold come near the baby; and have as little company as possible for the first three weeks. The mother should have plenty of time to read, rest, eat and sleep.

If the baby is kept on his abdomen, with the room cool and the air free from tobacco smoke or gases, and is given the right food at the proper intervals, the parents should not worry about the amount of sleep he gets. If his environment and health are good, the baby will get enough sleep. As a rule, a normal newborn will sleep from ten o'clock in the evening until six o'clock in the morning. He will be nursed and go back to sleep until nine-thirty when he gets his bath and is fed at ten; then back to sleep until two and then fed. After this feeding, the baby should stay awake and fuss or cry until six o'clock when he is fed again. From six until ten he may fuss or cry some or just stay awake. At ten he should be fed again and off to sleep for the night.

Chapter 6
From Birth to Two
(The Falling-in-Love Years)

When I was a young doctor, I used to meet with new parents at the hospital after the baby arrived. I knew that this first visit to a newborn baby might mean the difference between a stable and a well-adjusted child and a child who would never know security and self-reliance.

The first thing I said to the mother was, "This baby has come to live with you, not you with the baby. He needs to be trained into a system. If you were building an important business, you'd have a system, and building a human being is the most critical thing on earth. You're going to die one day and leave this little creature here. If you haven't built him a way of life, somebody's going to kick him around. That's the reason our jails are so full today. Those people didn't have a chance because they didn't have parents who taught them a way of life..

"The day this baby was conceived, everything was in one cell: its height, color, disposition, its whole life. If you took care of yourself during pregnancy--didn't drink, smoke, do drugs, or drink too much milk--at birth that baby is all it was meant to be. Now, if you don't feed him right and look after him properly until he's eighteen years old, he can never reach his full potential. This little baby has to have a system. There should be a time for everything."

After I have this talk with new parents, they go out to try to make a go of the most rewarding job on earth, developing a baby. If they have a system, they will have time for each other and will have a happy baby.

Sample of a newborn baby's schedule

6:00 a.m.	Diaper, swaddle, nurse, burp, and back to bed lying on his abdomen
9:30 a.m.	Bath and clean clothes--bathe him while he is lying on his abdomen
10:00 a.m.	Swaddle, nurse, burp, and back to bed for a four-hour nap
2:00 p.m.	Diaper, nurse, burp and let baby fuss, cry, play, or nap a little
6:00 p.m.	Diaper, nurse, burp and let baby fuss, cry, or play
10:00 p.m.	Diaper, swaddle, nurse, burp and off to bed for the night lying on his abdomen

Remember the following things: *Diaper the baby* while he is lying on his abdomen and when he is awake. *Swaddle the baby.* Fully open a baby blanket. Lay the baby down on his abdomen and position his head in one corner of the blanket. Fold the opposite corner over his feet. Leave his arms in their natural position so he can use them as he nudges his way around on the bed. Grasp the third corner of the blanket and wrap it across one arm. Bring the fourth corner around and wrap it around the other arm. Swaddling keeps the baby warm and makes him feel secure. *Nurse the baby.* Breast-fed babies will nurse seven to ten minutes on each breast. Bottle-fed babies can get their formula in 15 to 20 minutes. Never prop a bottle up in the bed for a baby to nurse or allow him to feed himself as he gets older. Until a baby is weaned, he should always get his nourishment while resting in his mother's arms. *Burp the baby.* Burp the baby after he finishes nursing the first breast. Allow him plenty of time to get a good burp. After he has nursed the second breast, his second burp can come when you put him to bed lying on his abdomen. When you burp, use Dr. Denmark's method or put him over your shoulder and pat his back until the air is expelled. Make a special effort to keep the baby awake from 6:00 to 10:00 p.m. *Put the baby to bed for the night.* After the 10:00 p.m. feeding, make certain the baby has had plenty to eat, is clean, has burped, his clothing is comfortable and fitting for the temperature in the room, and he is lying on his abdomen. *Leave the room and turn out the light,* always making sure you have the bed prepared the way Dr. Denmark directs. *Do not pick the baby up until 6:00 a.m.* (Madia Bowman, the mother of eleven, says it takes resolve to refrain from picking your baby up, but if you will endure, the baby will comply.) Don't forget that it only takes doing a thing three times in the same manner and a baby will expect that routine to continue. (See Chapter 10--Gem #3 and Gem #5)

Each day the way the baby is held, the type environment he is subjected to teaches him that his mother and father are not afraid and there is no need for him to fear. Having his food on time and at regular intervals, he has no fear of starving. With a time to sleep, a time to play, a time to eat, he feels secure.

From birth through the second month

The normal baby will cuddle close to his mother as a little kitten cuddles and will eat, sleep, and cry the normal amount each day; and that is about all he wants to do for the first three months. He likes to be talked to and sung to. He is dependent on his mother for everything.

Then he begins watching his mother's face as she talks, and as she moves her mouth and raises her eyebrows, he will do the same thing. Then he begins to carry on a cooing conversation with his mother and he seems to understand all she says; he smiles when she smiles and cries when she looks angry.

Third-Month Birthday

Time for a schedule change

At three months the baby is examined and a new schedule worked out. The baby has gained one ounce a day since he was a newborn and has started talking back to you in a little babble, smiling when you smile.

He has grown four inches. The amount of milk he takes is now eight ounces at six, ten, two, six and ten and he sleeps all night. He has one or two formed stools each day. He holds his head up, and the body is firm and pink in color. The baby is happy, moves over the bed, follows light, recognizes the different members of the family, and laughs out loud.

The mother is advised to put the baby on a pallet on the floor so he can have more freedom of movement and learn to crawl, a thing that is so important in the development of the body. She is advised to keep the baby out in the open as much as possible and to talk to the baby in clear well-formed words.

At twelve weeks you may notice your child stays awake longer, doesn't cry as long, and has begun drooling. Drooling is an indication that the child's saliva now contains ptyalin, the enzyme that enables the liver to change starch into sugar. It is time to begin slowly introducing foods into his diet. The drooling stops when he learns to swallow his saliva.

It's time to introduce solid foods

At this visit, solid food is started, with one new food each week to ascertain if he is allergic to these new foods.

Try one new kind of food at a time and observe the infant over the next four days for any signs of allergic reaction. If no reaction such as rash, diarrhea, asthma, eczema, vomiting, hayfever, a clear running nose, or

excessive crying occurs, you can assume there is no allergy and you can
begin to increase the amount of tested food.

Any abnormal condition should be recorded. You can then try the food
in question one month later and check for a similar reaction. Introduce
the food three times at one-month intervals. If the reaction occurs each
time, you may assume that the child has a lifetime allergy to it.

Baby's first solid food

Week 1 - Cereal is started first with one-fourth teaspoon at ten, two and
six, increased each day until two tablespoons are given at ten,
two and six.

Week 2 - Fresh banana is started in the same way and increased to two
tablespoons at ten, two, and six.

Week 3 - Apple sauce or prunes will be started in the same way and
increased to two tablespoons at ten, two, and six. (If the stools
are hard, prunes will be started; if the stools are too soft, apple
sauce is started.)

Week 4- Green beans or carrots are started in the same way and
increased to two tablespoons at ten, two, and six.

Week 5 - Beef or liver is started in the same way and increased to two
tablespoons at ten, two, and six.
Always breast-feed the baby at ten, two, and six before giving
him his meal. A bottle-fed baby will eat the meal and then be
given eight ounces of formula.

Prepare baby's food properly

All of baby's food must be fresh, cooked, and well pureed in a food
processor, using enough water to make the food the right consistency.
The consistency varies with the baby as some babies like the food rather
stiff and others like it soft.

Avoid using salt or spicy seasonings..

One can buy store-bought baby food, but it will be very expensive.
Invest in a food-processing machine and prepare your own baby food.
The savings will be immense.

If you choose to buy already prepared baby food, purchase un-mixed
varieties. Combination foods contain too much starch. For example, buy
beef and carrots in separate jars, not as beef stew.

Another positive aspect of making home-cooked baby food is that you
can choose the best cereals, meats, vegetables, and fruit available at the

market. You will be assured your baby is getting the highest quality and most nutritious food available.

One may ask, "How were babies fed before electricity and food processing machines?" The answer to that question is that mothers chewed for their babies until they were able to chew for themselves. This was before Louis Pasteur told mothers about germs. When a mother chewed for her baby, the food tasted sweet as the bread in the morsel she chewed with the other food changed into sugar in the mouth, making the morsel sweet, and babies like food that has a sweet taste.

Mix and serve all the foods stirred together

Measure out the proper amounts of each individual food you are serving and stir them together in a bowl. By your mixing all the food together, the baby cannot just take the sweet fruit and leave off the meat and vegetables. The food all tastes good and is an excellent way to ensure that baby receives a balance of all the necessary nutrients.

All of the mixed food should be heated until it is sterile. After it is cooled down, but still warm to the taste, it can be fed to the baby with the spoon with which it was stirred while heating, and fed out of the container in which it was heated. This makes less work for the mother and we can be sure the food is not contaminated. Some babies will not eat all that is prepared and many babies will eat more.

Some mothers make a week's worth of food at a time and freeze it in ice cube trays until needed. Others fix a couple of days' worth and keep it in the refrigerator.

Only one planned nap now

The nap should be continued from ten in the morning to two in the afternoon, with no other planned naps, and a strict schedule should be maintained if the mother wants a secure baby. No baby can feel secure unless he knows what to expect, and keeping a good schedule from the day a baby is born is the way security is taught. A mother with a plan builds a baby with a life that he knows how to use. This early advice to a young mother may save her home.

At the end of the three-month visit, the mother is advised to return when the baby is five months old.

Fifth-Month Birthday

Time to change schedules again

When the baby is five months old, he is brought back. The baby is fat, happy, laughing out loud, handling his toys well, can almost sit alone, can make his way over the floor, but cannot crawl on his hands and knees very well. He has gained three-fourths of an ounce a day since his last visit and is two inches longer.

At this visit he is put on three meals a day and nursed at seven, twelve-thirty, and six. All of the baby's food should be cooked, pureed, mixed together and sterilized in the same manner as was directed for the three-month-old baby. The food should always be served warm as cold food slows up the digestive process.

Each new food should be added in the same manner as at three months to ascertain if he is allergic to any food. If he is allergic, it will be discovered as each new food is added.

Three meals a day

Breakfast -	3 tablespoons protein
7:00	3 tablespoons starch
	2 tablespoons fruit
	1 banana

Lunch	3 tablespoons protein
12:30	3 tablespoons starch
	3 tablespoons vegetables
	2 tablespoons fruit
	1 banana

Dinner	3 tablespoons protein
6:00	3 tablespoons starch
	3 tablespoons vegetables
	2 tablespoons fruit
	1 banana

Breast-fed babies nurse before getting these meals. Bottle-fed babies get eight ounces of formula after these meals.

Some babies will not eat this much food and some will eat more. The amount a baby will take varies and if he wants more, more should be mixed in the same proportion, or less if he wants less. There can be no set amount as metabolism will vary. One thing to remember is that the food should always be mixed in the right proportion, and the baby should be the one to decide how much he wants.

Acceptable proteins are lean meat, eggs, or black-eyed peas. Other beans may be used occasionally, but black-eyed peas are the superior legume because of their high protein content.

Acceptable starch is cereal and potatoes.

Leafy or green vegetables are best to use because of their high iron content. Other vegetables may be interspersed with them.

An effort should be made to get the baby to eat, but he should never be forced and made to cry and be unhappy about what he has to eat. Eating must be a happy time if the baby is to be normal.

We have a new nap time and bedtime hour

At five months, a three-hour morning nap schedule from 9:30 to 12:30 should be maintained. Baby may catnap on his own in the playpen or car seat but should begin weaning himself from sleeping in the afternoon.

Encourage him to stay awake by keeping him in the living room or kitchen so he can watch family activity and play with his toys.

After the six o'clock evening nursing and mealtime the five-month-old should be put to bed for the night. He should sleep until seven the next morning.

It's time to learn to drink from a cup

It is time to begin giving baby sips of water from a cup. There's never any need to give it in a bottle. It takes practice, but they can learn to drink from a cup at an early age. I wouldn't give a child anything to drink except water after weaning.

Allow no fruit juices, carbonated drinks, or snacks between meals

Don't give your baby juice, carbonated drinks, or snacks between meals. Children who eat between meals get potbellied and anemic. Their stomachs never have a chance to empty, so they're always hungry but never hungry enough to eat a decent meal.

I had a little boy in my office not long ago. I tested his urine and I've never seen that much sugar in any human's urine. "Where in the world is he getting this sugar?" I asked his mother.

"We don't let sugar come into our house," she said.

"What does he drink?"

"Apple juice. I make it myself."

"What do you do with the pulp?"

"I throw it on the mulch pile."

I calculated that the child was getting eight ounces of pure sugar daily. I'm sure his eyesight was ruined.

"But it's natural sugar!" his mother said.

What sugar isn't natural sugar? The sugar mashed out of canes is natural. Everything on earth is natural! She was taking all the pectin, cellulose, and protein in that apple and throwing it away. The only thing the child was getting was the sugar and water.

People don't understand that children don't need juice. Why not buy the apple instead of just the juice? Why not buy the orange or the carrot and get the whole thing?

The family should not drink anything but water. Fruit juices stress the kidneys and produces highly alkaline urine that can cause burning, itching, and even urinary-tract infections. Drinking water exclusively can sometimes cure a bedwetting problem.

Time to start immunizations

At the five-month check-up the baby is given the first diphtheria-whooping cough-tetanus vaccine and the first polio vaccine.

The first shots shouldn't be given before five months because the baby's immune system hasn't developed enough to respond effectively. (See Chapter 10--Gem #1)

Your baby should be examined for possible illness before having the vaccinations. Don't have a sick baby vaccinated.

Vaccinations are safe and vital to your child's health; they should be administered in the deltoid muscle of the arm. Massage the area well after administering.

Let's talk about thumb-sucking again

As I have said previously, for the first three months of life a baby swallows air and has colic and the thumb is used as a pacifier...as a desire for comfort. After three months the thumb sucking will usually cease if the diet is correct.

However, if the baby has used his thumb with his colic or because of any upset mental or physical state, he goes for his thumb again when he feels the discomfort from his teeth as they start coming through. It feels good to rub his sore gums with his little soft thumb. This continues until the two-year molars are through, for there is never a time from five months of age to two years that the gums are not swollen.

The way I handle thumb-sucking is never to encourage or discourage it. I teach the parents never to bring the subject up or start pulling out the thumb and making an issue of the matter.

If a young baby has a stomachache, he has a reason to suck his thumb and the cause of the stomachache can be determined if the doctor and mother will try to find it.

Sixth-Month Birthday

On his six-month birthday the baby is given the second diphtheria-whooping cough-tetanus vaccine and the second polio vaccine. (See Chapter 10–Gem #1)

A description of a six-month-old baby

At six months the baby begins to crawl, but he wants to be in his mother's presence. She can sit and sew for hours with the baby happy on a pallet but when she leaves the room, the baby will cry.

This is annoying to a mother who does not understand the stages in a child's life but the crying is a compliment to her, showing that she and the baby have a normal mother-baby relationship. The baby is happy at nursing time and feeding time is a pleasure; he likes to eat and the mother likes to see him eat.

During the first six months of a baby's life the clothes, if they are soft and comfortable, will not affect the child's life. They may be any color or be made in any style. Boys and girls may be dressed alike. The clothes may be long or short; the only thing that matters is that they are comfortable.

At six months there is a definite change. The clothes must be short enough to allow the child freedom to crawl. At this time the style or color, or the fact that they may be girl's or boy's clothes does not affect the child. All he wants is comfort and the freedom to crawl.

Seventh-Month Birthday

The baby can say "dada," can crawl, and can sit alone. He has gained one-half ounce a day since his last visit. The diet remains the same. He is given the third diphtheria-whooping cough-tetanus vaccine and the third polio vaccine. (See Chapter 10–Gem #1)

Eighth-Month Birthday

It's time for a BIG change

At eight months he is back in my office again. At this visit he can say "bye-bye" and "dada," pulls up on his knees, weighs about ten pounds more than he did at birth, his head and chest measure about the same-- around seventeen inches--he is about twenty-nine inches long, not fat but firm, and, as a rule, he has six teeth.

At this visit the mother is advised to take the baby off the breast if he is a breast-fed baby, or off the bottle if a bottle baby. The child should not be given any more cow's milk. He should be given water from a cup. (See Chapter 10–Gem #4)

Foods the baby can and cannot have

The mother is advised to start feeding the baby small portions of food that she prepares for the family, but to be sure to puree it well and continue to mix the food.

The baby can have beans, squash, beets, cabbage (and other members of the cabbage family if cooked only ten minutes), black-eyed peas, green peas, tomatoes. But he should have no nuts, raw peaches, berries, melons, corn, new potatoes, or bought ice cream.

To repeat, breast-feeding or the formula is to be stopped, and only water should be given with each meal. The mother is advised as to the value of warm food, that cold food slows up the digestive process, and the soothing effect of warm food is important.

She is reminded that feeding between meals will cause a delayed emptying of the stomach and the baby, if fed between meals or closer than five and one-half hours, will become pot-bellied, be a feeding problem, and perhaps, develop anemia. One cannot stress too much the value of a good feeding schedule and a well-balanced diet if one wants to give a child a chance.

There should always be a cup of water on the table for the baby, and no food or drink should be given between meals except water. The meals should be at seven, twelve-thirty, and six.

The baby should be fed sitting up in a high chair before the family eats.

Happy First Birthday

At one year the baby is checked and at that time he is walking, talking and feeding himself with some help. He must continue his schedule of pureed food as was introduced at eight months. His weight is about twenty-two pounds, his height thirty inches, his head nineteen inches, and his chest nineteen inches.

At one year a baby likes to please his audience. A normal baby at one year of age with a normal mother is the best example of true happiness on earth. If a baby is born well and has a mother who loves him enough to nurse, hold, rock, sing, speak quietly and kindly, he has learned the greatest lesson of love and security.

The complete dependence on mother has been evident for the past twelve months. Baby has liked to be fed by her, dressed, bathed, carried in her arms, rocked, talked to, and played with. The mother can now make the baby laugh, wave bye-bye, do a pat a cake, or do anything she tells him to do.

Naptime can be shortened

His nap is from 10:00 to 12:00 noon with no afternoon naps and he goes to bed immediately after he has his dinner. His meals are always spaced five and one-half hours apart, with no food or drink between meals except water.

Continue to feed the one-year-old in the same manner you have fed him since he was eight months old and I will not see him again until he is eighteen months old.

Respect Me! I know who I am

At one year or at the time when a child is first walking, there is a big change. A boy seems to know he is a boy, and a girl seems to know she is a girl. When a little girl is dressed in a beautiful dress, she will show a marked feeling of pleasure, and she knows she is beautiful. She likes to look in the mirror and admire herself. A little boy seems to throw his chest out when he is dressed like a boy with his hair cut like a boy's. He will admire his looks as much as a little girl admires her looks. A little boy who is made to wear long hair and girls' clothes after one year never seems to get over that curse.

A boy who after one year is dressed like a girl as a rule is a bad child. If this is carried into the negative period of a boy's life--from two to six--

he becomes destructive and wants to fight all the time to show people that although he may dress or wear his hair like a girl, his parents can't make him act like a girl.

When one of these little children is brought into my office for the first time, wearing long curls, white high-top shoes, and fancy clothes, I may say, "What a beautiful little girl." And the mother, always with a moronic-type smile, will say, "Oh, no. This is my son. He is not a girl and if he stays around long, you will find that out. He hates to be called a girl."

And this is true. If we are around him very long, we will soon think he is demon-possessed because he must show us that his appearance has caused people to pass the wrong judgment on him, and he must prove to the world he is not a girl.

I have had the opportunity to follow these children from birth to adult life and they never seem to get over this experience. One would say that a mother who would do such a thing to a child is not a normal mother. I am sure that no normal mother would ever do anything to a child to handicap him, but there are many selfish or abnormal women who have babies, and their children do not have a chance to develop normally. They are under the curse of a bad parent, the most unfortunate thing on earth. The stigma of being called a female when one is a male cannot be forgotten if a child is subjected to this for a long time.

Many females seem to be dissatisfied with their sex, but I have never seen a male who would change into a female. So a boy should be dressed as a boy after he is one year old. His hair should be cut in a boy's style, and he should never be referred to as looking like a girl.

How parents can ruin a little girl

Parents I knew had one beautiful daughter. The second baby was to be a boy, they would say, and they made plans for a boy. But when the baby came, it was another beautiful girl. Their friends teased them and they laughed and called this little girl their "boy." They dressed her like a boy, and she had boy toys. They had lots of fun calling her a boy and would continue to say, "I just can't get her to wear girl clothes or to play with dolls or play with girls. We have to buy her boy toys and boy clothes."

This little girl was just as beautiful as her sister at birth, but the parents continued to talk about her masculine behavior and to confess that they could not do anything about it. At twenty years old she was still wearing men's clothes and a man's haircut. She walked like a man. Women were afraid of her, and men had no place for her. So her life was a failure. She played the game of being a boy so long she could not change.

Eighteenth-Month Birthday

Starting to show some independence

The period of the child's being completely dependent on the mother-- and enjoying it--begins to show evidence of breaking about the eighteenth month. The little fellow wants to hold the spoon and feed himself and begins to show a temper if he can't.

Papa and mama come again and they are very happy with this fine baby. He is a big boy, talking, walking well by himself, plays with his toys, can climb on top of the tables, can open and close doors.

The age to be carefully watched

Eighteen months old is an age when a child must be watched more than at any other time for he has very little judgment about what he eats or drinks, hot stoves, or high places. His body is fat, but he has gained only two pounds in six months and one and one-half inches in height; he has sixteen teeth.

The feedings are the same as at eight months and one year and he maintains his two-hour morning nap. At this visit the parents are advised to come back when the baby is two years old.

One last schedule review

Newborn	Nurse	- 6-10-2-6-10
	Naps	- 6:30 - 9:30 (3 hrs.)
		- 10:00 - 2:00 p.m. (4 hrs.)
	Meals	- None
	Bedtime	- 10:00 p.m.
3 Months	Nurse	- 6-10-2-6-10
	Nap	- 10:00 to 2:00 (4 hrs.)
	Meals	- 10:00 2:00 6:00
	Bedtime	- 10:00 p.m.
5 Months	Nurse	- 7:00 12:30 6:00

Nap	- 9:30 - 12:30 p.m. (3 hrs.)
Meals	- 7:00 12:30 6:00
Bedtime	- 7:00 P.M.

8 Months

Nurse	- Baby is weaned
Nap	- 10:00 - 12:30 p.m. (2 1/2 hrs.)
Meals	- 7:00 12:30 6:00
Bedtime	- 7:00 P.M.

12 to 24 Months

Nap	- 10:00 - 12:00 noon (2 hrs.)
Meals	- 7:00 12:30 6:00
Bedtime	- 7:00 P.M.

Dr. Denmark instructs not to give a child mashed or whole food until he has 8 molars. Introducing mashed or whole foods before this time will irritate the baby's stomach. Plan to continue feeding pureed food through the twenty-fourth month.

Summing up the baby from birth to two

From birth to two, if a child is fed right and trained right and has a good schedule, he is very dependent on his parents. He eats well and likes to do things to make his parents happy, and will do all kinds of tricks to get his parents and their friends to laugh.

If you ask him to sing for daddy, he will sing and if you ask him to do some stunts for his mama, he will do that. He will eat what you prepare for him and sometimes ask for more. He will eat more the first two years than he will eat for the next four.

Chapter Seven
Years from Two to Six
(The Negative and Discipline years)

At the second birth date, mama and papa return with little Johnny. "Well, how is that fine boy today?" "Well, doctor, I don't know. Something has happened to him.

"Maybe we just don't know how to handle him, or we have done something wrong. He has completely changed. Every time we tell him to do something or to eat his food, he says, 'No,' and he sticks to it. We have tried talking to him, we have tried letting him get a prize, and we have tried spanking also. We have tried making him do without something he really wants, like the dessert, and nothing works.

"He will not eat enough to keep a bird alive. Look at his legs. Those beautiful little chubby legs are just getting skinny. No matter how attractive I fix the food, he refuses it. I have tried playing games with him to get a little food down and I have threatened to give his food to his dog. Papa will try racing with him at the table, but he will just sit there and play in his food and not put one bit in his mouth.

"He has temper tantrums when he can't have his way, and he whines and cries at the least interference with his desires. We are really desperate; he has been a perfect child for two years and now it seems we have struck a stone wall. Do you think we should go to a psychiatrist? The trouble must be with us."

"Now, the first time you came into my office you were in just as bad a state; you were ready to give up. That worked out and this will also if you understand your problem. You have been good parents and have made this little boy a good body, so we must not fail at this point. Your problem is not so big if you only understand a two-year-old."

At two years every normal child begins to live a negative life. He rebels at every command and this will last for four years or until he learns the value of obedience.

From two to six he is braver than he will ever be. He is brave enough to try anything, so that makes this period in his life the most important teaching period. If the laws of life are taught well at this period, we have a good foundation on which to build a man or woman.

Who's to teach a child during his negative and discipline years?

The parents and grandparents should do this teaching during the negative period of a child's life. If a Smith wants to grow a Smith, a Smith must teach a Smith how to be a Smith from birth to six years of age. This teaching process requires love, patience, consistency, example, time, prayer--but the pay-off is great.

No minute of the day from birth to six years can be wasted if we are to develop a well-adjusted child. He is in constant motion all of his waking hours. There is a stubbed toe, a bumped head, a skinned knee, a broken doll, a torn dress, a lost toy, a glass of water on the floor, a bumped nose, and, if more than one child, there may be a few good fights. These mishaps not only need medical care, but the child must be taught by each of these experiences that the thing he did to get hurt was his own fault and how he can avoid this mishap next time and how he has to pay for every transgression.

From conception to six years of age is the most important time in a human life and parents must not miss one opportunity to make this period as perfect as possible.

We may be casual about some things, but we cannot be casual about this child who has come to live with us. We have no way to know who he is or where he is going, but this short stay with us must prepare him for the life he is to live, and we must make it so perfect he will never have reason to look back on this time as a curse, but on the contrary...as a great blessing.

Mother, don't make excuses

An overworked statement by mothers who don't want to take this great responsibility of training a child in this negative period is, "My child needs to be with other children. He is too much of a mama's baby, and I need to get away from him."

Another statement I hear often is, "Doctor, there are no children in our block, and I just had to send him off so he could learn how to play with other children." Oh, how these mothers think up excuses to put the training job on somebody else when they don't want the job!

All this is an excuse to get out of this great responsibility and tedious job of teaching a negative child how to live. The reward that comes to a mother who has spent six years teaching her child a good way of life is the greatest reward on earth.

I say nobody but the parents can do this job as it should be done; and in the development of a child there is no way to go back and start over. Each period of development is different and once that period is gone, the training the child should have had at that time and didn't get cannot be given.

The great harm resulting from the day care or baby sitter is that the child is not privileged to live with the mother during his negative period when he will say "no" to a two-hundred-pound papa or mama and stick to it even if it costs him a spanking. He can't learn these lessons that he is a subject instead of a king except with his parents.

Parents, you must exercise discipline

The child from two to six will learn all the discipline and the value of discipline he will ever learn. That is why he should live with his parents at this all-important period in his life. He will not act without an audience and his parents make the only audience that matters. If he is sent out of the home, he will not rebel for he does not have the proper audience. This business of rebellion and learning what it gets him is a lesson that cannot be missed.

Don't build a "rejection complex" in your child

If mothers could only see what they are doing to their children to make them develop a "rejection complex" by sending them out of the home before they are ready to go, surely they would make a greater effort to avoid it.

Every child deserves a chance but I know from more than seventy years of working with children that there are thousands who have never had a decent chance in life. I don't mean a chance at wealth and the things money can buy, but the blessing of a good mother who loves the child and realizes that the march of life is always forward and the opportunity missed today is gone forever.

As I just mentioned, the statement I hear over and over again is "Doctor, my child is getting to be too much of a mama's boy and will not let me get out of his sight." The child knows mama is rejecting him, so he clings closer and closer and cries out at night, dreaming he is left out or deserted. I have never heard this statement from a good mother, and I have never seen a child with a "rejection complex" who was not really being rejected.

We hear the statement again and again, "No mother should be tied down with a house full of kids." No woman who really wants to be a mother is ever "tied down with kids" and the only mother who is "tied down" is the mother who wants to get away. A real mother never has the feeling that she is being punished by having children, but she feels that she has been blessed with the greatest opportunity on earth.

A child should never leave home before six

Children have to leave home some time, and six years of age is not too late. We should not push them out of the nest until they are ready to fly. Physically and mentally no child is ready to go before six and some considerably later.

Between two and six is a parent's great opportunity to teach the important lessons of honesty, truthfulness, love, fair play, health habits, parental authority, respect for elders, good manners, and many other lessons that will prepare him to be ready to meet life out of the home when he is six.

It is in these years of a child's life that parents make or break him. It is during this time the most important things are learned: manners, fear, hate, love, faith, all the things that count in making a person secure or insecure, happy or unhappy, well or sick, and, maybe I should say, rich or poor.

Life is such a short day, and it is hard to see why we are not willing to give our children a chance by doing this day right. The greatest need of today or any day is parents who love their children enough to give them a chance to have a good body, good manners, a deep respect for others, and an ever-thankful attitude toward God and man. All this has to be taught.

A neglected plant can never be what it would have been if it had been started right and that is true of a child. Life is built up one day at a time. A child who is taught good manners and customs from birth has a treasure that money cannot buy.

By six a child has learned a "way of life"

The chief examples a child has the first six years of life are his parents and grandparents. He learns a way of life, which may be good or bad, but we can't argue with a little boy six years old about his way of life; for what his parents have taught him he believes is right. Six-year-olds are ready at this age to practice what they have learned in their homes. They are ready to see if the training they have had will work outside the home.

When my child started to school, she had learned a way of life; and it was interesting to hear her ask why other children behaved as they did. One night at supper she said, "Mama, the teacher had us answer some questions about our home life...if we washed our teeth...ate with the family...what time we went to bed; and do you know Jean stays up until ten o'clock and I go to bed at seven! I want to stay up tonight."

I said, "All right, you may, but the reason I like for you to go to bed early is because you will feel like getting up early and have breakfast with us and be ready to go to school. If you go to bed that late, you will have to sleep late; and you would not see Papa before he goes to work. You may try it tonight." About eight o'clock I noticed she was very quiet and it was not long before she said, "I wish Papa would go up with me and put me to bed."

There are rules to learn for effective parenting

1. The first thing I tell parents to do is to write a little sign and paste it across their bedroom mirror letting it read this way, "I will never do or say anything to my child that I would not want done or said to me." As I have said, he is living a negative life that will last four years. He will rebel to show you he is not about to be a baby any longer and nothing you have done makes him this way. This behavior pattern is just as normal as cutting teeth.

2. Never give a child a command that you can't carry through and never give a command in a manner you would not want to be commanded. Every command parents give a child must be carried through or the child loses respect for them, and always remember that there are a few things we can't make a child do. We can't make him eat, sleep, or eliminate, nor can we make him stop sucking his thumb.

3. Be Patient –

Patience, patience, patience...a mother needs to be so patient. I don't remember my mother ever being in a hurry or raising her voice at any one of us. She never made us feel we were working her to death, and I never heard her say, "You children are wearing me out!"

How did she stay so patient with twelve children? I think if You had been in my office today, you'd wonder how I stay so calm. There were babies crying in both side rooms, mamas slapping and yelling. I could get awfully upset. I could lose my temper at the parents and say, "Don't come back if you won't follow my advice."

I think my mother handled it just the way I do; she had self-control. If you don't have it, you'd better find some. If a mother raises her voice, the children will, too. Sometimes I'm asked, "Dr. Denmark, what makes my children so bad?" "Go look in the mirror," I say. "You get apples off apple trees."

4. Never ever nag - This negative behavior in a child's life is often blamed on a new baby, as it is often the case that about the time a child turns two, there is a new baby in the house. I hear this statement over and over, "My child was perfect until the new baby arrived; being jealous of the new baby has completely changed his life."

No, the new baby in a home is not the reason that a two-year-old changes. The new baby could be a contributing cause for trouble as the mother starts saying, "Don't bite the baby; don't touch the top of his head; don't throw toys in the baby's bed; don't cry and wake the baby up; don't wet your pants and make work for me when I am trying to care for the baby; go out and play so I can look after your little brother; hurry up and eat for I must feed the baby."

Now all these suggestions give the two-year-old a chance to cause trouble because he will react with a strong negative response to any suggestion, baby or no baby. The mother should not make all these suggestions if she does not want the problem.

Many times a mother creates a real hate for the new baby by the two-year-old in her constant nagging, because he is at a stage in his life when he will fight back no matter how big the commander is. We should never suggest evil to our children, and we could save them a lot of punishment. Neither the new baby in the home nor any other excuse we have when we see our perfect baby give up his perfect way of life is the reason, and we must know that these excuses we use are issues that have been suggested to the two-year-old that he can use to show he is not a baby any more. The greater the nagging, the greater the problem.

5. Restrain - Children must be restrained to teach them self-control and to make them see how their acts affect them and their fellow man. We can't afford to teach children that every desire they have must be satisfied at any cost.

Children must be guided and they must be inhibited, and they must learn this lesson while they can take it. When we inhibit a child from two to six, he may cry and have a temper tantrum, but he learns that lesson and in a few minutes will be happy and love us. If this happened to an adult, it would not be so easy unless he learned about being inhibited as a child. The earlier children learn they can't have everything they think they want, the better it is.

6. Punish if necessary. I often tell the parents of my patients that if they love a child, they will punish him. Love appears heartless at times. When a child is rolled off to the operating room crying, it looks heartless but we love him enough to hear this crying if the operation is necessary to save his life.

Help! How do we get this child to eat?

When a child reaches two years, his growth almost stops. He has gained thirty pounds in the past two years and nine months and will gain only three pounds in the next twelve months. He has grown thirty-two inches in the past two years and nine months and will grow only three inches in the next twelve months and maybe not that much.

He does not need to consume more than one-fifth as much food as he did at the time he was one year old. So you see he is not really hungry and it is not hard for him to hold out when you try to force him. The things we have to do become work; the things we want to do become play; and eating should not be work.

Food should be served on the child's plate in small portions, never discussing his likes and dislikes before him, but, if you know a food is unappetizing to him, just don't put it on his plate; you would not want it on yours. After the plate is served, return thanks and then talk about anything except food.

When you and your husband have finished the meal, clear the table and never say, "Johnny, why did you not eat your meat or carrots? That will make you big like Daddy." Just be happy about the whole thing and never mention the food, no matter how little he ate, and give him no food or drinks except water until the next meal.

If you find that he is eating no food off his plate except his potatoes, don't make an issue of that; just stop cooking potatoes for a while. If he just eats bread, stop giving him bread for a while but don't say to him, "I am going to stop the bread if you don't eat your other food." That provides him a challenge and nothing is quite so great as a challenge to a two-year-old. He will tackle any challenge and he goes in to win but, if you make a threat, you must be strong enough to carry it through or you destroy your child's respect for you.

He must have a balanced diet, and he will get that if you leave off the things he should not have and never let him eat or drink between meals. Once you say, "You can't have your dessert unless you eat what is on your plate," be sure to carry through.

Don't worry about the amount of food he eats but about the type and quality of food he gets. Every day I hear parents say, "Doctor, I would give him anything he might ask for just to get something in him." Eating time should be the happiest time of the day and it can be if the parents will not nag any more than they would like to be nagged.

How much sleep does a child two to six require?

All the research that has been done on sleep shows that afternoon naps make poor night sleepers. A child two to six years of age needs an average of twelve hours of sleep. He should be awakened at seven o'clock for breakfast and have no naps during the day. He will then be ready to go to bed after dinner at six-thirty to seven o'clock.

It's important for a child to go to bed early enough so papa and mama can have a break in the evening.

When I was a young, inexperienced doctor, a mother brought her two little daughters into my clinic and claimed it was impossible to get them to bed. She wanted me to prescribe a sedative for them.

I was puzzled and kept questioning her to determine the cause of her children's sleeplessness. Finally, I asked, "What time do they get up in the morning?"

"About 11:30," she responded.

"Well then, they shouldn't go to bed until 11:30 p.m.!" I told the mother. I advised her to get them up at 7 and give them breakfast. If she did that, they would be ready to go to bed at the right time.

Wet Beds and Wet Pants

No child over two years old will soil his pants if he can help it and, when a child continues to have soiled pants, he should have a good examination and the reason found...for there is a reason.

The same is true with respect to a child wetting his pants or the bed after two years of age. A mother will say her little girl keeps her pants wet and seems to be afraid to urinate. On examination the child is found to be red and very sore in her vulva and when she starts to urinate, it burns so she cuts it off and there is a constant desire to go and a constant fear of burning. If the mother would examine her little girl, she would see why she had wet pants.

The child may use the toilet paper wrong, pulling the paper forward and smearing the stool in the vulva, causing an infection; or she may be getting something she is allergic to that causes the rash; or she may be getting too much citrus or tomato which may make the urine alkaline and cause the burning. In some of these cases the labia minora have grown together and the urine has to be forced out of a small opening which causes pain.

A mother should check her child at bath time and if she finds some abnormal condition, she should see a doctor at once, as there are many reasons that a child cannot control the urine. Infection, malformation, and small bladders are very common in the urinary tract. A few things we can do to keep these little girls from getting into trouble are: Teach them how to use the toilet paper, keep them clean, give them no drinks except water. If there is trouble after these three simple things have been done, then the child should see a doctor. Girls don't want to be wet.

The same is true with respect to boys. They should be examined and kept clean and not allowed to drink all kinds of sweet drinks, carbonated water, cow's milk, or enough citrus to cause an alkaline urine.

Diapers should not be used after two years. There is always a reason for wet beds and wet pants and parents may be responsible for much of this. They permit the child to drink all day things he should not have, and never examine him to see if he is irritated or cannot stand to empty his bladder.

A schedule of three meals a day and no drinks except water has saved many of my little patients.

No more thumb sucking

When a mother comes to me with the thumb sucking problem after the child is two years old, I assure her that she is the cause of the trouble and that she must convince the child that she does not care if he does use his thumb. And the way to do that is to have him come in each day, wash his hands clean, sit on a chair and suck his thumb for at least thirty minutes, making this statement to him, "You have got to suck your thumb thirty minutes, each day by the clock." But we must be sure that we are ready to give up our nagging and be sure we are sincere in the act. This will never fail if carried out at two years if we are firm and always follow through.

At the end of the second year if the thumb is still used, the parents are beginning to talk about the act and pull the thumb out, make all kinds of threats, and use the most harmful statement that can be used before a child, saying, "I can't stop my child from sucking his thumb." When the parents say, "We can't stop him," he has to keep on because they have confessed he is greater and more powerful than they are. So the thumb sucking becomes an issue. He sucks because it creates a situation that provides him an audience and as long as there is an audience, there is acting. This acting will not end at the end of the negative period of the child's life if there is still an audience. I had one boy patient who sucked his thumb for twenty-one years or until he was married. His parents had made such an issue of it he could not afford to stop.

The only reason I would favor the breaking of the thumb sucking habit is to eliminate pinworms. At about two years of age children begin to play with other children and other children's toys that may be covered with pinworm eggs. The average child over two years who continues to suck his thumb, bite his nails, or put his hands in his mouth has pinworms. The eggs of these worms are everywhere and they stick to the hands.

I have had wonderful success with older children who suck their thumbs or bite their nails by explaining to them how impossible it is to get rid of the worms as long as they keep putting their fingers in their mouths. But I always tell them to make up their own minds, that, if they don't want the worms, they will have to give up the nails and thumb. Nagging is the devil's best weapon and the average person will not discontinue what he is doing if he is continually nagged.

Teach a child the art of meeting people

The art of meeting people must be taught. Often in my office I speak to a child, only to have him sit there in a sullen manner and not respond. Through training this attitude in the child must be changed if he is to be well adjusted later in life.

Sometime ago I was invited to a home and had an opportunity to see what this family had accomplished in a short time. They showed us a beautiful office with everything that could be bought to make it perfect for a businessman. As to the home itself, there was a television set in every room, the beds were self-styled, the floors were covered with the best carpets. Then we went out to see the cars--two of the biggest and finest. Then we had a visit with the family.

The little three-year old boy sat there alone on the floor playing and did not speak to us or show any interest in our speaking to him. He did not say one word to us the entire evening. When dinner was announced, he did not come to the table but got a dish of corn flakes and walked around over the house eating them, his only food for that meal. He was pale and pot-bellied.

This family had everything it takes in a physical way to be happy, but they neglected the thing that would have brought them the greatest happiness. In addition, they have handicapped a helpless child in not training him in a way that he could be happy. A child at three should know how to meet people and should be taught by that time good eating habits. This child is three years behind and, when he enters school, he will either be a bully or will shrink back and not be seen, for he has not been taught how to meet people and how to make people love and admire him.

Children are happier when you help them make their toys

The average child of today has a cabinet full of toys he never plays with at all, toys that were bought to show him how much he was loved by a parent who did not have any time for him.

The happy children are the little boys or girls who have parents who have time to make a doll dress or a doll, or time to saw some wheels off a log to make a wagon, or take an orange crate and show them how they can make a playhouse, post office or hospital, and create all the equipment out of things they make.

These fortunate children are also the children who know how to help with the housework, will learn to save money, help pack boxes for the less fortunate, or help make a present for Grandma.

These children are the ones who learn the art of giving.

Make time for reading, singing, and story telling

Babies seem to be soothed by reading or singing and as soon as they are able to talk, they like to be read to and have us tell them stories of our childhood, as they let their little minds fill in with their imagination. Soon they can tell us imaginary stories that show that their minds are developing. A child who is read to and talked to and has stories told to him soon wants to read and get into this wonderful world of thinking things out and solving problems in his own mind.

Progress is built on imagination and this imagination cannot develop if we see it all as we do on television and in the movies. We have to read and then fill in, think out, visualize, determine in our own minds how it worked, learn to want to solve problems and figure out things on our own. Reading, to be enjoyed, must be started early with the right book presented at the right time. As we read, so we live.

A story read by a parent or grandparent to a little child with the lesson that comes in the story is a good way to teach. A child who is started right will sit for a long time on a parent's or grandparent's lap listening to a good story. There can never be any better training than this, and children who live in homes where mama and papa, grandma and grandpa have time to let them relax on a good soft lap and teach them by the story method are truly blessed.

No parent or grandparent should ever be too busy to miss this greatest of all opportunities. A child who has a good story or a sweet little song at bedtime will not likely have nightmares.

Prepare your child for his first day of school

When a child at six starts to school and has learned from his parents how to say yes ma'am, yes sir, thank you, good morning, how are you, yes please, no thank you, have this chair, you go first, let me help you, I will close the door; to get up and offer a chair to an older person; to listen when talked to; never to interrupt a conversation without saying "pardon"; to let a lady enter the door first; to stand firm on an issue when he knows it is right; to respect rules and regulations of the school; to feel that school is a privilege and not a task; to know and respect other people's rights and other people's property, and recognizes that other people have a right to their own opinion; to stand firm in the way he was taught right from wrong--when he does all this, he is truly the child of choice and should be because he will be the leader of tomorrow.

He may not be the leader of the majority of the people, but he will be the leader of the group that wants a better world in which to live. When children of this type become men and women, they can speak with authority and people will listen.

Chapter 8
Ages Six to Twelve
(The Learning Years)

If a child has been trained right from birth to six, then from six to twelve is the easiest, the most pleasant, the happiest, and the most rewarding period in his life. It is like a beautiful oasis in a desert after passing through the negative and discipline period from two to six.

The normal boy and girl from six to twelve like to please and like to listen to their elders talk. They are collectors of stamps, shells, snakes, frogs, coins, and their room walls may be covered with pictures of ball players or presidents. At this age you may find a boy's or girl's room filled with what parents call trash, but to this young person every small item is important and should not be misplaced or spoken of lightly.

He is kind to animals and his playmates, he will take turns, will share his toys, is ambitious, and anxious to learn. He gets interested in scouting, likes to build, talks about what he would like to do as a man and is interested in his health.

After a child is six, if we have not made him develop a complex by constant nagging, talking, forcing and bribing, he will eat well; in fact, he will eat twice as much as he did from two to six. He will gain weight and height and start a fast period of growth that will last for two years. The appetite levels off then, and he makes a gradual gain and eats a moderate amount until he reaches adolescence, when the appetite becomes enormous--more so for boys than girls; but both eat well if they practice the laws of good health and do not eat between meals so the stomach can empty as it should.

Continue a three-meal schedule

Many homes have changed their kitchens into snack bars with tall stools and eating has become a short order restaurant-type operation with each person giving the orders and mama or papa filling the orders. How different it is when the meals are prepared and placed on the table, with the family all seated at one time, and papa gives thanks to God for what they have to eat! They are taught by this one act that eating is a privilege and not a task. The table is a wonderful place for a family meeting and a great school.

It is almost a daily occurrence for a mother to bring in a school child with a complaint going like this: "Doctor, the teacher called me in and she thinks my child must be sick for he has lost interest, does not finish his work, is not happy, and seems sleepy."

As a rule, I find on examination some infection and anemia and on questioning the mother find that the child has no regular schedule and the diet is poor. I have seen many of these children who are fussed at about their school work make good students when I could get the mother to feed them right, sleep them right, help them each night with their school work, and tell them they are somebody and not run them down.

When we are trying to help our child, we must not try to make him play but we must make him feel well enough to want to play. We must not try to make him learn, but make him feel well enough so he can learn. We must not make a child eat, but make him well enough to want to eat, and this is all so simple if we will just think a little and know how the body works. And, no matter how much we would like to change his body, it still operates on a natural system that cannot be changed. The child must have the right food at the right time in the right atmosphere.

Be in close contact and be a good listener

Children need to be in close contact with their parents, and they must feel free to discuss any subject with their parents. If a child has been taught that the parents will listen to his questions, no matter how small or personal they may be--and will keep his secrets-- the child will come to the parents with his problems and let them guide him as he seeks to decide between right and wrong. There should be time and patience with all questions; and the answers should show the child what the end results would be with a certain act.

Answer questions immediately and give reasons why

When a child begins to ask questions, he must be given answers. We should teach our children to question. Some parents get angry when a child asks the question, "Why should I do what you say?" and sometimes this question is answered with a spanking or the reply, "You do what I say because I say so."

A child has the right to know why he has to do a thing. Children should be required to do as the parents say, as the parents are their masters and they must learn obedience; but, when parents refuse to let their children question, they are starting them off on the wrong road.

Every answer to a question should carry a reason if a child is to develop and find his place in life. I had one mother who always had the same answer to all her child's questions. The answer was always "Because." That child developed the habit of asking the question and always ending with "Because." He answered his own question since "Because" seemed to be the answer to all questions.

The answer to a question doesn't suffice if it is simply; "You can't do that because it is wrong." No, that answer is not good for children in this age group because they want to know the reason for things. Why a thing is wrong must be given along with the answer.

Children should be taught and encouraged to ask the reason for things and they should be given concise, definite answers; and each question should be answered when the interest is there.

Expose expose expose

From ages six to twelve, parents should do all they can to expose their children to the best possible way of life, art, music, nature, science, church, school, perfect home, love of their homeland and the flag, to open their eyes to the beauties of this world.

If a child at this period shows an interest in a subject that would be good for him, he should be exposed to this subject as much as possible. If the interest would not lead to something good for the child, the parents should take time to explain to him what an interest in this subject would lead to, for at this age a child will listen and learn.

Teach teach teach - Your child is now willing to listen

This period from six to twelve is the time to teach because it is the time the child is willing to listen. This is the period in a child's life when parental suggestions and advice are best accepted and followed. It is during this period that a child will listen and ask questions and want help in his plans; he likes to work with his parents and have his parents work with him.

We must teach our children the way to eat, the way to walk, the way to sleep, the way to talk, the way to dress, the way to meet people, the way to keep house, the way to make money, the way to spend money, the way to treat their elders, the way to treat their superiors, the way to read and what to read, the way to worship God, and many, many more things.

Who is teaching and what is your child learning at school

When we select teachers for our schools--those who are to teach from the first grade through the sixth--we should select the type people we would like our children to use as models for their lives. We cannot stress this too much. I am sure that the teacher in this period of a child's life has been the making or breaking of many children.

Teachers who instruct children at this age should be of the highest type. They should be an example for the child to live by. A child in this age group has more admiration for his teachers than at any other age in the entire educational period and in many instances will listen to the teacher's reasoning in preference to that of the parents.

Teachers, as well as parents, must help all they can during this six years of a child's life when the child is so eager to find all the reasons for things and when his mind is receptive to reasons. They should never be taught by word or example a way of life or a reason for life that would not be good for them or for the world in which they live.

Teach a child how to analyze questions

Between six and twelve, a child begins to question his parents as to why they live as they do. Parents must be ready with a reason if they hope to make their child secure. In a world with so many different ways of life, there must be a reason that Papa pays his debts and the father of his friend, Johnny, does not. There must be a reason that Papa drinks and smokes, claiming it all well and good, while the teacher says it is bad to do these things that harm his body and make it less efficient.

A child should be taught to analyze every question that comes up in this manner:

1. Would this act make my body and life better or worse?
2. Would this act hurt another human being or thing?
3. Am I doing, as I would like to be treated?
4. Is this an act of a man or a coward?

Every day thousands of questions like how to dress, eat, talk, work, spend money, or save come up and a child has to make decisions. He has to decide whether his way of life is really best or whether the way his friends and schoolmates behave is best.

A child must be taught to listen but, most important of all, he must be taught to think for himself. Just because Lenin said communism is the perfect way of life does not make it true, and I would regard him as an authority and a specialist on the subject of communism.

Teach good study habits

When school days start and the children have to get lessons, numerous problems arise in many homes. When should they get their lessons?

When a child gets home from school, they should get out and play, or do the work that is required of them, until around five o'clock. By then they will have been out and away from schoolwork long enough to be able to study again. Then they should get their lessons before dinner and be ready for bed soon after dinner.

As they grow older, they do not require as much sleep and many have to do some studying after dinner, but that is not as good a time to study as before dinner.

When children work for money

From six to twelve, children want to work for money, and no job seems too hard. They will cut grass or carry papers. They want to own things, have dogs, cats, horses, tree houses, boats, have a way to ride; they want to have their own room.

From two years of age to the grave, a human being who is really alive likes a challenge and things that come easy don't seem very important. If a boy has to cut the neighbor's lawn to get money to take piano lessons, he will practice; if he has to carry a paper route to earn money to buy a microscope, he will take care of it and use it.

Teach good money management

If a child works outside of the home and earns money, this should be his, and he should be taught how to spend his money. Children should be taught early that they must not spend all the money they make if they are to be good business people as adults.

They should be taught that a portion should go back to the Giver through the church to help people who cannot help themselves and a portion should be saved for a time when they may need it to pay for something that takes a big sum. Then they should learn how to invest and make money and the great lesson of buying things that are worth what they cost.

A child should learn to say to himself, "Do I need what I want today more than I will want what I may need tomorrow?" Children must be taught that there is a tomorrow that will have needs like today, and that money saved today will make happy tomorrows.

A short time ago a mother and father brought in five little boys to be checked. One of them said, "Doctor, hurry and finish with us for we are going to Sears."

I asked what they were going to buy.

He said, "I don't know but I will find something to buy."

I said, "Son, you should learn this one lesson. You should never buy if you have to find something to spend your money for. You should not buy until you need something."

A child must be taught to need a thing before he spends his money for it.

Teach that it is more blessed to give than to receive

Children should also be taught that it is more blessed to give than to receive. This is a hard lesson to learn but, if started early, it can be learned.

They should be taught that a selfish person is never happy, but the greatest happiness comes when one makes others happy.

Teach a child gracious manners

The first day in school for a child who has not been taught how to meet and respect his elders may be his downfall.

The little boy who enters school and is able to say, "Good morning, Miss Smith, how are you?" and when Miss Smith says, "How are you, John?" and he answers, "Fine, thank you," and he says "Yes, thank you," "No thank you," "Pardon me," "May I have," "Yes, sir," or "Yes, ma'am," and many more phrases of culture and refinement that have to be taught the first six years of a child's life--that boy is off to a good start.

A child must be taught a gracious manner and an attitude of respect for his age and his elders if he is to be accepted by his elders and his age. This training has made life easy for those who practice the art, and lack of it has made life difficult for all too many boys and girls.

It is easy to love beauty and love, but it takes a good actor to accept the vulgar and untrained. Many times in all walks of life we see a person who may not be the most capable one in the group, but that person knows the art of meeting people and is happy and makes others happy. This must be taught from birth through training and it cannot be taught from books.

Teach how to address people properly

Our children should be taught by our example to address people by the right title, and should be taught to address their elders as Mr., Mrs., Aunt, Uncle, or by the title they hold.

We have a casual way of meeting people now that is not good. We go to a party or to any place where we meet people we have not met before, and the method of introducing the stranger is, "Mary, meet Jane."

When we meet people, we want to know who they are. Maybe Jane has worked for years to get a husband so she can be Mrs. John Smith, the wife of the office manager. She has earned a title and she should be introduced as Mrs. John Smith, the wife of the office manager. Then we have something to start on; we know she is married and her husband is an important man.

Meeting people is so much more pleasant if we know who they are, i.e., Mrs., Miss, General, Colonel, Major, Doctor, Lawyer, Cousin, Aunt, Uncle, Teacher, Husband, Wife, and it is no trouble to introduce a person in a manner that makes the guest feel good and saves many embarrassing situations. They have a title and they are somebody. "Jane" or "Joe" really means nothing.

Are you the person you want your child to be?

To every mother I would say: Examine your conduct and how it affects your child. Examine your schedule in the home and how it affects your child. Study the diet you give your children. Are you the person you want your child to be?

Would you have liked your mother to be the mother you are? Are you busy trying to make a better world for other children and neglecting yours? Are you working yourself to death making money to buy things for a child who is not taught to appreciate things? Are you teaching your child manners, something that will give him or her a better chance than will money? Are you really teaching him by example and word the value of a good body?

Are you teaching your child to question and to make decisions? Do you speak to your child as you would like to be spoken to? Are you making a nobody out of your child by telling him he is no good? Do you really trust your child and let him know you do? Are you willing to train your child and not leave the job to someone else? Have you taught your child that he must accept the body and mind he has and develop it to its greatest capacity?

If we are to save our country, we must teach our children a constructive way of life. The job is too big to be shifted to someone else. Parents are the God-planned trainers and man has never been able to change this.

Chapter 9
Adolescence
(The Independent Years)

Parents must know that at adolescence there is a great change in the glandular system in these young people. They gain pounds in a few months and they may grow several inches in a year. In a year's time there has to be a complete change in the type of clothes, and the shoe size may go up two to four numbers. It takes time to get adjusted to this size change.

They are called lazy, clumsy, and gluttons. They are not lazy but are really tired, for it takes time to develop strength sufficient for them to carry all the new weight. They must not do too much resting as they cannot then develop the strength they need, but they must have some interest that will keep them active until the body is strong enough to work without so much effort. They are clumsy because they have to learn how to use this big body.

In boys the feet seem to just kick up the rug or hit the table leg and upset the water. It takes a long time to get this big body adjusted to graceful living. They are not gluttons; it takes a great deal of food for this large body so the parents have to learn a new way of cooking to supply the adolescent's needs.

At this age a child comes to the point in life when the parents cannot completely dominate. Up to this time in the life of a child who has been reared by good parents, the child has been willing to let the parents rule as king and queen. His physical body is small in comparison to the parents', and he feels the need of a protector. His parents have been that protector for twelve or more years

At adolescence, human beings are neither adults nor children; they do not fit into either group. They have the minds of children and the desires of adults. They want to be free to run their own lives but they are not mentally or physically mature enough to do that.

Young people want to explore, they want adventure, they want to excel, to go higher on the mountain, deeper in the cave, faster in the car, stay up later into the night, leave home, and make their own way. This drive they have is normal, yet they are led to believe that it is something new, something modern; and, because their parents have passed through this stage and the drive is over, they are old-fashioned.

A good picture of an adolescent is a young colt. He can't be still; he kicks up his heels and gets hung in the fence. He is not doing this to get in trouble but he is just trying to see what he can do. That is so true of young people. They are trying to act like adults and they don't know how many mistakes these adults made before they learned how to live.

A struggle between good and bad

At adolescence the child seems to be the most sensitive to good or bad, right or wrong. Young people feel this and get very disturbed. Thousands of rebellious thoughts come into the adolescent's mind, such as: Why don't you go out and do as you please? Don't be a mama's boy. You are old enough to think for yourself. Education is not everything. Try out these things that adults do. You have a right to drink and smoke if you like. You have a right to have a car. You should not let people tell you when to come in.

Parents must take time to explain to these young people that this is nothing new, but these thoughts and suggestions have been happening to adolescents since the beginning of time; and that at this time in their lives they have to learn to take each suggestion made by the devil and study it out and decide for themselves what they will do with the suggestion made. That is what makes adolescence such a big problem.

Children must be taught from birth that in man there is a spirit to do good, a spirit to do bad, and himself as the solver. He is the only person who can decide which road to take.

If he is not helped by the parents, doctor, preacher, and teacher to understand these suggestions and the source of these suggestions, the child may become a juvenile delinquent. The parents must say to this young person. "There is a great fight for you between good and bad, and you are the only person on earth who can decide which force will control you--good or bad." Young people should be made to see that this time in their lives is one when they are the only persons held responsible for their acts by man or God. They may try to use their parents, school, church, and environment as an excuse for their acts, but it will not work. They are now old enough to decide whom they will follow--God or the devil.

There's a price to pay for bad choices

Young people should be taught that they can come to their parents and other adults for advice, but for them to develop into normal adults they must make the decisions as to their way of life. We must show them how adults live and use this statement over and over again, "I can advise you, but you have to make the decisions and be willing to live with what they bring."

The fact that a young person's friends are doing wrong will not lessen his punishment. He must learn that the way to be happy is to understand early in life about the two forces in the human body and always to decide for the right.

If he wants to do wrong and follows advice that sanctions his action, he will still have to suffer for his wrong. It must be made plain to our adolescents that the laws of God will not let us put the blame on parents, teachers, school, or church for our acts. If we harm our fellow man or ourselves, we have to pay the price.

No matter how much our parents would like to serve the sentence for us; that is not permitted by God or man.

Parents, have you done a good job?

I hear this story over and over again in my office. A mother and father with a teenage -child will say to me, "We can't do anything with this child; we are helpless."

That statement is really the truth. What can a mother and father do with a sixteen-year-old boy or girl? It is easy for them to say that as long as the child stays in their home, he must do what they say, but it will not work unless the parents have taught the child from birth to respect, honor, and obey. The job can't be started at sixteen. A boy or girl at this age cannot be made to do good; they must want to do the right thing.

Four factors that help adolescents decide good over evil

There are four factors that make it easy for these young people to decide for good instead of evil:

1. First, to have sixteen years of good training by parents who are an example of what they want their children to be.

2. Second, to teach them from birth to make decisions. For example, we should not say, "Don't touch that stove," but say, "If you touch that stove, you will get burned." "If you destroy your toy, you will want it one day, and we can't buy you another." Day in and day out, we should teach our children to make decisions.

3. Third, we should make our children know that we have confidence in them. Lack of confidence has destroyed many wonderful people. For instance, there are parents who say, "He will not tell me the truth; he will not keep up with his school work; he will not go to school; he will not do anything I tell him to do; the boy next door is so perfect, but my son doesn't care about anything but to go spend money." An adolescent who hears these statements from parents or teachers has nothing to live up to, and he has nothing to lose; nobody has any confidence in him so it matters not what he does. If an adolescent knows that somebody really has confidence in him and expects him to make the right decisions, he will take time to think when a suggestion is made that will betray the confidence of this parent, teacher, preacher, girl friend, boy friend, good neighbor, or whoever the person may be.

4. Fourth, in helping young people decide for good, let them know that we were once adolescents and we had every suggestion made to us that is made to our children and that we had to decide which road to take; that we had every feeling about our parents that our children have about us, and that there is nothing modern and there is nothing old-fashioned in the behavior of the human race.

More about showing confidence

The one thing above all others that will destroy a wholesome parent-child relationship is a feeling of distrust on the part of the child for the parent or the parent for the child. If a child knows his parents trust him and believe in him, it is hard for him to do wrong; but, if he knows they are watching him and expecting him to do wrong, it is easy.

The mother of one of my patients called one day crying. She had been a perfect mother and had developed a son who was as nearly perfect as any boy could be.

She said, "Doctor, I am heartbroken; I want to talk to you."

I asked her what the trouble was.

"I would rather come out to your office and talk there," she answered. She came over and we had the following conversation:

"You know we have tried our best to train our son by example, and now he is sixteen and has changed so much I can't believe he is my son," she said.

"Give me an example of what you are talking about."

"He will tell a lie."

"No--you can't use that word against that fine boy I have had as a patient for sixteen years; let's soften that statement a bit. You mean he does not tell you the truth. The word 'lie' will make him a bad boy, and I know he is not bad. How does this untruth come about?"

"Well, we let him have the car since he is sixteen now, so he goes out at night and I stay up to kiss him good night. When I go to kiss him, I ask him if he has been driving too fast, if he drank with the boys, or smoked with them. He answers 'no' to all these questions--and I know he does these things."

Then I said to her, "If your husband came home tonight and asked you if you had been out with the man next door, it would hurt you so bad to think he did not have any more confidence in you than that, you would not want to live with him. That is in reality what you are doing to your son. You have taught him that you doubt his living up to his training. He knows you would not ask him these questions if you had any confidence in him. He has nothing to live up to.

"If your husband told you that you were the poorest cook in town, you would not worry about making your meals beautiful and good, for there would be no incentive to try. You have one of the finest boys I know, and you are destroying him by making a nobody out of him.

"One day you two go out to lunch--just you two--and have a good talk about the younger generation. Tell him how disturbing it is to read and see so much about how many young people decide to follow the devil rather than God, but let him know just how much confidence you have in him.

"Tell him how important it is for a young man to think and decide for himself what he wants in life and make it clear that after a young man reaches sixteen, his parents can't make his decisions any longer. And say to him that you have been so anxious about him that you have shown him you did not have the confidence in him a mother should have in her son, but from now on you will not stay up until he comes in, and you will never ask him about his conduct for you know you can depend on him no matter where he may be."

I saw that mother several months later and she said things had really changed. When her son found that she loved him enough to trust him he could not help doing the right thing.

Continually remind your teenager

Teenagers have to be continually reminded that when two people marry, build a home and have children, the parents are the king and queen in that kingdom--and must reign supreme--and the children in that home must love, respect, and obey as long as the parents provide the home and the money that pays for their keep.

Then, when the children are mentally and physically able to go out and make their own home, the parents will grant them the right to a home like they have had and will not interfere with the way they run their home.

If adolescents get this picture, as a rule they begin to think and adjust their lives to this way of life. I have parents come to me with their adolescent problems who will make this statement, "As long as they stay in my house, they have got to do what I say." That is the way it should be, but that statement can't make it so. It is best to say to your adolescent, "Now, son (or daughter), you should never do or say anything in our home that you would not want your son or daughter to do or say in your home."

Do the things you do best and follow your interests

Young people ask the question every day, "How can I know what I want to do with my life?" There is only one answer to that question. They should do the things they do best and follow their greatest interests.

They must ask themselves, "Will this interest be an honor to my parents, my country, and my God?" If not, they should try to find an interest that will honor parents, country, and God for there cannot be lasting happiness in a career that falls below that standard no matter how much it provides in this world's goods.

We should not worry about our child not having a fixed goal but should help him to see that what he does today is important, whether it is cutting the grass or baking a cake and that he should do each job well and follow his greatest interest remembering that the only way to win is by working.

There is no known career on earth that is not honorable if it pleases man, country, and God. This is a great lesson to teach our children. If they can't climb to the top of the highest mountain, they should do the best they can; and to climb to the top of a hill, if it is the best they can do, is just as honorable in the sight of the Great Judge.

My career story

My daughter said to me one day, "Mama, I don't know what I want to do. I am all confused. You always knew you wanted to be a doctor."

No, as a child I did not know a woman could become a doctor but I loved to see things live. I would pick up flowers that had been thrown out as dead and put them in water and see them come back to life. I would help a little sick chicken, or get a grasshopper out of a spider web, or help my father doctor a sick cow. I would make salve for the sores on my little brothers and sisters and the little colored children on the farm. I would hang on the lot fence for hours watching a sick horse, or would pick up worms in the road to keep them from being killed by the traffic, always trying to save life, from the smallest plant to the largest animal.

My family and my friends were sure I would be a milliner and make hats, for that was what I seemed to do best-- make doll hats and dress hats for all the family. I also liked to sew, and dressmaking seemed to be a natural interest. Each year my interest changed, but the desire to make creatures and things live and to know why they had to be sick and die was my greatest interest and one that never changed.

Through grammar school, high school, and college the study of animals, man, chemistry, and physics was a great joy, but the study of music and language was a task. In college a great teacher, Dr. Macon, had the same interest so he let me set up a little private anatomy laboratory where I could study these things out myself. It was then I acquired the nickname "Doc," with no idea of becoming a doctor as there was no school in the South that would admit a woman to the study of medicine at that time. I thought teaching would be the only thing I could do. In that little laboratory I learned a great deal.

I finished college and tried teaching for two years, but that was not my field. I sent my application in to medical college, but it was not acknowledged. The day for medical school to open I was there and asked to be admitted but was refused on the grounds that the school had fifty-two students already and there was room for only thirty-six so it would be out of the question for me to get a place.

I asked them to just fix me a place in any corner and take me on a trial basis for a few days. So the officials of the school got together that night and decided to let me stay. They had one married man and one Yankee boy nobody wanted to work with so they put us three outcasts together. (This was a Southern college.) A married man in school at that time was not at all popular and a Yankee less so, and even less than that, a female student.

We three started on a cadaver and became good friends, had great fun and soon we were taken in by the entire class. My four years there passed like a day because I was doing the thing I wanted to do.

It's your child's life--let him live it

We must not say that our child will be a doctor, lawyer, preacher, or follow any other specific career. If we have a desire for his life, we should expose him to this career as much as possible and do no talking about what we are going to do with his life, but always talk about what he is going to do with his own life. Let's give our child a chance by example, not by force.

If we plan our child's life and talk it all the time when the child is not capable or is not interested in the life we plan, the child always feels his parents think he is a failure.

As a child grows older and begins to have genuine interest in art, music, law, farming, medicine, teaching, or thousands of other ways of life, the parents should encourage each of these interests. The interest may be for a day or it may be for a lifetime. The parents should not over-emphasize the interest with too much talk or force, but should let it work out gradually.

Too much interest on the parents' part has killed off many promising careers. It is best to let the child want the career or way of life and be willing to sacrifice to get it.

Teenagers want parents they can brag about

When children reach adolescence, they begin to judge their parents and find fault with the way they dress, act, and live. It is almost as common an occurrence to have these adolescents come to me with the parent problems as it is for the parents to come to me with the adolescent problems.

This is the way it goes: "Doctor, Mother comes to school with tight pants on that she should not wear even at home, and I am so embarrassed." "Doctor, I wish you would talk to Mother and Daddy about their smoking.   They tell me it is wrong, yet they are killing themselves, and mother's teeth are so dark and her skin so ugly.   She could be a beautiful mother if she would do the right thing."

I would say that any young person would rather have parents whom he could brag about than any other thing.

Summing up the adolescent

Children entrusted to our care should be taught the decorum, the manners, the customs that would give them the best chance to be good citizens and the best chance to be good parents.

Then each child should be taught that after all the help his parents have given him and all they have done to make his life a success, he himself must select his way of life and must decide what road he will take in life. The road to better the human race or the road to degrade the human race are his choices: to be a builder or a destroyer.

Parents can't make these choices for their children for the reason that each individual has been endowed with knowledge and wisdom to enable him to make his own decisions.   The most vulgar, immoral parents in my office would select for their children a perfect life if they could give it, even though they were not willing to be examples and give them a chance.   But the child must select his own way of life.

Chapter 10
Special Gems of Wisdom

Gem #1 - DPT Shots

A Special Note About Dr. Denmark!

One of Dr. Leila Denmark's greatest accomplishments was her work over an eleven-year period on the vaccine for pertussis. She received the 1935 Fisher Award for outstanding research in diagnosis, treatment, and immunization of whooping cough.

The shot (the P in DPT standing for pertussis) is the same shot given routinely to infants today.

Because of the longevity of Dr. Denmark's practice, she has probably vaccinated more children than any other physician in the world today.

Thank God for immunizations

In my youth a child was taken to a doctor for only one thing; he was sick with a fever. He had some disease--diphtheria, whooping cough, typhoid, diarrhoea, scarlet fever, pneumonia, or some other sickness. These illnesses took up all of the doctor's time. As a rule they were long-lasting and the doctor had no way to treat them except in a palliative way. There were no cures and the child had to build his own antibodies to cure himself, and the doctor tried to keep the child alive until he could cure himself.

Today these diseases do not worry a doctor because we don't have many of them any more. We have learned how to immunize against most of them and the others can be cured in a short time through use of our good drugs. I often say to my young mothers, "You should say a word of thanks each day for immunization and good drugs and for the blessing that your child does not have to suffer the long deadly illnesses of years gone by."

Immunize for DPT and polio at 5 months, 6 months, and 7 months

When I was doing my research on vaccine for pertussis I found out something that was critical. I began by vaccinating a pregnant mother, thinking I could immunize the baby inside her. The antibody response was no good. After birth, when the baby was a month old, I gave him a shot, but it didn't work; at two months it didn't work and so on. I began to get a wonderful response about the fifth month. I discovered that it was not until the child is five months old that his immune system is mature enough to respond effectively.

It takes three DPT shots to be fully immunized. The shots should be administered to the baby, along with polio, at 5 months, 6 months, and 7 months.

After the initial DPT shots, the child won't need a tetanus shot for ten years unless he receives a wound in a horse lot or from a gunshot or a rusty nail. For safety sake, you may want to repeat the booster every ten years.

Gem #2 - Food for a Day Plan

Another Special Note About Dr. Denmark!

The excellent health Dr. Denmark has enjoyed for more than one hundred years is convincing testimony to her understanding of what a body truly needs. Good nutrition is absolutely fundamental to health and happiness. A growing child particularly needs three balanced meals a day.

Dr. Denmark's Food for a Day Plan

Breakfast *(7:00 A.M.)*	*Lunch* *(12:30 P.M.)*	*Dinner* *(6:00 P.M.)*
Protein	Protein	Protein
Starch	Starch	Starch
--------	Vegetables	Vegetables
Fruit	Fruit	Fruit
Water	Water	Water

Daily nutritional needs

Protein -   Each meal should contain high-quality protein. If anyone has difficulty getting moving in the morning, consider whether he is eating enough protein at dinner.

Starch -   *Every meal should contain a starch. Whole grains and potatoes are the best sources. Homemade whole-grain breads and cereals are a great addition to any family's diet.*

Vegetables- *At both lunch and dinner, a child needs a serving of vegetables especially green and leafy ones that contain iron. Alternate them with yellow vegetables like carrots and squash. Frozen vegetables are convenient and contain few additives or salt. Cooked vegetables are as good as raw ones and are actually easier to digest.*

Fruit -   *Fruit is important, but other foods are more necessary. When a family is limited in its food budget, bananas and apples may be the best choices.*

Water -   *Don't drink anything but water and drink when you're thirsty. So many are saying we need eight or more glasses of water a day. I don't think that is necessary. There is actually something called water intoxication. The blood can get so diluted that there are not enough electrolytes to make the heart beat.*

What about

Desserts -   *A sweet dessert once or twice a week won't hurt, but children should not expect to have them every day. Dessert on Friday night or for Sunday dinner makes the meal special and gives children something to look forward to.*

Sugar -   *Honey as a sweetener is far superior to sugar, but even sugar in limited amounts is not harmful to the average child. Everything's good until man makes it bad. There's nothing wrong with sugar unless it's eaten to excess.*

Dairy   *Dairy products are much overrated In the American diet;*
Products -   *they should never be a meal's main ingredient. Cheese isn't a good meat substitute, yogurt and cottage cheese not much better. A little cheese sprinkled on top of a casserole, ice cream at a birthday party, or milk in a white sauce occasionally won't be harmful, but guard against regular consumption of dairy products in general.*

Calcium -   *Most foods contain plenty of calcium. A lot of widows develop osteoporosis in their old age, but it's not for lack of* calcium. Without husbands to cook for, they snack and don't eat a balanced diet. Osteoporosis is caused by a lack of vitamin D necessary for the body's utilization of calcium. Vitamin D is obtained through sunshine, meats, vegetables, and codfish.

Fruit Juices -   Fruit juices should be eliminated because of their concentrated fructose content. It's preferable to give a child fruit rather than juice. Fiber and protein in the pulp provide a much more balanced food. Juice stresses the kidneys and produces highly alkaline urine that can cause burning, itching, and even urinary-tract infections.

Nutritious   Meals should be spaced five and a half hours apart,
Snacks -   allowing time for the stomach to empty. If a child snacks throughout the day, that never happens. The stomach will not release un-digested food other than sugar, so his body is unable to make use of what he eats and he is constantly hungry. He also may be "pot bellied." Even nutritious snacks should not be permitted between meals.

A young doctor's attitude

In conversation with a young pediatrician at a medical meeting, I remarked that the most important thing a pediatrician should do is teach a mother how to feed and care for her children. I emphasized how much better it was to teach them how to keep their children well rather than simply hand them another prescription.

In response to my words the young man threw up his arms and said, "They don't pay us for that!" You know, it might be better to take a child to a vet. Vets insist on good nutrition for their patients. The vet is very cognizant of the fact that food means everything.

Gem #3 - Let Your Baby Cry!
Our home was much happier within a week

*Story written by Nora Dolberry Pitts - Before taking my first baby to Dr. Denmark I had been nursing her on demand and allowing her to sleep when she would. If she cried for more than five minutes, I picked her up to comfort her. By the time she was three months old my nerves were shattered from lack of sleep, my husband was wondering if he would ever have a meal and clean clothes again, and I was feeling desperate.

Dr. Denmark had me put my daughter on a schedule, assuring me that it was not only all right to let her cry but that it was actually good for her. Crying helps clean out the nose and strengthens the lungs.

Within a week, we had a much happier home. The baby and I were both sleeping all night. My outlook improved. I was no longer "leaking" through the night. I was soon able to prepare good, balanced meals for us all using Dr. Denmark's schedule as a guideline. It was comforting to know that what I fed my family would be building healthier bodies. With my once-colicky baby contented in her playpen, Mommy was able to catch up on the housework.

*Used by permission

If your baby isn't sleeping through the night--answer these questions

Some infants take longer than others to begin sleeping through the night. If your baby is one of those, ask yourself, "Am I following Dr. Denmark's schedule consistently? (Consistency is vital.) Is my baby positioned on his abdomen so he feels secure? Am I keeping his bedroom quiet? Do I need to exercise self-control and persevere a few more nights?"

Use your discretion, remembering that normal, healthy infants do cry even if nothing is wrong. Many things can wake a baby up. Check for fever, a stuffy nose, diaper rash, or abnormal bowel movements. Is baby gaining weight normally?

After ruling out the above you might try giving him a little formula at ten o'clock after you nurse him. You may be tired and not producing enough milk in the evening. Mix one tablespoon of powdered formula with two ounces of sterile water (yielding two ounces of formula).

If he drinks the entire amount, feed him two and one-half ounces the next night after nursing. Continue increasing the amount every night by one-half ounce until he leaves a little in the bottle. An infant will not drink too much. Minor supplementing may be all it takes to help baby sleep until six. (See Gem #5)

Gem #4 - All About Cow's Milk

The lower animals do not take milk after the sucking period. The cat has milk for six weeks, the sea lion fifteen days, the dog not more than twelve weeks, the calf for a very short time, and on and on it goes.

All animals wean their young as soon as they are able to eat, and they never have milk again. They never have bad teeth and do not develop anemia as the human race does.

Squirrels have milk for a short time and never again and they can open a hickory nut with their teeth. If a cat is fed only cow's milk after it is weaned, it will develop severe anemia. This is true of all domestic animals.

A year-old German shepherd that has been fed as a dog should be fed, on meat and vegetables, will have one hundred per cent hemoglobin and six million red cells. If on the same diet one quart of cow's milk a day is added, in two months the hemoglobin will have dropped thirty per cent and the red cells in the same proportion. If the dog is put on a diet of cow's milk only, he will not live two months. I know because I have made this experiment.

The exact reason for this reduction in red corpuscles and hemoglobin and the marked increase in white corpuscles is not known, but it does occur; and it is not because the animal is not taking other food, for dogs and cats with their regular diet have still developed anemia. But in the animals that are fed cow's milk only, the anemia develops much faster and is far more severe.

This is evident in the pregnant mothers of today. They usually eat well after the first three months, but some develop severe anemia before the nine months are up. These mothers are often advised to drink cow's milk to make the baby better and supply extra calcium, but if the diet is proper, the milk not only is not needed but will be harmful.

One observation I have made over the years is that when we open the long bones of a chicken that has been fed large amounts of cow's milk, we will find the medullary cavity filled with a complete network of fine spicules of bone that almost obliterates the medullary cavity and decreases the amount of marrow until it is almost dry.

In a normal chicken that has not been fed cow's milk, this marrow can be removed almost in one piece and there is very little evidence of bone formation in the medullary cavity. The marrow is a long, very vascular mass that resembles a blood clot.

I have never been able to compare the medullary cavities of the long bones of a baby that has had great quantities of cow's milk with the medullary cavities of a baby that had human milk and was weaned after the seventh month and then given a normal diet of meat, vegetables, fruit and cereal. I am sure, however, that in the case of the anemic, milk-fed-child, the medullary cavities are filled with fine spicules of bone from the excess calcium and phosphorus consumed, and that this is the reason it takes so long to get a normal hemoglobin. All of this excess bone has to be reabsorbed and the marrow has to grow back to the normal amount.

Drinking too much milk after weaning will produce anemia

My theory is that too much calcium inhibits absorption of iron. There has been a lot of research done on anemia. We know what causes it in calves--feeding them milk beyond the weaning point to make veal.

By eight months a baby should be weaned, eating plenty of pureed food, and drinking water from a cup. After weaning you don't need to add cow's milk or formula to his diet. It can produce anemia..

A proper diet for an anemic child

Children with marked anemia will clear up on good food when cow's milk is omitted and they are fed on a five and one-half-hour schedule.

The diet I have used with hundreds of anemic children has been meat with each meal, beef, lamb, chicken, fish, liver, meat-base formula; vegetables three times a day, black-eyed peas, cabbage, okra, broccoli, cauliflower, squash, beets, green beans, et cetera; fruit, bananas, apples, pears, prunes. The starch consists of whole grain cereal or sweet potato and some white potato (but not too much), corn meal mush (which is one of the best), whole grain breads, brown rice, and no drinks except water.

For the first month the gain in hemoglobin will be between ten per cent and twelve per cent--not very fast--but after the child has made enough blood and the bone marrow has had a chance to return to normal, the increase in hemoglobin becomes much faster.

70% hemoglobin seems to be the normal now

I read an article recently written by an internal medicine man saying a seventy per cent hemoglobin seems to be the normal now, and that was about the highest he could get.

Of the new patients that come to my office and the ones I see in the clinic, I would say that seventy per cent hemoglobin would be about the average and fifty per cent would not be uncommon. It is a frequent experience to find children with hemoglobin as low as thirty per cent.

When a child has a thirty per cent or seventy per cent hemoglobin, he has a seventy per cent or thirty per cent deficiency in every cell in his body. The cells cannot live without blood and in order for the cells to produce at their maximum, they must have the maximum amount of blood.

Gem #5 - Formulas

We cannot make a mother nurse her baby any more than we can make a mother stay home and train that baby. So we come to the problem that is taking a great portion of the doctor's time and thoughts.

The little babies who cannot be fed the way nature planned for them to be fed create a big problem. We can be assured that no two babies can be fed just the same way, so each baby is a new problem and must be worked out as a problem all his own.

How to feed a baby from a bottle

I would never feed a baby a formula more concentrated than human milk and never feed closer than four hours.

We must be sure the milk is diluted properly and is warm and the nipple cut so the milk comes easily. (This should be a crosscut one-sixteenth inch both ways.) The baby should be held in the mother's arms snugly and when the baby pulls, she should pull back on the bottle so he can strip the milk out as he does on the breast. The breast is elastic and when the baby pulls, the breast pulls and the baby strips the milk out. If the nipple is placed in the baby's mouth and not pulled as he sucks, he has to mash the milk out and he does not get the proper sucking act. It should not take a baby more than fifteen minutes to take a bottle; and the longer he sucks, the more air he swallows through his nose.

Rubber nipples can be injurious to the tongue

Nursing too long on the bottle injures the epithelium on the tongue and the mouth. If you look at the tongue of a baby who is allowed to nurse a nipple of any kind for a long time, you will see that the taste buds are flat and the tongue is red and more susceptible to thrush. Also, I am sure the tongue burns and the taste is not normal. Nature made the human breast nipples the softest part of the body. The covering over the nipple is like velvet and we have never been able to make a nipple that could simulate the normal human nipples; therefore, we should not let a baby suck on a rubber nipple for a long time and injure his tongue. It takes effort to nurse and if a baby is allowed to nurse for a long time, he gets tired.

If the baby is small and weak, one might think he should be allowed to nurse for a long time, but that is not true. The smaller and weaker babies are the ones that should not be worn out with long feeding periods. The longer they suck, the more air they swallow and the more colic they have. So the feeding period should be carried out right and should not be haphazard.

Don't feed a baby a whole-milk formula

Cow's milk has ten times as much calcium and phosphorus as human milk and the baby is not developed enough to utilize this large amount of ash. So, if the baby is fed that type formula, he may spit up or have diarrhoea, or constipation, or colic, and in a very short time you will find that the growing areas of the bones are much enlarged. The wrists, ankles, and ends of ribs become enlarged, the head takes on an angular appearance and the baby develops anemia because of the marked increase of bony formation in the medullary cavity of the long bones. A whole-milk formula is too high in butterfat. A newborn cannot digest that much fat. With a formula of that type, the proteins are too high. The baby is not able to eliminate the by-products of that much protein and the baby can become ill.

How we can make cow's milk more digestible

Dr. Kim Merritt determined some years ago that by the addition of enough lactic acid to form a curd and neutralize the buffer in cow's milk, the milk was made far more digestible. In 1928 we used lemon juice to form the curd and neutralize the buffer, which seemed even better as the curds were smaller and digestion was faster. The baby was started on half skimmed milk with an equal amount of water, enough acid to cause a curd, and enough carbohydrate added to make it simulate human milk. The amount of fat was gradually increased and the amount of water decreased until at eight months the baby was taken off the bottle.

An evaporated milk formula

To make an evaporated milk formula, start with one part milk, two parts sterilized water, and enough carbohydrates to bring the sugar up to the equivalent of human milk. A good starter would be six ounces evaporated milk, twelve ounces sterilized water, and two tablespoons dextrose. Give a newborn three ounces at six, ten, two, six, and ten o'clock. If the baby takes all of the three ounces, next time make up enough to put four ounces in each bottle in the same proportion until the baby eventually gets eight ounces at six, ten, two, and six o'clock. The formula will be assimilated much better if you add one teaspoon of lemon juice to each eight ounces of formula, or twelve drops of lactic acid to each eight ounces or enough to make a curd--after the formula is cold.

Making a formula from fresh cow's milk

The same formula as above could be made from fresh cow's milk using two parts milk, one part water, and for the first three months, taking off half the cream. Boil the milk and water five minutes in a covered boiler and when cold, add the lemon juice or lactic acid and the dextrose. The milk should form a fine curd and separate.

Powdered milk formulas

There are many powdered milks that work well. From some of them the ash has been removed to simulate human milk and the animal fat has been replaced with vegetable fat. If these milks are diluted right and given in a diluted form to start with, they are well tolerated if the baby is not allergic to milk or the sugar that is added.

If all else fails try my "witch's brew" formula

If a baby is allergic to cow's milk, I try goat's milk and if that does not work, I try one of the soy bean preparations. If that does not work, a meat-base formula would be tried. If the baby continues to cry, spit, have abnormal stools, rash--and if no other reason can be found to cause the trouble except the food--then I try my "witch's brew," prepared as follows: one cup brown rice, two quarts water, cook two hours, rub through sieve, add enough water to make two quarts, one teaspoon salt, four tablespoons dextrose, four tablespoons Knox Gelatine, boil three minutes, and give as much as the baby will take at six, ten, two, six and ten. This has saved many babies. We always make up two quarts as it can be kept safely for two to three days; and it is some trouble to prepare.

Supplementing mothers breast milk

The amount of milk a baby consumes is determined by his individual needs. If a child is gaining well and seems content, don't be concerned about the sufficiency of your breast milk. If the baby isn't gaining well and you're worried about his not getting enough, you can weigh him before and after nursing. During the first two weeks, most babies should weigh three to four ounces more after nursing. When he is six weeks old, he should weigh approximately eight ounces more after nursing. Most children continue to drink approximately eight ounces until they are weaned if pureed foods are introduced at the proper time.

If your child isn't receiving enough breast milk, you should supplement with formula, but always nurse first. (Otherwise your breast milk will quickly dry up.) After nursing, offer him however many ounces of formula he is lacking. For example, if your three-week-old gains only two ounces after nursing, offer him approximately two ounces of formula at the first feeding. If he drinks the entire amount increase it by one-half ounce at the next feeding. A baby won't drink too much formula. You can continue increasing the amount by half-ounces until he leaves a little in the bottle. That way you can be certain he's receiving all he needs.

Try a cow's milk formula first. If the baby spits up constantly, has eczema or diarrhea, switch to a soybean formula. Keep trying until you find one that works. If you're using formula that is intended to be diluted with water, add a little more water than the directions indicate on the can until your baby is three months old. Instead of one can of water to one can of formula, use one and one half cans of water to one can of formula. After your baby is three months follow the directions on the can.

Gem #6 - SIDS (Sudden Infant Death Syndrome)

I've practiced medicine for more than seventy years, and I've never had a SIDS (Sudden Infant Death Syndrome) baby because I insist that mothers place their infants on their stomachs and instruct them how to make the baby's bed correctly.

There was a man who received a grant to study SIDS and did a lot of his research in countries where babies sleep on sheepskins. I can imagine one might smother if he were placed on his stomach with his face buried in thick wool. That particular researcher concluded an infant should always be placed on his back or side.

I had a patient not long ago who was about four months old and had been put in one of those devices that kept him propped on his side. Four months old and he couldn't hold his head up because he had never used the muscles in his neck! His right arm was weak and the side of his head was very flat.

There are a lot of things that might make a baby die. A baby with meningitis can die in his sleep. But I don't believe an infant can get what we call SIDS unless he is placed on his back. An infant on its back is in constant danger of asphyxiating on its own spit up. The child may burp up a mouth full of milk and breathe it into his lungs, choking himself to death. It only takes a little thing to choke an infant to death.

Gem #7 - Administering Antibiotics

When we first began using antibiotics, patients went to the hospital every three hours for an injection. The results were miraculous. Later, we discovered that taking oral doses every three hours was as effective.

As time went on, physicians decided adhering to a strict three-hour schedule was too much trouble. Beside, parents didn't like waking up at night. But there is simply no way for an antibiotic to be effective unless it is kept in the bloodstream.

Antibiotics don't kill germs; they keep them from multiplying. To be most effective, the medication has to be kept in the bloodstream by dosages given at regular intervals around the clock. Missing one by fifteen minutes can greatly decrease the medication's effectiveness. If they are always given on time you can expect to see a difference in your child's condition in thirty-six to forty-eight hours. If the child is recovering from flu, it may take a little longer. The regimen must continue for at least seventy-two hours, but it is seldom necessary beyond that.

Steve, will you help me tonight?

Story written by Madia Bowman - Steve, both Leila and Joseph have bad throats, and Dr. Denmark has put them on penicillin. Will you help me tonight? If you dose them at twelve o'clock, I'll do it at three. Don't forget to reset the alarm clock for me. You know what she says about missing a dose."

I've talked to scores of moms who are skeptical of antibiotics. They have related story after story of children taking them for weeks, even months. Often their pediatricians have tried several different kinds, progressing from cheap to very expensive varieties. Still their children do not respond. I hear of maintenance dosages, tubes in the ears, yeast infections.

It's a mystery to me why pediatricians have departed from the original system of administering the antibiotics that Dr. Denmark uses. Instead of the typical four doses per day for ten days, we follow Dr. Denmark's preferred regimen.

As a result, our use of antibiotics is short-lived and highly effective. In over twenty years our eleven children have never needed tubes in the ears and have almost never had elapses. I seldom have had to repeat a round of antibiotics. This mom is convinced that the original way is the best.

Administering antibiotics Dr. Denmark's way is admittedly more difficult than the four-daily-doses routine. It is critical that the medication be given precisely on schedule, so it takes discipline on the part of the parents--remembering to set the alarm, getting up in the middle of the night, dealing firmly with a sleepy, resistant child. Inconvenience, however, is a small price to pay for the benefits received.

Gem #8 - Digestive Disorders and Enemas

Some doctors would lose their false teeth if they heard my advice about enemas--but enemas certainly do work!

One doctor told me, "Enemas went out with the Greeks!" Not so. My patients use them with great success. And I've never had a child develop Reye's syndrome who was treated with enemas.

Purpose of Enemas

Vomiting and diarrhea are immediate signals that the body is trying to cleanse itself of bacteria or food poisoning. Giving medication merely to stop the symptoms is not a wise method of treating intestinal disorders. The foreign matter needs to be expelled to enable the body to recover quickly.

In most cases enemas are particularly effective in treating digestive disorders. They help stop vomiting and diarrhea, prevent dehydration, and are an effective guard against Reye's syndrome. Reye's syndrome is caused by vomiting and diarrhea after which the blood becomes so thick it clots (vascular coagulation). Enemas can prevent thickening of the blood.

If a child cannot keep down fluid and has diarrhea, enemas prevent dehydration because fluid is absorbed through the colon. The chemical makeup of Dr. Denmark's enemas soothes the stomach and restores the balance of electrolytes. Enemas can also help bring down a high fever by replenishing vital body fluids.

How to administer a standard enema

(1) Purchase an enema bag kit from the pharmacy.

(2) Give a dose of Milk of Magnesia. This will prepare the digestive tract to receive the enema. (1/2 teaspoon for 0-6 months; 1 teaspoon for 6 months-6years; and 2 teaspoons for 6 years-adult.)

(3) Wait two hours. If the patient vomits the Milk of Magnesia within ten minutes, repeat the dose once and then leave him alone.

(4) Boil some water and let it cool down to body temperature.

(5) Prepare the enema water as follows: (8 oz. boiled water with 1/4 teaspoon baking soda for 0-1 year; 1 pint boiled water with 1 teaspoon baking soda for 1 year-6 years; 1quart boiled water with 2 teaspoons baking soda for 6 years-adult.)

(6) Administer the enema. Hang the solution-filled enema bag and expel the air from the tube by letting a little water flow from the nozzle. Pinch off the tube quickly to prevent wasting the rest of the solution. Put Vaseline on an appropriate size nozzle. Lay a child across your lap and carefully insert the nozzle 1 to 1 1/2 inches into the rectum. Point the tip toward his navel and let the water go in slowly. It is best not to let the solution be expelled for ten minutes. Hold the baby's buttocks together to prevent early expulsion. Administer the enema gently without forcing. Sliding the nozzle slightly in and out of the rectum will better allow the water to flow. The sooner the enema is administered, the more effective it is in cleansing the digestive tract of offending food or bacteria because there has been less time for absorption. Start with the Milk of Magnesia right after your child first vomits, and two hours later administer the enema. Don't wait for repeated vomiting.

With excessive vomiting and diarrhea the body may absorb most or the entire enema instead of discharging it. Absorption prevents dehydration. When a child is given an enema, he may expel the solution up to twelve hours later in the form of watery stools. If he is still having frequent, watery stools after twelve hours, they should be attributed to diarrhea, not the enema.

Retention enema (Tea Enema)

If the patient continues to vomit and cannot retain fluids after you have given a standard enema, a retention enema may be needed to prevent dehydration and restore the balance of electrolytes.

Follow this procedure:

(1) Put a single teabag in ten ounces of water and boil for three minutes. Stir the tea bag around in the water and remove.

(2) Mix 1 cup of the tea solution in 3 cups of boiled water. Stir in 1/2 teaspoon baking soda, 1/2 teaspoon salt, and 2 tablespoons dextrose* or white Karo syrup.

(3) Administer the above mixture at body temperature and give 1 cup as an enema every two hours for four doses.

> *Example: 1 cup at 10:00 a.m.*
> *1 cup at 12:00 noon*
> *1 cup at 2:00 p.m.*
> *1 cup at 4:00 p.m.*

All ages have the same dosage--even infants. It's best if the enema solutions are retained for ten minutes before expulsion.

There is no question in my mind that enemas have saved us at least half a dozen trips to the emergency room. With severe vomiting, I resort to the retention enema and it works wonders. Usually by the second dose, vomiting has stopped.

*Dextrose is a sweetener made from corn and can be purchased at any health food store.

My husband is a believer

*Story written by Jan Winchester - I grew up on Glenridge Drive near where Dr. Denmark had her office. I now have five children from one month to eight years old. Though we live in Dallas, I have never taken my children to a doctor here. I go back to Atlanta often, and we go see Dr. Denmark.

On one occasion when our family was on a ski trip to Colorado, we called Dr. Denmark. My husband had become very ill. The Denmark Milk-of-Magnesia treatment worked wonders. He even shared it with the CEO of his company while they were in New York on business. The man thought he was crazy, but it was that or the emergency room.

He chose the treatment and is now a believer. The lives Dr. Denmark has touched are many. I thank God so much for her.
*Used by permission

Gwen's Final Note: I highly recommend that you obtain Madia L. Bowman's book, *Dr. Denmark Said It!* It is an excellent reference book that will help you give treatment and identify illnesses that will frequently confront your family.   All of the combinations and recommendations in Madia's book come directly from Dr. Leila Denmark.

Dr. Denmark Said It! is one of those "must have books" for your library. You can order it by logging on to www.drdenmarksaidit.com

Credits

Introduction

1. *Dare to Discipline*, by Dr. James Dobson. Copyright 1970 by Tyndale House Publishers, Wheaton, Illinois. Used by permission.

2. From *Help! I'm A Parent!* by Bruce Narramore, Copyright © 1972 by The Zondervan Corporation. Used by permission.

3. Adapted from the article, "Want Bright, Happy Kids?" by Daniel Q. Haney, a wire story of The Associated Press which appeared in The Denver *Post*, February 23, 1976.

Parents Make Children - Chapter One

1. Reprinted by permission from *The Christian Family*, by Larry Christenson, published and copyright 1970, Bethany Fellowship, Inc., Minneapolis, Minnesota 55438.

2. From *Child Sense; A Guide To Loving, Level-Headed Parenthood*, new and expanded edition, by William E. Homan, M.D., © 1969, 1977 by William E. Homan, M.D., Basic Books, Inc., Publishers, New York,

3. From *A Woman's World*, by Clyde M. Narramore, Copyright © 1963. The Zondervan Corporation, Publisher. Used by permission of the author.

4. From *Best Loved Poems of the American People*, by Hazel Felleman. Copyright 1936 by Doubleday & Company, Inc., 245 Park Avenue, New York, N.Y. 10017. Used by permission of the publisher.

Daddy and Mother - Chapter Three

1. From *A Dictionary of Illustrations* by James C. Hefley. Copyright © 1971 by Zondervan Publishing House. Used by permission.

Daddy Bee - Chapter Four

1. Reprinted with the permission of Arbor House Publishing Company, Inc., copyright © 1971 by Bennett Olshaker, M.D.

2. Reprinted by permission of Hawthorn Books, Inc., from *Parents On Trial* by David Wilkerson, copyright © 1967 by Hawthorn Books, Inc. All rights reserved.

3. From *You Can Be a Great Parent!* by Charlie Shedd. Copyright 1970 by Charlie W. Shedd. Used by permission of Word Books, Publisher, Waco, Texas

4. From *Man of Steel and Velvet* by Aubrey, Andelin, Page 105, paragraph 4. Used by permission.

5. From *Knight's Master Book of New Illustrations* by Walter B. Knight. Copyright 1956. Wm. B. Eerdmans Publishing Co., Publishers. Used by permission

6. From *Help! I'm A Parent!* by Bruce Narramore, Copyright © 1972 by The Zondervan Corporation. Used by permission.

7. From *Help! I'm A Parent!* by Bruce Narramore, Copyright © 1972 by The Zondervan Corporation. Used by permission.

Mother Bee - Chapter Five

1. An excerpt from Dr. David R. Reuben's article, "Why Husbands Cheat on Their Wives," in the April 1972 issue of Woman's *Day* copyright © 1972 by Dr. David R. Reuben. Reprinted by permission of Harold Matson Company, Inc.

2. *Leaves of Gold*, by Clyde Francis Lytle. Revised Edition 1962. Coslett Publishing Company. Used by permission.

3. From *Christian Family*, by Dr. Hugo McCord. Copyright © 1968 by *20th Century Christian*, 2814 Granny White Pike, Nashville, Tennessee. Used by permission of the author and the publishers.

4. Used by permission from Tracey Rogers.

5. From *What Would Jesus Eat?* by Don Colbert, M.D. Copyright © 2002, Thomas Nelson Publishers Used by permission

6. From *Healthy Kids* by Marilu Henner Copyright © 2001, HarperCollins Publishers Inc. Used by permission.

7. Same as # 5

8. Same as # 6

9. Same as # 5

10. Reprinted by special permission, from the January 1975 issue of *Prevention* Magazine, Emmaus, Pennsylvania. © 1965 by Rodale Press, Inc.

11. Same as # 6

Be Co-Workers - Chapter Six

1. From *The Discipline of Well Adjusted Children* by Grace Langdon and Irving Stout, © 1952 by Grace Langdon and Irving W. Stout. Used by permission of The John Day Company, Publisher.

2. From *Child Sense: A Guide To Loving, Level-Headed Parenthood*, new and expanded edition, by William E. Homan, M.D., © 1969, 1977 by William E. Homan, M.D., Basic Books, Inc., Publishers, New York.

3. Taken from *The Marriage Affair*, edited by J. Allan Petersen. Copyright 1971 by Tyndale House Publishers, Wheaton, Illinois. Used by permission.

4. Reprinted by permission of Hawthorn Books, Inc., from *Parents On Trial* by David Wilkerson, copyright © 1967 by Hawthorn Books, Inc. All rights reserved.

5. From *You Can Be a Great Parent!* by Charlie Shedd. Copyright 1970 by Charlie W. Shedd. Used by permission of Word Books, Publisher, Waco, Texas.

6. Same as #3

7. Reprinted by permission from *The Christian Family* by Larry Christenson, published and copyright 1970, Bethany Fellowship, Inc., Minneapolis, Minnesota 55438.

8. From "Christian Family Living" by Hazen G. Warner. Copyright © 1958 by Graded Press.

9. Same as #7

10. Excerpt from "Don't Be Afraid to Demand," by Arthur Gordon. Copyright 1961 by Fawcett Publications, Inc. Used by permission.

11. Same as #10

12. Quoted from the article, "The Winner Who Can't Stop Losing," by Pam Pollock Bruns, copyrighted and published by *Redbook* Magazine (July 1972). Used by permission.

13. Same as #7

14. Same as #7

Love - Chapter Seven

1. Reprinted by permission of Hawthorn Books, Inc., from *Parents On Trial* by David Wilkerson, copyright © 1967 by Hawthorn Books, Inc. All rights reserved.

2. From *"Washington Parent Magazine,"* Article Bonding and Attachment - - When it Goes Right, by Dr. Lawrence B. Smith, L.C.S.W. - C., L.I.C.S.W. Used by permission.

3. From THE BREASTFEEDING BOOK by William and Martha Sears. Copyright © 2000 by Martha Sears, R.N. and William Sears, M.D. By permission of Little, Brown and Company, Inc.

4. Same as # 3

5. From *Logical Consequences* by Dreiker & Gray. Meredity Press, New York, New York. 1968.

6. From "Christian Family Living" by Hazen G. Warner. Copyright © 1958 by Graded Press.

7. Material on "levels of love" by Robert H. Schuller is from *Power Ideas for a Happy Family.* Copyright © 1972 by Robert H. Schuller. Published by Fleming H. Revell Company. Used by permission.

8. Same as # 6

9. From *Child Sense: A Guide To Loving, Level-Headed Parenthood,* new and expanded edition, by William E. Homan, M.D., © 1969, 1977 by William E. Homan, M.D., Basic Books, Inc., Publishers, New York.

10. Same as #9

11. Same as # 9

12. Same as # 6

13. Same as # 9

14. From *Christian Family,* by Dr. Hugo McCord. Copyright © 1968 by *20th Century Christian,* 2814 Granny White Pike, Nashville, Tennessee. Used by permission of the author and the publishers.

15 Excerpts from "This Too I Shall Give" by Ruth Graham, December 1965. From *Decision,* © 1965 by the Billy Graham Evangelistic Association. Used by permission.

16 R. Lofton Hudson, *Growing a Christian Personality.* (The Sunday School Board of the Southern Baptist Convention, Nashville, Tenn. 1955). Used by permission.

17, From *The Art of Loving* by Erich Fromm. Copyright 1956. Harper & Row, Publishers, Inc. Used by permission.

18. From *Help! I'm A Parent!* by Bruce Narramore, Copyright © 1972 by The Zondervan Corporation. Used by permission.

19. Same as #15

20. Taken from Dr. Laars I. Granberg's article, "It Makes the Home Go 'Round," Copyright 1964, The Church Herald. Used by permission.

21. From *How to Parent,* © Copyright 1970 by Fitzhugh Dodson, by permission of Nash Publishing Corporation.

22. Same as # 6

23. Same as # 18

24. Same as # 18

Obedience - Chapter Eight

1. Reprinted by permission from *The Christian Family,* by Larry Christenson, published and copyright 1970, Bethany Fellowship, Inc. Minneapolis, Minnesota 55438.

2. *Dare to Discipline,* by Dr. James Dobson. Copyright 1970 by Tyndale House Publishers, Wheaton, Illinois. Used by permission.

3. Same as #1

4. From *Child Sense:* A Guide To Loving, Level-Headed Parenthood, new and expanded edition, by William E. Homan, M.D. © 1969, 1977 by William E. Homan, M.D., Basic Books, Inc., Publishers, New York.

5. *Between Parent and Child* by Dr. Haim G. Ginott, Copyright 1965. The MacMillan Company, Publisher. Used by permission of Dr. Alice Ginott, Executor.

6. Same as #1

7. Same as #4

8. Same as #4

9. Same as # 2

10. Same as #1

11. Excerpt from *The Home: Courtship, Marriage and Children* by John R. Rice. Copyright 1946. Used by permission.

12. Same as #1

Independence - Chapter Nine

1. Reprinted by permission from *The Christian Family* by Larry Christenson, published and copyright 1970, Bethany Fellowship, Inc., Minneapolis, Minnesota 55438.

2. Same as #1

3. *Between Parent and Child* by Dr. Haim G. Ginott, Copyright 1965. The MacMillan Company, Publisher. Used by permission of Dr. Alice Ginott, Executor.

4. Same as #1

5. From *How To Parent,* © copright 1970 by Fitzhugh Dodson. By permission of Nash Publishing Corporation.

Good Habits - Chapter Ten

1. From *Christian Family,* by Dr. Hugo McCord. Copyright © 1968 by *20th Century Christian,* 2814 Granny White Pike, Nashville, Tennessee. Used by permission of the author and the publishers. Accounts 1 and 2 adapted, with permission.

2. Scripture taken from the New English Bible.

Work - Chapter Eleven

1. *Leaves of Gold,* by Clyde Francis Lytle. Revised Edition 1962. Coslett Pusblishing Company. Used by permission.

2. *The Mother's Book,* edited by Caroline Benedict Burrell, copyright 1911 by University Society Inc.

3. *Faith in Families* by Evelyn Millis Duvall. Copyright 1970. Rand McNally & Company, Publisher. Used by permission.

4. Same as #1

Communicating - Chapter Twelve

1. From *Adventures in Parenthood* by Taliaferro Thompson. © 1959 by C.D. Deans. Used by permission of John Knox Press.

2. From *How to Parent,* © Copyright 1970 by Fitzhugh Dodson. By permission of Nash Publishing Corporation.

3. Adapted from the article, "Just Listen to Him, Mother," by Charlotte Mize, in the June 1969 issue of *Christian Woman.* Used by permission.

4. Adapted from *Easy to Live With* by Leslie Parrott, pp. 36-37, Copyright 1970 by Beacon Hill Press. Used by permission.

5. From the Kansas City *Star.*

6. From *A Dictionary of Illustrations* by James C. Hefley. Copyright © 1971 by Zondervan Publishing House. Used by permission.

7. Reprinted by permission from the July/August issue of *Moody Monthly.* Copyright 1968, Moody Bible Institute of Chicago.

Together - Chapter Thirteen

1. From the article, "Worship, Family Style," by Howard Headricks, Copyright 1966 by the Navigators. By permission of The Navigators.

2. Used by permission.

3. Reprinted by permission from the July/August issue of *Moody Monthly.* Copyright 1968, Moody Bible Institute of Chicago.

4. "What Will My Boys Remember?" by Phyllis C. Michael included in *Poems for Mothers.* Copyright © 1963 by Phyllis C. Michael. Used by permission.

5. Same as #3.

6. Reprinted by permission of Hawthorn Books, Inc., from *Parents On Trial* by David Wilkerson, copyright © 1967 by Hawthorn Books, Inc. All rights reserved.

7. Revised Standard Version

8.*Leaves of Gold,* by Clyde Francis Lytle. Revised Edition 1962. Coslett Publishing Company. Used by permission.